Social Economy in China and the World

Thirty years of economic transformation have turned China into one of the major players in the global capitalist economy. However, its economic growth has generated rising problems in inequality, alienation, and sustainability with the agrarian crises of the 1990s giving rise to real social outcry to the extent that they became the object of central government policy reformulations.

Contributing to a paradigm-shift in the theory and practices of economic development, this book examines the concept of social economy in China and around the world. It offers to rethink space, economy, and community in a trans-border context which moves us beyond both planned and market economies. The chapters address theoretical issues, critical reflections, and case studies on the practice of social economy in the context of globalization and its attempt to create an alternative modernity. Through this, the book builds a platform for further cross-disciplinary and cross-boundary dialogue on the future of social economy in China and the world.

With examples from Asia, North America, Latin America, and Europe this book will not only appeal to students and scholars of Chinese and Asian social policy and development, but also to those of social economy from an international perspective.

Ngai Pun is Professor of the Department of Applied Social Sciences at the Hong Kong Polytechnic University.

Ben Hok-bun Ku is Associate Professor and program leader of the Master of Social Work (China) program in the Department of Applied Social Sciences at Hong Kong Polytechnic University.

Hairong Yan is Associate Professor, Department of Applied Social Sciences, Hong Kong Polytechnic University.

Anita Koo is Associate Professor, Department of Applied Social Sciences, Hong Kong Polytechnic University.

Routledge research on social work, social policy and social development in Greater China

Series editors:

Angelina Woon-ki Yuen-Tsang, Ben Hok-bun Ku and Ngai Pun

Hong Kong Polytechnic University

This series focuses on issues related to the rapid social change in contemporary Mainland China, Hong Kong, Macao and Taiwan. Comprising contributions from diverse disciplines, the series will explore and respond to the impacts of marketization, globalization, urbanization, modernization, migration, technological change, consumerism, dualism and disasters on people's livelihoods, well-being and social life in Chinese societies.

1 **Mobile Communication and Greater China**
Edited by Rodney Wai-chi Chu, Leopoldina Fortunati, Pui-lam Law and Shanhua Yang

2 **Hong Kong's Governance Under Chinese Sovereignty**
The failure of the state–business governing alliance after 1997
Brian C. H. Fong

3 **Asset-Building Policies and Innovations in Asia**
Edited by Michael Sherraden, Li Zou, Ben Hok-bun Ku, Suo Deng and Sibin Wang

4 **Social Economy in China and the World**
Edited by Ngai Pun, Ben Hok-bun Ku, Hairong Yan and Anita Koo

Social Economy in China and the World

Edited by Ngai Pun, Ben Hok-bun Ku, Hairong Yan and Anita Koo

Routledge
Taylor & Francis Group
LONDON AND NEW YORK

First published 2016 by Routledge

2 Park Square, Milton Park, Abingdon, Oxfordshire OX14 4RN
52 Vanderbilt Avenue, New York, NY 10017

Routledge is an imprint of the Taylor & Francis Group, an informa business

First issued in paperback 2020

British Library Cataloguing in Publication Data
A catalogue record for this book is available from the British Library

Library of Congress Cataloging-in-Publication Data
Social economy in China and the world / edited by Ngai Pun,
Ben Hok-bun Ku, Hairong Yan and Anita Koo.
pages cm. – (Routledge research on social work, social policy and social development in greater China ; 4)
Includes bibliographical references and index.
1. Economics–Sociological aspects. 2. Economic development–Social aspects. 3. Economic development–Social aspects–China. 4. China–Social conditions. 5. China–Economic conditions.
I. Pun, Ngai, 1970–
HM548.S6135 2015
306.0951–dc23 2015004948

ISBN: 978-1-138-85797-1 (hbk)
ISBN: 978-0-367-59847-1 (pbk)

Typeset in Times New Roman
by Wearset Ltd, Boldon, Tyne and Wear

Contents

Figures

Tables

Contributors

Editors

Ngai Pun, Professor, Department of Applied Social Sciences, Hong Kong Polytechnic University. Her research interest is globalization, migration, labor, gender and social economy in China. She has published extensively in *Modern China, China Quarterly, China Journal, Global Labour Journal*, etc. Her representative work is *Made in China: Women Workers in a Global Workplace* (2005) and *Inside Foxconn: Apple and the Struggle of Chinese Workers* (forthcoming). She is also chief editor of two social economies volumes in Chinese: *Social Economy in China: Beyond the Imagination of Capitalism* (2013) and *Alternative and Social Economy in Hong Kong* (2013).

Ben Hok-bun Ku, Associate Professor, Department of Applied Social Sciences, The Hong Kong Polytechnic University; Vice Director, Peking University-Hong Kong Polytechnic University Social Work Research Center; Executive Editor, *China Journal of Social Work*; Associate Editor, *Action Research*. He heavily engages in practice and action research in China. He endeavors to advocate participatory research methodology. He has been involved in China's rural development for about 15 years and has written extensively on topics related to rural development, cultural politics, participatory design, social exclusion and marginality, and social work education.

Hairong Yan, Associate Professor, Department of Applied Social Sciences, Hong Kong Polytechnic University. She is the author of *New Masters, New Servants: Migration, Development and Women Workers in China* (Duke University Press, 2008). Her current interests include China–Africa links, agrarian changes and the food sovereignty movement. She is conducting research on rural China in globalization, focusing on China's soybean crisis as a case study.

Anita Koo, Associate Professor, Department of Applied Social Sciences, Hong Kong Polytechnic University. Her research interest is education, employment, and social economies in Hong Kong and China. She is one of the editors of *Alternative and Social Economy in Hong Kong* (2013).

Contributors

Craig Borowiak, Associate Professor, Department of Political Science, Haverford College.

John Clammer, Professor, Institute for Sustainability and Peace, UN University in Tokyo.

Pauline F.Y. Chan, Lecturer, Department of Applied Social Sciences, Hong Kong Polytechnic University. She is currently the convenor of the Hong Kong Social Economy Alliance.

Li Changjiang, MA, Department of Sociology, Peking University. He is currently working as a NGO organizer in mainland China.

Chen Yi Yuen, PhD candidate, Department of Applied Social Sciences, Hong Kong Polytechnic University. She received her MA in sociology at Renmin University of China in 2011 and her BA in social work at Huazhong University of Science and Technology in 2009. Her research interests include agrarian change and food security in China.

Denison Jayasooria, Principal Research Fellow, Institute of Ethnic Studies, National University of Malaysia (UKM) and Deputy Chair, Asian Solidarity Economy Council.

Doris Lee, Southeast Asia Coordinator, No Chains; PhD candidate, Department of Asian and International Studies, City University of Hong Kong.

Liu Chi-wei, currently CEO of the Food Policy Research Institute, Taipei. He received his PhD in sociology from SUNY at Binghamton. His primary research interests are the sociology of agriculture and the political economy of agrarian change. In addition to publishing journal and conference papers, he has also received several honors for his work, including the 2013 Golden Tripod Book Award.

Lu Huilin, Associate Professor, Department of Sociology, Peking University.

Ma Yuna, Assistant Professor, Department of Social Work, China Youth University for Political Sciences.

Marguerite Mendell, Professor, School of Community and Public Affairs, Concordia University.

Carl Ratner, PhD, has worked as a co-op activist since the 1970s and is Vice-President of the largest consumer cooperative in California. He has written several books and articles on co-op practices and theory. His latest book is *The Politics of Cooperation* (Nova, 2015).

Richard H. Rudolph, Professor, University of Massachusetts Boston, retired. He is currently Chair of the Rail Users Network and director of several organizations, including the Massachusetts Energy Alliance, PTSI Transportation, and the Maine Rail Group. He is also a lead team member of the Cumberland County Food Security Council.

Andrés Ruggeri, Director of Documentation Center of Workers' Recovered Enterprises, Faculty of Philosophy and Letters, University of Buenos Aires, Argentina.

Devi Sacchetto, Lecturer in Sociology of Labor, Department of Philosophy, Sociology, Education and Applied Psychology, University of Padova, Italy. His research interests concern migration and labor processes, and he has published on topics of delocalization of production to Eastern Europe, migration and agriculture in Southern Europe, and seafarers' working conditions.

Marco Semenzin, PhD student at the Department of Philosophy, Sociology, Education and Applied Psychology, University of Padova, Italy. His research interests include the study of migration and the sociology of organizations. He is co-author (with Andrés Ruggeri) of *Las empresas recuperadas en la Argentina: ocupar, resistir, producir* (forthcoming).

Tsai Pei-hui, Assistant Professor, Graduate Institute for Social Transformation Studies, Shih Hsin University, Taiwan. She is General Secretary of Taiwan Rural Front.

Terence Yuen, currently Research Coordinator at the Centre for Civil Society Studies at the Chinese University of Hong Kong. He is also the founder and CEO of the Hong Kong Institute of Social Impact Analysts, a membership organization promoting the use and implementation of a new social value accounting framework that supports the development of a commons-based economy. He researches social economy, social impact assessment and the collaborative commons.

Preface

Thirty years of economic transformation have changed China and turned it into one of the major players in the global capitalist economy. However, China's economic growth has generated rising problems in inequality, alienation, and sustainability. The crises that gave birth to experiments in social or solidarity economy are the "agrarian crises" of the late 1990s, and the continuous migration and labor conflicts, both being problems of systemic sustainability. "Agrarian crisis" refers to the intertwined problems in sustaining rural production, rural community, and rural livelihood. Three decades ago, the rural reform instituted a separation between ownership and management of farm land. While the ownership of farm land remains collective, the reform made land use and management rights household based. Since the 1990s, much of rural China has seen a decline in agricultural production, the fragmentation and atomization of community life, and difficulties in community cultural reproduction. The family-based peasant economy could neither achieve productivity nor sustain social reproduction, making it difficult to increase the farmers' income, and impossible to develop economic activities other than agriculture in rural areas.

The "agrarian crises" gave rise to social outcry and threatened stability, thus becoming the object of central government policy reformulations, including subsidies and other reform measures. To be sure, recent reform efforts have to some extent mitigated the crises. However, the predicament still remains and exists in economic, communal, and cultural dimensions. In short, household-based agricultural production faces an uncertain future in the context of the marketization of productive materials (seeds, fertilizers, pesticides, etc.), loss of rural talents to the cities, and globalization of capital.

With the opening of coastal China to foreign investment and export-oriented industries that are in great need of cheap labor, large numbers of internal rural migrants emerged. Massive flows of rural migrant workers emerged in the mid-1980s and have been expanding ever since, leading to China's rise as a "world factory." China's development as a "world factory" has created serious potential risks, despite its contribution to economic success. The export-oriented industries are highly reliant on global demand and cheap domestic labor. If there are wild swings in the international market, China's economic growth and employment will be seriously affected. Meanwhile, the domestic market demand is weak due to persistently low labor wages, dimming the prospects for sustainable economic development. Low agricultural output led to a massive flow of rural labor, especially young labor, to the city, which further hampered the development of agriculture and rural areas, and caused social problems like "unprotected migrant workers," "left-behind children," "split families," "unattended elderly," "empty village communities," etc.

Currently, China is at the crossroads of its future development. Confronted by the social inequality and ingrained social contradictions that have been engendered by the development of the market economy over the past 30 years, it is high time for us to reflect on the current mode of development. The capitalist mode of development is obviously not people-centered, but instead controlled by large corporations and capital. The realization of profit thus becomes the sole goal, which ultimately creates disjunction with other forms of local socio-economic development. Not only does this mode of development hamper social development; it cannot resolve the contradictions that are deeply embedded in contemporary Chinese society. We argue that a globalized economy serving the interests of transnational corporations would only result in worsening environmental degradation, deepening exploitation of labor, and further eroding of indigenous cultures and knowledge.

The recent global financial crisis compels us in China and elsewhere to re-examine the neoliberal thought on development that has dominated China for several decades. This thought, characterized by de-collectivization, globalization of capital, deregulation of the economy, privatization of state assets, and lessening of social welfare provisions seriously impacts the livelihood of Chinese peasants, migrant laborers, and the urban poor. Rethinking the rise of China and its social and ecological impact, it is imperative for us who are critical of capitalist ways of development to ponder on alternative economies and other modernity.

This volume is an attempt to rethink space, economy, and community in a trans-border context. It is about reflexively placing China in an alternative world development context that endeavors to move beyond the planned and market economies. The case studies of social or solidarity economies in China and in the world provided in this book were born out of common efforts to counteract the negative social impact of fast global capitalism. In April 2013 we held an International Forum, "Rethinking Economy: Social/Solidarity Economy in China and the World," in Beijing. Leading scholars from Asia, Australia, Europe, Canada, the USA, and Latin America were invited to provide insights into theories of alternative economy and community, experimental and reflexive practices on the ground, and historical review and critique of social economy. Such debates and exchanges were recorded and efforts made to root social or solidarity economy in China and the world in more reflective ways.

In the context of the current economic crisis, this book is far less interested in critiquing the market economy as an end in itself than in constructively exploring an alternative sustainable economy that could strike a balance between economic and social development. Today, the development of social or solidarity economies has reached a critical stage that requires a comprehensive study to evaluate their achievements, as well as to understand the challenges and dilemmas they face. Such a study will facilitate efforts to have collective discussions and to search for solutions. Across the transnational border, new rural cooperatives and alternative economic initiatives are budding and social economies are attracting renewed interest. These are grassroots-based social practices that strive to connect economy with community in new ways.

In contrast with the market economy, the principles of social economy should be people-centered, community-based, cooperative, democratic, as well as upholding a vision of a new society in which production is not for profit-making and consumption, but for servicing the needs of the people. This book strives to contribute to a paradigm-shift in the theory and practices of economic development, as our case studies on social economy show models that organically and sustainably integrate economy with society and community. Our cardinal concerns are how to reconnect the economy with social development, supplement free trade with fair trade, and replace giant and monopoly corporations with social enterprises and cooperatives. Through this approach, we anticipate an "embedded" market that upholds the integrated principles of economic development, social equality, and environmental protection.

This book is divided into three parts. Part I seeks to revolutionize economic ideas and promote new thinking on the economy in China and the world. Amartya Sen, the 1998 Nobel Prize winner in economics, has propounded the revolutionary idea that the quality of life should be measured not by wealth, but by freedom and equality. Supplementing this idea, we suggest that the economy is not about money, a predominant ideology in reform-era China, but about human creativity, development, and participation that ensure the well-being of common people and the sustainability of nature.

In Part I, it is generally agreed that globalization has exerted a major transformation in trade, production, and other economic activities, creating a disembedded market, detached from local communities, which leaves little room for exploring alternatives. The deregulation of the world economy, enabling economic activities to cross political boundaries and allowing unrestricted movements of capital and commodities, has been considered as an act of deceptive neoliberal hegemony that has reduced government intervention, allowed the market to dictate pricing, and widened social and economic inequalities between North and South. These debates have led to the emergence of social or solidarity economy as an alternative strategy for challenging the free market ideology.

Three chapters in Part II contribute to our understanding that the failure of the market economy lies in the inevitable domination by capital, the commodification of people and land, and the destruction of society and the environment. On the other hand, the main weaknesses of the planned economy and the decline of the co-op movement in the West are due to high-level centralization, bureaucratic management, and the lack of motivation and autonomy among workers in the production process. By contrast, the social economy can avoid the pitfalls of the two economic systems. Social economy is not fundamentally about the accumulation of capital. Instead, it is an economic model which re-embeds the economy within social relations. Social economy is democratic, non-monopolistic, and truly prioritizes the developmental needs of communities and individuals. Cooperatives (producer and consumer cooperatives), social enterprises, fair trade, community economy, and collective economy are all concrete examples of social economy.

We seriously engage in alternative models in Argentina, Quebec, the USA, Italy, and some of the Asian countries in Part II that transform the outdated belief in the survival of the fittest as the principle of economic development. In addition to transforming our thinking on the economy, Part II, by introducing six case studies, contributes to a shift in development models from the capitalistic approach to the cooperative and communal approach. Conventional development strategies tend to emphasize competition, entrepreneurship, and individualism, or employ a problem-centered approach that focuses on seeing what the community lacks and what external assistance is needed for development. The new, alternative approach holds that social development must be built based on the change of production mode, redistribution, cooperation, and capacities and assets that already exist within communities or collectivities. Democratic participation, collectivity, respect, equality, and mutual help are regarded as essential for any development model that is sustainable and people-centered. This new approach would not only emphasize sustainable development within local communities, but would also empower communities to develop partnerships with counterpart communities in the world.

Beginning in the late 1990s and due to economic regression and high unemployment, a number of social or community economic projects emerged in Hong Kong and Taiwan. The economic problems brought by the Asian financial crisis have not only exposed the vulnerability of the local free market economy, but also presented a strong challenge to the existing minimal welfare system. The flourishing of socio-economic projects is situated at this particular historical conjuncture. In Part III, we provide case studies on Hong Kong and Taiwan, and demonstrate that since the late 1990s an increasing number of local NGO organizers and trade unionists have shown interest in experimenting with social economic projects. Various kinds of social enterprises, cooperatives, and community-based economic activities have been established since then. In many projects, organizers and participants have endeavored to broaden the meaning of "economy" and "economic practices." For example, the skills of many unemployed or underemployed participants are valued and the services they provide could be traded under an equal, fair, and communal relationship in the cooperatives. It builds up individuals' self-confidence, while reinforcing a sense of mutual assistance and solidarity among participants. In the context of exchange, they go beyond conventional market exchanges that seek maximization through money transactions. For example, the Community-Oriented Mutual Economy project (COME) in Hong Kong, also called the community currency project, uses the "time coupon" to replace "money," to make reciprocity a key basis for communal relationships. This new form of exchange reinforces practices of "sharing" and collective enhancement of social capital as the basis of community-building (Yuen and Chan, Chapter 14).

Three chapters in Part III are born out of emerging grassroots experiments in China, but its proximity with Hong Kong can enable fruitful exchanges in ideas and experiences of social economy, as well as linkages between some cooperatives in South China with Hong Kong. Social economy was introduced to mainland China in the mid-1980s, but was shelved as an academic concept. During recent crises, however, alternative social experiments have emerged in rural and urban settings, making "social economy" a live social practice and igniting discussions in academic writings, policy proposals, and social work practices. Out of this predicament grew grassroots efforts to form cooperative organizations. Currently, 200,000 cooperative organizations, with a total of 11.54 million members, exist among 200 million households in rural China. Although the number of "real" and active cooperatives is far less than 200,000 and many are struggling, rural China has embarked on exploring alternative ways to form relations among economy, community, and culture (Yan and Chen, Chapter 11). Specialized cooperatives are also organized by vegetable producers, fruit growers pig farmers, etc. These specialized cooperatives work together at different levels according to their own conditions and decisions. Some cooperate in purchasing production materials, as aggregated purchases fetch discounts or allow the cooperative to cut out the middlemen and source directly from suppliers. Some extend their cooperation to finance, marketing, and sales. Others cooperate both in farming and food processing.

Cooperatives are organized not only in the economic sphere – technical training, production, marketing, finance – but also around culture-based activities, such as women's handicraft co-ops and performance troupes involving senior villagers. Cultural cooperatives promote communal solidarity and cultural reconstruction. Many cooperatives have evolved from specialized cooperatives (e.g., in finance) to comprehensive cooperatives (e.g., involving finance, production, and cultural activities). Cooperatives might be organized within the village community, but trans-village or trans-township federations of cooperatives also exist. Whereas some cooperatives are organized to benefit from an economy of scale, others are rethinking the relationship between production, sustainability, and community, and have experimented with green or organic farming. With the assistance of volunteers and activists, some handicraft and organic food producer cooperatives have been fostering the formation of urban consumer cooperatives in mainland China.

The reality of mixed economies in mainland China makes it a fertile ground for experimentation with social economy, especially in the setting of collective villages. The impulse for such experiments joins grassroots efforts and a theoretical rethinking of the economic processes in relation to community, people, and sustainability. We recognize that social or solidarity economy as social practice is only at its inception and a consensus has yet to be reached about a theoretical definition of social economy in the Chinese context. While some are promoting "social economy" for its potential to create jobs and maintain stability at a time of financial crisis, others, inspired by the concept of social economy, place "social economy" in a future-oriented social vision and argue that it belongs to the emerging social economy that is a third sector, autonomous from the public/state sector and the private/market sector. Grassroots experiments place social economy hand in hand with community self-governance and the expansion of civic participation. Admittedly, there is a lack of coherent principles in defining what constitutes social economy. Yet this creates an openness that is conducive to discussions and debates about the space, pathways, and future for social economy.

In short, in this book we have invited scholars and practitioners to contribute writings related to theoretical issues, critical reflections, and case studies of the practice of social economy in the context of globalization and its attempt to create an alternative modernity. Through this attempt, we hope to build a platform for further cross-disciplinary and cross-boundary dialogue on the future of social economy in China and the world.

This book is supported by the research project, "Forging New Trans-Border Links: Social/Community Economies in Hong Kong and the Pearl River Delta," Strategic Public Policy Research, 2010 to 2012, and Li and Fung Social Policy Fund.

Reference

Wright, Erik O. 2006. "Compass Points: Towards a Socialist Alternative." *New Left Review* 41, 93–124. Available online at: www.ssc.wisc.edu/~wright/Published%20writing/New%20Left%20Review%20paper.pdf.

Part I

Rethinking economy

1 Social economics and economic anthropology

Challenging conventional economic thinking and practice

John Clammer

This chapter represents a preliminary attempt to outline the conditions, not for solidarity economies (of which many examples exist in the form of numerous experiments worldwide), but for something that should underpin them, notably a solidarity *economics*. Whereas an inductive economic theory may, to an extent, be derived from existing solidarity or social economies, this chapter argues that it is also necessary to attempt the construction of an alternative (to conventional, classical, or neoliberal economics) *foundational theory*, one that builds new and holistic socio-economic theory, not from the assumptions (many of them philosophical and psychological) or existing practices of market economies, but from the aims and principles of the creation of a solidarity economy. A solidarity economy is understood here to be one that is life enhancing in the fundamental sense that economics is simply a tool for the creation of other and largely non-economic ends – human conviviality and equality (including, importantly, gender equality), ecological sustainability, creativity, happiness, health, security, trust, cooperation, and community. Methodological individualism, profit maximization, and the consumerism of mainstream capitalist economics are consequently subordinated to a considerably broader and holistic conception of human needs, people's relationship to nature, and the organization of society. This last point is vital because the notion of a solidarity economy is meaningless unless contextualized in a total environment of solidarity politics, psychology, culture, social organization, and a fundamentally ecological worldview. Solidarity economics consequently implies a broad movement of social transformation that cannot be confined to "economics" in a narrow sense. In light of these thoughts, where might we start our search for such a theory of solidarity economics?

I have argued at length elsewhere (Clammer 2012) that attempts to define and move toward actually creating solidarity economics (a body of theories) and a real solidarity economy (a set of practices and institutions embodying and expressing solidarity economics) would substantially benefit from drawing on the structure and experience of both historical and existing alternatives (i.e., neoliberal capitalism and socialist systems that share its materialistic, productionist, and industrial characteristics), economic systems, and the social, cultural, and ecological bases on which they have sustained themselves, often over long periods. Such a body of knowledge exists, although it is rarely if ever drawn on in either theoretical debates regarding solidarity economics or in practical attempts to embody such economics in social practice. This body of knowledge is economic anthropology.

Economic anthropology is the comparative study of economic systems, often but not always on a small scale, existing largely outside of the paradigm of classical Western and neoliberal economics, although, since the onset of colonialism and globalization, spatially and temporally coexisting with economies based on such neoliberal principles. Economies range over numerous types, including shifting agriculture, subsistence farming, hunting, gathering, and fishing, mixed economies where more than one mode of production exists simultaneously, and transitional economies where money-based and quasi-capitalist elements are beginning to enter traditional and non-monetized economies. This latter situation is typical in colonialism, "development," and with the spread of modern forms of globalization. In addition, certain economic anthropologists and numerous sociologists have studied communes, cooperatives, and other forms of intentional communities (e.g., Veysey 1973; Hall 1978) and forms of social movements that embody widespread socially transformative intentions (e.g., Melucci 1996) and alternative forms of production, distribution, and exchange that they embody; for example, community currencies, farmers' markets, barter, and other forms that fall outside of or exist parallel to the mainstream market economy (Bakshi 2009).

Such studies are potentially of great significance for solidarity economics because they reveal the range of actually or historically existing real "alternative" economies by showing that non-capitalist economic systems are entirely possible, and, rather than allowing such economics to float in an abstract theoretical vacuum, they root it by embedding it in the social, cultural, and ecological milieu in which they exist, and out of which we have been considerably torn in the context of the capitalist, industrial, and consumerist systems in which most of us now lead our lives. They also show that it is possible to create economic systems that are ecologically sustainable and that nurture rather than destroy the solidarity-based and equitable social relationships on which many of these systems are based (Plattner 1994; Narotzky 1997).

Economic anthropology provides the basis for deriving a contemporary solidarity economics. It does so in a number of crucial ways, including (1) showing the theoretical parochialism of neoliberal economics by demonstrating empirically that resources exist for rethinking economic life along radically non-capitalist lines; (2) showing that economies with trade and exchange exist without the "market," as that term is currently conventionally understood; and (3) showing that an essential key to any solidarity economics, and a key entirely missing from conventional neoliberal economics, is the articulation of economic factors with ecological factors, cultures, values, and social practices. It does so by showing that actual and historically tested alternatives to both capitalism and industrial socialism exist, although many of these alternative systems are small in scale, and the issue of scaling up their lessons to meet the needs of large and complex societies must be addressed. If effectively exploited, economic anthropology can become a vital fertilizing element in stimulating fresh thinking of any viable form of alternative or future economy, based as it is on the study of actually or recently existing systems, rather than on utopian or futuristic systems, and how they have managed their relationships with the increasingly hegemonic capitalist system. Even when they have failed to sustain themselves, much can be learned from the survival of solidarity economies on how economies interact and how some have successfully defended themselves against the intrusion of alien values.

The huge range of economic systems that have existed prior to or outside of capitalism (see Forde (1963) for one of the classic surveys) illustrate several factors that any successful solidarity economy must consider. The first of these is that economic life is embedded in social practices, ontologies, institutions (which may be religious or otherwise apparently "non-economic"), and cosmologies. Economic life separated from these factors rapidly becomes destructive of community, values, and cultural practices, creates new patterns of inequality, and is ecologically unsustainable, as we see clearly from the hugely negative impact in all of these spheres of contemporary globalized capitalism and its immediate predecessors such as slave and plantation economies. Conversely, the subject matter of economic anthropology shows that it is possible to have a highly adequate economic life and level of subsistence while respecting cultural values, avoiding the stress that the neoliberal model places on both ecology and people, and placing the fulfillment of genuine and non-spurious human needs and the preservation of nature at the center of life. For example, a major theme in a substantial proportion of current alternative economic thinking is that of localization (McKibben 2007; Shuman 2000) or even of subsistence (Bennholdt-Thomsen and Miess 1999). In the economies studied in economic anthropology, almost inevitably, such economies are already local, drawing on easily accessible regional resources, engaging in trade only when necessary, rarely requiring the transport of resources over long distances, eating locally and seasonally, cultivating local crafts and skills, and consequently achieving high levels of self-sufficiency.

Economic anthropology and the economics of happiness

Conventional economics is in many ways a "virtual science" that creates what it purports to describe rather than actually discovering it in the real world, and which defines for itself and in its own solipsistic terms (rather than identifying what people actually mean by them) essential terms such as "happiness," "satisfaction," "needs," or "progress," and even "poverty," and has self-servingly promoted economic growth in GNP terms as a proxy for human progress and happiness (Carrier and Miller 1998). However, empirical studies conducted from outside of this closed framework reveal a different reality. GNP, for example, is currently well known to be a poor indicator of anything but itself (Naess 1993, 111–116). Studies by sociologists and anthropologists have shown that, in relation to poverty, whereas the reduction of extreme poverty is an urgent and essential goal, once any given country has achieved a moderate per capita income, further increases generate a negligible increase in perceived well-being. Recent studies on what is currently being termed the "economics of happiness" convincingly show that once basic material needs are met, a key factor contributing to happiness and emotional health is the desire for strong communities. In one such study (Diener and Seligman 2004), whereas the super-rich unsurprisingly scored highly on a life satisfaction scale of 0–7 (scoring an average of 5.8), the other highest groups with almost identical scores were the Inuit people of northern Greenland (5.99), the Pennsylvania Amish (5.8), and the semi-nomadic Maasai of Kenya and Tanzania (5.7). The lowest scoring group were Calcutta pavement dwellers (2.9), scoring lower than slum dwellers who, although certainly living in extremely poor physical conditions, had a sense of community, and even of solidarity with one another. In the United States, whereas GDP per capita has trebled over the second half of the twentieth century, satisfaction levels have remained flat, and crime, anxiety, depression, and evidence of psychological and emotional dysfunctions have increased substantially, as has depression (including among children), by more than 10-fold.

Solidarity economics and economic theory

It is established that the basis for most abuses directed at the Earth and its human and biotic communities is the deeply distorted and distorting economy that has been allowed to grow, and which, rather than being our servant, has become our master, successively colonizing almost every level of life and consciousness. Whatever adjustments or protests we might make at other levels of our existence (political, cultural, or spiritual), these will not fundamentally affect our rapidly deteriorating ecological or social justice situation, unless we address in basic and unequivocal ways the nature, operation, and effects of that economic system, and propose workable alternatives to it. "Solidarity economics" has emerged to achieve this goal: an economics devoted not to the expansion of private profit, regardless of ecological and human cost, but to the promotion of human solidarity, the achievement of social, economic, and ecological justice, care for the Earth as our only home, and the creation of a sustainable, humane, and culturally rich future for all the inhabitants of our planet. However, to achieve this, whereas individual examples of "social entrepreneurship" and the many solidarity-promoting social and economic experiments that are occurring worldwide are critical, they will not survive the onslaught of globalized monopoly capitalism, unless they can coalesce into a viable alternative system, which is unlikely, given the diverse, scattered, and democratic nature of the movement toward a solidarity economy. What we also require, and currently mostly lack, is an economic *theory* capable of undermining and providing a viable and powerful alternative to the classical economics on which neoliberal capitalism is based. Economic anthropology, by showing that economic systems can be approached on a comparative basis, demonstrates that different assumptions and value systems underpin those "alternative" systems that are completely at variance with conventional economic thinking.

Alfonso Cotera Fretel (2009, 88–89) suggested much the same:

> The vast scale of these solidarity economy practices shows the enormous potential they could have to reorient economic and political processes.... Unfortunately however they are dispersed and isolated, many not even recognising themselves as expressions of new economic relations and quite unable to project their capacity to confront sub-national, national and regional processes. Efforts to produce theory expressing the reality and proposals of the solidarity economy are still limited.

This last point is crucial. Although we can endlessly produce increasingly more examples of innovative social enterprises, with each valuable in its own right and local context, we cannot confront the dominant system without a theoretical basis to solidarity economics that is as equally convincing as the theoretical underpinnings of classical economics.

Drawing on our knowledge of the possibilities of alternative economies, derived from both historical experience and economic anthropology as well as from an analysis of the failures and violence of neoliberal economies and industrial socialist systems, we can confront the assumptions of conventional economic theory and begin to develop an alternative that can answer the questions that will inevitably be directed toward it by the powerful lobby committed to the theory and practice of neoliberalism.

Neoliberal economics is based on assumptions regarding human nature that are far from being universal. The belief that the desire for material gain, competition, and the profit motive are basic aspects of human psychology and behavior can easily be disproven by the simple comparative exercise of examining through anthropology the experience and practice of other societies. Numerous examples of such societies are available based on cooperation, the notion of conviviality brought into discourse by Ivan Illich (e.g., Overing and Passes 2000), sharing (see Sahlins 1972, a now classic study), and the egalitarian distribution of tasks and resources, in which pure economic gain is always subordinated to the harmony of the group, excessive wealth and inequalities are frowned upon, and those who do possess wealth do so to redistribute it through feasts, the Potlatch, and other devices designed to ensure the flow of resources through the community and their constant circulation. Societies based on gifting rather than on individual profit seeking are not uncommon (Godelier 1996), and the sociology of giving rather than of receiving is a neglected but crucial aspect of any alternative economic theory (Berking 1999).

We suggested that neoliberal economics is a virtual science, based on creating what it purports to describe; that is, it actually creates through mechanisms such as advertising and commodification the characteristics that it then claims are universally true of human nature on which it then bases its own marketing and desire-creating strategies (and theory subsequently based thereupon). Neoliberal economics fails to answer basic questions such as why human beings desire things (other than for purely functional reasons) in the first place. It assumes that among the possible reasons, only one – status seeking – is paramount, when anthropology clearly shows, as does the study of the psychology of material objects (Dittmar 1992), that such material objects fulfill numerous cultural functions. This includes identity formation at the individual and group levels, embodying memories as expressions of creativity, as the material for play, as objects of exchange, and of generosity as in gift societies, where giving and reciprocating are primarily related to establishing and nurturing social bonds, in which context the gifts themselves are largely symbolic. Such societies are by no means always small in scale: contemporary Japan is an adequate example of a society in which an extensive gift economy coexists with, modifies, and draws on the larger capitalist economy in which it is embedded (Clammer 1997).

Neoliberal economics suffers in that, although it represents itself as a science (and much of the work conducted in this field is arcane, mathematical, and entirely inaccessible to the layman, reinforcing this image), it is actually entirely non-holistic in its analysis of human and social behavior. Anthropology has always argued for an integrated view of human societies, one in which the different facets of a total society – its social structure, value system (including religion, ethics, and aesthetics), material culture including its products, fashions, foods, industry, technology, and agriculture, its political system, and its economy – are seen as a single system, a whole in which any one facet is embedded in all the others. Neoliberal economics violates this holism by emphasizing the exclusion of the others for only one facet: the economic. We face today the remarkable situation in which the economy has colonized all these other spheres: the "value" of art is measured primarily in financial terms, and the "success" of an artist by the sale-ability of her or his works and the price that they fetch at an auction. Religions measure their "power" by the number and size of their churches or temples, and by the amount of giving by the members donating to the organization. Almost every element in social and cultural life today is measured through economic success. Areas seemingly outside of the market such as art and religion are not the only areas affected: universities and scholars have also had to bow to this pressure in searching for research grants, funds for buildings, and in the design of their curricula. In the United States, approximately 50 percent of all students enrolled in university-level education are in business studies or economics, often as a preparation for law school, leading to a career in which the practice of law involves the lucrative defense of private property, not the seeking of justice. A major role of solidarity economics is to roll back this process and to recolonize ever-increasing areas of human activity with practices and values that reflect human centeredness and ecological responsibility, rather than the artificially created demands of the market (itself a virtual concept). All economies create subjectivities, ways of understanding the world, the self, and others, and neoliberal economics has created what in historical and comparative terms must be among the strangest and narrowest. It is consequently not simply an economy, but in reality a hegemonic system or form of totalitarianism, disguising itself as a creator of a culture of choice, when the only choices are actually between the things and images that it itself manufactures, approves, advertises, makes available, and socially and culturally supports through a network of status, approval, and "fashionableness."

Underlying neoliberal economics is a set of fundamental concepts that ascribe to it its apparent power. These include terms such as "efficiency," "productivity," "profit," "GNP," and "money." At first sight, such concepts appear definable and measurable until they are subject to both philosophical and anthropological scrutiny. We then find that they have little substance, unless rooted in particular cultural and value-system contexts. Money, for example, is a highly abstract concept, and in practice it takes numerous forms, from the stone money of Micronesia to the community-based currencies that are currently proliferating in the industrial world, such as LETS, HOURS in Ithaca, New York, BREAD in Berkeley, California, and Tianguis Tlaloc in Mexico City (Prelinger 2002). Efficiency and productivity are entirely relative to what one wants to gain from a given situation. For the peoples of highland New Guinea, "productivity" meant production with newly introduced steel tools resulting in exactly the same amount of food and artifacts that used to take considerably longer when using traditional stone tools, and devoting the time this saved to cultural activities, particularly dancing. The notion of efficiency is in any case not simply comparative. It is also true that conventional neoliberal economics is fundamentally inefficient in that it does not account for the true cost of its activities. "Externalities" such as air, water, bio-system services, long-term environmental impact, cost of waste disposal, and the use of non-renewable natural resources are not accounted for in the neoliberal economics model. These common resources being used or abused for private profit are, however, the heritage of all humankind and our fellow creatures. Critiques are now emerging on the use of such conventional indicators of economic "progress" by such measures as GNP, and proposals now abound for more accurate assessment tools such as the Genuine Progress Indicator (GPI), which factors in ecological costs and other externalities absent from the neoliberal economic model.

All this is to say nothing of the social costs of the neoliberal economics. Critiques and analyses of globalization, for example, are now so extensive that they do not bear repeating. Their basic conclusion may be summarized as rising inequalities both between and within countries, biased trade patterns monitored and enforced by the WTO in favor of the major actors, the widespread displacement of people, the destruction of natural economies, massive negative ecological impact, the promotion of poverty and loss of social safety nets, and the creation of an increasingly homogenized culture of consumerism and passive spectacle generated by powerful and transnational media organizations, in many cases constituting what Naomi Klein (2007) has characterized as "disaster capitalism." The critique is only the first stage: in having identified these issues; the problem then becomes to rectify them through an alternative economy. This is again where the question of culture enters: we have already argued for a holistic position in which economy and culture are seen as a single inter-penetrating system. Culture involves not only the production of images, objects, and performances, but also values. Of central significance here is the question of what type of society we want to create. In the neoliberal economic model, values other than those defined in a circular manner as "economic" are normally excluded as irrelevant to the construction of economic models. This is an inversion of the situation in which we should be living: we have allowed the neoliberal economic model to drive out non-economic values (or else to simply consign them to the marginal category of personal beliefs), rather than values defining what we want from an economy, and how we might then best organize that economy to obtain those values and their social, cultural, and institutional expression. Considerable discussion has been devoted in economic anthropology to the concept of rationality (e.g., Godelier 1966), and it is apparent from comparative studies that rationality is not an abstract term: it is relative to the tasks that must be achieved, and the most efficient ways of doing so. Neoliberal economics has forced on us one particular understanding of economic rationality, essentially that of the profit motive, even at the expense of the environment on which all human life and economic activity depends, whereas anthropology reveals to us many rationalities, leading, as history has proved, to sustainable, socially harmonious, and culturally vibrant societies in which humanity and nature come before profit and "efficiency."

This critique of neoliberal economics and advancing beyond it to the creation of viable alternatives implies alliances between solidarity economics and other forms of alternative economic thinking. These theories include the relatively new field of ecological economics, the localization and bio-regionalism movements, the transition movement (Hopkins 2008), and faith-based economic thinking, such as Islamic (Jomo 1993; Naqvi 1981), Buddhist (Schumacher 1973), and Gandhian-inspired economic alternative movements (Rao 1970; Kappen 1990), related movements such as the Indian Swadhyaya movement (Srivastava 1998), post-development thinking (Rahema and Bawtree 1997), the many forms of experiments in creating sustainable communities worldwide, and areas apparently outside of economics, but actually closely related, such as environmental law, sustainable architecture and urban planning, and ecologically responsible forms of agriculture such as permaculture and bio-dynamic agriculture. Furthermore, to complete the holistic approach, alliances must also be formed with artists, cultural workers, people in alternative media such as People's Radio and independent filmmakers, who will be the people to create the actual cultural content of a new economy, and the society that it supports and enables. Anthropology, as well as the study of the numerous literary utopias that populate world literature, shows how this is possible. In many anthropological societies, the division of labor is minor (an artist may also be a farmer or a hunter), often in the way of class divisions. However, other forms of hierarchy may exist, often based on expertise in a particular practical or cultural sphere, and with a cultural life in which all participate both as performers and spectators, where sport, if it exists at all, is non-competitive, and in which a close knowledge of and connection to nature – what today might be called ecological literacy – is considered an essential part of any child's education. Both developed alternative economic models exist; for example, progressive utilization theory (PROUT) founded by the Indian thinker P.R. Sarkar (Maheshvarananda 2003), and the collection and review of both anthropological data and the literature on these models, as well as the so-called new social movements, which show that a lively and extensive body of thought on economic alternatives already exists and is constantly enlarging (some, which have existed for generations, are now mostly forgotten and require recovery, such as the seminal work of the Gandhian-inspired economist J.C. Kumarappa in his major work *Economy of Permanence*). Likewise, the growing body of literature on a post-corporate world must urgently be incorporated into a fresh mode of thought on solidarity economics (Korten 1999, 2006; Theobald 1999), as does the development not only of a new economic theory but also of methodologies for examining the world and its economic aspects that do not share the assumptions of the neoliberal economics, but which help conceptualize and imagine new social futures beyond the narrow paradigm (e.g., Gershon 2009).

Here are also a number of theoretical challenges. The argument against an anthropological approach is often that many of these smaller economies and their social practices are difficult to "scale up," to meet the realities of contemporary large and typically highly urbanized societies. This objection seems to express more of a lack of imagination than an actual empirical difficulty, and alerts us that numerous practical steps must be addressed. The real issue may, instead, be the "scaling down" of the overly large and, in many ways, out-of-control economies of the capitalist world, and of the unmanageable urban centers they consistently generate. A generation ago, a major theme in developmental thinking was the theory of "human needs," an idea that was never refuted, but disappeared from both mainstream and alternative discourse, largely because of the inroads of postmodernism, with its argument that there was no such thing as human nature, or that any human essence actually exists, and that consequently the idea of needs was essentialist. In relation to solidarity economics, however, it seems crucial to resurrect the idea of human needs, considering cultural, historical, gendered, and other distinctions, because without a conception of genuine human needs, a clear notion of what objectives a solidarity economy is pursuing cannot exist. Likewise, much of the existing theory in solidarity economy and its cognates (e.g., community currency movements) assumes the existence of *community*. The problem is, however, that existing forms of capitalist economy have largely destroyed such social formations. The rebuilding of such communities, likely along new lines (in relation to traditional forms of community that were often patriarchal and contained their own internal mechanisms of injustice and inequality), then becomes the sociological correlate of the building of solidarity economies. This is particularly true when we recognize the impact of new technologies on the constitution of society and the existence of new forms of "virtual communities" created through the Internet and other forms of communication-at-a-distance. Therefore, a whole new set of issues arises, of how to create an economic system that is genuinely sustainable (*future*-oriented rather than *progress*-oriented), in which gender equality is central (no more "economic *man!*") because the study of economic anthropology and communes clearly shows that existing forms of solidarity economy do not necessarily guarantee gender equality (or, for that matter, abolish racism or ageism), in which numerous other social and policy adjustments would be necessary, such as an appropriate educational system, a political system (e.g., socialist, eco-socialist, or liberal democratic), the role of the cultural aspects of life, including religion, and the envisioning of cultural life under the regime of a solidarity economy, and the mechanisms of transition from the existing order to such a future state. Central among these issues is that of all economics: the conception of *value.* In a solidarity economy, value cannot obviously be reduced to money, nor necessarily to the Marxist notion of the labor theory of value. Rather, *value* in an economic sense and *values* in a much broader sense must be related in new ways.

Solidarity economy between past and future

Economic anthropology helps us to think against the grain of our currently impoverished social vision, and particularly the all too common belief that globalized capitalism is the only possible form of economic life in a post-socialist world, and that "there is no alternative." Anthropology exposes us to the rich range of social, cultural, political, and economic alternatives that have existed, and in numerous cases continue to exist, despite the inroads of international consumer capitalism and its degraded and commodified culture. A strange feature of contemporary life is that we have allowed the illegitimate colonization of the social, the cultural, and even the realm of values by a particularly impoverished and socially unjust form of economics: what the German social theorist Jürgen Habermas has called the "colonization of our life worlds." If the task at hand is now the decolonization of those worlds, one tool to help us is economic anthropology. The role of solidarity economics is then truly potentially revolutionary, transforming not only economic life in the narrow sense but also the subjectivities, cultures, and institutions that constitute an organic social whole.

Although we cannot, and in a democratic sense should not attempt to define in advance the "ethnography of the future" and its specific social, political, and cultural arrangements, we can certainly draw on the experience, history, and knowledge regarding the social and economic arrangements of societies that have achieved long-term ecological sustainability and high degrees of social equity and harmony. Post-industrial and post-capitalist theorists can learn considerably from the study of actual non-capitalist societies in framing fresh socio-economic possibilities and models for the future, which, if it is not to be simply a replaying of the present, is likely to resemble in numerous crucial respects at least some societies that have been studied by economic anthropologists. Similarly, social movements, about which a considerable amount of sociological and anthropological data now exists, have much to teach solidarity economics and social entrepreneurs regarding the mobilization of resources, often in socially unfavorable conditions, motivating people to action, and the reasons for which such movements often fail, things that may also be learned from the study of communes and cooperatives.

A field that should be closely related to solidarity economics, but often completely separated from it, is that of "development." This is undoubtedly in part because much conventional development is based on neoliberal economics, and thus tends to generate the same types of institutions, economic education, and economic theories as found in existing developed capitalist societies, partly because of a perception of the violence of so much conventional development because it displaces people, destroys nature, disrupts traditional social patterns, and creates unemployment and hyper-urbanization with its attendant pollution, congestion, and waste, and partly because, for all the strivings of conventional economists, the central problem of poverty on a massive scale remains unsolved. However, opposed to such pseudo-development are alternative forms alert to the failures of the past and willing to take new theoretical and practical directions. One of the most effective statements of this is in the work by Francois Perroux (1981), who argues the need for what he terms "integral development": rather than the imposition of development plans from outside, the stimulation of capacities for "auto-creation." In his model, this move has several key elements: the creation of an economy based on genuine human needs and which overcomes the pattern of overconsumption characteristic of contemporary rich economies with its attendant, highly negative impact on nature; overcoming the current crisis of (alternative) theory, or what he terms the "poverty of theory" in both the neoliberal economics and alternative camps; that there has to be a sociological foundation for any workable economy; and that any morally acceptable economy has to be both for all people and for the "whole person." To achieve this requires a radical revision of economics for the "new development" that needs to be integral and endogenous, and to emphasize the vital significance of culture, to stand against the destruction of physical and intellectual potentialities, to contain a deepened and expanded concept of well-being and welfare (*bien-être*), and to move beyond hedonism and materialism. For Perroux, the basic problem is capitalism (or at least big capital), and the loss of the vital connections (or perhaps their distortion) between the social and the economic. The solution can lie only in a fundamental reorientation: modified forms of the neoliberal (e.g., "third way") and growth paradigms have been proven not to work and to actually deepen the crisis. Rather than the economy being at the center of our conception of a good society, human potentialities, fundamental and genuine needs, transcendence, and values should be the core, with the economy existing essentially to serve these needs.

Therefore, linking development to solidarity economics highlights the issues that solidarity economics must confront in expanding its reach to both the already capitalist and the "developing" world alike. Anthropology, having historically concentrated mostly on the economic aspect, contains a vast body of information and insight into the organization of such societies, the consequences of their contact with colonialism, globalization, and monetized societies, and the ways in which they have traditionally managed their relationships internally, with their neighbors through trade, and with nature. We are currently in a global crisis of unprecedented proportions: environmental breakdown, conflicts, resource depletion, rising populations, loss of biodiversity (much of it vital to human well-being as well as having intrinsic value), an erosion of cultures, and the loss of cultural and linguistic diversity. The so-called developed world is also unwilling to restrain itself in its patterns of consumption, militarism, and unsustainable growth and energy generation, with much of the developing world set on a path to emulate the rich world, and both coexisting with scandalous poverty and levels of social and gender exclusion, racism, and a lack of medical, cultural, and educational access. All of this is accompanied by psychological strains, what Max Weber long ago called the "disenchantment of the world," including the loss of magic and mystery that particularly accompanies the widespread destruction of nature or the living in de-natured environments, and a widespread tendency to address all of these ills with managerial "solutions," rather than with social imagination. For social imagination, numerous sources exist: utopias, science fiction, and, as we suggest here, the study of actual and historical societies that have achieved, at least on a smaller scale, much of what we strive for. The great issue for the future (and it contains the ecological issue) is how to achieve humane and sustainable economies and societies without devolving into consumerism, or, posited differently, of how to solve the poverty of much of the globe without reproducing the greed and materialism of most of the already rich world. This requires what Herbert Marcuse a generation ago called the "education of desire," and, as we have argued, economies and subjectivities are deeply embedded in each other. Achieving the goal of solidarity economy is a necessity if our species is to survive and flourish on this planet. Although he may have been wrong in other respects, Karl Marx was undoubtedly correct in arguing that if the economy does not determine culture, it is certainly the main formative influence over it. To create a culture of conviviality requires an economy of conviviality, and of economic and social justice: the two are inseparable.

References

Bakshi, Rajni. 2009. *Bazaars, Conversations and Freedom: For a Market Culture Beyond Greed and Fear.* New Delhi: Penguin Books India.

Bennholdt-Thomsen, Veronika, and Maria Miess. 1999. *The Subsistence Perspective: Beyond the Globalized Economy.* London: Zed Books.

Berking, Helmuth. 1999. *Sociology of Giving.* London: Sage.

Carrier, James G., and Daniel Miller, eds. 1998. *Virtualism: A New Political Economy.* Oxford: Berg.

Clammer, John. 1997. *Contemporary Urban Japan: A Sociology of Consumption.* Oxford: Blackwell.

Clammer, John. 2012. *Culture, Development and Social Theory: Towards an Integrated Social Development.* London: Zed Books.

Diener, Ed, and Martin E.P. Seligman. 2004. "Beyond Money: Toward an Economy of Well-Being." *Psychological Science in the Public Interest* 5(1): 1–31. Available online at: www.psychologicalscience.org/pdf/pspi/pspi5_1.pdf.

Dittmar, Helga. 1992. *The Social Psychology of Material Possessions: To Have Is to Be.* Hemel Hempstead: Harvester Wheatsheaf.

Forde, Cyril Daryll. 1963. *Habitat, Economy and Society: A Geographical Introduction of Ethnology.* New York: E.P. Dutton.

Fretel, Alfonso Cotera. 2009. "Visions of a Responsible, Plural, Solidarity Economy in Latin America and the Caribbean." In *A Non-Patriarchal Economy is Possible: Looking at Solidarity Economy from Different Cultural Facets*, edited by Marcos Arruda (pp. 87–90). Rio de Janeiro: Alliance for a Responsible, Plural and Solidarity Based Economy (ALOE).

Gershon, David. 2009. *Social Change 2.0: A Blueprint for Reinventing Our World.* West Hurley, NY: High Point/Chelsea Green.

Godelier, Maurice. 1966. *Rationalite et irrationalite en economie* [Rationality and Irrationality in Economy]. Paris: Francois Maspero.

Godelier, Maurice. 1996. *L'Enigme du don* [The Enigma of the Gift]. Paris: Librairie Artheme Fayard.

Hall, John R. 1978. *The Ways Out: Utopian Communal Groups in an Age of Babylon.* London: Routledge & Kegan Paul.

Hopkins, Rob. 2008. *The Transition Handbook: From Oil Dependency to Local Resiliance.* Totnes: Green Books.

Jomo, Kwame Sundaram, ed. 1993. *Islamic Economic Alternatives: Critical Perspectives and New Direction.* Kuala Lumpur: Ikraq.

Kappen, Mercy, ed. 1990. *Gandhi and Social Action Today.* New Delhi: Sterling Publishers.

Klein, Naomi. 2007. *The Shock Doctrine: The Rise of Disaster Capitalism.* New York: Picador.

Korten, David C. 1999. *The Post-corporate World: Life after Capitalism.* San Francisco, CA: Berrett-Koehler.

Korten, David C. 2006. *The Great Turning: From Empire to Earth Community.* Bloomfield, CT: Kumarian Press.

Maheshvarananda, Dada. 2003. *After Capitalism: Prout's Vision for a New World.* Copenhagen: Proutist Universal Publications.

McKibben, Bill. 2007. *Deep Economy: The Wealth of Communities and the Durable Future.* New York: Holt Paperbacks.

Melucci, Alberto. 1996. *Challenging Codes: Collective Action in the Information Age.* Cambridge: Cambridge University Press.

Naess, Arne. 1993. *Ecology, Community and Lifestyle.* Translated and edited by David Rothenberg. Cambridge: Cambridge University Press.

Naqvi, Syed Nawab Haider. 1981. *Ethics and Economics: An Islamic Synthesis.* Leicester: The Islamic Foundation.

Narotzky, Susana. 1997. *New Directions in Economic Anthropology.* London: Pluto Press.

Overing, Joanna, and Alan Passes, eds. 2000. *The Anthropology of Love and Anger: The Aesthetics of Conviviality in Native Amazonia.* London: Routledge.

Perroux, Francois. 1981. *Pour une philosophie du nouveau developpment* [For a New Philosophy of Development]. Paris: Aubier/Les Presses de l'UNESCO.

Plattner, Stuart, ed. 1994. *Economic Anthropology.* Stanford, CA: Stanford University Press.

Prelinger, Megan Shaw. 2002. "How Parallel Economies Are Working Against Global Capitalism." In *The Anti-Capitalist Reader: Imagining a Geography of Opposition*, edited by Joel Schalit (pp. 175–185). New York: Akashic Books.

Rahema, Majid, and Victoria Bawtree, eds. 1997. *The Post-Development Reader.* London: Zed Books.

Rao, Vijendra Kasturi Ranga Varadaraja. 1970. *The Gandhian Alternative to Western Socialism.* Bombay: Bharatiya Vidya Bhavan.

Sahlins, Marshall. 1972. *Stone Age Economics.* Chicago, IL: Aldine.

Schumacher, Ernst Friedrich. 1973. "Buddhist Economics." In *Toward a Steady-state Economy*, edited by Herman E. Daly (pp. 231–239). San Francisco, CA: W.H. Freeman.

Shuman, Michael H. 2000. *Going Local: Creating Self-Reliant Communities in a Global Age.* New York: Routledge.

Srivastava, Raj Krishnan, ed. 1998. *Vital Connections: Self, Society, God: Perspectives on Swadhyaya.* New York: Weatherhill.

Theobald, Robert. 1999. *We DO Have Future Choices: Strategies for Fundamentally Changing the 21st Century.* Lismore, NSW: Southern Cross University Press.

Veysey, Laurence. 1973. *The Communal Experience: Anarchist and Mystical Communities in Twentieth-Century America.* New York: Harper & Row.

2 Mapping social and solidarity economy

The local and translocal evolution of a concept

Craig Borowiak

Currently, approximately six years after the 2008 world financial crisis began, economies worldwide are still reeling from its effects. The cascading effects of foreclosures, forestalled retirements, diminished savings, high levels of unemployment, ballooning fiscal deficits, sovereign debt debacles, dwindling export revenues, and currency instability, among other woes, have drastically reshaped economic geographies. Nonetheless, despite all the damage it has wrought, the 2008 financial crisis may have also opened up new vistas of economic possibility as communities have been forced to find new ways to meet their needs. In tough times – today, as always – reciprocity and social solidarity often help people survive. In recent years, experiments with alternative, solidarity-based economic practices have proliferated worldwide as populations grapple with hardship and attempt to re-envision economic futures that are healthier for communities and the environment. Cooperatives, community-supported agriculture (CSA), community currencies, community land trusts, and social enterprises are only a few examples of initiatives that prioritize social norms such as equity, social and ecological sustainability, cooperation, workplace democracy, and community-based development above profit maximization, private ownership, and competition.

Although initiatives such as these are altering local economic landscapes, they typically fall out of mainstream studies of the economy, which focus instead on state budgets, for-profit capitalist enterprises, and the market economy. Furthermore, to the extent that these entities are studied, they tend to be treated in isolation from one another. Thus, worker cooperatives are studied independently from consumer cooperatives, which are studied independently from social enterprises, community gardens, CSAs, credit unions, and so on. This piecemeal approach contributes to the further underrepresentation of such economic practices in empirical and theoretical research and to the perception that they represent, at best, small niches in the economy. For numerous practitioners and activists, however, the value of these diverse practices and their interconnections is far more apparent. In many countries, these organizational forms and practices have begun to coalesce into a self-identified movement promoting the social and solidarity economy (SSE).

This chapter chronicles the emergence of the social and solidarity economy framework and maps the rise of a global solidarity economy movement, from its purported origins in Europe and Latin America to the creation and consolidation of an intercontinental network for the social and solidarity economy. This narrative draws particular attention to three counterhegemonic features of this movement and its framework. First, the movement's commitments to local self-determination, participatory development, and non-reductive modes of solidarity make it a model of cosmopolitan organizing and economic development that contrasts sharply with the centralizing, hierarchizing, and universalizing tendencies of mainstream development paradigms. Second, the movement draws energy from the observation that reciprocity-based non-capitalist practices already exist in even the most capitalist of economies. It seeks to support and build an awareness of such practices, and to create new opportunities for further experimentation. In this respect, the movement discloses and validates economic alternatives that are otherwise obscured within mainstream economic paradigms. Finally, given its breadth and flexibility, the social and solidarity economy framework provides a basis for building conceptual and material connections among otherwise highly diverse practices spanning the economic cycle. Against hegemonic frameworks that would isolate and then render these alternatives economically marginal, the social and solidarity economy framework reflects a more holistic approach that regards the diverse economic practices as mutually constitutive of a larger segment of the economy. The movement is consequently able to recognize the substantial and broad community impacts that diverse economic alternatives have when they are conceived together rather than separately.

This chapter comprises two sctions. The first is a description of the histories of the social and solidarity concept and movement, including some of the definitional variations that characterize the movement. The second section outlines the counterhegemonic implications of the movement and provides a description of the various tactics the movement has used to make solidarity economy practices visible and to foster connections among them. This includes a discussion of conceptual, geographic, and economic mapping strategies, as well as a discussion of more qualitative studies involving the narration of particular case studies.

History of social and solidarity economy

What is social and solidarity economy? The composite expression "social and solidarity economy" itself reflects a convergence of two related concepts – the "social economy" and the "solidarity economy" – with distinct, albeit overlapping histories, which are described as follows.

Social economy

The concept of social economy (*économie sociale* in French) has a longer pedigree, dating at least as far back as the early nineteenth century. In the 1830s, liberal French economist Charles Dunoyer described social economy as a way to augment political economy (by which he meant the new economic paradigms inspired by Adam Smith and David Ricardo, among others). In the 1850s, at a time of greater worker mobilization and cooperative development, socialist Auguste Otte conceived social economy not as an augmentation, but as a substitute for political economy. Around that time, French sociologist Frédéric Le Play drew greater attention to the concept with the founding of both the *Société Internationale des Etudes Pratiques d'Economie Sociale* and the *Revue d'Économie Sociale*. Thereafter, around the turn of the century, Charles Gide and Leon Walras further elevated the academic and public profile of *économie sociale*.[1] Both defined the concept as the "science of social justice" in contrast to the "science of utility" that characterized classical political economy. For them, social economy was complementary to the market economy in that it provided for social needs left unmet by the market. Gide in particular highlighted the role of cooperative and solidarist economic relations (Moulaert and Ailenei 2005; Demoustier and Rousselière 2006).

The concept seems to have fallen from public attention in the mid-twentieth century, arguably because of the rise of the modern welfare state, only to re-emerge again in the 1970s, this time under conditions of economic hardship combined with skepticism regarding the capacity of either state planning or capitalist markets to provide for social needs. The pioneering work by Henri Desroche and Claude Vienney in analyzing the common characteristics of cooperatives, associations, and mutual societies helped reignite interest in the concept of social economy (Vienney 1994; Desroche 1983, 1991; Laville *et al.* 2007). Social economy came to represent an alternative way to meet social needs that do not involve state redistribution or competitive markets organized around profit maximization; in other words, beyond being simply economic activity with a social purpose, it came to be interpreted through the analytic division of the economy into three distinct sectors: the state sector characterized by planning and public service, the market sector characterized by private action and profit orientation, and the third sector, which was characterized by self-help, mutualism, and social purpose. The social economy came to refer to voluntary and community-oriented economic activities falling into the third sector, outside of the for-profit market sector in one aspect, and the state-based public sector in another. Specifically, social economy came to refer to the specific organizational forms of mutuals, cooperatives, and associations. As Defourny and Develtere (1999) described it, social economy may be delimited in two ways. First, it may be defined according to the types of organization that participate. The three primary organization types are cooperative organizations, mutual aid societies, and associations. Second, an alternative way to define social economy is according to a set of key principles. This includes co-ops, mutual aid societies, and associations that (1) place services to members or to the community above profit; (2) have autonomous management; (3) have democratic decision-making; and (4) give primacy of people and work over capital in the distribution of revenues. Unlike the "non-profit sector" – a term in wider use in the United States and other Anglophone contexts – the concept of social economy is not exclusive of for-profit enterprises as long as they follow cooperative principles.

Outside of Francophone Europe, the social economy concept has been developed to include a broader set of practices. The British activist and theorist

John Pearce (2003), for example, adapted the three-sector model in ways that both extend the meaning of the third sector (what he calls the third system) beyond only social economy, and extend the meaning of social economy to include various entities in addition to mutuals, co-ops, and associations (Figure 2.1).

For Pearce, what defines the third system is the principle of reciprocity, which he opposes to the profit motive and planning that characterize the first and

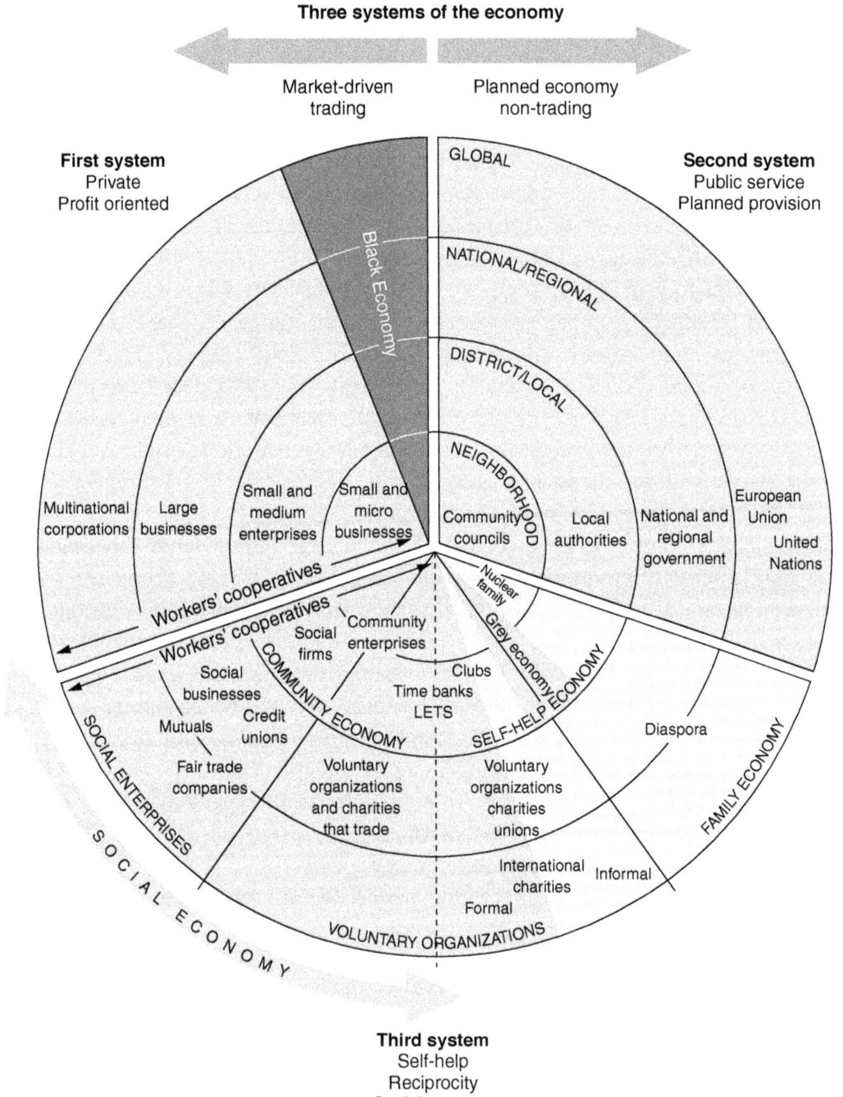

Figure 2.1 The three systems (source: Pearce (2003, 25). By permission of the Calouste Gulbenkian Foundation).

second systems, respectively. Defined in terms of reciprocity, the third system includes family- or kinship-based economies as well as social economy. In social economy, Pearce includes entities such as time banks, fair trade companies, and social enterprises.

In Canada, social economy similarly includes hybrid economic forms that span the state and the market sector. Examples include social enterprises, community economic development, public sector non-profit organizations, and state-subsidized cooperative elder and child care (Amin 2009; Quarter *et al.* 2009; Mendell and Neamtan 2010). In this respect, social economy has more directly come to resemble what is elsewhere called the "solidarity economy," a concept that is described as follows.

Solidarity economy

Compared with social economy, the concept of solidarity economy has a considerably shorter history. Although the concept of social solidarism had been developed in the early twentieth century by figures such as Charles Gide in France, the contemporary concept of solidarity economy appears to have first been developed in the mid-1980s by sociologists Luis Razeto of Chile and Jean-Louis Laville of France, who had independently posited the concept to visualize, analyze, and propagate the transformative economic practices that were emerging worldwide (Razeto 2010; Laville *et al.* 2007; Laville 1994).

In Latin America in the 1980s, the combination of authoritarian rule, a regional debt crisis, and neoliberal policies had caused significant social and economic hardships and dislocation for numerous communities. In Chile, as in many other countries in the region, unemployment was high, and the state offered little welfare support. Furthermore, the legacy of civil war and authoritarian reprisal in the region had led to disenchantment with revolutionary forms of resistance, and the 1973 coup that had installed Pinochet in power had foreclosed the possibility of achieving socialism through formal democratic institutions. After spending the post-coup years in Italy, where he gained experience with the cooperative movement there, Razeto returned to Chile to find numerous local communities innovating with alternative economic practices to cope. Collective kitchens, community service centers, labor workshops, labor exchanges, and cooperatives were only a few of the new, popular, economic initiatives organized around the collective strategies of survival and social justice. In this context, Razeto began organizing meetings under the framework of the Program for Labor Economics (PET). In such a meeting, a local community member coined the expression "solidarity economy," thus combining the principles of solidarity (advocated by the Church) and those of economic development (advocated by NGOs) (Razeto 2010). Adopting this terminology, Razeto then theorized solidarity economy in opposition to development models centered on either the state or the assumption of individualism and profit maximization. He underlined the importance of reciprocal relations and the sense of belonging often found in traditional societies. He called for an "economy of solidarity" organized around cooperative endeavors to satisfy common needs and to achieve the well-being of local communities. In such an economy, economic enterprises would embody cooperation, co-responsibility, communication, collaboration, and community, all of which help constitute what Razeto calls "Factor C" (1998, 2010). His concept was not to dispense with the state and market sectors of the economy, but instead to devise methods to spread cooperation into those sectors. His idea was not to overthrow capitalism so much as to resist its monological imposition, and to infiltrate its operation through cooperative principles. This notion of *economia solidaria* was subsequently adopted by other activists and academics in Columbia, Brazil, Argentina, and across Latin America, where it has continued to flourish (Coraggio and Arroyo 2009; Mance 2002; Rodríguez-Garavito 2006).

Around the same time that *economia solidaria* was being introduced in Latin America, French sociologist Jean-Louis Laville introduced *économie solidaire* in continental Europe. Economic hardship was again a prime motivator. In Europe, however, the key reference points were not traditional economies, authoritarian states, and the dislocations induced by neoliberal austerity measures, but instead the crisis of the Keynesian welfare state that was generating a reconfiguration of state–economy relations, as well as the growing influence of civil society in the economy, not merely as an adjunct to the state and the market but as a complementary pole (Evers and Laville 2004; Laville *et al.* 2007). In the mid-1980s, Laville used the language of *économie solidaire* to intervene in ongoing research on social economy in Europe. As opposed to those who focus only on the organizational forms of cooperatives, mutuals, and associations, Laville used the concept of *économie solidaire* to prioritize the normative commitment to reciprocity and solidarity as a strategy for social integration. He also used it to highlight the need to extend cooperative principles so that they would apply to the public and market sectors of the economy in addition to the third sector. What mattered most for Laville was not, for example, whether an organization was organized as a cooperative, but rather whether it organized its activities around social solidarity and reciprocity (Laville *et al.* 2007). Laville's conceptualization of *économie solidaire* influenced social economy research across much of Europe (particularly in Francophone countries) such that solidarity economy and social economy are now frequently combined into one expression: *l'économie sociale et solidaire.* This is also how the concepts appear in transcontinental networks promoting the movement.

The spread of the social and solidarity economy movement

Taken together, and to an extent along separate tracks, the Latin American and Francophone European perspectives have built momentum around the notion of the social and solidarity economy (SSE). The framework has been adopted and theorized by practitioners, activists, and academics across the globe as a way to comprehend and foster value-based, socially embedded economic practices and to build linkages across geographies and economic sectors. With the spread of the SSE concept, several new transnational networks have been formed. Vibrant SSE networks may be found across Western Europe. The Latin American Solidarity Economy Network (*Las Redes Latinoamericanas de Economía Solidaria y Políticas Públicas*) has been in place since 1998. An Asian Social Solidarity Economy Forum was formed in 2007. New networks have been forming in Africa, including in Francophone West African countries such as Senegal, Mali, and Burkina Faso. In Canada, Quebec has been a pioneer with its SSE campaigns and networking. In the United States, the U.S. Solidarity Economy Network (USSEN) was founded in the spring of 2007.

On a global level, the first "International Meeting for the Globalization of Solidarity" was held in 1997 in Lima, Peru. This first meeting allowed activists of the social solidarity economy from around the world to meet and exchange their experiences and ideas on the subject. The meeting resulted in a declaration opposing development models built around cutthroat competition and advocating the creation of a solidarity economy that incorporates "cooperation, collective sharing, and action," in addition to "putting the human being at the centre of the economic and social development" (RIPESS 1997). The movement then received a substantial boost with the creation of the World Social Forum (WSF) in 2001. The WSF meetings catalyzed discussions regarding alternatives to capitalist globalization and considerably facilitated regional and global networking among civil society actors involved in alternative economic organizing. In 2001, a second International Meeting for the Globalization of Solidarity was held in Quebec. This resulted in the founding of the Intercontinental Network for the Promotion of the Social and Solidarity Economy (RIPESS). Subsequent RIPESS conferences have been held in 2005 in Senegal, in 2009 in Luxembourg, and in 2013 in Manila. RIPESS provides institutional stability for the movement worldwide and now includes over 60 social and solidarity economy networks and groups in its framework. Other major international conferences on the SSE have also been organized outside of the RIPESS structure. In 2011, for example, an International Forum on the Social and Solidarity Economy (FIESS) was held in Montreal. In May 2013, the U.N. Research Institute for Social Development held a conference on "the Potential and Limits of Social and Solidarity Economy." Momentum clearly exists behind the SSE concept, which is sustained by a combination of a backlash against the alienating and disruptive effects of neoliberalism, the rise of ethical consumer consciousness among the middle class in rich nations, new networking opportunities made available by globalization, the appeal of pragmatic alternatives that eschew ideological battles between the state and the market, and the efforts of young people to adapt their lifestyles creatively to the realities of ecological change and the limits of growth.

Mapping counter-hegemonic implications of the SSE

Having briefly described the evolution of the SSE concept and movement, I now turn to three methods by which the SSE challenges capitalist and statist hegemonies. First, it embraces a decentralizing pluralism that counters the monological and hierarchical tendencies of dominant development paradigms. Second, it makes existing economic alternatives visible in ways that they are not within mainstream economic paradigms. Third, beyond merely recognizing existing economic alternatives, the SSE provides a framework for building further solidarities across diverse geographies and economic sectors. This allows us to view the SSE as non-marginal to the economy, and also to further develop the SSE across its diverse instantiations.

Solidarity across diversity

As this narrative begins to reveal, a considerable variation exists within the SSE movement. Diversity may even be considered to be one of the SSE's defining characteristics. The movement's diversity comes in many forms.

Linguistic diversity exists. This is a multilingual movement that spans world regions. Spanish, French, Portuguese, Italian, and English dominate international SSE discussions, but the movement also reaches many national, local, and indigenous language groups in East, South, and Southeast Asia, as well as indigenous language communities across the Americas. The linguistic differences can present a barrier to communication and cooperation, particularly when translating from the international network into local languages. In numerous parts of Asia, for example, English is the dominant language for transnational networking, but many, if not most, participants in SSE practices speak only their native tongue. Despite such difficulties, the SSE movement nevertheless accepts, on principle, the importance of respecting linguistic diversity, and, where possible, it takes measures to enable participants to communicate in their own languages.

In addition to linguistic diversity, terminological diversity also exists, even within the same language. I have already presented the differences between the terms *social economy* and *solidarity economy*. Although the two concepts overlap, each conveys a slightly different meaning. Numerous other concepts are currently in use that reference similar types of socially embedded economic activity. Examples of alternative frameworks include *local living economy*, *community economy, community economy development*, *people's economy*, *cooperative economy*, *pluralist commonwealth*, *new economy*, and *buen vivir*. Many more terms exist, each with its own advocates, and each providing a unique framework for conceiving and validating alternative economic practices. Certain concepts, such as *local living economy*, *community economy*, and *community economic development*, prioritize localism and communal attachment, without necessarily highlighting solidarity across communities and localities, and without necessarily indicating the dangers associated with communal exclusions.[2] Other terms, such as *people's economy*, a term that appears to find a stronger footing in certain Asian contexts, is more suggestive of an anti-hierarchical populism that is grassroots, without being limited to particular communities. *Cooperative economy*, in turn, ascribes greater emphasis to the formation of cooperatives, although the expression may also be more broadly read as support for cooperation. *Pluralist commonwealth* and the *new economy* are concepts that have gained some traction in the United States. Both are broadly inclusive of a substantial variety of economic activities in ways that are relatively non-threatening to vested capitalist interests. *Buen vivir* is a concept that has drawn attention across parts of Latin America, particularly in Bolivia and Equador, where it has been incorporated into constitutional law (Gudynas 2011). The concept taps into indigenous traditions and is suggestive of an alternative model of development in which well-being is tied to both community and nature. In certain respects, these terms and concepts compete with the SSE to define the movement. Tensions may emerge when one category of economic activity is included in one framework, but not in another. For example, in the United States, the *pluralist commonwealth* and *new economy* frameworks include employee stock ownership plans (ESOPs), whereas the local solidarity economy network does not. From another perspective, however, these different methods of conceptualizing alternative economic practices all have affinities with one another in their support for alternatives. Together they form a constellation of concepts that stands apart from the neoliberal economic principles that govern prevailing models of economic development.

Beyond its terminological and linguistic variations, the SSE movement is also shaped by diversity in the way the SSE is operationalized. The definitional work and research that exist on the SSE are directed mostly by practitioners, with universities serving only a complementary role. Because of the newness and grassroots character of the movement, as well as the diversity of participants and languages, defining the concept of solidarity economy is not an easy task. Rather than searching for a single definition, it is more appropriate to examine solidarity economy's plural meanings.

As the SSE concept has spread, its meaning has been adapted to local contexts. In Francophone Europe, for example, as mentioned, the distinction between social economy and solidarity economy remains crucial, and therefore it is critical to discuss both. There, too, the definition of social economy is closely tied to the third sector, and to associations, cooperatives, and mutuals (Moulaert and Ailenei 2005). In Quebec, despite sharing the French language, the distinction between social economy and solidarity economy has less importance. This is partially because social economy is interpreted more broadly to include hybrid economic forms spanning the three sectors. Greater attention is ascribed, for example, to multi-stakeholder cooperatives and social enterprises operating with partial support from both the government and civil society. In the United Kingdom, a particular focus is placed on progressive financial institutions and social enterprises coping with a weakened welfare state (Murray 2009; Amin 2009). In Brazil, in contrast, the language of solidarity economy dominates that of social economy. There, solidarity economy is strongly associated with worker self-management and reflects the country's history with liberation theology, worker factory takeovers, and the landless worker movement (Singer 2006; Arruda 2009; Mance 2002; Wolford 2010). To be considered as part of solidarity economy by the Brazilian Secretariat for the Solidarity Economy, an organization must reflect four principles: solidarity, economic activity, cooperation, and self-management (Figure 2.2).

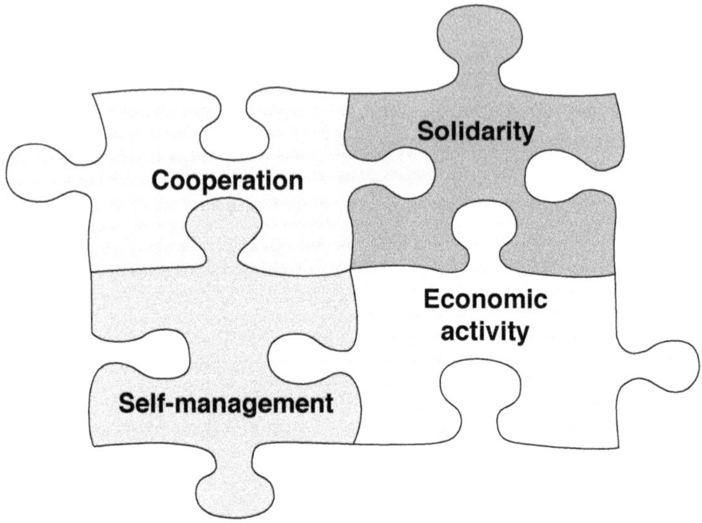

Figure 2.2 Solidarity economy characteristics, Brazilian Secretariat for Solidarity Economy (source: adapted from Brazil Ministry of Labor and Employment (2008)).

In Mexico, community currencies, barter networks, and craft cooperatives have a higher profile. There, symbolic ties to indigenous histories and traditions are also prominent, as evidenced in the use of Aztec symbols on community currencies and in the organization of barter arrangements modeled on pre-Columbian traditions. Across much of South, Southeast, and East Asia, SSE is strongly associated with micro-credit, fair trade, and social enterprises (Jayasooria 2013). In the United States, the U.S. Solidarity Economy Network (USSEN) has defined the SSE broadly around the following set of six core principles:

1 Solidarity, mutualism, and cooperation.
2 Equity in all dimensions: race/ethnicity/nationality, class, gender, and LGBTQ.
3 The primacy of social welfare over profits and the unfettered rule of the market.
4 Sustainability.
5 Social and economic democracy.
6 Pluralism and organic, bottom-up development.

From these principles, a provisional typology of SSE entities has been generated (see Table 2.1).

Here, the entities are organized under labels that indicate whether they are primarily modes of consumption, production, finance, exchange, or governance.

Table 2.1 U.S. typology of solidarity economy entities

Alternative consumption	*Alternative production*	*Alternative finance*	*Alternative exchange*	*Governance*
Consumer cooperatives	Worker cooperatives	Credit unions	Fair trade networks	Participatory budgeting
Buying clubs	Producer cooperatives	Community development credit unions	Community-supported agriculture and fisheries	Collective community management of resources
Co-housing	Volunteer collectives	Peer lending	Complementary currencies	
Intentional communities	Community gardens		Barter networks	
Housing cooperatives	Collectives of self-employed		Free-cycle networks	
Community land trusts	Unpaid care work		Time banks	

Source: U.S. Solidarity Economy Network (2012).

This categorization by organization type has appeal in the United States. It has less appeal in contexts where solidarity economy practices are more informal, and where large entities that are legally constituted as cooperatives act in abusive rather than in solidaristic ways.

Generally, in developing and agrarian economies, interpretations of the SSE concept tend to be influenced by traditional or indigenous economic practices, which are often informal and which, in their own ways, have consistently offered points of resistance to the intrusion of capitalist markets. In industrial or post-industrial settings, by contrast, the SSE concept is more closely associated with more formal modes of organization and with the formal principles of the modern cooperative movement. Furthermore, as Ash Amin describes, in developed market economies with strong welfare states, the SSE is viewed as a parallel system, capable of prospering alongside both the state and capitalist markets. In left-leaning countries with weaker market economies and weaker states, however, the SSE is considered to offer more radical post-capitalist possibilities (Amin 2009, 15–16). These variations appropriately reflect differences in culture, context, and history. Different communities have various struggles, different economic positions, different relationships to markets and the government, and different traditions on which to draw. It would in fact be unusual if one definition were applicable everywhere.

Despite this diversity in the way the SSE is operationalized in different regions, it is still possible to identify a loose set of shared values. The underlying objective is one of re-embedding economic relations within the social relationships of cooperation and reciprocity. It is a desire to center economic activity on human needs, rather than on the insatiable desire for profit. As Brazilian economist Marcos Arruda (2004, 2) describes:

> It [solidarity economy] is economic activity organized for safe and sustainable individual and collective self-development, which implies the shared satisfaction of needs and wants and the co-management of the people share in common – the home, the community, the district, the county, the ecosystem, the country, the planet. It is an ethical, reciprocal and cooperative way of consuming, producing, financing, exchanging, communicating, educating, developing which fosters a new way of thinking and living.

Such articulations of principle provide a general orientation without much specificity regarding what does and does not count as SSE. One of the most interesting things about the movement is the manner in which participants have embraced both the loose normative generalities and the variations in meaning across countries. They see the different definitions themselves as a reflection of solidarity across differences. Beginning from decentralized local contexts, new translocal solidarity economy linkages are being built and institutionalized in ways that work toward as much convergence as is possible, but without the expectation that a uniform definition can or should be achieved or imposed. As Brazilian activist Ana Mercedes Sarria Icaza stated,

> To speak of a solidarity economy is not to speak of a homogeneous universe with similar characteristics. Indeed, the universe of the solidarity economy reflects a multiplicity of spaces and forms, as much in what we would call the informal aspects (size, structure, governance) as in qualitative aspects (levels of solidarity, democracy, dynamism, and self-management).
>
> (Miller 2006, 14)

This brings me to a primary way in which the SSE offers a counterhegemonic alternative. As a paradigm for development (or, more appropriately, as a model of "post-development," as theorized by Escobar (1995)), the SSE contrasts sharply with the hierarchical and centralizing models that have long characterized international development institutions. For centuries, models of cosmopolitan emancipation, whether conceived as economic or spiritual emancipation, have been imposed from a cultural and economic center on subjected peoples, most often with little regard for the perspectives of those meant to be emancipated (Mignolo 2000). This has certainly been true for the ascendance of international development models and institutions in the twentieth century. Dominant economic development programs have been hierarchical, centralized, and universalizing while discounting the voices and perspectives of subjected and subaltern populations who do not speak the master language or who do not share the hegemonic epistemologies (Santos 2005). By contrast, the SSE movement's open embrace of difference, in addition to its principled commitment to respecting cultural, linguistic, and historical contexts and to promoting local self-determination and self-governance, both lends it a flexibility that helps it sustain itself and engenders a rooted and critical form of cosmopolitanism.

Making economic alternatives visible

The SSE challenges capitalist hegemonies in another manner: it makes economic alternatives visible as alternatives. This is particularly crucial owing to the occlusion of alternatives by what J.K. Gibson-Graham refer to as the "capitalocentrism" of contemporary discourse. The economic activity validated by neoclassical economics represents only a minute fraction of human efforts to meet needs and fulfill desires, and yet the prevailing economic discourse would have us believe that capitalist markets either saturate our existing economies or provide the only viable prospect for statist and developing economies. In their response to capitalocentrism, Gibson-Graham (1996, 2006) call on us to "read for difference," by which is meant that we should interpret economic practices in ways that emphasize how they depart from rather than conform to the capitalist norm, thereby yielding an image of our economic landscape as populated by a great diversity of economy forms. Once we are able to recognize such diverse economies, Gibson-Graham argue, we will be better able to find openings for projects of non-capitalist invention and to construct different types of economic community. The SSE movement may be seen in this light; it is making visible – it is visibilizing – non-capitalist alternatives that already exist.

This visibilizing function is particularly crucial owing to the legacy of the Cold War and the contemporary patterns of globalization. During most of the twentieth century, cooperativist theory was overshadowed by collectivist experiments with state socialism and centralized economies. Such experiments proved, in many instances, to be both politically oppressive and economically unsustainable. The collapse of centralized economies subsequently left a void regarding the envisioning of emancipatory political economies. Once state socialism was removed, it became unclear what alternatives to capitalism remained. Consequently, in the two decades since the fall of the Berlin Wall, the global political economy has been dominated by what Boaventura de Sousa Santos (2005), following Franz Hinkelammert, has called the conservative utopianism of neoliberal globalization. Instead of a utopianism that uses a vision of the world as it *could be* as a way to elucidate the shortcomings of the world *as it is*, the neoliberal worldview has relished the triumph of capitalism over communism while rejecting the viability of alternatives to present-day reality. It is utopian because it views capitalist economies as the best of all possible worlds. It is conservative because it denies possibilities outside of the present reality, which is narrowly construed. Between state socialist dystopias and neoliberal conservative utopias, the SSE offers new avenues for social, economic, and political restructuring.

How does the SSE movement perform this counterhegemonic function of visibilizing economic alternatives? One way is by narrating case studies of particular initiatives in ways that draw out their solidaristic character. The bulk of published material on the SSE consists of edited volumes containing numerous qualitative examples. Conferences and symposia on the SSE are similarly replete with presentations and images of particular case studies. Presenting qualitative case studies is a useful approach to conveying optimal practices and to expanding the realm of the possible for practitioners for whom the cases reveal different ways of conducting business.

In addition to case studies, some of the most interesting work being conducted on the solidarity economy to date involves mapping. Numerous participating networks have undertaken mapping initiatives that resonate with our own. Of these, Brazil's is the most comprehensive. In 2005, the Brazilian Forum on Solidarity Economy (FBES) partnered with several universities and the federal government to pioneer a solidarity economy mapping project. Hundreds of interviewers from universities and civil society visited tens of thousands of worker-controlled and -managed enterprises countrywide, searching for information regarding their history, management, economic activity, difficulties, and needs. The research project was intentionally designed according to a model of participatory management that required consensus building at different stages of the project. The FBES generated a searchable database and map that allows policy development, networking among solidarity economy entities, and enhanced public visibility. Figure 2.3 shows an image from Brazil's solidarity economy mapping platform.

Other SSE mapping initiatives may be found in France, Italy, Spain, Germany, Luxembourg, and Quebec, among other regions. Figures 2.4, 2.5,

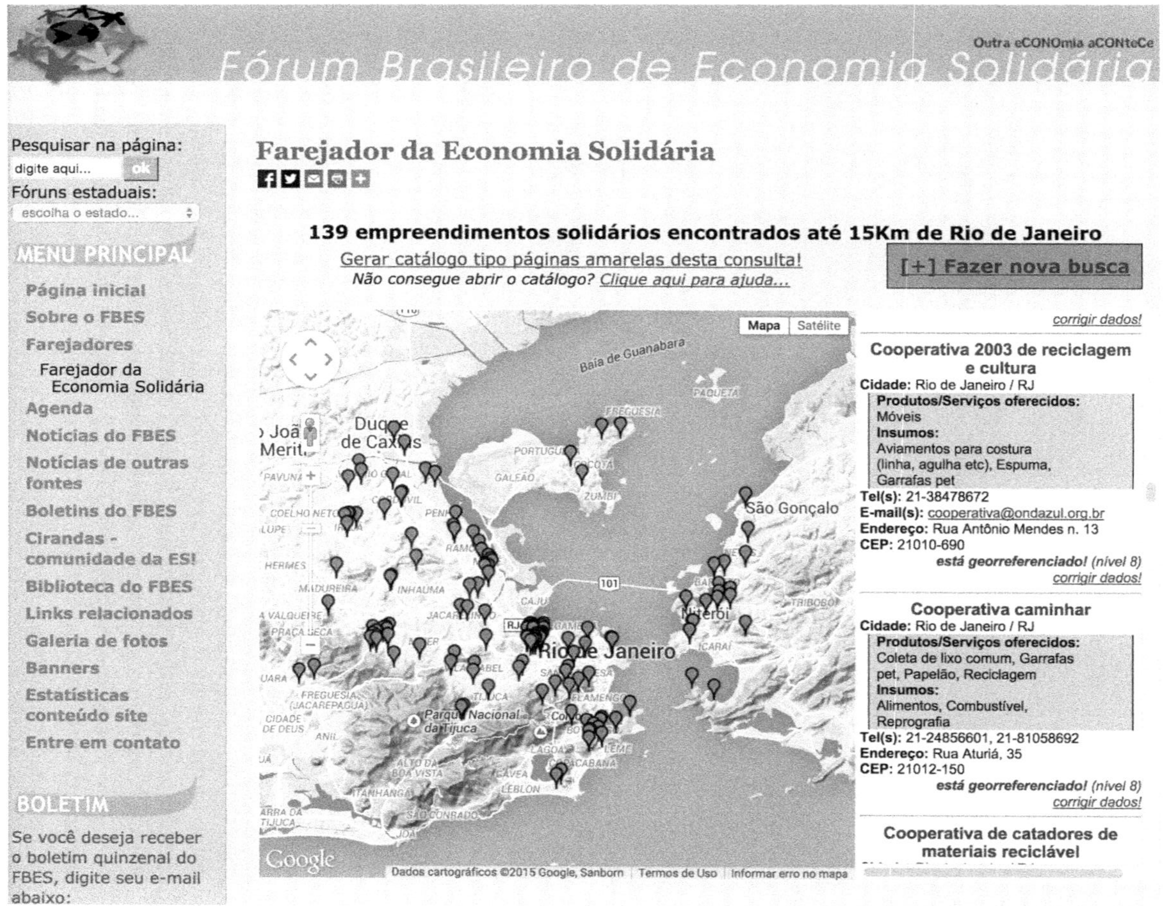

Figure 2.3 FBES: map of the Brazilian solidarity economy (source: FBES (n.d.)).

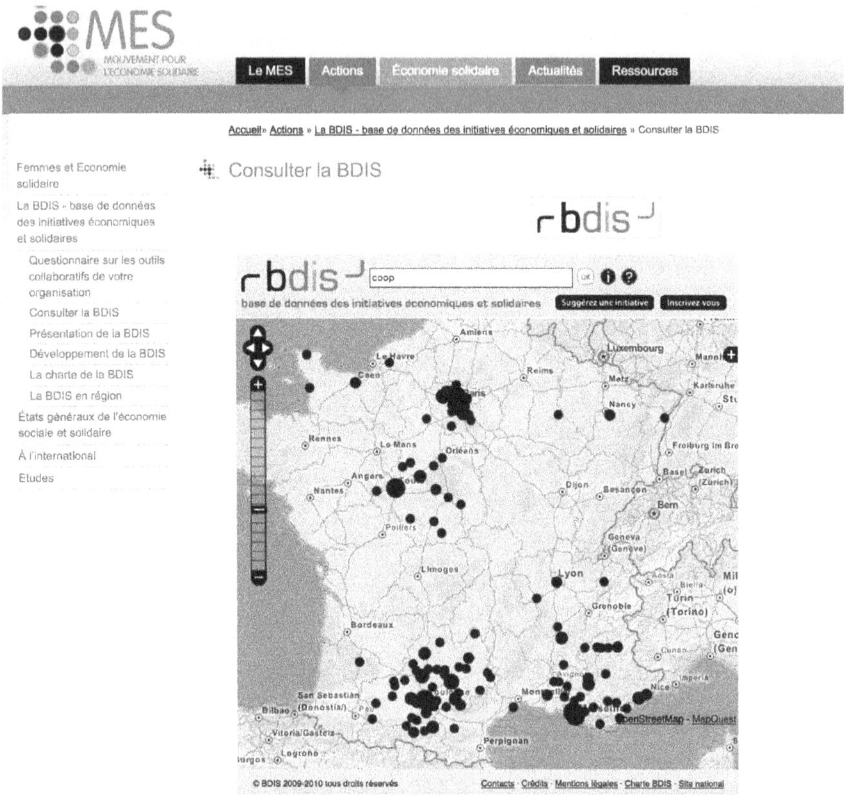

Figure 2.4 BDIS: map of the French solidarity economy (source: BDIS (n.d.)).

and 2.6 display images of the mapping platforms in France, Italy, and Spain, respectively.

All of these maps incorporate participatory practices that enable the mapped organizations themselves to maintain the databases. This enhances the sustainability of the mapping platforms and further instantiates the movement's commitment to local self-determination. In the United States, provisional mapping projects have been undertaken in a few regions, including Massachusetts, New York, New Jersey, and Philadelphia. Figure 2.7 shows a snapshot of the mapping platform created by Solidarity NYC. They do not yet have the functionality or the participatory character of the other countries' mapping platforms, although plans are in development.

Similarly to the general movement, the mapping initiatives have been designed in a decentralized fashion. They deploy differing technologies, use different computer languages, and generate their own boundaries, definitions, data-gathering methods, and inclusion criteria. The networks simultaneously continue

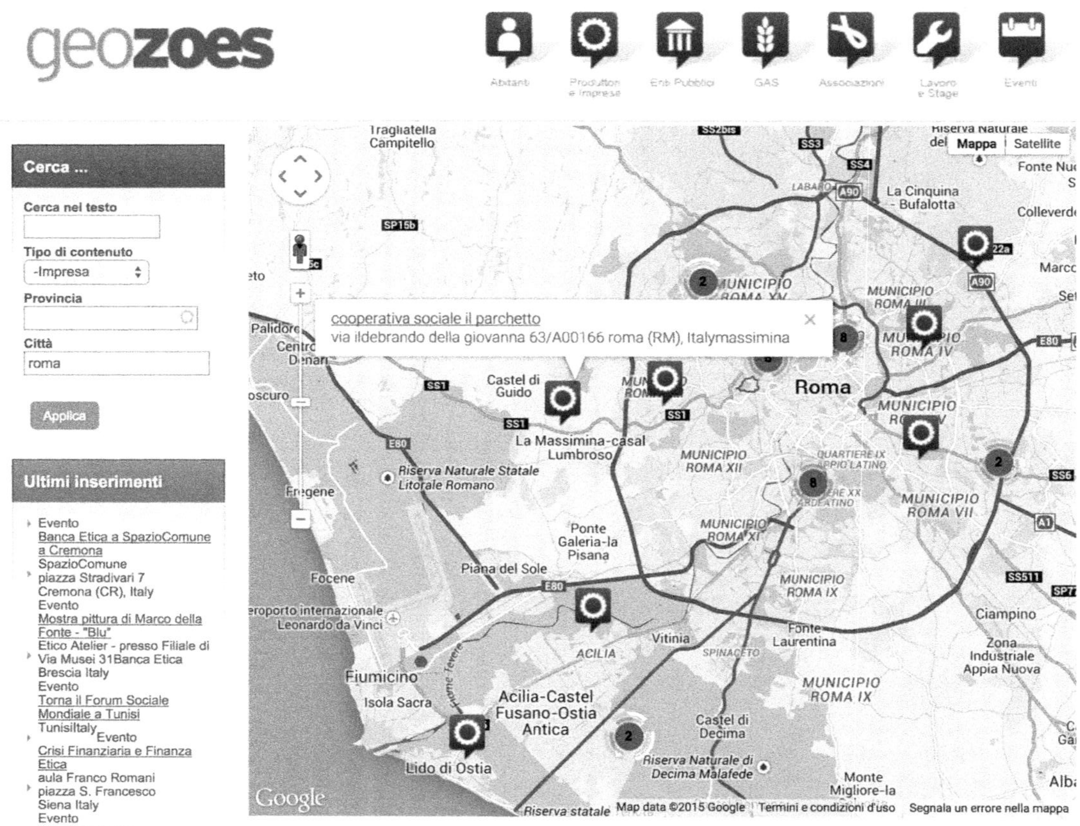

Figure 2.5 ZOES: map of the Italian solidarity economy (source: ZOES (n.d.)).

Figure 2.6 REAS: map of the Spanish solidarity economy (source: REAS (n.d.)).

to learn from one another. In another example of solidarity across difference, RIPESS has launched a new initiative – ESS Global – which aims to make the different mapping platforms interoperable without requiring a centralized database or a universal set of definitions. The movement recognizes that a solidarity economy should have meanings and applications appropriate to local contexts and, rather than forcing conformity, it is adapting technology to accommodate the differences.

Building the SSE across the economic cycle

ESS Global's effort to generate interoperability across various platforms is one innovation in SSE mapping. Another may be found in efforts to use mapping technology to develop SSE supply chains. Beyond merely building an awareness of existing SSE alternatives, the movement seeks to encourage the development of new practices and the strengthening of existing practices. One manner in which it achieves this is by representing the SSE as spanning economic activity across the economic cycle. It reveals the possibility of exercising solidarity among initiatives that would otherwise not discern or build the connection. Ethan Miller (2010) generated a map that has been influential in the United States by illustrating the diversity of initiatives and how the movement spans the whole economic cycle from production to consumption to disposal (Figure 2.8).

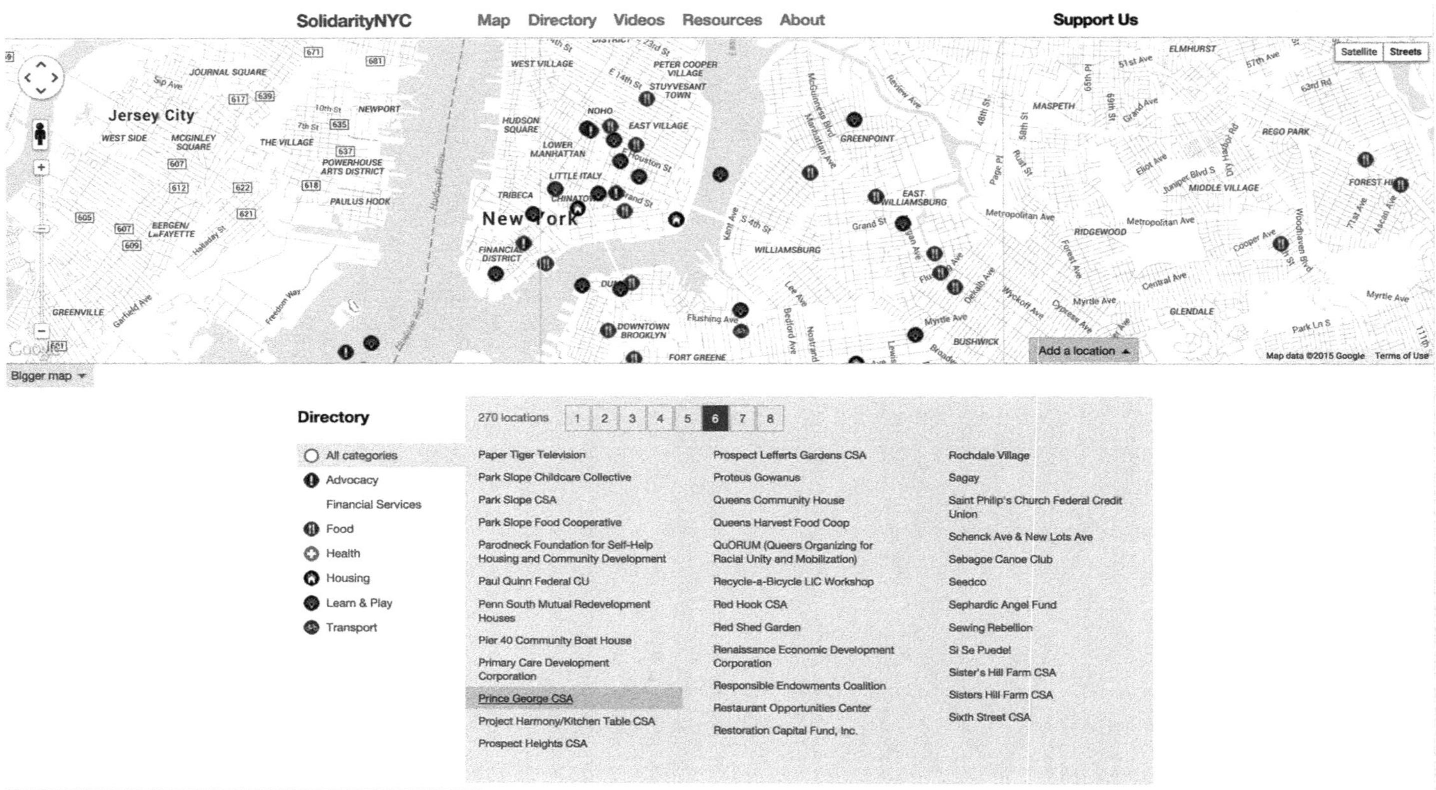

Figure 2.7 SolidarityNYC: map of the solidarity economy in New York City (source: SolidarityNYC. Map design by Dan Phiffer, Georgia Bullen, Mia Pears, and SolidarityNYC).

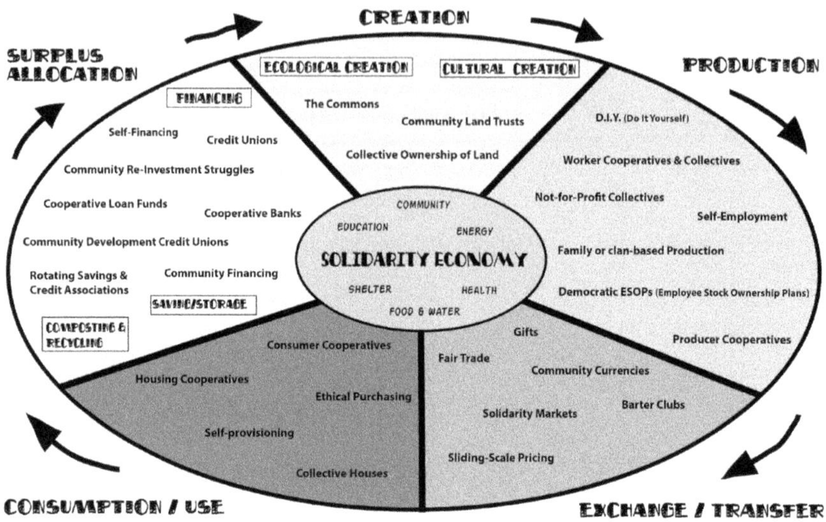

Figure 2.8 The solidarity economy across the economic cycle (source: Miller (2010, 32)).

This type of conceptual mapping invites the viewer to regard the SSE as a single, internally diverse sphere of economic activity. It invites solidarity across economic stages. If we consider "solidarity" to mean the sense of a common struggle among participants in otherwise different occupations, movements, social positions, and practices, the solidarity economy movement seeks to build solidarity in at least three ways. First, it seeks to cultivate a sense of common struggle among individuals within organizations and initiatives. Second, it seeks to build networks of solidarity among like-minded organizations and initiatives. Third, it seeks to generate solidarity between such groups and the marginalized within society. To adopt cooperatives as an example, the movement seeks to build solidarity among members of a cooperative, among cooperatives and related initiatives, and between cooperatives and broader society, particularly the lowest stratum of society who may or may not actually participate in cooperatives. Rather than viewing the diverse initiatives in isolation, the solidarity economy framework allows us to view them as part of a common effort in transforming the economy. It also helps generate channels for participants in such initiatives to network with one another, sharing experiences and developing shared agendas. In brief, it engenders commonality with diversity. This type of conceptual mapping has an analog in the mapping platform being developed by the Brazilian Solidarity Economy Movement. Called "Cirandas," this platform does not act only as a portal for geographically mapping SSE entities; the Brazilian movement has also made it a site for networking and for developing supply chains and encouraging exchange. They aspire to use it to encourage solidarity economy markets in which consumers, producers, and suppliers can find and

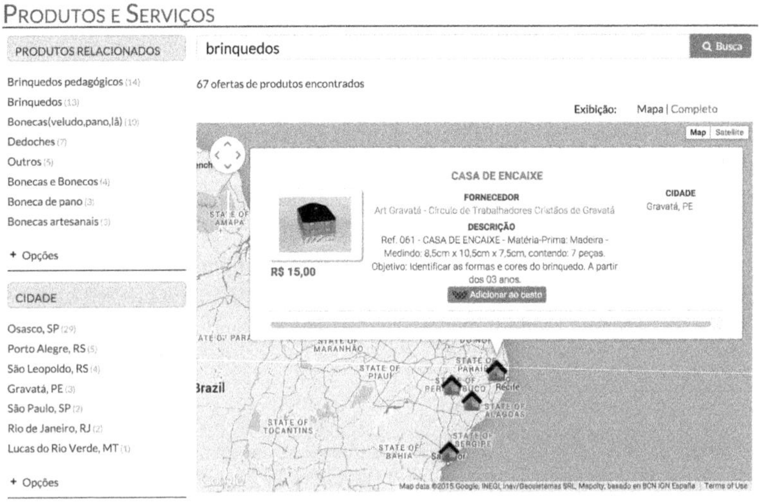

Figure 2.9 Cirandas: mapping and building solidarity economy supply chains (source: Cirandas (n.d.)).

contract with one another. Figure 2.9 displays a snapshot of Cirandas' marketplace function.

As shown in Figure 2.9, the image is a Cirandas.net site for a solidarity economy organization named Art Gravatá that produces toys. The site displays the company's mission, location, products, price composition, and contact information. Cirandas is searchable according to location, product type, and solidarity economy characteristics.

These types of initiative that aim to map the SSE geographically and conceptually and to foster new networks, consumer–producer connections, and producer supply chains provide a challenge to dominant perspectives that focus narrowly on individual economic sectors, and that regard values-based economic alternatives as marginal to the larger economy and as incapable of substantially scaling up.

Conclusion

This chapter has described the evolution of the concept(s) of the SSE and the spread of the SSE movement. It has also highlighted certain ways in which the SSE defies hegemonic paradigms of economic development. Not everyone will find such interventions compelling or sufficient. For many critics of capitalism, the state is the only force capable of significantly countering the concentrated power of capitalists and the destructive effects of capitalist markets. Conversely, for some critics of authoritarian regimes, free markets are the only adequate approach to counter the concentrated power of officials and the repressive apparatus of the state. In its own manner, the SSE seeks to leverage social power against the preponderance of both market power and state power in our economies (Wright 2010). In this way, it offers emancipatory frontiers that break the familiar binary of the state versus the market. The movement's potential as an economic alternative lies not only in the generation of entirely new economic relations, but also in its ability to put existing non-capitalist economic relations into motion. The movement draws its energy not from revolutionary theory or a utopian vision of a classless society; rather, it roots itself pragmatically in the proliferating number of economic experiments already occurring worldwide. I have also demonstrated how, by naming alternatives, making them visible, mapping them, and fostering connections among them, the SSE can establish itself both in the present and in the future as far more than a niche in the broader economic landscape.

Notes

1 At the 1900 Paris World Fair the social economy had its own pavilion. Charles Gide described it as a "cathedral" (Defourny and Develtere 1999, 11).
2 In their own use of "Community Economy," Gibson-Graham directly and usefully engage the problem of exclusive communities (Gibson-Graham 2006).

References

Amin, A., ed. 2009. *The Social Economy: International Perspectives on Economic Solidarity*. London: Zed Books.

Arruda, M. 2004. "Solidarity Economy and the Rebirth of a Matristic Society." Paper presented at the panel "Towards People's Economy: Realities and Strategies from Local to Global" at the 2004 World Social Forum in Mumbai, India. Available online at: http://base.socioeco.org/docs/doc-7390_en.pdf.

Arruda, M., ed. 2009. *A Non-patriarchal Economy is Possible: Looking at Solidarity Economy from Different Cultural Facets – Asia – Latin America – North America – Europe*. Rio de Janeiro: ALOE. Available online at: http://aloe.socioeco.org/IMG/pdf/Non-patriarchal_economy_is_possible.pdf.

BDIS (*Base de Données des Initiatives Économiques et Solidaires*). n.d. "Consulter la BDIS [BDIS (Database of Economic and Solidarity Initiatives)]." Available online at: www.le-mes.org/Consulter-la-BDIS.html. Available under a Creative Commons Attribution-Share Alike 2.0 (France) license at: www.creativecommons.org/licenses/by-sa/2.0/fr (last accessed on February 15, 2015).

Brazil Ministry of Labor and Employment. 2008. "Sistema de Informações em Economia Solidária – SIES [Information System in Solidarity Economy – SIES]." PowerPoint. Available online at: http://portal.mte.gov.br/data/files/FF8080812B35FA90012B45A6D-C262FA5/Apresentacao_SIES_2008.ppt (last accessed June 14, 2013).

Cirandas. n.d. "Produtos E Serviços [Products/Services]." Available online at: www.cirandas.net/search/products?display=map&profile=cirandas.net (last accessed February 12, 2015).

Coraggio, J.L., and M.S. Arroyo. 2009. "A Path to the Social Economy in Argentina: Worker Takeovers of Bankrupt Companies." In *The Social Economy. International Perspectives on Economic Solidarity*, edited by A. Amin (pp. 139–155). London: Zed Books.

Defourny, J., and P. Develtere. 1999. "Social Economy: The Worldwide Making of a Third Sector." In *Social Economy. North and South*, edited by J. Defourny, P. Develtere, and B. Fonteneau (pp. 25–56). Brussels: De Boeck.

Demoustier, D., and D. Rousselière. 2006. "Social Economy as Social Science and Practice: Historical Perspectives on France." In *Ethics and the Market: Insights from Social Economics*, edited by B.J. Clary, W. Dolfsma, and D.M. Figart (pp. 112–125). Abingdon, Oxon: Routledge.

Desroche, H. 1983. *Pour un traité d'économie sociale* [For a Social Economy Treatise]. Paris: Coopérative d'édition et d'information mutualiste.

Desroche, H. 1991. *Histoires d'économies sociales. D'un tiers état aux tiers secteurs, 1791–1991* [Stories of Social Economies: From a Third State to the Three Sectors, 1791–1991]. Paris: Syros.

Escobar, A. 1995. *Encountering Development: The Making and Unmaking of the Third World*. Princeton, NJ: Princeton University Press.

Evers, A., and J.L. Laville, eds. 2004. *The Third Sector in Europe*. Cheltenham: Edward Elgar.

FBES (*Fórum Brasileiro de Economia Solidária* [Brazilian Forum of the Solidarity Economy]). n.d. "Farejadores [Sniffer]." Available online at: www.fbes.org.br/farejador (last accessed on February 12, 2015).

Gibson-Graham, J.K. 1996. *The End of Capitalism (As We Knew it): A Feminist Critique of Political Economy*. Minneapolis: University of Minnesota Press.

Gibson-Graham, J.K. 2006. A *Post Capitalist Politics*. Minneapolis: University of Minnesota Press.

Gudynas, E. 2011. "Buen Vivir: Today's Tomorrow." *Development* 54(4): 441–447. doi:10.1057/dev.2011.86.

Jayasooria, D., ed. 2013. *Developments in Solidarity Economy in Asia*. Malaysia: Asian Solidarity Economy Council. Available online at: www.rencontres-montblanc.coop/sites/default/files/devlopments_in_solidarity_economy_in_asia_denison_jayasooria_2013.pdf.

Laville, J.L. 1994. *L'économie solidaire. Une perspective international*. Paris: Desclée de Brouwer.

Laville, J.L., B. Lévesque, and M. Mendell. 2007. "The Social Economy: Diverse Approaches and Practices in Europe and Canada." In *The Social Economy: Building Inclusive Economies*, edited by Antonella Noya and Emma Clarence (pp. 155–187). Washington, DC: OECD. doi: 10.1787/9789264039889-en.

Mance, E.A. 2002. *Redes de Colaboração Solidária* [Network of Solidarity Collaboration]. Brazil: Editora Vozes.

Mendell, M., and N. Neamtan. 2010. "The Social Economy in Quebec: Towards a New Political Economy." In *Researching the Social Economy*, edited by L. Mook, J. Quarter, and S. Ryan (pp. 63–83). Toronto, ON: University of Toronto Press.

Mignolo, W.D. 2000. "The Many Faces of Cosmo-polis: Border Thinking and Critical Cosmopolitanism." *Public Culture* 12(3): 721–748. doi: 10.1215/08992363-12-3-721.

Miller, E. 2006. "'Other Economies Are Possible!': Organizing toward an Economy of Cooperation and Solidarity." *Dollars & Sense* 266: 14–16.

Miller, E. 2010. "Solidarity Economy: Key Concepts and Issues." In *Solidarity Economy I: Building Alternatives for People and Plane, Papers and Reports from the 2009 U.S. Forum on the Solidarity Economy*, edited by E. Kawano, T.N. Masterson, and J. Teller-Elsberg (pp. 25–41). Amherst: Center for Popular Economics.

Moulaert, F., and O. Ailenei. 2005. "Social Economy, Third Sector and Solidarity Relations: A Conceptual Synthesis from History to Present." *Urban Studies* 42(11): 2037–2053. doi: 10.1080/00420980500279794.
Murray, R. 2009. *Danger and Opportunity: Crisis and the New Social Economy*. Online Publication Series. NESTA and Young Foundation. Available online at: www.nesta.org.uk/sites/default/files/danger_and_opportunity.pdf (last accessed June 14, 2013).
Pearce, J. 2003. *Social Enterprise in Anytown*. London: Calouste Gulbenkian Foundation.
Quarter J., L. Mook, and A. Armstrong. 2009. *Understanding the Social Economy. A Canadian Perspective*. Toronto, ON: The University of Toronto Press.
Razeto, L. 1998. " 'Factor C': la solidaridad convertida en fuerza productiva y en el factor económico [Factor C: The Force of Solidarity in the Economy]." Luisrazeto.net. Available online at: www.luisrazeto.net/content/el-factor-c-la-fuerza-de-la-solidaridad-en-la-economia-entrevista (last accessed June 13, 2013).
Razeto, L. 2010. "Esteban Romero's Interview with Louis Razeto, May 2010." Interview. Solidarity Economy Resources. Haverford College. Available online at: http://cborowiak.haverford.edu/solidarityeconomy/wp-content/uploads/sites/3/2013/07/Interview-with-Luis-Razeto_May-2010.pdf.
REAS (*Red de Redes de Economía Alternativa y Solidaria* [Network of Networks of the Alternative and Solidarity Economy]). n d. "Portal de Economia Solidaria. Mapa [Portal of the Solidarity Economy Map]." Available online at: www.economiasolidaria.org/entidades/mapa. Available under a Creative Commons Attribution 3.0 Unported (Spain) license at: www.creativecommons.org/licenses/by/3.0/deed.es (last accessed on February 11, 2015).
RIPESS (Intercontinental Network for the Promotion of the Social and Solidarity Economy). 1997. "Lima Declaration." Available online at: http://base.socioeco.org/docs/declaration_lima_eng.pdf.
Rodríguez-Garavito, C.A. 2006. "Solidarity Economy and the Struggle for Social Citizenship in Times of Globalization: A Study of the Cooperatives of Informal Garbage Pickers in Columbia." In *Another Production is Possible: Beyond the Capitalist Canon*, edited by B. Santos (pp. 43–69). London: Verso.
Santos, B. 2005. "The WSF: Toward a Counter-hegemonic Globalisation (Part I & II)." In *World Social Forum: Challenging Empires*, edited by J. Sen, A. Anand, A. Escobar, and P. Waterman (pp. 235–245, 336–343). New Delhi: Viveka Foundation.
Singer, P. 2006. "The Recent Rebirth of the Solidary Economy in Brazil." In *Another Production is Possible. Beyond the Capitalist Canon*, edited by B. Santos (pp. 3–41). New York: Verso.
Solidarity NYC. n.d. "Solidarity NYC Map." Solidarity NYC Website. Available online at: www.solidaritynyc.org (last accessed June 14, 2013).
USSEN (U.S. Solidarity Economy Network). 2012. "Working Group on Mapping the Solidarity Economy." Unpublished study.
Vienney, C. 1994. *L'économie sociale* [The Social Economy]. Paris: La Découverte.
Wolford, W. 2010. *This Land is Ours Now: Social Mobilization and the Meanings of Land in Brazil*. Durham, NC: Duke University Press.
Wright, E.O. 2010. *Envisioning Real Utopias*. New York: Verso.
ZOES. n.d. "Geozoes" [Geographic Equi-sustainable Zone]. ZOES website. Available online at: www.zoes.it/geozoes. Available under a Creative Commons Attribution-NonCommercial-ShareAlike 2.5 (Italy) license at: www.creativecommons.org/licenses/by-nc-sa/2.5/it (last accessed on February 11, 2015).

3 Rethinking the politics of the mainstream co-op movement

Carl Ratner[1]

Introduction

The co-op movement seeks to be a structural alternative to capitalism. It seeks to develop new forms of economic ownership and management, social responsibility, and sustainable use of natural resources. I ask whether co-ops in their current direction and organization can accomplish this task. In Foucauldian terminology, I problematize co-ops as a form of social organization or governance. I demonstrate that the current, predominant politics (and conceptual ideal) of co-ops are incapable of realizing cooperative, progressive ideals, despite their good intentions. The reason is that leading co-op organizations have adopted a conservative, reformist politics that is complicit with political and economic institutions of capitalism. These politics hamper the development of cooperative *praxes* in smaller, local co-ops that are guided by the leaders.

This chapter contributes to the literature that examines the politics of social movements (Bryer 2012; Hale 2013). Political critiques of co-ops have general political import for all reform movements – in education, health care, ecology, peace, justice, and civil rights. It reveals the limitations of reformist social change. The critique indicates that all progressive social change requires fundamentally challenging the politics and economics of capitalism (see Park 2011).

A political analysis of co-ops is a structural-institutional analysis. It evaluates the organizational structure of cooperative institutions – both their internal structures and their external associations; it analyzes power groups that advance particular interests, forms of ownership, forms of management, and forms of work/participation. Institutional structures are the level at which politics of cooperation are formed and implemented. This kind of analysis is also called Power Structure Analysis. It is not only a descriptive tool; it educates people about the power groups that shape their lives and that must be replaced. Ignoring power, politics, and structure allows these to persist without challenge.

The structural-institutional analysis of the co-op movement identifies leading organizations which shape the structure of the movement through their financial, organizational, intellectual, and political might. I focus on leading co-op associations such as the International Cooperative Alliance and the National Cooperative Business Association, as well as giant producer and consumer co-ops such as Land O'Lakes dairy co-op, the National Council of Farmer Cooperatives, and the U.S. Overseas Cooperative Development Council. These bodies sponsor co-op conferences and webinars: they fund cooperative research institutes, provide grants for co-op projects, produce voluminous materials that define cooperative issues and provide guidelines for action, and they have deep political ties within government that create a legal framework for co-op practices. These leading institutions are central to the politics of cooperation practiced by co-ops and by the populace at large.[2] Studying these leading organizations is as important as "elite studies" of the upper class are for understanding the forces that affect subaltern subgroups and quotidian practices in a nation's social system. Indeed, I shall use the methodology of elite studies, such as Domhoff's, to detail the specific, myriad interlinking interests and associations of mainstream co-op leaders.

To understand why the movement is the way it is, its structure must be elucidated in a way that focuses on leading organizations. Unfortunately, such analysis is rare. The co-op movement is presented as a series of small, local, independent, egalitarian enterprises that practice a spontaneous, "bottom-up," natural, universal form of cooperation. This ideology of "localism" masks politics and power that are wielded by large institutions over an institutional structure. Ironically, the coverage of cooperative structure and politics is inversely proportional to their real existence. The larger, dominant co-ops that wield enormous power over small, local co-ops through dominating the co-op structure and promulgating a particular cooperative politics are rarely studied, while small, local co-ops that wield little power over the structure are the focus of much research. This chapter aims to invert this epistemological/methodological inversion.

It is crucial to understand the politics of cooperation because they shape the praxis of cooperation. This point will be documented with examples throughout this chapter. Cooperation, like all behavior, is political in that it is grounded in politics of cultural institutions, embodies these politics in its specific practices, and functions to reinforce/promulgate cultural politics (Ratner 2012). Improving the praxis of cooperation requires elucidating and reorganizing the politics of cooperation in the leading cooperative institutions.

The cooperation that is practiced by the mainstream co-op movement is political: it is a particular form of cooperation which is organized by leading organizations to suit particular interests and objectives. It is not natural, normal, universal, and given. Elucidating the politics of co-ops and cooperation affords the opportunity to deconstruct and reconstruct them by other organizations to suit more progressive and different interests and objectives.

Of course, leaders' influence is not absolute. Many co-ops may still depart from their direction. However, the leading politics and praxes exert widespread influence that must be understood and corrected.

A central point of this chapter is that the cooperative form has been infiltrated by corporate, neoliberal politics. Observers of the co-op movement should not be beguiled by the (general) co-op form into overlooking its (concrete) neoliberal features that undermine genuine cooperation. This chapter additionally asks the deeper question of why the cooperative form becomes infiltrated by neoliberal politics. We conclude that the extensive infiltration is due (in this case) to inherent deficiencies in the mainstream cooperative form itself. We will analyze foundational cooperative principles to demonstrate this deficiency. This central deficiency in the concept of cooperatives and cooperation mandates a new cooperative form based on new politics and foundational principles.

Methodology

To understand, and advance, the politics of cooperation, I will analyse the following:

1. The organizational structure of the mainstream international cooperative movement that is led by large producer and consumer co-ops, and rich, politically connected, co-op associations such as the National Cooperative Business Association and the International Cooperative Alliance.
2. The politics of leading, large producer and consumer co-ops, including their interlocking business associations/networks.
3. The politics of the National Cooperative Business Association, including its interlocking associations/networks with large co-ops, government agencies, and think tanks.
4. Flaws in the founding cooperative principles.

The structure of the mainstream international cooperative movement

The distribution of co-ops in the United States is summarized in Table 3.1. This shows the predominance of consumer co-ops and the paucity of worker co-ops (1 percent of total cooperative firms) with an average employment of 10 workers.

The movement's institutional structure is dominated by the International Cooperative Alliance (ICA), which is the umbrella organization for many co-ops and co-op associations in the world. Its 277 members include the massive Italian LEGA Association, the (North American) National Cooperative Growers' Association, Credit Union National Association, and the National Cooperative Business Association (NCBA) which is the umbrella organization for most North American cooperatives (it also has extensive outreach to third world co-ops, described below). The NCBA's membership includes individual co-ops, as well as the U.S. Confederation of Workers' Co-ops, with all of its member co-ops.

The ICA influences this extensive set of organizations through providing funding, resources (reports, templates), political connections, conference venues, and publications through organizational networks, layers, and levels.

The ICA is also influential beyond its immediate membership roster and associates. It devotes enormous resources to providing templates that define sectorial co-ops such as housing co-ops and agricultural co-ops. The ICA defines the

Table 3.1 U.S. cooperatives by type: summary of key economic indicators

Cooperative type	*Assets*	*Wages*	*Firms*	*Employees*[b]	*Memberships*[a]
	(million dollars)			*(thousands)*	
Worker[c]	128.02	55.41	223	2.38	55.14
Producer	23,632	2,970	1,494	72.93	714.65
Purchasing	1,126,848	2,902	724	130.35	6,133
Consumer	1,975,805	19,085	26,844	650.65	343,969
Total	3,126,414	25,013	29,285	856.31	350,872

Source: NCBA (2012).

Notes

a One member can belong to multiple cooperatives, so does not necessarily represent a unique individual.

b Employment is reported in terms of full-time employees. Two part-time workers are reported as one (full-time) employee.

c Member numberrs are higher than employment figures because (a) member numbers include part-time workers, but employment figures represent the number of full-time positions; (b) some cooperatives reported their membership but not their employment figures.

characteristics and criteria for what qualifies as a cooperative – its famed seven principles. These are adopted by co-ops who are not affiliated with the ICA. Naturally, individual co-ops use the ICA's framework somewhat distinctly; however, the general parameters of the framework are pervasive. The reason is that at this point the ICA framework is the main game in town. There is no alternative cooperative system with a substantially different social and political philosophy of cooperation.

Nor is there an alternative organized faction within the ICA which presses for a social and political philosophy that is different from the mainstream (e.g., one which researches socialist forms of cooperation, is invited to present its perspective at co-op conferences, and publishes a newsletter that debates and diversifies mainstream ideas and practices).

One pillar of the co-op movement's structure is large producer and consumer co-ops. They wield enormous power, especially through their dominance of the market, their co-institutions, their political connections with government, and their partnerships with umbrella co-op associations such as the National Cooperative Business Association (NCBA) that transmit their influence through the system to small, local co-ops.

Large consumer and producer co-ops

Large consumer and producer co-ops are influential in the co-op movement because their enormous material presence and resources shape the practices and programs of small, local co-ops. Just as large corporations dominate the economic landscape of small firms through financial pressure, resources (grants, conference venues, program funding, media programs, and templates), modeling, and political influence, so large co-ops shape small ones in the same ways. In addition, large co-ops interlock with international and national cooperative associations such as the ICA and NCBA, where they provide financial, organizational, and conceptual/intellectual resources to the ICA/NCBA for projects with small, local co-ops. Large consumer and producer co-ops influence small, local co-ops directly, and also indirectly through the mediation of the ICA/NCBA – just as large corporations influence small ones directly and also indirectly through the government that large corporations control.

Recreational Equipment Inc. (REI)

REI is the nation's leading outdoor equipment outlet and largest retail cooperative in the United States. REI is important because it is the largest consumer cooperative in the United States, with two million active members. REI CEO Sally Jewell was selected by President Obama in 2013, to be Secretary of the US Department of the Interior. This was hailed by the NCBA as an important official endorsement and expansion of cooperatives. Unfortunately, REI is a corrupted, corporate co-op. This character must be analyzed as a reflection of fundamental problems with cooperative politics.

A former REI store owner described REI as follows:

> Members have virtually no say over the way things are done today, and the co-op's monolithic, self-perpetuating board of directors has changed the organization's bylaws to make insurgency virtually impossible.
>
> At some point, REI's board of directors changed the bylaws to make it virtually impossible for anyone not of their choosing to join their ranks. These days, if you'd like to get onto the board, you must win the approval of its nominating committee, a subcommittee of the board. Failing that, you must gather the signatures of 1 percent of the co-op's active membership, about 21,000 names. To make things just a little more challenging, the co-op won't let you even peek at the membership list, which they say is not released for privacy reasons.
>
> But let's say you're stubborn and willing to stand outside an REI store and gather member signatures for six months or so. Your name will, indeed, be placed on the ballot clearly distinguishable from the board-nominated, board-endorsed candidates.
>
> With "choices" like that, it is small wonder that the percentage of members voting each year has been declining steadily: 14 percent in 1980, 5 percent in 1999, 4.3 percent in 2000, 3.9 percent in 2001, 2.9 percent last year, and 2.8 percent this spring.
>
> The company closed its Seattle garment manufacturing facility in 2000 and moved the work to Mexico, where the wages were a fraction of those in the U.S.
>
> (Ryan 2006)

In 2004, REI CEO Madsen's compensation was US$1.3 million. It consisted of US$515,000 in base pay, US$80,221 in profit sharing and pension money, US$6,480 in allowances such as a car, US$397,480 in annual incentive, and US$380,033 in long-term incentives.

Sally Jewell became his successor. She earned US$1 million as REI's chief operating officer. According to REI's executive compensation web page, as CEO in 2010, her compensation was US$2,281,764, about 100 times the average REI employee's. Prior to her employment at REI, Jewell worked for nearly 20 years in the banking industry, most recently serving as president and CEO of Washington Mutual's Commercial Banking Group.

Jewell was also on the board of directors of Avista Corporation, a Spokane-based power utility, from 1997 through 2003. U.S. Securities and Exchange documents show that in her last full year as an Avista board member, Jewell held more than 15,600 shares in the utility and received $50,000 in director's fees. Needless to say, these are not cooperative practices that qualify Jewell as a praiseworthy cooperator.

Four new board members of REI are officials in capitalist corporations. One was president of Hannaford Supermarkets, a leading supermarket retailer in northern New England that operates 181 stores in five states. Another board member is the regional vice president and chief medical officer for Sutter Health's East Bay Region in California, an affiliate of one of the largest health care associations in the nation. Another is CEO and president of AMC Entertainment, Inc. He has 30 years in management, marketing, sales, and operations with global consumer brands including Starbucks Coffee Company, Frito-Lay, Pepsi-Cola Company, and Procter & Gamble. The fourth is the president and chief executive officer of SITEL Worldwide Corporation, a global customer care outsourcing provider. All of these backgrounds represent anti-cooperative, capitalist values and interests. None of them prepares these board members with a solid cooperative perspective. On the contrary, their backgrounds inexorably lead them to align cooperativism with capitalism.

At REI, executive compensation is pegged to corporate standards instead of cooperative principles. According to REI's web page,

> Current director compensation is $46,000 per year, with an additional fee of $1,000 per meeting. In recognition of the significant work and responsibilities associated in leading the board, the board's chair receives an additional $10,000 for this service to the co-op. The chairs of the Audit and Finance, Compensation, and Nominating and Governance Committees receive an additional $5,000 per year in recognition of the responsibilities of the positions.

These compensation agreements of REI directors and executives violate a tenet of co-ops that they promote equalitarian relations and volunteerism.

REI is better than the average capitalist corporation. It is a green company and spends money maintaining outdoor areas for recreation. However, it is a corporate co-op, run by corporate executives who practice corporate management (and compensation) with little knowledge of, interest in, or practice of genuine cooperation. A green corporate co-op is still a corporate co-op. Misrepresenting corrupt, corporate co-ops as genuine co-ops misleads the co-op movement and its potential allies into inadequate, pseudo cooperation.

Other corporate co-ops reveal this in detail.

CHS co-op

CHS cooperative is the USA's largest member-owned cooperative. It is "one of the nation's leading farmer-owned cooperatives," according to the NCBA's December 2012 *eCooperator*. CHS is the largest producer co-op in the USA, consisting of over 1,000 member co-ops. But CHS is much more than a farming co-op. It is also a leading energy and foods company that operates petroleum refineries/pipelines, and manufactures, markets, and distributes Cenex® brand refined fuels. CHS earned US$25.3 billion in revenue in 2010. Indeed, CHS's mission is "To grow company profitability and stockholder value" (CHS 2013a). This is not a cooperative mission. CHS sells preferred shares on the New York Stock Exchange! Purchasing unlimited voting shares violates the signature cooperative principle of one member, one share, and one vote. Yet CHS is a member of the NCBA.

The president and CEO of CHS co-op is Carl Casale, who was a former executive vice president and chief financial officer for Monsanto Company from September 2009 until December 31, 2010. Prior to that he was executive vice president, Strategy and Operations for Monsanto from 2007 to 2009 and executive vice president, North America and Latin America North for Monsanto from 2003 to 2007, and vice president, North America from 2000 to 2003. As CEO he authorized US$150 million in cash and trade incentives to Latin American farmers to encourage them to use Monsanto's Roundup. Casale's compensation in 2011 was US$1.7 million. Casale moved directly from Monsanto's CEO position to the CHS leadership on January 1, 2011. At his farewell from Monsanto he praised the company: "I'm incredibly honored to have had the opportunity to work at Monsanto Company," Casale said. "This company is the demonstrated leader in seeds and traits."

With Casale at the helm, CHS sponsored a managers' conference from February 9–11, 2011 at which CHS executives shared the podium with the executive vice-president of Monsanto and the president of Koch Industries, the notorious, reactionary corporation that funds reactionary political movements in the USA.[3] Casale's executive compensation at CHS in 2012 was US$6,750,711 – not exactly a cooperator's salary (http://investing.businessweek.com/research/stocks/people/person.asp?personId=550664&ticker=MON:IM).

CHS lobbies on behalf of the commercial fertilizer industry. CHS produced a brochure entitled "The U.S. Fertilizer Industry and Climate Change Policy" (CHS 2013b) The brochure acknowledges that the fertilizer industry is an energy-intensive industry that uses large amounts of natural gas and emits significant carbon dioxide. Yet the brochure insists on maintaining this system and rails against regulating or transforming it.

> It is critical to our nation's food security and meaningful environmental improvement that Congress align climate with energy policy. This means not imposing a climate change policy that renders U.S. nitrogen manufacturing uncompetitive, drives natural gas prices higher.... Congress needs to consider the dramatic impact climate change policies could have on our national food security.... Any new U.S. climate change policy must deliver environmental progress *without* harming the economy.

This is typical conservative, corporate rhetoric that seeks to contain environmental legislation within the capitalist status quo. There is no transforming the economy in line with ecological needs, nor any recognition of the destructive influence of current energy policy on food security (which even the CIA recognizes).

Clearly, CHS's reactionary environmental agenda will affect the cooperative agenda that CHS promotes. This includes the CHS Foundation and its Center for Cooperative Growth.

To wit: CHS organizes a CHS Directors' Conference for Cooperatives (CHS 2013b). It focuses on business leadership and industry outlook and insight. The sessions are designed for boards of directors to attend together, with outcomes including improved board quality, decision-making, and cooperative profitability. One workshop, in 2011, explored market attractiveness analysis and "Power of Five Forces" analysis, including:

- bargaining power of the customer;
- bargaining power of the supplier;
- competitive rivalry;
- threat of new entrants;
- threat of substitutes.

This is the language of competitive capitalist business. The CHS vision of cooperatives sits squarely within the capitalist rubric. CHS could never endorse a politically radical and politically engaged co-op that sought to transform capitalist industry and the production of commercial fertilizer.

This corporate, reactionary CHS foundation is welcomed by the NCBA onto its board of directors in the person of William Nelson, President of the CHS Foundation and Vice President of CHS, Inc. CHS is additionally embraced as a stalwart of the co-op community by the Cooperative Development Foundation (CDF) which has made CHS a partner organization.

The CDF administers the Co-op Hall of Fame as an affiliate of the NCBA, located in its building and holding its induction ceremony at the NCBA's annual conference. The CDF/NCBA admitted retired CEO of CHS, Inc., Noel Estenson, into the Co-op Hall of Fame in 2011! This unconscionable action by the CDF/

NCBA disguises the anti-cooperative essence of CHS; it also mystifies the public about what cooperation is.

The National Council of Farmer Cooperatives (NCFC)

CHS is a member of the National Council of Farmer Cooperatives. Unsurprisingly, the NCFC practices the same corporate-co-op politics as CHS, though on a larger scale of influence because it is an umbrella council of numerous "co-ops."

The NCFC's president, Charles Conner, was George Bush's acting secretary of agriculture. He was Mitt Romney's agricultural advisor during the 2012 presidential campaign. Conner worked directly with President George W. Bush and his senior staff to formulate domestic and international food, trade, security, and energy policy – which was pro-capitalist and militaristic. In addition, he directed a successful World Trade Organization (WTO) and NAFTA trade case against the Government of Mexico, forcing it to allow heavily subsidized high-fructose corn syrup from the U.S.A. to overwhelm its domestic sugar industry. While Conner was deputy secretary of the United States Department of Agriculture, on April 24, 2005, hundreds of family farmers and rural and urban community leaders with National People's Action (NPA) protested at his home to tell Conner and the USDA to end corporate welfare and stop cutting food assistance programs that help America's neediest families. Conner had rebuffed written invitations from NPA to meet with its national leadership.

As president of the National Council for Farmer Cooperatives, Conner supported Monsanto's 2010 attempts to win USDA approval for its genetically modified alfalfa (Barrett 2012). In January 2011, Obama's USDA deregulated Roundup Ready alfalfa without conditions (CBI 2011; Charles 2011).

The NCFC opposed the Clean Water Restoration Act that would regulate farming chemical runoff. The NCFC expressed its anti-environmental interests through a position statement against the Act by the Waters Advocacy Coalition of which the NCFC is a member, alongside the National Mining Association and the National Association of Manufacturers.

Clearly, the National Council of Farmer Cooperatives is a corporate co-op, deeply embedded in corporate capitalism. Yet this is never mentioned by leading co-op associations. On the contrary, they welcome the NCFC as a model cooperator. The NCBA invited the NCFC onto its marketing committee. The National Cooperative Steering Committee, which administered the International Year of the Co-op – chaired by NCBA CEO Paul Hazen – invited the NCFC to become a member where it joined the NCBA, the US Federation of Worker Cooperatives, the Overseas Cooperative Development Council, and the National Cooperative Grocers' Association. (This is as unconscionable as UN Secretary General Ban Ki-moon recently inviting Bank of America's chairman onto the UN's group on sustainable energy for all, despite BofA being the largest funder of mountain-top removal coal-mining.) All of these leading associations (including the Federation of Worker Co-ops) worked amicably with the NCFC instead of publicizing its nefarious character and disavowing it. The Mid Atlantic Cooperative Council also "proudly partners" with NCFC.

Land O'Lakes co-op

Conner was joined in his support for GM alfalfa by a member of his board of directors Chris Policinski. Policinski is the CEO of Land O'Lakes dairy co-op. Land O'Lakes is another leading producer co-op with the same politics of cooperation as the others we have identified. The NCFC, CHS co-op, Land O'Lakes, and the NCBA are all interlocked. Land O'Lakes, like CHS, is a member of the NCBA.

Land O'Lakes also produces animal feed, as well as seeds and crop protection products including herbicides, pesticides, and fungicides. Land O'Lakes has a subsidiary, Forage Genetics International, that developed Roundup Ready alfalfa in conjunction with Monsanto (www.landolakesinc.com/stellent/groups/public/documents/web_content/ecmp2–0126651.pdf)! These are the seeds that Land O'Lakes sells to its thousands of farmer cooperators whose cows eat the GM hay and produce genetically modified dairy products that Land O'Lakes sells. GMO seeds are not only ecologically and nutritionally destructive, they reinforce the political economy of private agribusiness that concentrates agricultural ownership of resources in exclusive, anti-cooperative corporate hands.

Land O'Lakes CEO Policinski joined Conner as agricultural advisor to arch-conservative capitalist presidential candidate Romney in 2012.

In 2012, Land O'Lakes co-op issued a policy statement: "We oppose any efforts by EPA to regulate emissions of greenhouse gases under the Clean Air Act," and "We oppose the Chesapeake Bay TMDL requirements proposed by EPA that would require Chesapeake Bay states to aggressively constrain [farming] discharge and pollutant load allocations to farmers" (Land O'Lakes 2012).

In June, 2010, Land O'Lakes Cooperative Inc. and two subsidiaries agreed to pay US$25 million to settle a class action alleging that they were part of a long-running conspiracy between trade groups and agricultural companies to drive up the price of eggs by limiting production. Similarly, on September 26, 2011 several dairy consumers filed a class action lawsuit on behalf of consumers alleging that various dairy companies and trade groups – including Land O'Lakes – combined to form Cooperatives Working Together (CWT) in order to engage in a price-fixing scheme that inflated the price of milk. According to the complaint, this scheme resulted in over US$9.5 billion of unfairly and illegally obtained profits. According to the lawsuit, between 2003 and 2010 more than 500,000 young cows were slaughtered under CWT's "dairy herd retirement" program in an effort to reduce the supply of milk and inflate the price. The complaint further alleges that the program, which primarily bought out smaller farmers and instructed them to kill dairy cow herds, increased the profits of agribusiness giants (COK 2013). CWT members produce and sell more than 70 percent of the milk consumed in the U.S.A. Here, a cooperative worked to monopolize an industry, drive out small producers, increase profit, and impoverish consumers. Land O'Lakes co-op was a key player.

The NCBA rewarded these activities by inviting Land O'Lakes to co-sponsor the 2012 Induction Ceremony of the Co-op Hall of Fame. The NCBA also inducted Land O'Lakes, Inc. President and Chief Executive Officer, John Gherty, into the Co-op Hall of Fame (as it inducted a CEO of CHS co-op). The Hall of Fame is an affiliate of the NCBA that is administered by the Cooperative Development Foundation, which is a partner of the NCBA – and of Monsanto-linked CHS. This induction into the Co-op Hall of Fame occurred after Land O'Lakes released its GM alfalfa in 2005.

Neoliberal cooperativism

My analysis has revealed that corporate capitalists, think tanks, and the government agencies they control have invented a form of cooperativism that serves their political-economic interests. I dub it "neoliberal cooperativism." It is a particular cultural-historical-political form of cooperation that works within capitalism and legitimizes its evils.

The NCBA and ICA promote neoliberal cooperativism as genuine cooperation by partnering with and honoring neoliberal leaders.

For instance, the ICA recently held an "International Summit of Cooperatives" from October 8–11, 2012 in Quebec. It invited corporations such as Google, IBM, Microsoft, and Ernst & Young (auditing firm) to sponsor the Summit (the sponsors are displayed on the Summit website) (ICA 2012). This invitation elicits two pregnant questions that reflect on the social philosophy of the co-op movement: (1) why leaders of the world cooperative movement would choose to invite capitalist corporations to sponsor a major cooperative event; and (2) why the corporations accepted the invitation to sponsor the Summit, given their capitalist, anti-cooperative interests and practices. Answering these questions is pivotal for understanding the nature of cooperation that ICA and its associates advance.

Corporate sponsorship of the International Summit of Cooperatives

Corporate sponsorship of the co-op Summit reveals a congruence between (1) their politics, (2) their concept and practice of cooperation, and (3) the cooperative praxis of ICA and its associates.

The sponsors' politics are public knowledge. Microsoft has been fined over US$2 billion for criminal practices. Ernst & Young accounting giant has been sued by *New York's attorney general for helping Lehman Brothers disguise its financial condition for more than seven years, while collecting more than US$150 million in fees from the firm.* The two New York companies worked together from 2001 until Lehman's collapse in 2008. The lawsuit, led by New York Attorney General Andrew Cuomo, alleged that the firms engaged in practices to temporarily erase as much as US$50 billion in Lehman assets. This often occurred near the end of a quarter, allegedly making the company look much healthier than it really was. In June 2009, Ernst & Young paid US$109 million to settle investor claims that it failed to uncover a US$2.7 billion fraud at HealthSouth Corporation. In December 2009, the firm and some of its partners paid US$8.5 million to settle Securities and Exchange Commission allegations that they knew or should have known about fraudulent accounting by Bally Total Fitness Corporation. On December 3, 2012, Canadian regulators said Ernst & Young had conducted improper audits of Sino-Forest Corporation in the years before fraud allegations brought down its client, and the accounting firm said it reached a settlement in a class-action suit by Sino shareholders. Dimitri Lascaris, a partner at Siskinds LLP and co-lead counsel for the investor class action, said he believes the auditor settlement, at C$117 million (US$118 million), was the largest of its kind in Canadian history. Ernst & Young spent US$2,180,000 on political lobbying in 2011; 20 of their 21 lobbyists have previously held government jobs.

The insistent question is: Why would these corporations, which persistently exploit the political process and the business process to reap obscene profits, sponsor a summit of cooperatives? What does it tell us about cooperatives that they are attractive to bastions of neoliberal capitalism? Why do these capitalist bastions support co-ops when they would never support progressive groups such as Occupy, Wikileaks, unions, or socialist groups?

Co-op leaders believe that cooperation is more universal and appealing; it somehow makes capitalists forget their anti-cooperative interests, and elevates them to a higher social and ethical plane to which they naturally aspire "underneath" their capitalist tendencies. Co-op leaders believe cooperation is a transcendental, elevating phenomenon. However, transcendental cooperation is a myth. In reality, cooperation is concrete and political. The reason that capitalists endorse current cooperativism is that it is agreeable to their interests and practices – whereas these other forms of activism are not. Capitalist sponsors and speakers are barometers of mainstream cooperative politics. Cooperation does not transcend and elevate anti-cooperative practices and interests; on the contrary, it is permeated and perverted by them; they dominate it, it does not dominate them; their concreteness degrades it; its abstractness does not purify and elevate them.[4]

The co-op Summit validated this analysis by inviting the corporations into workshops and allowing them to frame cooperative issues. Ernst & Young actively participated in workshops at Summit 2012 and even drafted a pamphlet, "Enlightened Cooperative Governance: Balancing Performance with Broader Principles in Co-operatives and Mutuals" (Ernst & Young 2012). This pamphlet seeks to define co-ops as keeping pace with the capitalist economy. Here we have an empirical example of the way in which corporate praxis shapes the principles and practices of cooperativism. The title itself implies a conflict between performance and cooperative principles that must be balanced. It implies that cooperative principles are utopian and impractical, and must be adjusted or compromised with "real-world" economic performance, such as competitive profit margins. The language of the pamphlet frames co-op functioning in corporate terms:

> To stay competitive, co-ops and mutuals need to be able to quickly adapt to evolving market trends. The board therefore needs to be agile enough to make rapid business decisions – like acquiring a competitor or investing in the latest technology – all the while taking the time to listen to its members and maintaining member proximity.... Cooperatives and mutuals that want to remain competitive need to leverage the components of an agile governance structure.
>
> (Ernst & Young 2012, 8)

Ernst & Young's pamphlet about "enlightened governance for co-ops" replaces the cooperative ethos with a nondescript "listening to members" – who have not been educated to develop a cooperative ethos. The result is a co-op that works within, and works for, a capitalist economy: "In pursuing enlightened governance, co-ops and mutuals can inspire confidence in the marketplace, elevate their status and reputation as solid and unique business entities, and contribute to building competitive economies and cohesive communities" (Ernst & Young 2012, 15). Enlightened governance equals introducing a few humane values to capitalism – within the rubric of capitalism. Corporate involvement in co-ops is designed to pervert cooperation just as corporate involvement in organic food is designed to pervert organic standards in the interest of profit maximization. Framing cooperative practices and organizations within the limits of capitalism is the exact opposite of enlightenment, which analyzes and exceeds current limits (Foucault 1997).

Co-op leaders validate and facilitate the corporate framing of cooperative politics and practice. The Canadian Cooperative Research Network listed Ernst & Young's corporate approach to enlightened co-op governance on its web page under "articles of interest." Not a critical word appears in the notice. Co-op invitations to socially irresponsible corporations are a stamp of approval that obfuscates their evils. Co-op invitations acclaim corporations as trusted allies of co-ops. Invitations allow them to present themselves as cooperators. These actions by co-op leadership mystify and pervert cooperation (as compatible with capitalism), and they mystify capitalism (as compatible with cooperation).

The legitimating function of mainstream co-ops

Co-ops help capitalism to do its dirty work with impunity, without provoking rebellion, because co-ops are there to "pick up the pieces" and provide palliatives to the disenfranchised without condemning capitalism or trying to curtail or transform it. The NCBA/USAID Yaajeende project, for example, assists marginal Senegalese in desolate locations which corporations shun. Co-ops in the third world do the unprofitable dirty work of preparing the population and the infrastructure so that capitalist corporations may move in and profit. A 2009 publication from the Overseas Cooperative Development Council (OCDC) explains this:

> The urban-based private sector generally has had little experience dealing with the problems of rural areas. As a result, management sees it as risky and is reluctant to move in. However, once cooperatives have shown the way, private banks and other institutions (often catering more to the upper end of the income spectrum) do move into rural areas, which increase outlets and competition. So cooperatives may serve a catalytic role in bringing a variety of competing institutions into rural areas, which benefits all rural people.
>
> (Mellor 2009)

Co-ops are handmaidens to corporations; they save capitalism from itself; they supplement and sustain capitalism rather than negate it.[5]

Co-ops additionally promote the myth that social improvement can occur without political challenges to the capitalist mode of production.

Neoliberal cooperative politics stem from abstract cooperative principles

The foregoing examples of anti-cooperative, corporate politics of cooperation call for analysis of the reasons for this corruption and its acceptance. Have the corporate co-ops corrupted co-op principles, or are the principles inherently flawed so that they enable infiltration?

I argue that neoliberal, corporate infiltration of co-ops stems from an enabling, internal deficiency in cooperative principles: foundational cooperative principles misrepresent co-ops as a voluntary association of individuals, not a concrete cooperative collective. This allows non-cooperative praxes to qualify as cooperative if they are voluntary praxes. Non-cooperative voluntary groups such as corporations can legitimately insinuate their praxes into the rubric of cooperation/co-ops, and co-op associations such as NCBA must accept, honor, and promote non-cooperative praxes as cooperative because they meet the authoritative definition of a co-op. This is cooptation of cooperation that is inspired by cooperative principles.

This problem is evident in the definition of a co-op institutionalized in "The Statement on the Co-operative Identity" by the International Cooperative Alliance in 1995. A cooperative is defined as "an autonomous association of persons united voluntarily to meet their common economic, social, and cultural needs and aspirations through a jointly owned and democratically controlled enterprise." Co-operatives "are based on the values of self-help, self-responsibility, democracy, equality, equity, and solidarity. In the tradition of co-operative founders, co-operative members believe in the ethical values of honesty, openness, social responsibility, and caring for others."

Almost all of these descriptors (with one exception, discussed momentarily) characterize all voluntary groups, including corporations. To wit, a corporation is a voluntary organization; nobody is compelled to join it. Corporations practice open membership: anyone can buy shares. Founders and investors meet their common economic, social, and cultural needs and aspirations through a jointly owned enterprise. Founders and investors unite in *solidarity* to meet their needs. Corporate members and managers engage in *self-help* to actualize their aspirations: they make their own business plans, hire necessary staff, buy equipment, and finance their projects. Shareholders vote to decide on by-laws for their voluntary organization. They are autonomous in making these administrative decisions. No outsider dictates their decisions. Corporate law stipulates that corporations act honestly and openly. They are subject to audits to ensure transparency. Every corporation has some system for remunerating investors in proportion to their financial support for the enterprise. This is equity. And corporations are socially responsible in creating jobs and donating money to communities and political organizations. In these ways, corporations meet the definition of a cooperative! (Of course, corporations also violate these principles, but co-ops do also.)

This comparison reveals that co-op principles are actually principles of voluntary association, not a co-op. This eviscerates co-ops of genuine cooperation. It enables non-co-ops such as Monsanto to qualify as co-ops because they fulfill the pseudo "co-op principles" which are actually voluntary association principles. Eviscerating cooperation from co-op principles also enables co-ops to replace genuine cooperative praxis with non-cooperative praxis and claim cooperative status – as when they partner with capitalist corporations and conservative government agencies; when they pay exorbitant compensation to executives; when they recruit capitalist executives to run their organizations; when their members do not participate in governing it; and when management does not create a participatory environment for members.

The only significant difference between co-op and corporate praxis is that corporations allow one individual to have multiple votes according to the number of shares owned, whereas co-ops practice equality of voting rights, with each member only allowed one share and one vote. However, the anti-cooperative acts by corporate co-ops, NCBA, and even small, local co-ops (Ratner 2013), prove that this principle is inadequate to generate cooperation. Economic democracy of one shareholder one vote is formal equality of ownership; however, it entails no substantive content about the ownership. Equal owners may decide to implement all kinds of nefarious objectives and social relations – as voters in democratic capitalist elections vote against their own interests. Democracy is solely a decision-making process; it is not a content, nor does it necessarily generate humane or cooperative content. Formal voting equality may generate selfishness and acrimonious argument as it does in the U.S Congress.

Humane, cooperative content depends upon a concrete analysis and negation of existing social systems. This is what the focus of the co-op movement (and the progressive movement at large) must become. Democratic decision-making processes should be an auxiliary focus. Cooperation fosters true democracy, whereas democratic voting does not necessarily foster cooperation.

The formal equality of economic democracy is subverted in most co-ops by numerous rewards for unequal participation. A prominent example is patronage dividends where wealthier shoppers who purchase more products receive a greater patronage refund than poorer shoppers. Patronage dividends exacerbate inequalities of wealth. Another example is co-ops allowing members to invest through loans. Wealthy members invest more than poor members, and thus receive more interest. Indeed, the large majority of loans in any co-op are concentrated in the hands of a very few wealthy individuals who receive the vast amount of interest. Formal equality of economic justice mandates that each member receive the same rate of return on investment and patronage; however, disparities in the amounts of investment generate disparate amounts of wealth (Ratner 2013, 77–83).

The ICA's co-op principles are general/abstract to the point where they do not intimate or foster cooperation. Voluntarily forming an organization that is open to anyone is autonomous, honest, and donates to community groups, and allowing one member to have one vote is not tantamount to cooperation. The fact that a Muslim, patriarchal, Pakistani man, and a white supremicist American woman independently join an autonomous co-op and independently vote for directors who run an honest, open, socially responsible business does not entail cooperation among these parties. Cooperation is an organic social relation based on a particular social philosophy that is never specified in ICA's co-op principles. This silence guarantees deficient forms of cooperation.

ICA co-op principles silence, distort, mystify, and impede genuine cooperation. They extend co-op principles to non-co-ops and they make non-co-ops appear to be co-ops. They provide a benevolent cover for anti-cooperative parties and practices. This is how neoliberal politics come to infuse cooperation. "Co-op principles" are acceptable to diverse parties, including anti-cooperative ones, because they are devoid of any concrete form of genuine cooperation that would exclude non-cooperators and would require institutional and behavioral change. The popularity of co-op principles is due to their failure to promote genuine cooperation, not to their success in promoting it.

Advancing cooperation

Our political critique of co-ops shows that cooperation and economic democracy/justice are not simple, universal, taken for granted, neutral, or natural phenomena. They are fraught with specific politics that concretize their features and practices. These must be identified, evaluated, and improved. We must not make general statements urging and praising cooperation and economic democracy/justice, because they do not specify concrete politics and practices. Only a particular, concrete form of economic democracy and cooperation realizes progressive ideals and benefits.

To be truly fulfilling, economic democracy and economic justice must surpass abstractions, and they must surpass market social relations and commodity production/exchange. They must adopt an anti-capitalist, organic, collective praxis of cooperation. In other words, economic democracy must be qualified and concretized as *socialist economic democracy*, and economic justice must be qualified and concretized as *socialist economic justice* (Ratner 2013).

Developing an anti-capitalist, socialist politics of cooperation is the preeminent, urgent task for co-op activists and progressives. They can draw upon the praxes of Robert Owen and other progressive founders of the co-op movement. Owen was far more radical than contemporary co-op leaders. He founded the co-op movement in conjunction with the socialist movement and the union movement (Ratner 2013). A new cooperative politics, and cooperative form/concept, will also draw upon the collective social philosophy of Marxists and socialists (see Ratner forthcoming).

Anti-capitalist, socialist cooperators will work with organizations of the status quo in a principled manner that promotes the alternative praxis. It will not accommodate its praxis to capitalism as the mainstream co-op movement does.

Notes

1 www.sonic.net/~cr2.
2 I present examples of this influence and its effects in Ratner (2013).
3 This may be referred from CHS Inc.'s booklet "People," which has introduced the conference (CHS n.d).
4 In the same vein, capitalist corporations only accept environmentalism that is deformed to accommodate capitalist practices. Capitalists similarly promote health care "reform" only in the form of greater privatization of medical treatment (as in "Obamacare").
5 Park (2011) astutely explains that small-scale, local enterprises of any type cannot solve macro social problems. Consequently, any and all localism is necessarily marginal and unthreatening to the macro social system.

References

Barrett, W. 2012. "Mitt Romney, Monsanto Man." *The Nation*, September 12. Available online at: www.thenation.com/article/169885/mitt-romney-monsanto-man.

Bryer, A. 2012. "The Politics of the Social Economy: A Case Study of the Argentinean Empresas Recuperadas." *Dialectical Anthropology* 36(1–2): 21–49. doi: 10.1007/s10624–010–9190-x.

CBI (Council for Biotechnology Information). 2011. "Science Wins the Day: USDA Makes Science-based Decision to De-regulate Biotech Alfalfa." Available online at: whybiotech.com, January 31. www.whybiotech.com/?tag=biotech-alfalfa.

Charles, C. 2011. "Statement of Charles Conner – President and Chief Executive Officer, National Council of Farmer Cooperatives." Committee on Agriculture, US House of Representatives website. Available online at: http://agriculture.house.gov/sites/republicans.agriculture.house.gov/files/pdf/hearings/Conner110623.pdf (last accessed April 15, 2013).

CHS. 2013a. "About Us." CHS Official Website. Available online at: www.chsinc.com/portal/server.pt/community/1chs_facts/339 (last accessed April 15, 2013).

CHS. 2013b. "Crop Nutrients." CHS Official Website. Available online at: www.chsinc.com/portal/server.pt/community/6crop_nutrients/371 (last accessed April 15, 2013).

CHS. n.d. "People." CHS Official Website. Available online at: www.chsinc.com/portal/chs/server.pt/document/89271/4 (last accessed April 15, 2013).

COK (Compassion Over Killing). 2013. "COK Uncovers $9.5 Billion Price-fixing Scheme." COK Official Website. Available online at: www.cok.net/inv/dairy-lawsuit/ (last accessed April 15, 2013).

Ernst & Young. 2012. *Enlightened Co-operative Governance: Balancing Performance with Broader Principles in Co-operatives and Mutuals*. Ernst & Young official website. Available online at: www.ey.com/Publication/vwLUAssets/Enlightened_co-operative_governance/$FILE/Enlightened%20co-operative%20governance_EN.pdf (last accessed April 15, 2013).

Foucault, M. 1997. "What is Enlightenment?" In *Ethics: Subjectivity and Truth*, edited by P. Rabinow (pp. 303–319). New York: The New Press.

Hale, M.A. 2013. "Tilling Sand: Contradictions of 'Social Economy'" in a Chinese Movement for Alternative Rural Development." *Dialectical Anthropology* 37(1): 51–82. doi: 10.1007/s10624–013–9294–1.

ICA. 2012. "2012 Speakers." International Summit of Cooperatives website. Available online at: www.2012intlsummit.coop/site/speakers (last accessed April 15, 2013).

Land O'Lakes. 2012. "2012 Land O'Lakes Resolutions, Proposed." Signup4.net. Available online at: www.signup4.net/Upload/LAND10A/2012559E/PolRes2012%20draft.pdf (last accessed April 15, 2013).

Mellor, J.W. 2009. "Measuring Cooperative Success: New Challenges and Opportunities in Low- and Middle-Income Countries." NRECA International Programs. Available online at: www.nreca.coop/wp-content/uploads/2013/07/metrics-3.pdf (last accessed April 15, 2013).

NCBA (National Cooperative Business Association). 2012. "Co-op Research/Economic Impact." NCBA official website. Available online at: www.ncba.coop/ncba/about-co-ops/research-economic-impact (last accessed April 15, 2013).

Park, M. 2011. "Imagining a Just and Sustainable Society: A Critique of Alternative Economic Models in the Global Justice Movement." *Critical Sociology* 39(1): 65–85. doi: 10.1177/0896920511411319.

Ratner, C. 2012. *Macro Cultural Psychology: A Political Philosophy of Mind*. Oxford: Oxford University Press.

Ratner, C. 2013. *Cooperation, Community, and Co-ops in a Global Era*. New York: Springer.

Ratner, C. Forthcoming. *The Politics of Cooperation and Co-ops*. New York: Nova Publishers.

Ryan, A. 2006. "Who Owns REI?" *Seattle Weekly*, October 9. Available online at: www.seattleweekly.com/2003-06-18/news/who-owns-rei/.

Part II

Social economy in the world

4 Workers' cooperative movement in Argentina

Andrés Ruggeri

Introduction

Since the late 1990s, attempts at workers' self-management in companies have proliferated throughout the Argentine territory – in all sectors of the productive economy and services – and attracted enormous popular solidarity and the attention of researchers and activists. The commonly called "worker-recovered enterprises" (*empresas recuperadas por los trabajadores*, in Spanish (ERT)[1]) are companies abandoned by capitalists which have gone bankrupt, and workers attempt to take them over and self-manage them, with a primary objective of preserving jobs. The situation sets workers on a complicated and risky path, one that requires their maximum effort to succeed where capitalism has failed. In this context, the survival of the ERTs is useful to imagine how self-management may be achieved in adverse situations, strained by the logic of the capitalist market.

Recovered enterprises are a relatively recent phenomenon in Argentina and are closely related to the effects of neoliberal economic policy on the country's production structure and working conditions. Their emergence is directly connected to the massive shutdowns of factories and the consequent unemployment of millions of workers (Aspiazu and Schorr 2010; Kulfas 2003; Rebón 2004; Ruggeri 2009). Under these conditions, the first ERTs were desperate reactions by workers trying to keep their jobs in a way that would allow them to escape from the poverty and social marginalization which appeared to be their future destiny. The living conditions of unemployed workers were frightening for those who were at risk of losing their jobs. Desperate workers were driven to develop strategies for survival beyond old union tools that were no longer useful. The unions had lost all ability to pressure the owners to workers' demands in the context of massive unemployment, in a society in which employment had become a precious asset for the vast majority of workers (Harispe 2009; Azpiazu *et al.* 2010).

This process of neoliberal hegemony in which the ERTs were born was not independent from the process of capitalist globalization which introduced major changes to production and consumption structures, as well as to the organization of work and the role of the state apparatus (Antunes 2005; Harispe 2009). Argentina, possibly the Latin American country where the postwar "welfare state" had been more successful in ensuring an operational network of social security, was seriously affected by this global neoliberal hegemony, which was brutally manifested during the Carlos Menem government (1989–1999).

In the early 1990s, the Washington Consensus (Williamson 2004) established a wide range of neoliberal ideas that were generally adopted as unquestioned rules by most governments in the region. In most Latin American countries, so-called adjustment programs, privatization, downsizing of the state, and financial appreciation processes were carried out, heralding a bleak outlook by the mid-1990s (Basualdo *et al.* 2002). The old welfare states were swept away, crushing worker movements' achievements and subjecting society to the threat of massive unemployment. Neoliberalism soon generated a new society and a new model of state, but its character is regressive. Social and economic development is extremely uneven. The new neoliberal state apparatus broke up the old model, privatizing public enterprises and dismantling most of the social security systems that have been built up over decades. The global forces radically changed the role of the state, which became almost exclusively devoted to ensuring the interests of large economic groups.

In recent years, despite an increasing amount of resources devoted to the expansion and maintenance of social security or support networks, they were insufficient. Unemployment caused by the economy's escalating deindustrialization grew several times faster than the resources and structures created to contain it. As a result, marginal groups were socially unified under the category of "the unemployed"; they began to organize and press for their demands, leading to numerous forms of organization and the proliferation of micro-experiences, cooperative, and self-managed enterprises of all types.

This radical version of neoliberalism that has existed in Argentina since 1989 finally collapsed in December 2001, a few years before the spectacular global collapse that resulted from the implementation of this policy on an international scale. The country was not the only one to suffer this type of crisis, and it may be the most extreme case. In the rest of the world, expressions of resistance to what was being described as the global neoliberal system began to manifest, particularly in anti-globalization protests, as in popular governments that began winning elections in Latin America, especially since Hugo Chavez's victory in Venezuela in late 1998. This new context of resistance to global neoliberalism led many intellectuals and activists around the world to identify some of these popular expressions of resistance and reaction to the crisis in Argentina as part of a global anti-globalization movement (Petras *et al.* 2002; Schoijet 2006; Bowman and Stone 2009). However, what we have seen, and especially in the case of recovered enterprises, is that while the Argentine process is related to the global context, it has its own characteristics.

By analyzing the characteristics of the ERTs and their formation, especially political processes and changes in workers' subjectivities, we can assess the relationship between this movement and the possibility of a global struggle against capitalism. It is unquestionable that the Argentine and Latin American ERTs emerge more as a form of resistance against extreme situations stemming from a neoliberal crisis, rather than as an anti-capitalist ideological choice. But, at the same time, they also shed light on critical issues related to reformulating an economic and social project for achieving a worked-controlled economy.

Self-managed enterprises in Argentina

To evaluate the concrete phenomenon of worker-recovered enterprises, we collaborated with the Programa Facultad Abierta (Open Faculty Program) team at the University of Buenos Aires,[2] especially the data from the third survey of ERTs conducted in late 2009 and early 2010 (Ruggeri 2011b), compared to the previous two surveys done in 2002 and 2004 respectively (Programa Facultad Abierta 2003; Ruggeri *et al.* 2005).

Argentina had a total of 205 recovered enterprises at the end of the survey (2010), while in 2004 it had only 161, an increase of 44 in five years. This growth contradicts the widespread view that ERTs were exclusively the result of the 2001 crisis, and therefore represented a stagnant and declining process in subsequent years.

Today, the country's more than 200 self-managed enterprises provide jobs for some 9,400 workers. In the past four years – also in contrast with the image of the disappearance or mere survival of ERTs – more than 2,400 new self-managed jobs have been added, including those in recently created ERTs and additions to older ones. Forty-two percent of the ERTs belong to metallurgical or other manufacturing industries, 19 percent to the food industry, and 22 percent to non-production-related services, such as health care, education, and tourism. Most ERTs are categorized as small and medium enterprises (SMEs)[3] according to the number of employees, with an average of just over 30 members. The average worker's skill is quite specialized, but difficult to place outside of the industry in which they have spent most of their careers.

Long processes of struggle and occupation of factories and other workplaces have been observed in order to revive production, usually involving a number of months (more than nine for cases that began in 2001, and five for subsequent cases). These long-term conflicts have created obstacles to keep the highest qualified workers, or those whose skills command greater demand on the market (such as administrative and executive personnel). Thus, workers who remain in the ERTs are generally those who have no other chance of re-employment.

The profile of the workforce is made up of workers with a certain level of expertise and many years of service at the same company, with 5 percent being young adults, 75 percent over 35 years old, and 20 percent over age 55. Most of the survey respondents were male. The small presence of women is explained by the characteristics of the Argentine labor market as a whole, with certain industries and jobs occupied almost entirely by men (as in the case of metallurgical or printing industries, where the few women employed work in administration or cleaning). In other industries – such as education, health care, and the textile industry – a large number of female workers were employed, although these cases are far fewer in our sample.

Moreover, the ERTs are spread throughout the country, with a distribution that is closely related to Argentina's economic structure and the industries that were hardest hit by the neoliberal offensive of the 1990s. This is reflected in the fact that 50 percent of the ERTs are in the Buenos Aires metropolitan area, and most of those located outside the capital are in the industrial area of Santa Fe province. In the rest of the country, the ERTs are present in 15 of the country's 24 provinces.

Another important feature of ERTs is their legal conformation as worker cooperatives. According to our figures, 95 percent of cases were created under this legal form, while the remaining 5 percent comprise other types of cooperatives, undefined cases that are involved in conflicts, and cases of co-management between workers and former owners or other businesspeople. The choice of the cooperative form is favored for several reasons, such as lower taxes and the possibility of being recognized by a bankruptcy judge as "continued production" of a factory or business that has been declared bankrupt. As a cooperative, the members can operate legally on the market and enjoy protection over ownership of facilities, machinery, or other assets of the former company. Moreover, in forming a cooperative, workers can control the plant without being held responsible for the generally large, sometimes multi-million-dollar debts left by former owners.

In regard to health and social security benefits, however, ERTs have serious problems in ensuring workers' rights. This is due mainly to a lack of specific regulations that apply to these cases of cooperativized former wage workers. The absence of a specific law for workers' cooperatives places ERTs and other, similar cooperatives in a situation of legal ambiguity. Recently, this situation has increasingly become a subject of internal debate, given the "aging" process of recovered enterprises, with the majority of workers having been veterans when the self-management process began.

Regarding productivity, despite the efforts of their members, most recovered enterprises have not achieved the maximum productive output of their installed capacity. While significant improvement was made between the start of the operations and the first two years of work, subsequent expansion has been problematic and slow, and ERTs sometimes reach a point of stagnation. The reasons for this are diverse, including the disastrous state of plant and machinery in most cases, forcing workers to invest heavily to make it operational. These continuous or long-term investments are almost impossible in conditions of lack of capital, leading to situations of great sacrifice in which workers contribute their labor power without receiving an income that exceeds the threshold of survival. At the same time, this collective behavior – against the odds of market logics – shows an important level of maturity because it is a pledge of commitment to build the future development and progress of the self-managed enterprise.

Difficulty in breaking into the market is the main reason cited by ERTs for their economic problems. Even after several years of working, they have not been able to achieve sales levels that would allow them to make maximum use of their productive capacities. Most administrative and executive personnel who oversaw sales abandoned the enterprise amid conflict, and production workers must collectively take on their tasks. In some cases, ERTs resort to a form of subcontracting (*trabajar a façon*) in which a capitalist external to the company contributes prime materials and supplies and pays a fixed price for the final product. As product marketing is left to this businessman, the cooperative's profit levels are very low. However, in some very difficult cases, this is one option for allowing operations to begin.

One decisive factor in this situation is the role played by the state, which potentially has the ability to help prevent these problems from becoming obstacles that can lead to the failure of the enterprise. However, in addition to a legal system and a legislature that is very vulnerable to changes in "public opinion," which is not supportive of ERTs, the executive power at its different levels has yet to develop anything more than instruments for partial assistance. Some subsidies do reach the ERTs, representing support that is important, but not sufficient.

In addition, there is still no defined public policy that is consistent with the goal of consolidating workers' self-management. There is, however, a lack of legal framework which brings about two negative outcomes. On the one hand, it leaves too many aspects up to the judges to interpret and make decisions subjectively; on the other hand, it places the ERTs in illegal or precarious situations. Moreover, no development or training program exists that would give workers tools for collective management based on real situations.

Many more workers now confront the same challenges faced by millions of others during critical periods in Argentina: either they defend their jobs under self-managed forms, or they become part of the structurally unemployed sector, most of them workers who are ill suited for being reabsorbed into the labor market because of their age, gender, or trade.

Sustaining self-management in cooperativized economic production is not easy, but the starting point was much worse: shuttered businesses, unemployed workers who could not feed their families, rundown facilities, an absence of capital, a lack of involvement by the state, business fraud, and other elements that conditioned the beginning of ERTs. Despite all of this, in the past four to five years, the ERTs have increased in number and generated more than 2,400 jobs. They undertook solidarity-based cultural and educational initiatives, and provided work and dignity to their members.

Collective management mechanisms

What distinguishes enterprises that are self-managed by their workers from other types of enterprises is their main political and symbolic capital: the collective form of management. This process of self-management is dynamic and must be maintained voluntarily by the workers. The new collective enterprise emphasizes workers' decision and joint management practice.

While self-management is the most frequently cited characteristic of recovered enterprises, the specific ways it in which operates are not shown in statistics, nor adequately presented in case-by-case reports. We find that in each case, the dynamic nature of self-management, and how it is practiced, depend on the conditions of the original group of workers during the conflict that led to the ERT creation, its ability to achieve legal recognition despite many difficulties, the specific ways it uses to restart production, and the characteristics of the collective of former wage workers who now lead it. In particular, the intensity and nature of the initial conflict has been reported in several studies on the dynamic of self-management (Fajn 2003; Ruggeri *et al.* 2005). They show that a complex relationship has existed among the intensity of the conflict, direct democracy that workers need to establish collectively, and the egalitarian mechanisms that are used subsequently in dealing with questions related to decision-making and equality in work day and income levels. The studies also established a relationship between the ERTs that went through occupation processes and the possibility of facing political pressure (such as obtaining expropriation laws or other measures in its favor).

Given that almost all ERTs have adopted the cooperative form, they must take into account formal legal mechanisms that regulate the cooperative's operation, basically in terms of decision-making, which is essential for any self-management process. Cooperatives recognize two basic management bodies: the administrative council and the general assembly of members. In traditional cooperatives, the administration council holds the management power, while general assemblies are only involved in the preparation of annual reports and leadership elections. Everything else is decided by the council, and only one annual assembly is required by law. However, in the recovered enterprises, the relationship between the two bodies is totally different. Our research found a very different situation in the ERTs from that of traditional cooperatives in Argentina: only 8 percent of the surveyed ERTs said that decisions were made by the administrative councils. The vast majority gave their councils a variety of operational functions that, because of their immediacy, form of implementation, or routine nature, were impractical for assemblies to address. Thirty percent of ERTs explicitly said that the assemblies carry more weight than the administrative council. Sixty-two percent responded that their administrative councils were responsible for administrative, commercial, legal, and customer relations issues, and so on. According to these findings, administrative councils functioned more as the representatives and day-to-day administrators of the cooperatives' routine affairs, rather than as an authority equivalent to a board of directors, as sometimes happens in many traditional cooperatives.

The 8 percent where everything is decided by the administrative council coincides with the 8 percent that hold assemblies once a year. National legislation on cooperatives requires these annual assemblies, which should be minuted and are subject to external oversight. However, the reality for most ERTs is closer to the image that has become popular, and to the management model of using more frequent assemblies. An overwhelming 88 percent said they hold assemblies periodically, and, perhaps surprisingly, among them, 44 percent hold assemblies weekly and 35 percent monthly.

Evidently, the assemblies are very important for ERTs' workers. While some analysts attribute the importance of the assembly body to the expansion of direct democracy during the mass mobilizations of 2001 and 2002 (Fajn 2003; Rebón 2004), it is important to highlight other factors. We contend that the following findings are helpful for us to understand the current development of ERTs. The first is that the depth of the conflict cumulates to the dissolution of the previous forms of organization, both in hierarchical management and the trade unions. The profound changes in the structures of workers' relations occur. This leveling of social status of the members makes an assembly a more logical form for debate and decision-making. Second, assemblies are a constant element in working-class organization. Even bureaucratic union leaderships must use assemblies as a validation mechanism during labor conflicts. The assembly is a working-class tradition, not the product of crisis-related mobilizations or the emergence of new social movements. Of course, the fact that most ERTs were formed at the same time as those mobilizations may have promoted this practice during those years. Finally, an assembly is the most effective way of ensuring that members of a recovered enterprise participate in decision-making in the context of self-management. It is hard to think of self-management without assemblies, and the results of this research confirm this.

According to these data, the relationship between the regular bodies of cooperative management – the administrative council and the general assembly – acquire particular ways in ERTs that are more in line with their origins in workers' struggle for their jobs than with traditional cooperativism. The imprint of these origins and their class background appears clearly in the inverted traditional roles of council and assembly: while this may be true in many different ways and to different degrees, it tends to impose the weight of the collective of direct democracy over that of representative democracy.

However, reducing self-management to decision-making methods or workers' rights of equal participation does not take into account the repercussions that come with a production process that is different – although to various degrees – from that of the capitalist enterprise. Without ignoring the enormous difficulty and challenge involved in this transformation of the logic of economic production, it is worth examining the changes to the organization of work and the production process itself in the ERTs. This may be the aspects that most reveal the depth of change that occurs in workers' self-management.

In ERTs where attempts are made to democratize the production process itself, it is possible to go further than recovering jobs, and to envision a different conception of work and, therefore, a different logic of production and worker–worker relations as well as worker–society relations.[4] At the same time, this is the area where change is the most difficult, and where more factors are involved.

As we have discussed above, production conditions tend to vary from enterprise to enterprise, and the needs and shortages that emerge when production is restarted immediately pose the question of how to organize labor. The collective ability to begin the entire production process is a real test of workers' knowledge about the company's operation (both mechanical and non-mechanical dimensions) and their ability to overcome any potential obstacles.

In analyzing the internal workings of ERTs, we find complex and heterogeneous situations. An analysis of these data makes it possible to establish certain commonalities and to outline a starting point for a more complete analysis of management forms, work organization, and distribution of income among workers. It becomes clear that since the self-management dynamic is very complex, we will not limit our discussions to a single aspect (such as decision-making or equal income among workers), or a single moment of the whole organizational and laboring process.

At the same time, the heterogeneous solutions that ERTs workers apply to similar problems show that, at least for the time being, there is no single or right course of self-management. It is evident that, based on cooperatives' rules and traditional practices, no standard solution can be provided for a problem. Workers' creativity and effort in problem-solving is at times demanding.

All of us – social actors and academics who support these self-management processes, policy-makers, and workers themselves – have the opportunity to contribute to the development of a new type of production relations and management. We may broaden and enrich the first-hand experience of ERTs' members in walking together with them.

Rethinking self-management in the capitalist market

Although the concept of self-management is often utilized in a broad sense (Peixoto de Albuquerque 2003) for all types of social and political relations, here we try to limit it to cases of workers' economic management.

By self-management we refer to "workers' management of an enterprise's unit without capitalists or bosses, conducting their own organization of work under nonhierarchical forms" (Ruggeri 2009). In other words, self-management means that the workers collectively decide on the organization of the labor process, production norms, the use of surplus, and the company's relationship to the rest of the economy and society. It is important to note that we are talking about strategies of building new economic and social organizations, and supporting grassroots movements intersecting with working-class struggles to improve the living conditions of many workers, while we are still living in a larger capitalist society.

As mentioned earlier, the greatest difficulty with self-management cases like ERTs is the economic aspect: maintaining horizontality and solidarity while also being economically effective – and new definitions are needed for "effectiveness," "profitability," "growth," or "viability" that are not defined in market terms – to be able to achieve a decent life for workers.

Recovered enterprises, then, can demonstrate in practice the potentials and limits, in the current circumstances, of self-management as a social and economic practice. We are referring specifically to the economic conditions of self-management, analyzing concrete processes, not abstractions and idealizations. What are the conditions and problems for achieving self-management in ERTs? What solutions have been found, if any, and what progress has been made?

The theory, and the concept of self-management and its practical implementation, can be reconstructed and expanded in light of concrete experiences. For the first time in a long history, cases of self-managed enterprises like the ERTs in Argentina and other Latin American countries (including the new cases in European countries like Greece, Italy, and Spain) have become durable so that we are able to learn about their dynamics beyond a spotty existence at historical junctures.

Below is a brief breakdown of some of the key problems and solutions that workers have been experiencing in everyday practice; these are largely novel and not yet well formulated in academic circles.

Political and socio-economic context

Without taking into account the relations of production, the social and cultural logic, and the political context of self-management cases, any analysis of their problems would be an abstract, ahistorical intellectual process. In any circumstance of social transformation, understanding its context is critical to understanding its determinations and starting point. We have noted the neoliberal context in which ERTs emerged in Argentina, as well as their defensive, and reactive (rather than proactive) character. While workers' objectives were limited initially to responding to that reality, they have evolved and become more profound as a result of their conflicts with capitalist society and the market. By taking into account that political and socio-economic context, it is possible to understand the enormous difficulties faced by ERTs and to assess their achievements.

We note that the self-management process cannot be completely cut off from the influence of the capitalist market in which the company operates. The challenge is to preserve and develop a particular logic of economic rationality for self-management, even accommodating to the market's rules of competition. In that sense, even though workers feel like the "owners" of their labor process, they cannot break away from the ultimate reason of alienated labor: the production of commodities for exchange on a market whose logic and purpose is beyond their control. They alone cannot make up for the lack of a social order in which self-managed labor can exist without the hegemonic social relations created by capital. (But the creation of a protective market niche through "institutional purchase" of universities or churches may alleviate marketing pressures, and raise the exchange price of goods).

It would be a different scenario in a context of production relations where the market is not the main mechanism for the appropriation and distribution of production. The introduction of self-management enterprises in a mixed economy that is run by a socialist state would place the starting point for this process in a qualitatively different place, one which cannot be addressed here. A study of the Yugoslavian experience, with all of its historical limitations, may provide some basic clues (Jakopovich 2009).

Lack of capital

ERTs generally begin operating solely with their workforce, and, in some cases, with whatever raw materials remain in stock. Without access to credit it is very difficult for them to operate, except at the cost of enormous sacrifices, which are often borne by the members and their families. Some government subsidies exist to ease this situation, as briefly highlighted above, but results are unsatisfactory (Ruggeri 2011b).

How workers obtain the level of capital or financial resources to begin and maintain production is one of the most decisive and interesting aspects of these case studies. Channels for achieving this without exploiting workers (as in the gap-filling survival tactic through taking orders from bosses in subcontraction), and still meeting people's needs in an environmentally sustainable way, is, in fact, the main challenge of this form of management.

If self-managed enterprises are not based on capitalist accumulation, then they must implement an organizational way of life that controls, or even eliminates, the adoption of any type of capitalist logic that justifies the exploitation of workers in the workplace (and in the society). Democratic and solidarity-based management, with all of the complexity of its mechanisms for participation, is the foundation for generating a non-capitalist logic for guiding the ERTs.

In the Argentine context, an absence of that type of non-capitalist logic at the level of the national economy makes the task even more difficult. The practices of equality and collective management in ERTs constantly clash with the needs of the market, as well as with the values and ideas that workers have internalized from the capitalist culture in which they were born and have lived all their lives. So, who deserves to have more? Is the equalization of all fair and just? How do workers' inherited beliefs, cultural values, and (transformed) subjectivities work in the day-to-day functioning of ERTs?

The problem of self-exploitation, and the "external boss"

ERTs' lack of working capital, often combined with the difficulties in developing a marketing structure (which is clearly related to the previous point) and their small-scale operations, has forced a significant number of recovered enterprises to resort to production for third parties; that is, *a façon* work (Ruggeri 2009, 2011a, 2011b). In this case, a business or business owner, whom workers refer to as "the client," provides the raw materials and guidelines for production and rents, and the ERT's workforce and the use of machinery and facilities. This "external boss" then pays the ERT for its finished product at a significantly lower price than the price the ERT would earn if production were its own. In these cases, self-management is reduced to certain parts of the outsourced production process, and, what is worse, the surpluses go almost entirely to the indirect boss. We conclude that exploitation, in the form of the extraction of surplus value, is more hidden in these cases than in market relations: the boss possesses the working capital and takes the lion's share of the value created in production, while the self-managed collective is reduced to controlling only parts of the means of production and a small share of their labor value.

In a certain sense, this leads to "self-exploitation," a concept in academic circles that is frequently associated with recovered enterprises (Fajn and Rebón 2005; Heller 2004). In cases of *a façon* work, it is clear than the exploitation is being done by a boss disguised as a "client," and this is accepted by ERT workers due to the lack of a better alternative on the market. In other cases, self-exploitation is associated with long work days, maintaining features of the work process inherited from the former capitalist enterprise, low income, and other circumstances that are negative for workers, even when compared to their private business counterparts. However, these analyses of self-exploitation in ERTs generally equate self-managed workers with wage workers, ignoring all of the features characterizing ERTs: the factors that led to their creation, the state of the business, and the collective decision-making typical of these enterprises. They also fail to consider other circumstances involving the humanization of the workplace, such as comradeship, solidarity, and collective action. Even more significantly, these analyses do not address the basic question of whether or not ERTs have the essential element needed for exploitation: capitalist accumulation. Here we voice our counter-arguments or different perspectives. Definitely, the acute challenge is whether ERTs are, or can be, economically viable, in which workers' needs are relatively well satisfied.

Relationship to the market

Self-managed enterprises are an attempt to collectively solve problems of production, usually by taking on democratic forms of management, and guided by the logic of solidarity among workers and with society. That solidarity-based and egalitarian logic contradicts the logic of maximizing profits and market competition under the rules of capitalism.

However, the rhythms or more time-consuming process of internal democracy under workers' management, their ways of solving problems, and the solidarity exercised among workers and between workers and society cannot be protected from the encroachment of market competition, forcing self-managed enterprises to adapt at least part of their operations to market rules.

The way that these opposing logics are reconciled or adapted to each other is another powerful characteristic of ERTs, and one of ERTs' major problems. Despite having to comply with the rhythm and pace of production imposed upon them by the operation of the markets into which they are inserted, recovered enterprises try not to be subjected to other forms of exploitation that are widespread throughout the world.

For example, they attempt to maintain a work space that is humane, which is one of the major changes in the working conditions of recovered enterprises. Moreover, the inclusion of non-productive and solidarity-based activities in the enterprise's facilities, especially when these activities are related to the community – using collective work time, space, and organization for actions that are not part of the capitalist rationality – is an unusual form of altering the social functions of the enterprise and raising workers' awareness about their role in society.

The purpose of production is often debated among ERT leaders and members. Capitalist businesses seek capital accumulation, using different forms of organizing production to maximize self-interest by exploiting workers. By contrast, self-management enterprises must find a way to grow and operate under a rationale that does not seek this accumulation. It must strive to build a business that will allow workers to enjoy basic living standards, that will be able to provide jobs to others, and that will be socially integrated.

The labor process

Self-management implies a different dynamic in relations among the workers involved, not just in management decisions but also in the production process itself. It means that workers appropriate the labor process, with the possibility and obligation of changing the rules that govern the work process.

However, virtually none of the ERTs have made significant changes to the organization, pace, or characteristics of the labor process (Novaes 2007; Vieta 2009, Ruggeri 2009, 2011c). Those types or changes would require not only an injection of capital, but also the ability to dismantle the previously existing process and to re-create it under new conditions. The changes may be only a few but they are significant. These changes are related to workers' personal freedoms and the dignity that comes from knowing that they, the workers, really do control what is happening in the company. These changes are especially manifested in the characteristics, length, and pace of the working day, which is more humane than a typical work day for wage workers.

It is important to point out that these changes to the quality of working life do not make self-managed workers less productive; in fact, the opposite is true. When such changes can be made compatible with the efficient administration of the pace and organization of work, in most cases they lead to increases in production. In other words, labor productivity in ERTs, in our research, can also be competitive.

Production and technology problems

The relationship among the available technological tools, their role in the organization of production, and their importance when determining possibilities for changes in the labor process and the possibility of producing socio-technological adaptations (Novaes 2007) and what we refer to more broadly as social innovations (Trinchero 2009; Ruggeri 2009), are some of the richest and most complex aspects of the dynamics of self-managed enterprises. One of the major limitations for ERTs is how to organize self-managed production within a technological framework that was designed for capitalist accumulation. Technology is not neutral; its design, use, and even its dismissal are part of how relations of production are structured (Novaes 2007; Dagnino 2009). How machinery is arranged in a plant and how the chain of production is organized can (and in most cases does) imply the need for an authoritarian management structure to carry out the work and force a new structure to reproduce the former way of organizing production, restricting conditions for self-management.

Therefore, self-managed production is conditioned by an appropriation of production technologies designed for building social relations in a people-centered way. Socio-technological adaptation and social innovation allow workers to move to the new social relations they are attempting to build in their enterprises. This path is an extremely difficult one when it is not articulated by a state or research institution that has science and technology policies for including self-managed enterprises in a productive strategy with non-capitalist objectives.

Impact on local and community development

The impact of Argentina's ERTs upon local communities is not just economic in maintaining or generating jobs; it also has cultural and social dimensions. ERTs have made it possible to rebuild and create social ties between workplaces and local communities.

Most ERTs have not forgotten the enormous social solidarity they sparked among broad layers of the population, something that was critical to their recovery. They have engaged in solidarity-based activities with their local communities to reciprocate the solidarity and support they received during the conflicts that led them to become ERTs in the first place. These activities, which may appear to be anti-economic or irrational, include the lending of space and facilities for cultural activities, schools for the lowest income groups in the community, and donations and collaboration with social organizations and movements.

These are not strategies for winning political legitimation; they are workers' heartfelt way of giving back for solidarity received. These community actions, which differentiate from "corporate responsibility" PR shows, play a fundamental role in creating a caring community.

Conclusion

As enterprises that are neither state nor private and that are different from traditional cooperatives, ERTs have been developing genuine self-management in practice, despite many challenges and limitations. The ERT experience in Argentina may be useful for thinking about the reality and potential of self-managed labor beyond the abstract proposals of ideologues or jurists, and taking into account the common circumstances of Latin American workers.

This adoption of a diverse form of workers' sharing of tasks and lines of work, which were previously carried out under the contradiction between labor and capital, does not occur without resistance. Sometimes, we have observed a lack of commitment and responsibility on the part of some groups and individuals. The resolution of major obstacles, both internal and external, is not without conflict, and this may impact the viability of recovered enterprises.

The Argentine case shows that workers' management of production units is a difficult reality. But it is a reality for much of the past decade and is still ongoing. The lessons from these processes, involving not only hardship and suffering, but also joys and celebrations over workers' achievements, should nourish critical thinking that builds practices from the ground up. The alternative of the political economy is, and should be, guided by the logic of solidarity, breaking with the bondage of the self-destructive nature of capital flight, factory shutdown, and endless capital accumulation in global capitalism.

Notes

1 We use ERT in this chapter, instead of the English acronym, worker-recovered enterprises (WREs).
2 The Programa Facultad Abierta (Open Faculty Program) is a research and extension program directed by the author since 2002. It is attached to the Faculty of Philosophy and Letters of the University of Buenos Aires, Argentina. It specializes in ERT support, assessment, and research. Since 2004, the program has been managing the Documentation Centre of Recovered Enterprises, located in the facilities of the Cooperative Chilavert Graphic Arts, a recovered printing company in Buenos Aires.
3 PYMES (Pequeñas y Medianas Empresas) in Spanish.
4 Several researchers have addressed this point; see Fajn and Rebón (2005); Ruggeri (2009); Novaes (2007).

References

Antunes, Ricardo. 2005. *Los Sentidos del trabajo: Ensayo Sobre la Afirmación y la Negación del Trabajo* [The Senses of Work: Essay on the Affirmation and Denial of Job]. Buenos Aires: Taller de Estudios Laborales/Herramienta.

Azpiazu, D., and M. Schorr. 2010. *Hecho en Argentina: Industria y Economía, 1976–2007* [In Argentina: Industry and Economy, 1976–2007]. Buenos Aires: Siglo Veintiuno Editores.

Azpiazu, D., M. Schorr, and V. Basualdo. 2010. *La Industria y el Sindicalismo de Base en la Argentina* [Industry and Trade Unionism in Base in Argentina]. Buenos Aires: Atuel.

Basualdo, E., D. Aspiazu, M. Abeles, C. Arza, K. Forcinito, J. Pesce, and M. Schorr. 2002. *El Proceso De Privatización En Argentina: La Renegociación con las Empresas Privatizadas* [The Privatization Process in Argentina: The Renegotiation with Privatized Enterprises]. Buenos Aires: Página/12 and Universidad Nacional de Quilmes.

Bowman, Betsy, and Bob Stone. 2009. "La Cooperativizaciòn como Alternativa al Capitalismo Globalizador [Cooperativization as Alternative to Capitalism Globalizing]." In *La Economía de los Trabajadores: Autogestión y Distribución de la Riqueza: Selección de Trabajos Presentados al Primer Encuentro Internacional* [The Economics of Workers: Self Management and Distribution of Wealth. Choosing Jobs Presented by First International], edited by Programa Facultad Abierta (pp. 49–95). Buenos Aires: Ediciones de la Cooperativa Chilavert.

Dagnino, Renato. 2009. "Tecnologia Social: Ferramenta para Construir Outra Sociedade [Social technology: Another tool for building society]." Campinas: IG/UNICAMP.

Fajn, Gabriel. 2003. *Fábricas y Empresas Recuperadas: Protesta Social, Autogestión y Rupturas de la Subjetividad* [Recovered Factories and Businesses: Social Protest, Self and Subjectivity Breaks]. Buenos Aires: Centro Cultural de la Cooperación.

Fajn, Gabriel, and Julián Rebón. 2005. "El Taller ¿Sin Cronómetro? Apuntes Acerca De Las Empresas Recuperadas [El Taller without timer? Notes about the recovered companies]." *Revista Herramienta* 28. Available online at: www.herramienta.com.ar/revista-herramienta-n-28/el-taller-sin-cronometro-apuntes-acerca-de-las-empresas-recuperadas (last accessed January 25, 2006).

Harispe, Hernán. 2009. "Trabajo y Sindicalismo [Work and Unionism]." In *La Economía de los Trabajadores: Autogestión y Distribución de la Riqueza: Selección de Trabajos Presentados al Primer Encuentro Internacional* [The Economics of Workers: Self-Management and Distribution of Wealth: Selected Works Presented by First International], edited by Programa Facultad Abierta. Buenos Aires: Ediciones de la Cooperativa Chilavert.

Heller, Pablo. 2004. *Fábricas Ocupadas: Argentina 2000–2004* [Occupied Factories: Argentina 2000–2004]. Buenos Aires: Ediciones Rumbos.

Jakopovich, Dan. 2009. "Sources of the Democratic Deficit in the Yugoslav System of 'Self-Government.'" Z Net. Available online at: www.zcommunications.org/sources-of-the-democratic-deficit-in-the-yugoslav-system-of-self-government-by-dan-jakopovich.

Kulfas, M. 2003. "El Contexto Económico: Destrucción del Aparato Productivo y Reestructuración Regresiva [Economic context: Destruction restructuring the production system and timer]." In *Empresas Recuperadas: Ciudad de Buenos Aires* [Recovered Companies: Buenos Aires], edited by E. Hecker, M. Kulfas, F. Sanchez, M. Briner, and A. Cusmano (pp. 8–19). Buenos Aires: Secretaría de Desarrollo Económico. Gobierno de la Ciudad de Buenos Aires.

Novaes, Henrique T. 2007. *O Fetiche da Tecnologia: A Experiência das Fábricas Recuperadas* [The Fetish of Technology: The Experience of Recovered Factories]. São Paulo: Editora Expressão Popular.

Peixoto de Albuquerque, Paulo. 2003. *Autogestão* [Self-management]. In *A Outra Economía* [The Other Economy], edited by Antonio David Cattani (pp. 39–46). Porto Alegre: Veraz Editores.

Petras, James, H. Veltmeyer, J.C. Volnovich, P.V. Hazaki, and R. Castel. 2002. *Produciendo Realidad: Las Empresas Comunitarias: Grissinopoli, Río Turbio, Zanón, Brukman y Gral. Mosconi* [Producing Reality: Community Enterprise: Grissinopoli, Río Turbio, Zanon, Brukman and Gral Mosconi]. Topia Editorial. Buenos Aires: Colección Fuichas.

Programa Facultad Abierta, Facultad de Filosofía y Letras, Universidad de Buenos Aires. 2003. *Informe del Relevamiento de Empresas Recuperadas por sus Trabajadores* [Report of the survey of companies recovered by their workers]. Available online at: www.recuperadasdoc.com.ar.

Rebón, Julián. 2004. *Desobedeciendo al Desempleo: La Experiencia de las Empresas Recuperadas* [Unemployment Disobeying: The Experience of Recovered Companies]. Buenos Aires: Ediciones Picaso/La Rosa Blindada.

Ruggeri, Andrés. 2009. *Las Empresas Recuperadas: Autogestión Obrera en Argentina y América Latina* [Recuperated Enterprises: Worker Self-Management in Argentina and Latin America]. Buenos Aires: Facultad de Filosofia y Letras, Universidad de Buenos Aires.

Ruggeri, Andrés. 2011a. "Autogestión Obrera en Argentina: Problemas y Potencialidades del Trabajo Autogestionado en el Contexto de la Poscrisis Neoliberal [Workers' self-management in Argentina: Problems and potential of self managed work in the post-crisis context of neoliberal]." In *Cooperativas y Socialismo: Una Mirada desde Cuba* [Cooperatives and socialism: A look from Cuba], compiled by Camila Piñeiro Harnecker (pp. 272–300). La Habana: Editorial Caminos.

Ruggeri, Andrés. 2011b. *Las Empresas Recuperadas en la Argentina. 2010. Informe del Tercer Relevamiento de ERT* [The Recovered Companies in Argentina, 2010: Third Report of the Survey of ERT]. Buenos Aires: Ediciones de la Cooperativa Chilavert.

Ruggeri, Andrés. 2011c. "Reflexiones Sobre la Autogestión en las Empresas Recuperadas Argentinas [Reflections on the self-management in business recovered Argentinas]." *Estudios* 1(1): 60–79. Córdoba, España: Secretaría de Formación y Estudios, CNT-AIT.

Ruggeri, Andrés, Carlos Martínez, and Héctor Hugo Trinchero. 2005. "Las Empresas Recuperadas en la Argentina: Informe del Segundo Relevamiento del Programa Facultad Abierta [The recovered companies in Argentina: Report from the second survey, Open Faculty Program]." Buenos Aires: Facultad de Filosofía y Letras, Universidad de Buenos Aires.

Schoijet, Mauricio. 2006. *La Crisis Argentina: Los Movimientos Sociales y la Democracia Representative* [Argentina's crisis: Social movements and representative democracy]. México: SITUAM-Plaza and Valdés Editores.

Trinchero, Héctor Hugo. 2009. "De la Exclusión a la Autogestión: Innovación Social Desde la Experiencia de las Empresas Recuperadas por sus Trabajadores (ERT) [From exclusion to self-management: Social innovation from the experience of the companies managed by their workers (ERT)]." In *La Economía de los Trabajadores: Autogestión y Distribución de la Riqueza: Selección de Trabajos Presentados al Primer Encuentro Internacional* [The Economy of Workers: Self-Management and Distribution of Wealth: Selected Papers Presented at the First International]. Buenos Aires: Programa Facultad Abierta. Ediciones de la Cooperativa Chilavert.

Vieta, Marcelo. 2009. "Desafíos e Innovaciones Sociales en las Empresas Recuperadas por sus Trabajadores [Challenges and social innovations in companies managed by their workers]." Chapter 10 in *Las Empresas Recuperadas: Autogestión Obrera en Argentina y América Latina* [Recuperated Enterprises: Worker Self-Management in Argentina and Latin America], edited by Andrés Ruggeri (pp. 103–114). Buenos Aires: Editorial de la Facultad de Filosofía y Letras.

Williamson, John. 2004. "A short history of the Washington Consensus." Paper commissioned by Fundación CIDOB for a conference "From the Washington Consensus towards a New Global Governance," Barcelona, September 24–25. Available online at: www.iie.com/publications/papers/williamson0904-2.pdf.

5 La Alameda

"Guerrilla" struggles to make the Argentine economy social

Doris Lee

Introduction

Within the concept of "social economy" lies the implicit criticism that the existing neoliberal capitalist economy is insufficiently "social" – it fails to cater to the needs of all members of society; it excludes and leaves certain sectors of society deprived. The rise and development of the "social economy" is one response to and remedy of those gaps in human need created by the existing economic model. The social economy is an "economy" – yet with values and scopes that are contrary to those of the mainstream capitalist economy: values of people above profit, cooperation above competition, and of worker participation and workplace democracy.

The creation and sustenance of the "social economy" requires carving out a path in a hostile legal and discourse setting where precedence is given to that which extracts private corporate profits from labor and from the privatization of collective goods, including land. It may be debated (but will not be treated at length here) whether the aim and goal of the social economy is ultimately to replace and take over the whole existing economy (revolution?), or to simply create a parallel sphere that coexists with and complements the existing capitalistic market economy (Wright 2010).[1] In either case it requires struggle. Whether one is demanding a state role in the guarantee of employment, or the state's non-intervention in but legal recognition of workers' self-creation of employment and use of public spaces, struggle by workers and communities is constantly needed.

In such a task, civil society organizations are often the agents that push such struggle. I will rely here on the definition of civil society as "the sphere of ideas, values, institutions, organizations, networks and individuals located between the family, the state and the market and operating beyond the confines of national societies, polities and economies" (Anheier *et al.* 2001, 17, quoted in Kaldor *et al.* 2012).

Making the economy social

Here I examine how a civil society organization can be effective in making the economy social – or creating social economy. The historical path of one Argentine organization, La Alameda, is traced and examined in terms of what factors and variables have contributed to its achievements in making the economy social. The example of La Alameda is important because the field of social struggle and the "population" of civil society are filled with organizations that speak the same language about fighting poverty and the social exclusion of marginalized groups, yet appear to contribute to the status quo more than to radical change.

In Argentina: seeds sown and shoots grown

Argentina is a country that has been noted for the upsurge of social economy initiatives and structures of various types since its economic crisis of 2001 to 2002, and which has significantly retained many of the gains for its workers which had been achieved at that time (Ruggeri 2010). Among these were three significant phenomena relevant here: the *asambleas* (neighborhood assemblies), the recovered factories (or occupied factories) movement, and worker cooperatives. To some extent these were not entirely new, and did have roots in labor and community struggles carried out even prior to the economic crisis.[2] However, we want to examine what has enabled some organizations to continue their successes even after the crisis and once some of these phenomena have died down and lost their ability or even intention to change the external, fundamentally exploitative economic system (why the "seeds" indeed took root and became shoots that continued to grow).

In this section, I examine the methods and sources of power of the community organization La Alameda, in Argentina, which account for its many achievements in the past 10 years to limit the power of capitalists to exploit workers, particularly migrant workers, and which is currently most well known for its anti-trafficking achievements. "Making the Argentine Economy Social" means ensuring that the growth in the economy does not come at the expense of workers' lives and dignity.

The element of democratic consultation and participation of "stakeholders" (i.e., communities, migrant worker victims) is one of the factors contributing to the organization's strength and effectiveness in its mission of making the economy social by limiting the control of capital over workers and of the government also over citizens and workers. Aspects of the organization's source and use of resources is another key element. Through its methods and their success, La Alameda has demonstrated the potential power of an organization which insists on maintaining financial independence from external donors for its core activities, and which also functions as a substantially horizontally organized network.

La Alameda: introduction

La Alameda is the name of a community center, but also of an anti-trafficking NGO. It may be more accurate to label La Alameda as a worker and community service/advocacy conglomerate. In the building called La Alameda, activities are conducted, including weekly *asambleas*, union meetings, a community canteen providing free meals, worker education courses, and a garment production cooperative.

In just 10 years, the organization La Alameda has succeeded in making "slave labor" a term routinely used in mainstream media – in this way helping to make sex trafficking and abuse of migrant and child labor major social issues; achieving the support of the Cardinal of the Catholic Church (presently Pope Francis) as well as a wide group of media figures, and expanding its activist network even to other parts of Argentina where labor and sex trafficking are entrenched problems – all the while succeeding in achieving the escape and re-employment of countless migrant workers, closures of illegal sweatshops, and more.

La Alameda has also played a role in securing the inclusion of "excluded workers" and the "popular economy" as a sector under the main union federation in Argentina, the Confederación General de Trabajadores (CGT, or the General Confederation of Workers).

Below, I first examine the origins, development, and current patterns of operation of La Alameda. Then I discuss the relation of its finances and organizational structure and operations on its "success" in terms of activism, and how these fit into other debates on "successful organizations" and on revitalization of a bureaucratizing and rigidified union movement.

La Alameda: origin

The organization now well known as La Alameda originated as an *asamblea* of residents in the neighborhood of Parque Avellaneda, which was formed during the crisis and mobilizations of the public on December 19 and 20, 2001. This *asamblea* – a gathering of neighbors in order to solve the common problems of the community – was eventually called "20th of December." Until June 2002, it operated outdoors in Avellaneda Park, and focused on dealing with the pressing problems of that moment: the hunger and unemployment that had become rampant since the economic crisis and currency devaluation that had gripped Argentina since 2001. During that period, unemployment reached as high as 25 percent, the government was paralyzed, and workers even occupied factories out of desperation to keep their jobs, even at the cost of violent confrontations with police who would come to evict them; the *asamblea* responded by forming a community canteen to feed the hungry and also various cultural activities to support those neighbors in need.

From June 8, 2002, the *asamblea* began to function inside a bar which it took over – a bar called La Alameda that had been abandoned and remained unused for four years.[3] It continued its service of providing food for local residents in need, reaching up to 160 people served at each meal, and obtained the support of the City of Buenos Aires for the food, and the legalization of the community kitchen as a project of the Ministry of Social Development. Yet the *asamblea* had to fight against attempted eviction, and had to continue its fight in the courts to win expropriation of the site for its use as a cultural and community center.

Finally, in 2007, the site was expropriated by the city government and granted to La Alameda as a public utility. La Alameda (the *asamblea* now assumed the name of the bar) was one of the first *asambleas* to recover (occupy) a space and has also been one of the longest-lasting popular *asambleas* (Hauser 2004).

Since the takeover of the bar in 2002, the *asamblea* not only continued the community kitchen but also promptly established job creation projects – garment worker cooperatives were one of the priorities – to provide work for the garment workers who escaped from hidden sweatshops in the streets nearby and come to La Alameda for meals.

From 2005, La Alameda began a campaign to raise awareness among the Bolivian garment workers in the neighborhood about their labor and migrant rights. From then began the first lawsuits against slave labor and labor trafficking in hidden sweatshops that supplied the major clothing brands. To date, more than 100 brands have been charged with lawsuits for use of hidden sweatshops founded on slave labor and trafficking. Through the fight against these forms of production, garment workers have been rescued and reinstated in the formal labor market.

In 2007, Fundación Alameda (the Alameda Foundation), a legal aid organization, was established with lawyers in order to provide regular assistance to workers who had escaped from sweatshops, and to sue the sweatshop owners and brands that exploited them. It also aimed to give training to sympathetic lawyers and other concerned people who wished to join the struggle against garment worker exploitation, and to inform more sectors of the public about the truth behind so many fashionable brand names. By the end of 2007, La Alameda had already brought legal charges against 85 brands for exploitation of garment workers in sweatshops, forced servitude, and violation of the Law on Home-based Work. Since then, the number of brands that have been legally charged by La Alameda has reached 110.

From 2008 onward, La Alameda has also exposed the use of migrant labor, including child labor, in poultry farms by using hidden camera footage, which was a technique also often used in exposing the hidden sweatshops. As more and more workers learned of La Alameda's unrelenting and immediate support for workers in need, more workers would call upon La Alameda to assist them – and La Alameda would also continue to take the initiative – to expose workers being abused in their workplaces, under the inaction of police and labor inspectors.

In 2009, after making contact with Asian labor organizations, La Alameda initiated a joint global garment brand called No Chains to expand its work against exploitation in the global garment industry as well as to widen support for worker cooperatives.

Recently, a growing problem in the city of Buenos Aires – and a very grave problem also in other tourist parts of Argentina – has been the spread of organized prostitution and of prostitution houses where many of the sex workers have been trafficked. La Alameda has also been aggressive in exposing these places, and also, daringly, in exposing the links of these places to prominent politicians and government figures – one of the most scandalous cases being the connection of several brothels to a Supreme Court Judge named Raul Eugenio Zaffaroni.

Until today, La Alameda has been carrying out those attacks against exploitative employers and corrupt officials, while continuing to function as a local center serving local needs. On a given day, perhaps only about 40 people attend for the free lunches, rather than the 160 or so that would attend at the peak. In addition, importantly, the weekly *asamblea* at La Alameda still continues.

La Alameda: decision-making and agenda-setting

The central issues which this "NGO" tackles in its advocacy and legal and protest actions are determined first by the needs of the surrounding community. Thus, when the needs of the surrounding community were to feed large numbers of people and to create dignified employment for workers, this was the central focus of activity. However, as the economy began to recover and the problems shared by workers coming to the community canteen were more about exploitation in garment sweatshops, tackling that problem became the priority.

This character is quite different from many NGOs which are formed with a particular "issue" as their focus, and which, as a consequence of their funding, are incentivized to specialize narrowly in a niche and to distinguish themselves as experts to stay "competitive" when applying for funds.

As the organization gained a wider reputation for defending the rights of and assisting any migrant workers – or any workers – who wished to sue and expose their employer, inquiries would come from further away and from different fields, not only garment sweatshops. Furthermore, as La Alameda itself became more deeply involved in these struggles, as a natural consequence of its aim of solving problems in the community it would seek allies in different fields – the media, the Church, leftist organizations and political parties, student groups – to broaden their struggles and gain wider support for their desired legislative changes and for their attempts to effectively discipline offenders.

Internal democracy and space for debate

The weekly gathering to update the whole collective – the community, the activists of La Alameda, and all workers in the related cooperatives – on matters of ongoing struggles and to consult them on future activities ensures that the activities are never far from the stakeholders' interests and concerns.

The openness of the group to debate and sharing of tasks also strengthens trust in the leaders and core activists. The transparency to the outside also inspires great trust in the group, a trust which the public do not often share with politicians, unions, religious groups, and NGOs.

Financing and resources

The organization, during its 10-year history, has relied on several streams of financing for resources that it needs.

1 "Occupation" of what it needs. For example, the place La Alameda, which was first occupied by the *asamblea* and which went through a long process of legal battles to gain legal rights.
2 Recognition as a community service center, which was linked to other "benefits" for the community and for the center.

- A monthly subsidy provided by the City of Buenos Aires to provide free morning and lunchtime meals in the main activity space of La Alameda.
- Students who undertake internships or community service come to stay for periods of time and offer their practical help.
- People who have been charged with petty crimes and then sentenced to community service may complete their service at La Alameda.

3 Furthermore, sustained campaigns also to obtain services or materials from the government, such as aid for migrants who have been rescued from sweatshops.
4 Solidarity of sister/brother organizations. Left political parties are granted travel vouchers to travel by bus to other parts of Argentina. They give the leftovers to La Alameda for its activities in other parts.
5 Fundraising events such as parties and festivals.
6 One-off donations for particular needed items, such as machines, raw materials for production, or other urgent needs of workers. These donations may come from concerned individuals who sympathize with the work of La Alameda, or from entities such as the Swiss Embassy or a private foundation.
7 Income generated by the cooperatives that are based in La Alameda. Currently about 10 percent of the regular costs of La Alameda (electricity, the Internet, etc.) are paid by the cooperatives.
8 Pro bono services of activists who are workers with other sources of personal income, including professional lawyers.

One of the aspects which members of La Alameda believe has been key to their ability to gain public attention and sympathy for their work is the fact that the activists of La Alameda have all been working voluntarily, i.e., with no compensation from La Alameda for their work; on the contrary, many of the activists have cut down their working hours and thus their own incomes in order to free themselves for the tasks of La Alameda. For example, one of the main spokespersons and chair of the Fundación Alameda (Alameda Foundation), Gustavo Vera, works as a schoolteacher for a half day rather than a full day. Thus he earns his own livelihood, which itself is a low one, as he works voluntarily only half a day in order to spend more time for activism within La Alameda. Others also have foregone greater income opportunities in order to advance the work of La Alameda in the community; Tamara Rosenberg, who is the head of the garment worker cooperative 20th of December, is qualified as a psychologist and used to have her own consultation office; however, she worked with the other garment workers with very low incomes for several years in order to develop the factory and gain income through expanding the market for their goods and through work, rather than through charity. All other activists working in and with La Alameda also worked totally on a voluntary basis; however, as the volume of tasks has greatly expanded, especially over the past five years, three of the activists, Lucas Schaerer, Lucas Manjon, and Facundo Lago, have been given a small stipend in the past two years, subsidized by an external organization, since otherwise these activists may have to take up other full-time work which could prevent them from fulfilling their key roles and from continuing the high volume of work in the organization. These three activists have been handling the time-consuming, skilled, and essential tasks of producing videos, coordinating interviews and reports in the media, writing legal charges and press releases, organizing protest actions and advocacy-related events, and updating the La Alameda websites and the online monthly journal *Agenda Oculta* – their one-year-old journal dedicated to offering information and views about topics meriting public debate, which are hidden in society and minimized or ignored in mainstream media: trafficking, forced labor, corruption, etc.

Media strategy/public credibility

La Alameda relies very much on a branding strategy, much like a corporation.[4] They have a clear name, clear slogan, and clear logos. The slogan they use is "For a World With No Slaves, With No Excluded" – it is one which many can sympathize and assist with, regardless of political or religious leaning. The name they use, La Alameda, is repeated in every media statement, banner, and publication. With such a clear use of a name and slogan, and with their repeated appearances in media, backed up by video evidence taken with hidden cameras, workers or other sympathizers and allies in particular causes know where to turn to when they need assistance to escape from abuse, or to join in partnership in fighting against an abusive employer, or an unjust law or policy that would further subject workers to hardship.

The consistent use of its name La Alameda and constant appearance in the media, often in many media each week, has added tremendously to its ability to influence public discourse and gain allies for its efforts.

As a reflection of La Alameda's public reach, the blog of La Alameda has about 400,000 visits per year, while the online journal, *Agenda Oculta*, managed by La Alameda, has received 50,000 visits within a few months of launching the publication.[5]

The intensive efforts to gain "media power" – to gain influence over debates in favor of victims, to publicly shame violators, and gain support for legislative and policy changes – are mutually constructive to the aim and principle of La Alameda of staying politically and financially independent. The organization, which is not spending up to a quarter of its time, energy, and resources reporting and justifying its actions to a small group of donors on donors' terms, is compelled – and freed – to use far more of its time, energy, and resources in solving the needs of its "stakeholders" and mobilizing media and alliances in society to strike at the core problems.

Legal foundation

With the Alameda Foundation acting as a legal "wing" of La Alameda, the organization can battle not only in the field of campaigns and public education but with concrete data, concrete victims, and legal bases of action. Cases do not often end with conviction and punishment of the perpetrators; for example, many of the sweatshop owners who have been sued by La Alameda have been able to simply open again, even in the same location. Nonetheless, the cases accumulate and La Alameda keeps a constant media presence, and these add weight and legitimacy to La Alameda's demands to the public and to the legislature and government for systematic changes that genuinely protect workers from slave-like exploitation for profit.

The legal wing of La Alameda serves both as a service provision to exploited members of the community and as an important concrete technical support to enable making the economy social.

Ecumenical partnership/alliance-building

A natural extension of its work is conducting legal cases, giving training to the public, advocating in media and various platforms to address the roots of the concrete problems found in the community in which La Alameda is based – garment sweatshops, migrant exploitation, sex trafficking, drug trafficking, etc. In order to achieve concrete gains such as punishment and deterrence of violators and changes to the law to protect victims and eliminate exploitation, La Alameda constantly reaches out to allies, which range from church clergy, to art designers, to politicians.

Politics

La Alameda has indeed often worked in collaboration with politicians from different backgrounds – but generally those which are clearly pro-worker and against the exploitation and abuse of workers, especially migrants. For example, in the anti-trafficking and anti-mafia conference held in April 2013, organized primarily by La Alameda, politicians from various parties as well as representatives of union federations such as CGT attended and extended their commitment to work with La Alameda against trafficking and domination by the mafia. However, certain individuals who work for or with La Alameda may be affiliated to or members of one party, union, or another; La Alameda has for a long time kept the principle of maintaining its independence as a whole from any particular political party, while being willing to maintain links and alliances. This has been a contributing factor to the willingness of a wide range of social actors and members of the public to recognize La Alameda as a credible organization and advocate for exploited workers and neglected communities. Being independent of any particular political party, La Alameda did not face pressure to gain votes for "their party," thus remaining free from the tendency to exaggerate the organization's achievements and promises near election times, and to modify its position on a certain issue for the sake of more possible votes.

Following the initial writing of this chapter however, in June 2013, Gustavo Vera announced that, on behalf of La Alameda, he would join Pino Solanas and Elisa Carrió in their political party coalition called Coalición Sur to run as candidates in national and local elections. The coalition includes nine political parties and La Alameda, the NGO, and is the forerunning list within UNEN, a larger political space which includes three other lists/coalitions besides Coalición Sur. Although some supporters of La Alameda have expressed the wish to see La Alameda maintain its distance from politics, the commitment of La Alameda activists, foremostly Gustavo Vera, remains high toward principles of democracy, worker participation, and transparency. The future will tell whether participation in the legislature brings any dent in La Alameda's remarkably intense level of achievements.

Formula for success?

In the following sections, I will expand from observations about La Alameda to the typical problems that face organizations, including trade unions, that over time lose their capacity and legitimacy to carry out radical social change; touch on theories that offer explanations and predictions of whether an organization can stay radically powerful; and revisit the characteristics of La Alameda that are paralleled by other examples in the world – offering the hope that its "winning" characteristics are indeed replicable.

The question of how to maintain relevance and impact, and the social power to change the economy and society to workers' needs – this is the same question for NGOs and for unions, and has been a theme of deep reflection and sometimes acrid debate.

Since the unfolding of neoliberal policies around the world in waves since the 1990s, including privatization, outsourcing, subcontracting, and deregulation, and accompanied by concerted attacks on union power, social organizations and communities have been struggling for the means to counteract these attacks and restore decent livelihoods and some element of control over economic and social institutions.

Trade unions and their problems

In industrialized countries, trade unions have been a major social force to collectively protest and make demands, to protect workers from work accidents, insure against illness and old age, and advocate for fair working and social conditions. However, the unions have posed threats to government and capital's agendas and have been undermined through diverse ways, including legislative, political, and other indirect means. Furthermore, capitalists have found numerous ways to exploit cheap, unprotected labor – legal and illegal migrants, part-time and temporary workers, independent contractors, students, etc.; unions have not responded quickly and many are still focused on organizing formal workers in the workplace, or have become focused, for example, in the US, on gaining large membership numbers and influence in electoral politics.

The loss of the relevance and power of trade unions has forced many of them to search seriously for ways to recover, while some new or simply alternative forms of organization which also defend workers' rights have arisen. La Alameda, the Argentine organization described above, may be considered one such new form of organization, defending workers' rights together with communities and unions, yet not a union per se.

Organizations' tendency to oligarchy: can the "Iron Law" be broken?

The German sociologist Robert Michels presented what he regarded as the "Iron Law" of social organizations – that inevitably an oligarchy will develop in any democratic organization (Michels 1915). An "oligarchy" of elites assume leadership, the goals of the organization are modified, and the organization turns its focus on maintaining its existence. Indeed, the danger of the tendency exists; however, besides the above evidence across cultures and eras, of starfish-like decentralized organizations which do exhibit democratic decision-making, more recently Hanspeter Kriesi has identified four types of trajectories of movement organizations, based on the common core of the "new social movements" that emerged in Western Europe in the 1970s and 1980s (Kriesi 1996, quoted in Tarrow 2011, 212–213).[6] The four processes that Kriesi found an organization may go through in its development are as follows:

1. *Institutionalization*: combination of the formalization of the internal structure of a social movement organization with moderation of its goals (the pattern also identified by Michels in European social democracy).
2. *Commercialization*: transformation into a service organization or profit-making enterprise.
3. *Involution*: a path leading to exclusive emphasis on social "incentives" so that movement organizations end up as self-help groups or voluntary associations.
4. *Radicalization* – that is, becoming an ever more exclusive organization for the mobilization for collective action.

While social movements struggle against government and capital to make the economy responsive to human need and subject to greater democratic control by workers and citizens, in rolling waves of moves and counter-moves, government and capital continually make available myriad ways to disarm, coopt, and defuse movement organizations. However, it is not an inevitability that organizations follow that road to "survival" and allow their aims to be subverted and their activities tamed.

Organizations – and movements – exist that do recognize certain keys to maintaining organizations that do not lose their value to the movement (i.e., that keep their radical power to mobilize and strike at the core of their target, not at the mere surface).

The power of the starfish, the power of the guerrilla

In his 2006 book *The Starfish and the Spider: The Unstoppable Power of Leaderless Organizations*, Ori Brafman argues that decentralized and network-based operations and a certain type of people – "catalysts," rather than leaders who monopolize authority – are important for the success of an organization. The author shows, using examples of "winner" and "loser" organizations, including corporations but also organizations like Alcoholics Anonymous, how differences in the degree of the centralization of authority, centralization of resources, and the sharing or restriction of information, affected whether an organization would grow, or survive when attacked. The "starfish" (a decentralized network type of organization) could regrow parts when attacked, while the spider (a hierarchical organization with centralized authority, decision-making and resources) would be disabled if the center were attacked. Besides the decentralization of authority and sharing of information, also key are shared values or ideology, which is also related to having members who are self-motivated rather than reliant on external reward.

Brafman examined past as well as current examples for lessons to inform corporate management; for example, he also referred to the guerrilla tactics of the Apache warriors in battles against the colonial Spanish army.

Referring to the methods of guerrilla warfare, as opposed to conventional warfare, also suggests elements of success in fighting against a large, centralized authority such as a government. This is summed up succinctly in Wikipedia:

> [T]he strategy and tactics of guerrilla warfare tend to involve the use of a small, mobile force against a large, unwieldy one. The guerrilla force is largely or entirely organised in small units that are dependent on the support of the local population. Tactically, the guerrilla army makes small, repetitive attacks far from the opponent's centre of gravity with a view to keeping its own casualties to a minimum and imposing a constant debilitating strain on the enemy. This may provoke the enemy into a brutal, excessively destructive response which will both anger their own supporters and increase support for the guerrillas, ultimately compelling the enemy to withdraw.[7]

Indeed, not much explanation is needed to demonstrate how La Alameda does employ guerrilla-type methods of action. The organization is indeed small in the number of dedicated activists; nearly all participants have other paid jobs. Yet the members themselves are part of fluid larger groups of activity – for example, those who run the cooperatives, those who mobilize media, those who mobilize networks and the public for protests, etc. The group does make repeated small attacks on its targets: exploitative brands and factory owners, corrupt judges and politicians, and even the garment union federation SOIVA[8] – though it is a union federation and in principle La Alameda supports trade unions and the labor movement – is not above attack if it fails to protect workers that in principle are under its mandate.

Yet, possibly above all, the one characteristic of guerrilla warriors which gives them power over their enemies and which is shared by La Alameda is legitimacy that comes from support of the local community, through its success in presenting the evidence of abuses to the media, and its wide and steady alliance-building.

A final important factor in a social movement organization's capacity to bring about radical social change should be pointed out which merits its own attention – i.e., the impact of funding sources on an organization's goal definition – though it is to some extent implied in the process of institutionalization, which Kriesi identified as one of the trajectories of social movement organizations and which Michels viewed as an inevitability. This is all the more important in examining frankly the countries of Asia and Latin America (and other developing countries), where many of the active and prominent NGOs and trade unions are heavily if not exclusively reliant on external funds from donors based in the USA or Europe. Social movement organizations active in their local movements may or may not be aware of the impact upon their movement overall of their funding sources, since that external "non-profit" funding tends to steer the organization's activity toward donors' requirements and reporting to donors, instead of responding to ground-level needs to the maximum degree.

Impact of funding sources

In the book *The Revolution Will Not Be Funded*, US-based non-profit organizations from various backgrounds debated exactly the nature of the impact of non-profit funding upon organizations relying on them for their organization's basic work.

One of the main concepts used in the book is that of the non-profit industrial complex (NPIC). The NPIC functions as a means of controlling dissent – by incorporating it into the state apparatus, functioning as a "shadow state" constituted by a network of institutions operating what should otherwise be under the government remit, in areas of government and social services (Smith 2007, 9). Robert Arnove, for example, has argued in his book *Philanthropy and Cultural Imperialism* that foundations have a corrosive influence on a democratic society; they represent a relative and unregulated and unaccountable concentration of power and wealth which buy talent, promote causes, and, in effect, establish an agenda of what merits society's attention. They serve as "cooling-out" agencies, delaying and preventing more radical, structural change (Arnove 1980, 1 quoted in Smith 2007, 8).

The framework in which foundations fund organizations negatively impact social movements, according to the experiences of several of the contributors to this volume, most of which have been involved in organizing against violence against women, whether individual or state based. The reliance of non-profit organizations on external foundations for funding contributes to a form of organization which is ultimately unsustainable, not contributing to building up grassroots leadership and a mass movement capable of actually transforming society. Furthermore, the NPIC is seen to contribute to a social movement culture that is non-collaborative, narrowly focused, and competitive – as they must compete with each other for funding by promoting only their own work (Smith 2007, 9–11). It also encourages social movements to model themselves after capitalist structures rather than to challenge them (3).

On the other hand, grassroots fundraising – income generated from individuals, fees for services, and non-foundation sources – can become an organizing strategy itself, as well as a means to build a wider and stronger community base to determine the effectiveness of the organization itself (like a built-in monitoring and check-and-balance system). As stated by Project South, a social justice organization which learned the hard way how unreliable and politically controlling foundations can be and decided to re-focus on grassroots fundraising (Smith 2007, 1):[9]

> Fundamentally, economies are about the give and take of resources. In a community-based economy, resources flow from and return to the same community. Connecting organizing and fundraising allows those affected by the work of an organization to determine its course.
>
> (Guilloud and Cordery 2007, 109)

Thus Project South made financial independence – even partially if not completely – a principle and aim which supports the organization's intention to make real change in the community based on the needs, concerns, and perspective of the community. This meant that the organization also naturally collaborated with other organizations – jointly planning, coordinating, and paying costs of community events. This manner of raising funds while engaging with the community means that a culture of economic give and take is developed, one which places value on community, collaboration, and sharing of resources (Guilloud and Cordery 2007, 109–110).

The contrasting example of La Alameda confirms the power to change society that comes from independence from government or foundations, and from its tasks which themselves are directly generated from the problems of the community, and solved with the community's resources. Thus – and also mentioned in *The Revolution Will Not Be Funded*, refraining from entering a framework of salaried NGO work dependent on foundations has made the organization even more reliant on the community for enabling its work – in other words, the organizing and advocacy come before the fundraising, and even enable the fundraising.

In this final section, I briefly explain how the example of La Alameda shares parallels with worker centers in the US, and other organizations that operate in ways other than workplace-based organizing.

Relevant debates in the trade union movement

Decline of mainstream unions and union organizing

In the USA the trade union movement has been struggling also to tackle the impacts on workers and worker organizing from corporate globalization. In the book *US Labor in Trouble and Transition*, Kim Moody analyzes the reasons for the decline in the power of US labor, and prescriptions for revitalization of the labor movement (Moody 2007). Some of the reasons are macro-economic, but Moody places great responsibility on union leadership for the decline. Some of the major mistakes he believes they have made are brokering compromises and partnerships with employers, accepting deals that raised the welfare of a union elite but not that of the rank-and-file, and also investing excessive union resources and hopes in the election of favorable candidates for Congress or for president, which draws away from basic organizing work and serves to marginalize workplace militancy.

Rise of worker centers

Yet there is no lack of effort to counteract the weakness, bureaucracy, and unresponsiveness of organized labor in the US. Among the various attempts to tackle labor and employment issues outside of the US trade unions, a major attempt worthy of note is the trend of worker centers being established. This trend in the USA suggests that in the vacuum left by traditional trade unions, not only in Argentina but in the US and potentially in Asian countries too, experiments in organizing workers who have been excluded from unions or whose workplaces are dispersed or hidden are accumulating into movement wisdom and stirring unions into overdue reform and adaptation.

In the research by Janet Fine on US-based worker centers, which are defined in her project as community-based and community-led organizations that engage in a combination of service, advocacy, and organizing to support low-wage workers, she finds that they prioritize leadership development and popular education, and combine aspects of organization and movement, and regard membership as more a matter of active involvement and commitment to the center's work than of paying dues and formal registration. They mainly serve immigrant communities (and a few which are mainly African American), and help immigrant and low-wage workers to have a collective voice in public policy-making, and offer important bases for educating and organizing excluded workers. Similar to La Alameda, they serve and organize workers outside the workplace, they cater to workers who tend to be excluded or neglected in mainstream trade unions, they provide space for a variety of cultural as well as educational or work-related activities, and tend to prioritize reproduction of the movement by the continuous education and cultivation of new leaders. They combine efforts to thwart the dehumanizing effects of the current economic model while promoting the "social economy" – economic activities with social goals, with aims of reinstating the excluded into the economy with dignity and rights.

And in Latin America

To a significant extent, the example of La Alameda is one that is visible in many parts of Latin America. As Paula Rojas has written in her article "Are the Cops In Our Heads and Hearts?," many new models of organizing and of movement-building have appeared and been built up in various countries in Latin America over the past 15 years (Rojas 2007, 189). The *asambleas* and recovered factories phenomena in Argentina are significant examples, but there are also the Zapatistas in Chiapas, Mexico, and other horizontally connected community and worker movements in Brazil, Venezuela, Bolivia, and Ecuador. Some of the traits they share include the people's struggle for autonomy rather than attempts to seize state power, and collective production and decision-making in common spaces, demonstrating political work not only at election time or at NGO offices but in everyday life. And the work of building a mass base and mass movement may be slow but it would be true people power.

Conclusion

The level of worker organization and trade union ethic in the USA is far behind that of Argentina, and there are many factors accounting for the differences in the worker movements and for the development of the trade unions and other organizations that aim to protect workers' rights. Yet what is common across the USA and the countries of Latin America is the insidious search of capital for ways to exclude different categories of workers from rights as citizens, and for ways to exploit those excluded workers for cheap and docile labor. The emergence of social and solidarity economy in Latin America, the USA, Canada, European countries, and many places around the world reflects a counter-reaction to the divisions caused by neoliberal economic development.

Without doubt, organizational development is determined by a mixture of internal and individual (person-level) factors, and external macro factors such as the political context. Yet what I have examined in this chapter are the aspects of organization which an organization may decide itself – its aims, its membership practices, its manner, and criteria of fundraising to support its costs. Using the example of La Alameda in Argentina, it was possible to see the close relation between "success" in terms of responding to the community-level but also nation-wide problems of worker and migrant abuse, and the "light" guerrilla-like practices of the organization: horizontal decision-making, sharing of information within the organization, reliance on support from the community rather than on the risky amassing of wealth from certain external donors for core functions.

As the concept of social and solidarity economy is slowly being articulated and developed, it is already being encroached upon, in a sense, by government and business initiatives to couch business with social goals in terms of "social innovation" while continuing to minimize labor-related restrictions on entrepreneurs and to prevent unions from exercising rights to participation in management. It would be beneficial for those who see social and solidarity economy as the future necessary direction for worker and community struggle to realize the importance of keeping organizational strength and agility to always respond first to community needs, which may be done by ensuring that resources come from and go back to the community, and by staying cautious against the development of an organizational or movement "oligarchy."

Notes

1 Wright describes three methods of social change: ruptural, interstitial, and symbiotic change. The concept of social economy is not used in a narrow sense but could be achieved through all of those ways; what is certain is that it is oriented toward fulfilling social goals, not the pursuit of private profit.
2 In the words of Eduardo Murua,

> This movement began before the crisis; the movement of worker-recuperated enterprises began four years prior to the formation of the National Movement of Recuperated Enterprises [MNER]. What happened in 2001, that is, what it perpetuated, beginning with the financial crisis and the social crisis that this generated, was that all of the experiences of struggle of the labor movement – the movement of unemployed workers, the *piqueteros*, the worker-recuperated enterprises – finally became visible to society at large. It wasn't that these movements began with the financial crisis, but that all of this already started with what the neoliberal model generated, the model that was installed by the dictatorship of 1976 and that was continued by the subsequent formal democracies up to '95–'96. And it was then that there was a decision by a good part of the collectivity of workers to begin a method of struggle that included occupying factories and getting them to produce again, but his time under the control and management of workers. This was many years before the financial downfall.
> (www.workerscontrol.net/es/node/236 (last accessed April 15, 2013))

3 The following chronology of the development of La Alameda (which earlier was also known by the name of the garment worker union that was set up in La Alameda – Unión de Trabajadores Costureros (UTC)) is drawn in large part from Barattini's article (2010).
4 La Alameda has maintained a blog since February 2007. Available online at: http://laalameda.wordpress.com.
5 The website of Agenda Oculta is www.agendaoculta.net.
6 Drawing on data from France, Germany, the Netherlands, and Switzerland, Kriesi focused mainly on how the political context influenced the development trajectories of different types of organizations. However, I leave aside this area to focus on internal organizational factors.
7 Available online at: http://en.wikipedia.org/wiki/Strategy_and_tactics_of_guerrilla_warfare (last accessed April 15, 2013).
8 SOIVA: Sindicato Obrero de la Industria del Vestido y Afines, or Clothing Industry Workers' Union.
9 The Ford Foundation had approved a large grant to cover the general operating expenses of Project South but at a late stage reversed its decision because during the board approval process, one of the board members saw a support statement for the Palestinian liberation struggle on the organization's website.

References

Anheier, Helmut, Marlies Glasius, and Mary Kaldor, eds. 2001. *Global Civil Society 2001*. Oxford: Oxford University Press.

Arnove, Robert, ed. 1980. *Philanthropy and Cultural Imperialism*. Boston, MA: G.K. Hall.

Barattini, Mariana. 2010. "Trabajo esclavo y organización: el caso de la Unión de Trabajadores Costureros en Argentina." *Estudios Demográficos y Urbanos* 25(2): 461–481.

Brafman, Ori. 2006. *The Starfish and the Spider: The Unstoppable Power of Leaderless Organizations*. New York: Penguin.

Fine, Janice. 2005. "Worker Centers: Organizing Communities at the Edge of the Dream." *Economic Policy Institute Briefing Paper* 159, December 14. Available online at: www.epi.org/page/-/old/briefingpapers/159/bp159.pdf (last accessed April 15, 2013).

Guilloud, Stephanie, and William Cordery, Project South: Institute for the Elimination of Poverty and Genocide. 2007. "Fundraising is Not a Dirty Word: Community-based Economic Strategies for the Long Haul." In *The Revolution Will Not Be Funded: Beyond the Non-profit Industrial Complex*, edited by Incite! Women of Color Against Violence (pp. 107–112). Cambridge, MA: South End Press.

Hauser, Irina. 2004. "Los vecinos de Parque Avellaneda temen perder otra vez 'La Alameda'." *Página 12*, April 15. Available online at: www.pagina12.com.ar/diario/elpais/1-34118-2004-04-15.html (last accessed 15 April, 2013).

Kaldor, Mary, Henrietta L. Moore, and Sabine Selchow. 2012. *Global Civil Society 2012: Ten Years of Critical Reflection*. Basingstoke: Palgrave Macmillan.

Kriesi, Hanspeter. 1996. "The Organizational Structure of New Social Movements in Political Context." In *Comparative Perspectives on Social Movements: Political Opportunities, Mobilizing Structures, and Cultural Framings*, edited by Doug McAdam, John D. McCarthy, and Mayer N. Zald (pp. 152–184). Cambridge: Cambridge University Press.

Manjon, Lucas. 2013. Personal Interview, April 22.

Michels, Robert. 1915. *Political Parties: A Sociological Study of the Oligarchical Tendencies of Modern Democracy*, translated by Eden Paul and Cedar Paul. New York: The Free Press.

Moody, Kim. 2007. *US Labor in Trouble and Transition: The Failure of Reform from Above, the Promise of Revival from Below*. London: Verso.

Rojas, Paula X. 2007. "Are the Cops in Our Heads and Hearts?" In *The Revolution Will Not Be Funded: Beyond the Non-profit Industrial Complex*, edited by Incite! Women of Color Against Violence (pp. 197–214). Cambridge, MA: South End Press.

Ruggeri, Andrés. 2010. *Las Empresas Recuperadas en la Argentina. 2010: Informe del Tercer Relevamiento de Empresas Recuperadas por Sus Trabajadores*. Buenos Aires: Programa Facultad Abierta Facultad de Filosofia y Letras Universidad de Buenos Aires.

Smith, Andrea. 2007. "Introduction: The Revolution Will Not Be Funded." In *The Revolution Will Not Be Funded: Beyond the Non-profit Industrial Complex*, edited by Incite! Women of Color Against Violence (pp. 1–18). Cambridge, MA: South End Press.

Tarrow, Sidney G. 2011. *Power in Movement: Social Movements and Contentious Politics*. New York: Cambridge University Press.

Vera, Gustavo. 2013. Personal interview. April 22.

Wright, Erik Olin. 2010. *Envisioning Real Utopias*. London: Verso.

6 Democratizing capital

Social and solidarity finance in Quebec

Marguerite Mendell

Introduction

Dis-embedding has greater significance today as financial markets are dis-embedded from the real economy, which is itself increasingly dis-embedded from society. The consequences are borne by societies throughout the world, trying to dig themselves out of the financial crisis of 2008 and the current economic crisis in numerous countries. The most dramatic example today is the EU and several of its member states, notably Greece, Spain, and most recently, Cyprus. But economic growth has slowed in most parts of the world and unemployment rates are increasing. Countries are applying austerity measures at their peril and remain committed to market-driven solutions, despite their numerous failures throughout the world. Austerity is imposed upon countries already experiencing high rates of unemployment, cutbacks in state expenditures, and cancellation of numerous social programs. Welfare to work programs have replaced social programs in numerous countries, abandoning systemic approaches to reduce social exclusion and dysfunctional labor markets that can only be corrected with effective interventionist public policy measures and with a commitment to the public good. This is the context in which creative counter-movements are emerging, and in which those with a long history are now more visible, as the credibility of the dominant paradigm is tested by its continuous failures.

A word of caution is however necessary before celebrating the many new approaches to addressing increasingly complex social and economic challenges. Counter-movements driven by civil society are also confronting a different challenge that is sweeping across the world. In several countries, reducing the role of government has given rise to strong support for initiatives that reinforce this dis-engagement. This includes pressure to commercialize social service provision by NGOs and new hybrid forms of business with revenue-generating capacity, reinforcing the privatization of public services, many of which have already been outsourced or subcontracted.

The influence of Anglo-American support for social enterprise, social entrepreneurship, social business, etc. must be situated in this context, to distinguish initiatives spearheaded by citizens and social movements that exist or are emerging in many parts of the world that tell a different story. Rather than reinforce disengagement by government, many civil society organizations and movements are designing a new model, a new socially constructed economy re-engaging government in a collaborative process to re-embed the economy in society. In many cases, this is a pragmatic response by government hard pressed to find solutions. Civil society organizations and social movements are forcing government to move beyond binary options – more government/less government – to innovate and collaborate in creating new public spaces for policy formation and new approaches to policy implementation.

The social and solidarity economy (SSE) exists in many sectors of activity – from manufacturing, to natural resources, media, telecommunications, culture and the arts, and in a variety of social services including child care and home care, to name a few. Cooperatives and non-profit enterprises are very present in agriculture in the South, and increasingly in local food production and distribution – the growing community supported agriculture movement (CSA) in the North. Indeed, many social and solidarity enterprises respond to new needs that are not met by the public or private sectors, but they are also responding to an increased desire to work collectively. The diversity of economic sectors in which collective enterprises are present confirms this growing trend, especially among young people.

Several forces are driving the growing interest in the SSE: (1) the moral and ethical crisis of the capitalist model; (2) the search for alternative forms of economic production and service provision committed to societal well-being; (3) the democratic governance of social and solidarity enterprises and organizations; and finally (4) the proven viability of collective enterprises. The social and solidarity economy is testing the limits of the dominant paradigm. While driven by social movements and a diversity of civil society organizations locally, regionally, nationally, and internationally, its capacity to develop tools of transformation is forcing governments to participate in this process. As this chapter will demonstrate, the process of democratizing capital, of providing greater access to finance for the SSE, calls for many levels and layers of innovation, not least of which is an enabling policy framework. Democratizing capital requires a new mindset in government; it requires *dialogue* between social actors, including the private sector.

Research on the evolution of the social economy in Quebec describes this as a process of social innovation. I will do likewise by focusing on solidarity finance and how social innovation underlies the financial innovation it represents. The literature and terminology on social innovation is extensive, as are the ways in which to interpret and distinguish this process. While we probably do not need more terms to describe the innovation underlying the transformative capacity of the social and solidarity economy, "disruptive innovation" resonates with the rapidly growing social and solidarity economy internationally, and its ability to disrupt and transform ways of doing and ways of thinking. *Disruptive innovation* is a term used to describe producing goods and services for markets that are considered marginal and unprofitable by market players, that may actually drive out competitors as these products become more widely known and competitive, increasing demand beyond their initial target market.[1] If we limit this concept to developing competitive markets, examples include fair trade, local and community-based agriculture, and recycling, to name but a few that have changed patterns of consumption internationally. Many of the enterprises engaged in these activities are in the social and solidarity economy.

Disruption invites reaction; it inspires new thinking; it creates discomfort and forces change. Disruption does not settle into complacency; it is an ongoing process. In Quebec, this describes the social economy and its creative capacity to develop new goods and services, to form alliances and networks, to work across boundaries with all social actors, and to shape a new paradigm through this dynamic process.[2] Unlike private enterprise driven by a profit motive, social economy enterprises and organizations – cooperatives and non-profit organizations/enterprises – generate social and economic returns. They are rooted in community and are collectively managed. Democratic governance distinguishes SSE enterprises from private business, even those social enterprises that are privately owned. In Quebec, these objectives are embedded in a comprehensive and integrated system of social innovation that includes the many services required for social economy enterprises to emerge and to achieve their goals. Social economy enterprises, collective enterprises, require development tools and a solid institutional infrastructure. Access to capital, to investment, is critical for the development of the SSE. Democratizing capital not only refers to creating greater access to existing capital; it refers to institutional and organizational innovation within the financial sector. Democratizing capital is embedded in a larger process of economic democracy that "focuses on widening access and control over productive property of all citizens" (Conaty 2012, 4). Solidarity finance in Quebec is an important example of such a process that has increased its presence on financial markets while providing much needed access to investment capital for the social economy. It is part of a larger process of economic democratization of land, labor, capital (money), and knowledge.

The social economy in Quebec

In October 2011, over 1,600 participants from more than 60 countries gathered at an International Forum on the Social and Solidarity Economy (FIESS) in Montreal, organized by the Chantier de l'économie sociale, the network of networks representing the social economy in Quebec. This generated extensive dialogue and exchange of experiences, in particular, the diversity of policy regimes in different national contexts. It is clear that such exchanges are increasingly important as the social and solidarity economy (SSE) emerges in different parts of the world in the North and the South. Despite historical, cultural, political, and economic specificities of individual countries, common trends and/or needs are also part of this otherwise diverse international landscape. There is a great deal of interest in the social economy in Quebec. Because it is embedded in the socio-economic landscape of Quebec and is recognized as a significant economic actor, the social economy is considered a model or a "template" for other parts of Canada, and in many regions and countries internationally.[3] Today, it is also considered a counterpoise to the growing interest in social enterprise and/or social entrepreneurship in many countries that, unlike the social economy in Quebec, are often dis-embedded from their larger socio-economic context.

As noted earlier, today's vocabulary includes a cacophony of terms – social economy, solidarity economy, social enterprise, social purpose business, to name but a few. The growing interest in social enterprise internationally is encouraging the commercialization of non-profit organizations and the development of social purpose or public benefit businesses by the private sector. This "enterprise" focus is gaining ground in Canada and often conforms to prevailing global trends to privatize public services more generally. It focuses on individual initiatives and not on comprehensive approaches. The long history of the cooperative movement and its presence in numerous sectors of social activity is overlooked, as are the growing number of non-profit organizations that are meeting social needs with economic means, including the provision of public services not previously provided by the state or by the public sector.

The experience of the social economy in Quebec, especially over the past 15 years, allows for bold statements about its capacity to contest the dominant paradigm through practice. Its resilience in the face of the post-2008 economic crisis is testimony to the viability of the social economy as an alternative model of economic development and societal wealth creation.

In Quebec, the social economy includes more than 7,000 collective enterprises, both cooperatives and non-profit organizations, and enterprises in many sectors producing both goods and services. Its presence in natural resources and the environment is growing and a great deal of work is devoted to developing more opportunities in this sector. The effectiveness of the collective management of resources is validated by important research.[4] In Quebec, as elsewhere, the resource sector is under siege, be it in forestry, or in the reckless mining projects under way that will destroy ecosystems and displace communities. The domination of the extractive sector internationally raises the urgency for social economy alternatives. Access to capital allows the social economy to develop collective sustainable alternatives.

For the social economy to develop, it has to simultaneously promote collective enterprise and design new instruments to enable their emergence, consolidation, and growth. Challenges for the social economy today include commercialization and access to existing and new markets. Important work on social accounting and indicators is responding to the need for evaluation and adapted accounting measures. Procurement policies, integrating the social economy into the movement for socially responsible consumption, labeling or branding, purchasing portals, and trade fairs are among the many strategies in place to create markets for social economy goods and services.

The image of the social economy, often associated with activity on the margins of the economy or exclusively with non-market social services, is also a challenge, though this is changing with increased visibility, certainly in Quebec and across Canada. We have learned from the Quebec experience that for the social economy to achieve its objectives, it requires *institutional innovation*. It requires *deliberative processes*, in which actors participate in designing democratic strategies of transformation. In Quebec, alliances among social movements, labor, the cooperative movement, and the community or popular sector and, most significantly, the construction of an institutional context for *multi-stakeholder partnerships* and *distributed and democratic governance*, have been critical to its development.

Social economy actors are engaged in *institutional innovation* at several levels, not the least of which was the creation of a network of networks, the *Chantier de l'économie sociale* in 1997 and the development of enabling instruments – finance, training, enterprise services, public policy, and research. Practitioners are *re-embedding the economy in society*, designing sustainable approaches to development that respond to the needs and desires of communities and the appropriate tools to achieve this goal.

The institutional architecture or what is increasingly referred to as the *ecosystem of the social economy* in Quebec includes old and new social movements, collective enterprises, and territorial development intermediaries. The strength of the social economy is grounded in the capacity of its practitioners to work inter-sectorally, collaboratively, and to negotiate with different levels of government. The roots of this collaborative approach were established in the early 1980s and the creation of citizen-based community economic development organizations in urban neighborhoods struggling against economic restructuring and the recession. Social actions were transformed into economic actions as citizens' organizations defied the fatalism of both government and business by proposing strategies for economic revitalization. The struggle for greater equity and social justice was radicalized, as proposals undermined existing power relations among businesses and citizens and movements, as well as with government. The dialogue necessary to carry this out has endured, despite shifting political tides over the past two decades and a predominantly business-led agenda at the macro and global levels.

The legacy of the social economy in Quebec has deep roots, of course, in the cooperative movement and in social movements. However, citizen-based community economic development organizations that grew out of the early 1980s planted the seeds for what we refer to today as "*place-based strategies*" that require comprehensive policy to meet the needs of communities. They became sites for the integration of policy – labor market, enterprise services and business development, social integration through economic initiatives, and local revitalization and development. They also revealed the limits of homogeneous and undifferentiated programs designed in ministerial silos and the need for multi-stakeholder dialogue with social and economic actors. These initiatives also became important sites to resist the prevailing commitment to reduce the role of the state, by arguing for a different relationship between the state and civil society. These *place-based hybrid strategies* demonstrated the benefits of *working across boundaries* – inter-sectorally and with different divisions of government. The comprehensive and coordinated approach that characterizes the social economy in Quebec today is rooted in these earlier experiences, to which we will return below.

Architects of the social economy are *contesting the dominant paradigm through practice*, by challenging existing institutions through the creation of new ones that work, by creating networks of citizens who speak with *one voice*, despite the many sectors they represent. Resistance to institutionalization misses the critical need for hybrid spaces for dialogue, negotiation, and strategy design and for building political capacity. When institutional spaces exist, such as in Quebec, they can address the specificities of individual sectors and also develop coherent cross-sectoral strategies and tools, including finance.[5]

Institutional design is probably the most difficult challenge facing social economy actors. What has been achieved in Quebec through the establishment of the *Chantier de l'économie sociale*, the hybrid institutional network of networks in the social economy, demonstrates the need to mobilize and build cross-cutting or inter-sectoral relationships. Where networks exist, they have greater capacity to resist both the instrumentalization and the marginalization of the social economy; they have the political capacity to influence public policy and inspire larger institutional transformation.

Social economy actors in Quebec do not question the primary regulatory and redistributive role of the state. Quite the contrary; they call for a *new socio-political architecture*, for more *horizontal policy settings* to address the hybrid needs of the social economy within government, and for a *process of collaborative policy formation* that includes social economy actors. Growing reference to collaborative planning, policy dialogue, communities of practice, co-construction of public policy, all refer to the need for such processes situated in new institutional dialogic spaces.

The strategy to decentralize government, so common in many parts of the world, must include a shift in political culture that recognizes the indispensable knowledge local actors bring to the policy table and the consequent need for flexibility in program design and delivery. In Quebec, both the pragmatic and innovative capacity of civil society to address hard issues with concrete strategies and processes of implementation has had a significant impact upon the political culture and on institutional innovation. The actors are, in a real sense, writing the script. And while this occurs within a larger macro context that maintains its grip on the economy, in Quebec, government has come to accept that a dialogue with civil society is essential to respond to a complex and transforming socio-economic environment. These often conflicting forces need to be noted. What Karl Polanyi referred to as counter-movements or the "double movement" are destabilizing and forcing innovation (Polanyi 1944).

The social economy in Quebec embodies processes of change originating in civil society. Documenting these processes of change has great heuristic value. It demonstrates "the role of deliberate change in human institutions" and the "freedom to change institutions"; it is a form of resistance that moves beyond claims for resources and political space, beyond a politics of contestation to negotiate new social arrangements (Polanyi 1977; Mendell 2007). Indeed, the social economy exists within the dominant system but is driving change, however uneven this may be in different parts of the world and even within countries.

Situating solidarity finance in history

In an earlier paper that explored the evolution of solidarity finance internationally, we applied a historical perspective to situate the current development of new financial tools for the social and solidarity economy and for community-based initiatives (Mendell and Nogales 2012). We used the term "social finance" to capture the many financial institutions/organizations that in today's terminology seek blended value or triple bottom-line returns – economic, social and environmental. Too often, this is presented as a new phenomenon overlooking centuries of cooperative finance and social banking, for example. In Quebec, we speak of solidarity finance to refer to those financial institutions that invest exclusively in collective enterprise and development capital to refer to investment with socio-economic objectives but not only in the social economy, to distinguish this from traditional risk or venture capital. Together, this represents *socially responsible finance in Quebec* (Bourque *et al.* 2009). This chapter will focus on solidarity finance with reference to development capital since, in some cases, they overlap and/or the same institutions invest in both collective and private enterprise. The boundaries between them are permeable, which allows for the creation of innovative hybrids involving different institutions.

Quebec shares a long history of mutual aid societies, cooperative financial institutions, and credit unions with other parts of the world. The *Mouvement Desjardins* in Quebec, created at the turn of the twentieth century, was influenced by European experience, in particular, the *Raiffeisen Bank* in Germany established in 1864. Mutual societies were created in Europe long before in both Quebec and Europe. Mutual finance associations emerged in Latin America as well at the beginning of the twentieth century. These roots are embedded in solidarity finance in Quebec, notwithstanding the growth of the *Mouvement Desjardins* today into a global financial institution that was severely hit by the financial crisis in 2008 owing to its participation in global financial markets, investments in commercial paper, etc.

Social banks were also created to provide financial services to their communities. Also referred to as sustainable banking, these banks were created in the nineteenth century and, within Europe, they trace their history to Rudolph Steiner's vision of an "associative economy." These banks exist in many parts of the world and survived the 2008 crisis owing to their prudential practices and links to the real economy. They provide loans to developing countries and innovative tools such as sustainable trade credits to permit up-front financing to enable local producers to enter export markets and cover their costs while awaiting payment.[6]

In more recent times, innovations include micro-credit and micro-finance providing small loans to those who could not apply for bank loans or access any form of capital investment. The short history of micro-credit is well known, including its mitigated results in different parts of the world. As well, the skepticism many felt about its capacity to considerably reduce poverty has been confirmed. Micro-credit is only one among many tools necessary to help millions of people living in poverty throughout the world, and is grossly inadequate in addressing endemic poverty and social exclusion. Its ambitions were unrealistic, even if these small loans have certainly made a difference to the lives of many people. Many micro-credit institutions are well established and have developed the necessary social infrastructure to accompany borrowers. This is essential. Micro-finance institutions (MFIs) coordinate lending and serve as intermediaries, thus significantly mitigating risk for investors. However, critical evaluations of micro-credit experiences are revealing the limitations of a homogeneous approach to poverty alleviation without (1) enabling public policy measures, and (2) raising the capacity of micro-credit to leverage larger sums with the availability of a diversity of financial tools, thereby increasing its transformative potential. This capacity exists in Quebec, for example, but in many contexts it does not.

The enthusiasm for micro-credit in the early 1990s (the micro-credit revolution) is now expressed by the numerous and growing proponents of "impact investing," including large international financial institutions and investment banks eager to enter this growing market. Impact investing is distinct in its capacity to mobilize large pools of capital from institutional investors (pension funds, insurance companies, etc.), foundations, high net worth individuals, and increasingly from retail and investment banks. It is the new face of socially responsible investment that began as a means to filter negative investment opportunities. Impact investing is capitalizing on the large international SRI market to transform negative screening into pro-active or intentional investment in social enterprises and organizations with the capacity to achieve social outcomes while generating economic returns. It is not surprising that interest in impact investing has increased exponentially since the 2008 financial crisis as investors seek more "ethical" investment opportunities.[7]

In Quebec, impact investing is greeted with some perplexity given the history of investment with social impact and the creation of numerous innovative financial tools and institutions since the beginning of the twentieth century. In addition, government has been an important player in this process. Still, as impact investing makes its way into Quebec, much as micro-credit did in the early 1990s, it remains to be seen whether and how this surge of capital may be available for social economy enterprises. Because Quebec has a closer affinity with Europe and Latin America, the American and British influence that is shaping the impact investing market is not as strong as it is in other parts of Canada. A strong labor movement and the role of social movements and community organizations in Quebec, political alliances between diverse movements, an entrenched welfare state culture that limits the disengagement of government, and a history of dialogue among principal social actors – labor, government, business, and more recently, social movements and community organizations – distinguishes

Quebec from the political culture of the USA and the UK, and from other regions across Canada. *A history of mobilization and militancy underlies the democratization of capital and the history of solidarity finance in Quebec.* Thus impact investing finds an uncomfortable cultural fit in Quebec in these early stages; solidarity among social actors will determine how and where this capital will be deployed. That said, there are numerous community organizations in the "voluntary sector" that are transforming into social enterprises or social purpose businesses that will attract this investment. The landscape is shifting but the unity and cohesiveness of the social economy will determine how this new source of capital will best serve its organizations and enterprises in Quebec.

Despite the growth of social finance and an almost evangelical commitment to impact investing similar to the reception given to micro-credit over 20 years ago, access to capital remains a problem in many parts of the world; in fact, in all parts of the world. As we have learned in Quebec, and rather successfully, capital is not a homogeneous term. Much as mainstream investors have a variety of asset classes at their disposition, the forms of capital required by the social economy are also diverse. This is often not taken into account in the growing commitment to transfer more capital into impact investing today, for example. For the most part, available investment vehicles are largely limited to debt. In the case of the larger sums associated with impact investing, the only way to reach small or emergent enterprises or organizations is through intermediaries that are able to receive large sums and pool investments, thereby considerably reducing the risk to investors and deploying the capital to projects. To a large extent, most impact investing is from the North to the South.

Financial innovation in Quebec: embedded finance in the 1970s and 1980s

The development of solidarity finance in Quebec is a *process of democratization*, of designing financial institutions and savings and investment tools by social movements. As stated earlier, the history of the social economy in Quebec begins in the nineteenth century with the establishment of mutual aid societies and insurance companies. In the twentieth century, small agricultural producers established cooperatives and then joined with small producers and merchants to establish credit unions. This paved the way for the creation of the *Mouvement des caisses populaires et d'économie Desjardins*. Even if it has undergone significant changes over the years and competes with other financial institutions, its presence in every region and sector of the social economy demonstrates its commitment to an economy embedded in values of solidarity and collective well-being.

The credit union, *Caisse d'économie solidaire Desjardins* (formerly the *Caisse d'économie Desjardins des travailleurs et travailleuses*), created in 1971 by the labor movement, provides guaranteed loans to social economy enterprises and organizations. Its mission is to contribute to social justice and solidarity by supporting collective and social enterprise and the cooperative movement. Since its establishment, the *Caisse* has invested $442 million in more than 2,500 socially engaged enterprises. Its total assets today are $690 million. The *Caisse* invests primarily in cooperatives and non-profit organizations, including social and community housing. Total savings of its more than 12,500 members in 2009 were almost $500 million. Members include approximately 10,000 individuals and approximately 2,800 collective enterprises. The *Caisse* also created the *Fonds de soutien à l'action collective solidaire* – in which depositors forego their interest to benefit collective initiatives. These solidarity savings reinforce the mission of the *Caisse.*[8]

The 1980s was marked by the strong presence of civil society and social movements in economic development in Quebec in response to the recession, the crisis in the welfare state, and mounting rates of unemployment. The *Fonds de solidarité des travailleurs* (FTQ), a workers' fund, was established by one of the three large labor federations in 1983 to create and maintain jobs and contribute to the revitalization and development of communities across Quebec. The *Fonds* is an example of development capital. Its investment decisions combine social and economic objectives. For the *Fonds* to invest in an enterprise, these objectives have to appear in the company's social audit. The *Fonds* has created many different financial tools, including local development finance and a sectoral housing fund that also invests in the social economy.[9] Recently, it established the *Fonds locaux de solidarité (FLS)* that invests in the social economy,[10] affirming its commitment to citizen-based local development. While *SOLIDE*, the antecedent to the *FLS*, was created by the labor movement in 1991, it is an example of many "hybrid" funds that exist in Quebec in partnership with other actors and financial institutions. The *SOLIDE* and now the *FLS* includes the participation of the *Féderation québecoise des municipalités*, a network of municipalities across Quebec. Total investment by this local fund in 2011, a decade after its creation, was $91 million, creating or maintaining 27,418 jobs.

It is noteworthy that both the federal and provincial governments agreed to provide tax credits for investors in the *Fonds de solidarité.* In addition, these investments can be rolled into registered retirement savings with additional credits. This is an important example of enabling the public policy necessary to facilitate financial innovation. For government, the advantages are clear. Job creation and economic development also generate revenue for government.[11]

In addition to the strategic action taken by the labor movement to engage directly in socio-economic development and job creation, citizens mobilized in communities to construct coherent and integrated strategies to revitalize their local economies devastated by the recession and an already protracted period of deindustrialization and rising unemployment, the fate of most industrialized urban communities in North America and abroad at the time. Collaboration between the labor movement, community organizations, and the private sector also succeeded in bringing all three levels of government on board to create *Community Economic Development Corporations (CDECs)* in Quebec. The early CDECs were the model for 120 local development centers (CLDs) and 13 CDECs established by the Quebec government in urban settings across the province.[12]

Details of this remarkable mobilization and the ensuing *place-based, integrated, or comprehensive strategies* have been recorded by researchers and social actors. Several forces were at play; however, government involvement and support articulated through a process of negotiation, which continues today, was key. The *Fonds de développement de Montréal* (*FDEM*) was created in 1988 by the *CDECs*, the *City of Montreal*, the *Fonds de Solidarité (FTQ)* et la *Société de développement industriel du Québec*, now *Investissement Québec*, a public investment fund, following the international mobilization of actors engaged in local development. All three levels of government – municipal, provincial, and federal – participated in the initial capitalization of this fund.[13] While the FDEM does not necessarily invest directly in the social economy, it provides capital to small enterprises with demonstrated capacity to contribute to local development and vitality, and to create and/or maintain local jobs.[14] It is a historic example of social innovation. Civil society established a multi-stakeholder institutional space to develop and implement strategies for economic and social revitalization, and to engage major social actors and three levels of government in designing a financial tool to meet this objective. In today's terms, we would refer to this as a process of co-construction.

Since the 1980s, these local intermediaries have created and have had access to a variety of financial tools, including investment funds designated for the social economy. In fact, these intermediaries are examples of hybridity, where public, private, and community resources are combined in the financial tools at their disposal. What is even more important and significant in this narrative is that whatever form these tools take, be it government subsidy or investment in partnership with labor solidarity funds, for example, they were spearheaded by civil society organizations, and by citizens' movements.

The history of micro-credit in Quebec is also one of collective action. In the late 1980s, community organizers fought to gain access to credit for local micro-enterprises, red-lined by mainstream banks, and established the *Montreal Community Loan Association (MCLA)*, the first micro-credit institution in Canada in 1990 to meet this need. Unlike many micro-credit institutions internationally, the mandate of the MCLA was to provide finance for initiatives embedded in a socio-economic development strategy. Although it does not target collective enterprises, the MCLA is part of the solidarity finance landscape, both in its self-identification and in its contribution to community-based socio-economic development. Since its founding, the MCLA has issued $2.9 million in loans. It created 358 jobs and maintained 712 jobs (2011).[15]

Today, there is a network of micro-credit institutions in Quebec. The *Réseau québecois du credit communautaire (RQCC)*, formed in 2000, represents 23 community-based funds and loan circles across the province. Its mandate is to develop and promote community credit for well-being and to eliminate poverty. By 2012, members of the RQCC network had invested $10 million in communities across the province and had created or maintained 4,210 jobs.[16]

The network collaborates with all social actors – the labor movement, the social economy, the credit union movement, numerous government ministries, local development intermediaries, and the private sector. It has spearheaded and/or participated in innovative partnerships with other solidarity finance and development capital organizations and institutions to create more access to finance. This is an excellent example of retaining the original mission of micro-credit and micro-finance while developing its capacity to leverage more capital. Collaboration has included both the design of new financial vehicles and leveraging larger loans and investments from other social finance institutions, and even mainstream banks.[17]

In 1995, the *Confédération des syndicats nationaux (CSN)*, the second largest workers federation in Quebec, also created a workers' fund – *Fondaction, le Fonds de développement de la CSN pour la coopération et l'emploi* – to promote economic development in Quebec. It began its operations in 1996. In contrast with the *Fonds de solidarité (FTQ)*, *Fondaction* prioritizes investment in enterprises with participatory management, distributed control, and environmental stewardship. In 2012, the assets of *Fondaction* were $940 million; it had invested approximately $620 million in more than 100 small and medium-size enterprises (SMEs) and funds. Since its establishment, *Fondaction* has maintained or created, directly or indirectly, 27,848 jobs.[18]

Because the investments undertaken by *Fondaction* in SMEs are generally between $2 million and $5 million (although it can invest as little as $500,000), it created *Filaction, le Fonds pour l'investissement local et l'approvisionnement des fonds communautaires* in 2000 to meet the need for smaller loans (between $50,000 and $500,000), and to invest in community funds. *Filaction* manages the *Fonds de financement coopératif* created by *Fondaction* that invests from $100,000 to $250,000 in cooperatives and non-profit organizations.[19] *Fondaction* also invests in the *Fiducie du Chantier de l'économie sociale*, a new social economy patient capital fund.

The mid-1990s: a critical turning point for the social economy in Quebec

The second half of the 1990s was another turning point for the social economy. Prior to a *Summit on the Economy and Employment* convened by the government of Quebec in October 1996, a *Social Economy Working Group* was established to propose how the social economy could contribute to job creation and economic development in the province. The Working Group presented its report to the Summit and was invited to continue its work for another two years. Its initial mandate, which it surpassed, was to identify 20 social economy projects that would create 20,000 jobs in three years. In 1997, the Working Group was incorporated as the *Chantier de l'économie sociale*; in 1999, it became a permanent non-profit organization.

The work of the *Chantier* and its goals are embedded in community and shaped by its roots in militancy and mobilization. The *Chantier* is convener, coordinator, and developer. It has successfully built alliances and has won its struggle to be recognized as an organization representing *economic* actors. This was and is a remarkable victory for the social economy in Quebec. The view that the private sector is the only economic actor and, more so, the engine of economic growth was challenged by the *Chantier* which represents a diversity of sectors producing goods and services employing thousands of men and women. The social economy does not exist on the margins of the economy. It challenges private enterprise with a different business model. Most recently, the Government of Quebec passed framework legislation on the social economy in the fall of 2013, enshrining the identity and role of the social economy in Quebec society in law.

While the social economy is committed to poverty reduction, unlike the approach in the U.K. and the U.S. referred to earlier, it is well understood in Quebec that the social economy reduces poverty by creating economic opportunities in all sectors. Social economy enterprises in the service sector respond to needs that are not met by the private and public sector, such as affordable child care and home care. Social economy enterprises provide opportunities for disadvantaged workers unable to participate actively in the labor market. Government contributes significantly through financing and programs, transforming the logic of government from spending to investing in the public good.

In 1997, its first year, the *Chantier* created an investment fund for the social economy, the *Réseau d'investissement social du Québec (RISQ)* in partnership with the Quebec government and a few private investors. RISQ invests exclusively in the social economy through loans and loan guarantees up to $50,000. It has invested in approximately $14 million in 354 collective enterprises since 1997, creating 1,583 jobs and maintaining 2,921 jobs. In addition, 341 initiatives have received financial support for technical assistance from RISQ for a total of $1.5 million (2011).[20] As part of a *National Action Plan* to support the social economy in 2008, the Quebec government designated $5 million for RISQ to provide *pre-start-up loans* for social economy enterprises, acknowledging the importance of this kind of support. By 2011, $1.4 million of pre-start-up loans had been provided to 21 initiatives.[21]

Soon after the creation of the *Chantier* and RISQ, the Quebec government introduced both complementary state funds and established local intermediaries across the province to promote economic development, including the development of the social economy. This is an example of the institutionalization of collective action and the tensions which such institutionalization brings. In addition, as emphasized earlier, where these tensions persist, the risk of institutional isomorphism is considerably reduced. This is the history of some CDECs that engage in a *constant disruptive renewal of democracy*. It is not, of course, the history of the numerous new CLDs across the province, but because the majority of CLDs belong to an association, the collective memory of those who have been involved for a long time works to instill this into those working in newer centers, with some success.[22]

This experience underscores the importance of a strong, united, and autonomous network of social economy actors. The creation of regional poles across Quebec by the *Chantier* was strategic. The cooperative movement also has poles, so to speak, across the province. The *Coopératives régionales de développement (CDR)*, which promote the development of cooperatives, are represented in the social economy poles as well.

The twenty-first century: 2000 up until the present

Due to the integrated network developed by social economy actors in Quebec, they have the ability to identify potential areas for development in different sectors of activity and in different regions of Quebec. They also have the capacity to identify needs, gaps, fragile enterprises, and projects requiring support as well as those that will not succeed for a variety of reasons, including misalignment with the needs and desires of communities. This capacity considerably mitigates the risk of investors.

Two challenges were identified in 2003. The first was the absence of long-term capital for social economy enterprises, and the second, which, of course, followed, was developing a financial product to meet this need. It was clear that the availability of financial vehicles was limited to debt, preventing long-term planning, and also certain forms of investment, such as the purchase of real estate, for example. The process that led to the creation of a patient capital fund, the *Fiducie du Chantier de l'économie sociale* in 2007, is documented, and is a fascinating example of collaborative learning and design that included social economy practitioners and researchers. It also involved legal and accounting professionals, and learning from experiences in other parts of Canada and the U.S.A. that had not yet created long-term capital for community-based initiatives, but were useful examples of financial innovation and the *ability* to innovate, to disrupt.[23]

Today, the *Fiducie* provides access to patient capital or quasi-equity that is repayable after 15 years. The federal government provided the initial capitalization with a $22.8 million grant by *Economic Development Canada.* Investors (trustees) in the *Fiducie* today are the two labor solidarity funds, the *Fonds de solidarité* ($12 million) and *Fondaction* ($8 million), as well as the Québec government (Investissement Québec –$10 million). To date, the *Fiducie* has invested $30 million in 106 enterprises and has created 1,689 jobs.[24]

The *Fiducie* is a milestone innovation in solidarity finance in Quebec for several reasons. The most important, of course, is the availability of long-term capital to collective enterprises, which would otherwise not be possible. This required financial innovation embedded in a process of social innovation and collaboration between government and civil society. The alliance between the social economy and the labor movement was key. The role played by the Government of Quebec was innovative as well. It is an investor or a trustee through *Investissement Québec*, a state investment fund. The *Fiducie* has its own Board of Trustees but is the *Fiducie du Chantier de l'économie sociale*, much as RISQ is also a financial institution created by the *Chantier* with its own Board of Advisors. In both cases, the *Chantier* is present on the boards of these two organizations and the Board of the *Chantier* oversees their operations.

The *Fiducie* demonstrates the ability of social economy actors to evaluate the financial needs of enterprises and to design customized tools. Collaboration and partnership underlie the *democratization of capital* represented in this experience. The process is embedded in the mission of the social economy in Quebec. But it has also become a template demonstrating the effectiveness of collaboration and what we have called *a process of co-construction and democratization*. This applies to all the work and challenges of the social economy in Quebec. Knowledge mobilization, the design of new development tools, identifying research priorities, working with government to assure more effective policy formation, are all processes of collaboration, co-construction, and democratization, as horizontal dialogue and decision-making govern these processes.

Most recently, a partnership between *Capital regional et coopératif Desjardins (CRCD)*, both the federal and provincial government, the network of *Community Futures Development Corporations* and *Centres d'aide aux entreprises*, and the *Conseil québecois de la cooperation et de la mutualité*, the network of cooperatives in Quebec, have established a fund, *Co-investissement coop*, with \$30 million in capitalization to provide access to patient capital from \$50,000 to \$1 million to cooperatives in Quebec. The CRCD and the federal government's *Development Bank of Canada* have each contributed \$10 million; the Minister of Finance and the Economy, Quebec, \$4 million; *Community Futures Corporations (CFDCs)* and the *Centres d'aide aux entreprises (CAEs)*, \$5 million,[25] and the network of cooperatives and mutual aid societies (CQCM), \$1 million. At the time of writing, there is little information on this fund, as it was only established very recently. It adds to the possibilities of access to patient capital by cooperatives, though not by non-profit enterprises, and is part of the landscape of solidarity finance in Quebec.[26]

Figure 6.1 captures the embeddedness of solidarity finance in Quebec in a systemic approach. This approach is necessary to be able to effectively meet the capital requirements of social economy enterprises and to continue to innovate

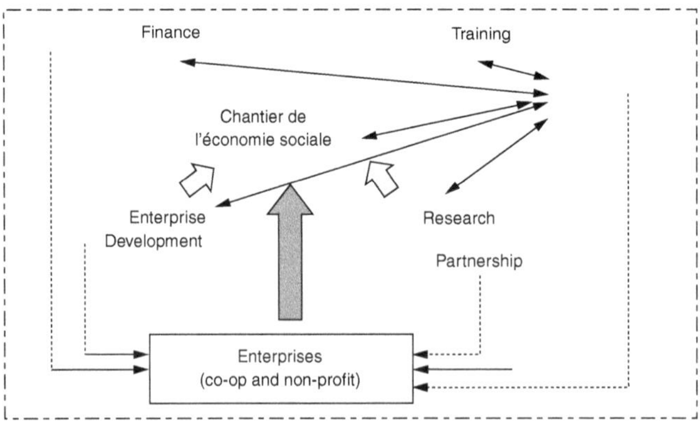

Figure 6.1 The co-construction of solidarity finance: a systemic approach (source: adapted from Mendell and Nogales (2003, 23)).

as those needs evolve and transform. The *Chantier* is at the center of this coherent system. It has created its own financial institutions and products, RISQ and the *Fiducie*, and is in the process of developing a housing fund for the social economy. The *Fiducie* also collaborates with solidarity finance and development capital institutions and organizations across Quebec, and is exploring the development of secondary markets and new financial products to increase the pool and diversity of capital available for collective enterprises. As Figure 6.1 demonstrates, the investment readiness of social economy enterprises is a priority. In other words, both the demand for and the supply of capital may be effectively and efficiently addressed in such a coherent institutional setting.

State funds available for the social economy

Government has been instrumental in supporting the development and growth of the social economy in Quebec. Even a short and stressful period following the fall of the Parti Québecois government and the election of the Liberal Party in 2003 ended when it became clear to the Liberals that the social economy in Quebec was well organized to resist attempts to reduce its capacity through cutbacks in support to the *Chantier* and to the numerous networks it represented. This does not suggest that there were no struggles, but the recognition of the social economy and its acknowledgement as an economic actor in Quebec led to many important government initiatives, all of which were co-constructed with actors. It also acknowledges the *Chantier* as representing this large network of actors and the dual capacity of sectoral networks, social movements, and development intermediaries (CDECs and CLDs) to negotiate on their own behalf and in the collective interest of the social economy. This is further reinforced by the collaboration of external actors (e.g., researchers).

As is clear from many of the examples given in this chapter, government has contributed financially and through public policy measures to solidarity finance and development capital institutions and organizations. It has also invested directly in the social economy principally through *Investissement Québec (IQ)* since its creation in 1997. The difficulty of clearly delineating state funds arises in several cases in which there are non-state partners. That said, IQ has created independent investment products that often complement other sources of finance. IQ also enters into partnerships with solidarity finance, the cooperative movement, *Desjardins*, and, most recently intermediaries such as the CFDCs.

In 2001, IQ created *la Financière*, designating $15 million for collective enterprises – cooperatives and non-profits. In 2003, IQ created the *Capitalization of Social Economy Enterprises Program* (*Programme pour la capitalisation des entreprises de l'économie sociale*), providing loans of between $25,000 and $500,000 and a moratorium on the repayment of the capital and interest for two to five years. A total of $3 million was invested in 2011 (capitalization loan or, in some cases, purchase of preferred shares). IQ estimated that these investments would contribute to the creation and/or maintenance of 244 jobs. In 2012, IQ created *IMPLIQ*, a new patient capital fund that paradoxically and potentially competes with solidarity finance institutions.[27]

Other examples of federal state funds noted earlier include *Community Futures Development Corporations* (*CFDCs*) established in 1987, that were also influenced by the CDEC model in Montreal. These intermediaries exist across the country and are located in low-income rural areas. Their reach is not as broad as the CLDs in Quebec. Where CFDCs and CLDs coexist within Quebec, the possibilities for state funding of local initiatives, including social economy enterprises, increases, as these intermediaries have investment funds. In Quebec, there are 57 CFDCs and also 10 *Centres d'aide aux entreprises* (*CAEs*), with assets of $250 million in 2012. They have provided $416 million in loans between 2000 and 2010. Together, they have created almost 20,000 jobs during this period and have provided approximately $416 million in loans to enterprises, both private and collective.[28]

In 2008, the Quebec government launched a five-year Action Plan (*Plan d'action gouvernemental pour l'entrepreneuriat collectif*) to support the development of the social economy.[29] Among the many commitments in this interministerial plan was the creation of the *Fonds d'initiative et de rayonnement de la métropole*, to promote urban social economy initiatives in the city of Montreal. The Government of Quebec allocated an annual amount of $850,000 available for the social economy from 2009 to 2014.[30]

To complicate this landscape even further, the former government, elected in September 2012, announced the creation of a Quebec development bank, the *Banque de développement économique du Québec (BDEQ)* to coordinate all government finance engaged in economic development. This project was rejected by Parliament and is off the agenda of the current government elected in the spring of 2014. That said, we note this initiative as another example where social economy actors were positioned to participate in the design of this public development bank.

CAP finance

After years of informal collaboration, a formal network of solidarity finance and development capital organizations and institutions, *CAP Finance*, was created in 2010. The founding members include the *Fiducie, Fondaction*, the *Fonds de solidarité*, the *Réseau de crédit communautaire, Filaction, RISQ*, and the *Caisse d'économie solidaire*. Together they constitute what we have called a network of solidarity and responsible finance.[31]

Why this network? Why another organization in an already highly networked and tightly knit social economy in Quebec? The founding members agreed that in 2010, these financial institutions had to distinguish their history, identity, and activity from the increasingly toxic financial sector and also to demonstrate their capacity to compete with mainstream finance, while challenging its culture and objectives. In its founding document, members of CAP Finance describe their commitment to reduce income inequality and the damage to the environment by providing access to capital to those enterprises that share these objectives. The time had come to "rethink finance and the economy." The creation of this network, write its founders, is not a response to the crisis. It is the result of many years of innovation and collaboration. The formalization of this collaboration provides a new perspective on finance by demonstrating another approach. Greater visibility of these experiences today is urgent. The mission of CAP Finance is to develop and promote solidarity finance and development capital; its vision is to make CAP Finance the reference point in Quebec for financing the social economy and enterprises committed to sustainable development. Because the composition of CAP Finance includes very large and smaller financial organizations/institutions with a great variability of assets and investment portfolios, its credibility is even greater, as mainstream finance has to acknowledge its significance.

Conclusion

This chapter is a narrative, a story of innovation, of disruption, of remarkable people and organizations that have designed a new socio-economic architecture that is in sharp contrast with the current reality of austerity measures that are reinforcing hardship, the propping up of failing institutions through massive bail-outs, outsourcing essential services to the market, privatizing resources, committing public funds to support extractive industries despite increasing knowledge about the damage to the environment and to human beings, hollowing out communities that require transitional policy support as industries and sectors disappear; the list goes on. Indeed, solidarity finance and the social economy will not reverse this process alone. But the experience in Quebec is telling; it is possible to develop financial institutions that are historically rooted in a different logic and that have been very successful in realizing their societal objectives.

I began this chapter by recalling the long history of mutual aid societies, cooperative finance, credit unions, and social banks in Quebec and elsewhere. They have existed in a parallel universe. Some have slipped over to the other side and participated in global financial markets to their peril. Hopefully, the heavy anchor of history will pull these institutions back to their origins. Today, the misguided notion that there is trade-off between economic profit and social engagement has been turned upside down. Financial institutions in the social economy have survived the crisis and are earning steady returns. As the financial crisis transforms into an economic crisis, this stability may, of course, be shaken.

Democratizing capital is at the heart of democratizing the economy. I would like to end with a few quotations from the *Charter* signed by the founding members of CAP Finance:

> The democratization of the economy cannot be realized without redefining the role of capital in economic development. Notwithstanding a growing preoccupation within Quebec society about social and environmental impact of development, there remains a big gap between these concerns and the behaviour of both individual and institutional investors. The timing is right

> for a transformation of these practices. The creation of this network increases the capacity of its members to distinguish themselves from mainstream actors in financial markets. The financial architecture represented by this network has an important role to play in reconstructing the sector. Creating this network is not a response to the crisis; it is the result of many years of innovation and collaboration. The formalization of this collaboration increases the possibility to respond individually and collectively to growing needs; it requires rethinking finance.[32]

It requires challenging the dominant paradigm through the increased visibility of the collective capacity of CAP Finance, its founding members, and those who will join this network to ease the work in rethinking finance by documenting their practice systematically and making this widely available. The history of solidarity finance and development capital in Quebec which I have synthesized in this chapter is an ongoing process of democratizing capital.

Notes

1 Disruptive innovation is a term referred to in the literature on management and business. We appropriate this term to describe the continuous and dynamic process of innovation that characterizes the social and solidarity economy. "In today's turbulent environment, leading disruptive innovation is likely more about *best principles* than best practices, and requires a disruptive approach to management itself." This quote has wide applicability beyond the management audience it is intended for (Kaplan 2012).

2 In Quebec, the term *social economy* refers to all collective enterprises. In other parts of the world, the social economy and the solidarity economy are distinguished. In the South, for example, the solidarity economy also refers to the popular economy, what was previously called the informal economy. Country-specific definitions and terms are important to allow for the diversity of experiences. The social and solidarity economy captures this diversity. As this chapter is about Quebec, the term *social economy* will be used throughout.

3 Needless to say, in China where the SSE is only beginning to be explored as a possible strategy for democratic processes of socio-economic transformation, the need for an international conversation inspired the conference for which this chapter was written. I will return to the *Chantier* and its key role in Quebec below.

4 The work of the late Elinor Ostrom, Nobel Laureate, for example.

5 Details on the *Chantier de l'économie sociale*'s role in democratizing capital are provided in the chronology of innovation in solidarity finance which follows and which is the theme of this chapter.

6 This was introduced by Merkur Cooperative Bank in Germany targeting forestry, agriculture, and fair trade (Mendell and Nogales 2012, 11).

7 A study by J.P. Morgan in 2010 estimated that between $400 billion and $1 trillion will be invested in impact investing over the next decade with profits of approximately $185 billion. These investments will be concentrated in water purification in rural areas, women's health, primary education, and in establishing financial services for those earning less than $3,000 per year (Mendell and Barbosa 2013).

8 www.caissesolidaire.coop.

9 www.fondsftq.com/. Total assets of the *Fonds de solidarité* in 2012 were $8.5 billion. The *Fonds* has invested $5.7 billion in 2,239 enterprises and has created or maintained 168,577 jobs.

10 The *Fonds locaux de solidarité* was formerly called SOLIDE, created in 1991. www.fondsftq.com/fr-ca/financement/fonds-locaux.aspx.
11 The tax credits given to subscribers to the labor solidarity fund were initially 30 percent by both levels of government. These were reduced to 15 percent. Today, the federal government announced a gradual reduction of this 15 percent with its eventual elimination. The province of Quebec retains this tax credit and the ability for further tax benefits for retirement funds. The actions by the current federal government have been severely criticized. In 2012, the total assets of the *Fonds de solidarité (FTQ)* were $$8.5 billion. They have created and/or maintained approximately 170,000 jobs in Quebec.
12 Local development centers (CLDs) were established in 1998 throughout the province of Quebec.
13 www.fdem.qc.ca/.
14 Investments by the FDEM range from $25,000 to $100,000. Since its inception, it has invested $2,965,790 (2012).
15 The average reimbursement rate for MCLA is 94 percent. www.acemcreditcommunautaire.qc.ca.
16 The average reimbursement rate for the entire network is 91 percent. www.rqcc.qc.ca.
17 It is well known that the high reimbursement rate in micro-credit and micro-finance is due to the many services offered by these funds to accompany the small initiatives and enterprises they finance. The *Fonds d'emprunt Québec* is expanding the services offered to include the ability to create micro-savings deposits and to offer micro-insurance. This *disruptive innovation* is a first in Canada as, up until now, micro-credit institutions could not provide banking or insurance services. Since we know the resistance of banks to small loans, this means removing considerable savings from mainstream banking, surely part of the process of democratizing capital in Quebec.
18 *Fondaction* will also be affected by the decision of the federal government to reduce and eliminate the 15 percent tax credits, noted in earlier discussion on the *Fonds de solidarité*. www.fondaction.com.
19 www.filaction.qc.ca.
20 Technical assistance support of $5,000 does not have to be repaid if the initiative is not feasible. It is repaid by those receiving this support who are able to launch their projects.
21 www.fonds-risq.qc.ca.
22 For information on the *Association des Centres locaux de développement du Québec* and its work, see www.acldq.qc.ca/.
23 This is rather ironic, given the numerous "innovative" toxic instruments in financial markets. Clearly, there is no resemblance, as the innovation in solidarity finance was in the interest of the initiatives requiring patient capital, not in the interest of the investors seeking speculative returns.
24 http://fiducieduchantier.qc.ca.
25 These are discussed in the next section of this chapter.
26 www.economie.gouv.qc.ca/ministere/salle-de-presse/communiques-de-presse/communique-de-presse/?tx_ttnews[tt_news]=7948&cHash=5ac1b1125d70d1a9fdfc86734d6d5322.
27 www.investquebec.com.
28 http://sadc-cae.ca.
29 Ministère des Affaires municipals et des Régions, Governement du Québec (2008).
30 www.mamrot.gouv.qc.ca/metropole/developpement/fonds-dinitiative-et-de-rayonnement-de-la-metropole-firm/.
31 http://capfinance.ca.
32 Ibid., M. Mendell translation (Mendell 2013).

References

Bourque, G.L., M. Mendell, and R. Rouzier. 2009. *La Finance Responsable au Québec: Portrait, Enjeux et Défis d'une Finance au Service d'un Développement Durable et Solidaire* [Finance Manager in Quebec: Portrait, Issues and Challenges of Finance at the Service of Sustainable Development and Solidarity]. Montreal: Éditions Vie économique, coopérative et solidarité.

Bourque, G.L., M. Mendell, and R. Rouzier. 2013. "Solidarity Finance: A History of an Emerging Practice." In *Innovation and the Social Economy: The Quebec Experience*, edited by Marie J. Bouchard (pp. 180–205). Toronto: University of Toronto Press.

Conaty, Pat. 2012. *Cooperative Money as a Commons: Convivial Technology for Economic Democracy*. Paper prepared for the First International Social Transformation Conference, University of Split, Split, Croatia, July 10–12.

Kaplan, Soren. 2012. "Leading Disruptive Innovation." *Ivey Business Journal*, July–August. Available online at: wwsg.com/wp-content/uploads/Leading-disruptive-innovation-Ivey-Business-Journal.pdf.

Mendell, M. 2007. "Karl Polanyi and the Instituted Process of Economic Democratization." In *Karl Polanyi: New Perspectives on the Place of the Economy in Society*, edited by M. Harvey, R. Ramlogan, and S. Randles (pp. 78–92). Manchester: Manchester University Press.

Mendell, M. 2013. "Comment se situe le Québec dans le mouvement de 'l'impact investing'? [How is Quebec in the movement of 'impact investing'?]" *Revue Vie Economique* 4(3): 28–34. Available online at: www.eve.coop/?r=18.

Mendell, M., and E. Barbosa. 2013. "Impact Investing: A Preliminary Analysis of Emergent Primary and Secondary Exchange Platforms." *Journal of Sustainable Finance and Investment* 3(2): 111–123. doi: 10.1080/20430795.2013.776258.

Mendell, M., and R. Nogales. 2009. "Social Enterprises in OECD Member Countries: What are the Financial Streams?" In *The Changing Boundaries of Social Enterprises*, edited by A. Noya (pp. 89–138). Paris: OECD. Available online at: http://dx.doi.org/10.1787/9789264055513-4-en.

Mendell, M., and R. Nogales. 2012. "Solidarity Finance." *Universitas Forum* 3(2): 1–18.

Mendell, M., B. Lévesque, and R. Rouzier. 2003. "New Forms of Financing Social Economy Enterprises and Organisations in Québec." In *The Non-profit Sector in a Changing Economy*, edited by A. Noya and C. Nativel (pp. 139–168). Paris: OECD.

Mendell, M., V. Bourdeau, R. Rouzier, A. Marchildon, and L. Campeau. 2010. *Portrait de la finance responsable au Québec* [Portrait of Responsible Finance in Quebec]. Coordination par Gilles L. Bourque. Montreal: CAP Finance and Chaire d'éthique appliquée, Université de Sherbrooke.

Ministère des Affaires municipales et des Régions, Gouvernement du Québec. 2008. *Économie sociale: Pour les communautés plus solidaires: Plan d'action gouvernemental pour l'entrepreneuriat collectif.* Quebec: Ministère des Affaires municipales et des Régions.

Polanyi, Karl. 1944. *The Great Transformation: The Political and Economic Origins of our Time*. Boston, MA: Beacon Press.

Polanyi, Karl. 1977. *The Livelihood of Man*. New York: Academic Press.

7 The struggle for public power in the United States

Richard H. Rudolph

The power struggle

Public power in the United States provides a model of alternative development which can help mitigate the negative economic, social, and ecological impacts of the global capitalist economy. While publicly owned utilities and rural electric cooperatives provide electricity to 46 million U.S. consumers, few scholars or social solidarity practitioners are aware of their existence nor of the role that they have played in providing electricity as a non-profit service, emphasizing efficiency and minimizing growth. The reform of existing public power systems and the creation of new ones could provide the missing political and economic bridge for a transition to least-cost policies and use of community controlled energy alternatives like solar, wind, and other decentralized technologies. It could also provide a model for democratization and reform in other countries where public power systems are run by national governments and are often unresponsive to local residents. The best options are local non-profit municipal systems and rural cooperatives run by elected officials and employee representatives with an open-door policy on information and voter control over investment in major programs and projects.

The power struggle over who controls the resource of electricity which has taken place during the past century and more continues to this day not only in the U.S.A. but in other countries as well. In Boulder, Colorado, for example, citizens have recently voted for public power, not for the usual reasons – better rates and more reliable service – but rather for democratic control of their power in order to advance the goal of becoming a carbon-neutral city. The City of Munich, Germany has also set ambitious targets for obtaining electricity from renewable sources from its municipal utility. The first goal is to produce enough green electricity through Stadtwerke Munchen (SWM, or Munich City Utilities) to meet 100 percent of household demand by 2015. The second is to generate enough electricity from renewables to meet all the electricity requirements of the municipality by 2025. While Munich's plans are exceptional even by German standards, SWM is a flag-bearer for the wider movement toward "recomunalized" and decentralized energy which places local utilities at the center of Germany's plans to consign electricity generated from nuclear and fossil fuel sources to the dustbin of history.

My purpose here is to not only describe the historic struggle for public power in the United States, but also to assess whether it has lived up to its potential for not only providing electricity as a non-profit service, but also allowing a process for debate over development options which enables local citizens to weigh social, economic, and environmental costs against the need for new power plants, energy efficiency, or alternative resources. This chapter will also examine the potential for new public power systems as well as other community initiatives to take control of their power supply.

The electric power industry is the most money-intensive, pervasive, and politicized business in modern America. Its course over the past century and more has been shaped by the struggle over who would control the resource of electricity, the geographic territories that went with it, and the increasingly central place it would occupy in the nation's economy. On one side were those who insisted that free enterprise was the only way to develop electric power systems. On the other side, forward-thinking individuals saw electricity as an essential resource which was best utilized according to common priorities.

The historical struggle of public power

The historic roots of public ownership can be traced back to a period before the American Revolution when the first municipal waters systems were established. Access to clean, reliable water supplies was fundamental to the physical health of a community. Public-minded individuals in the nineteenth century saw electricity as the same kind of resource. A flow of cheap, reliable electricity offered a boon to the economic health of a town's businesses and industries, as well as to its citizens (Rudolph and Ridley 1986, xi, 34).

According to popular myth, the Age of Electricity began in 1882 when Thomas Edison opened the first central electric generating station on Pearl Street in New York City. While other inventors were interested in selling individual power systems or providing the service at a fixed charge, Edison was the first to conceive selling electricity itself. He saw the growth of the business as dependent on the construction of central power stations, each generating and transmitting electric current to hundreds of thousands of customers, all paying operating companies year after year all their lives for a supply of electricity. Although Edison was a pioneer of electrical generation and transmission, it would be his assistant, Samuel Insull, who would develop the vertically integrated public utility which later proved to be an instrumental management model for utilities.

The first municipally owned electric lighting plant was actually set up more than three years earlier. The story began when Charles Brush of Cleveland, a pioneer who had developed a dynamo and arc lamp, signed a contract with officials of the Telegraph Supply Company and the City of Cleveland to provide electric street lighting in the public square. The success of this demonstration led the city fathers of Wabash, Indiana in the following year to put four of Bush's 3,000 candle power lamps on top of the courthouse dome, 200 feet above ground. The 10,000 or so individuals who converged on the courthouse on the moonless night of March 31, 1880 stood "over-whelmed with awe" when the dazzling light illuminated the houses, yards, and distant river. An eye witness reported that "the strange, weird light, exceeded in power only by the sun, rendered the square as light as midday. Men fell on their knees, groans were uttered at the sight and many were dumb with amazement" (Rudolph and Ridley 1986, 26–27).

Although most of the early municipal light plants were initially established to provide street lighting, it was not long before they sold current to private citizens. The city of Fairfield, Iowa, which had purchased a Brush dynamo and six 2,000 candle power arc lamps, expanded its operation so that it could sell electricity to its citizens by the end of the decade. A municipal plant in Danville, Virginia which began operations in January 1886 also supplied electricity for both commercial and public lighting.

In the 1880s, privately owned utilities first focused on lighting large cities, commercial establishments, and the homes of the very wealthy. As demand for electric lighting remained relatively low, however, they soon began to promote its use to electrify urban trolley systems to maximize daytime use of generating capacity built primarily for lighting streets at night.

As the number of central power stations multiplied and interest in business grew, deep-seated conflicts began to emerge among competing companies and between the companies and city governments. In an age of horse-drawn street cars, many regarded the franchises merely as concessions to perform a service. But in reality it meant a system of political favors in which corruption could be rank. With the coming of electric franchises, investment and competition increased – so did graft.

According to one observer in the late 1880s, nearly every city in the country had granted several electric light franchises to competing companies. Out of a belief that maximum competition between the companies would keep charges low, some city governments granted franchises to all companies desiring to supply electric services. As a result, these cities became ensnared in the wires of the new technology. The vicious infighting that occurred between companies resulted in increasing failure in service, higher costs, and gradual consolidation under companies that gained a political and economic upper hand. For example, in 1897, the Commonwealth Edison Company in Chicago swallowed up its 23 competitors virtually overnight, leading the *Chicago Tribune* to observe that, "Beginning this morning the sun and the Gas Trust [have] a monopoly of all the light with which Chicago is to be blessed" (Rudolph and Ridley 1986, 30–31).

Faced with the growing political and economic clout of these private electric companies, many local governments formed electric utilities of their own. By 1890, more than 150 towns were operating lighting and power systems, and in the following decade that number multiplied at a rapid pace. For the owners of private electric companies, the most disturbing fact about public power companies was that their charges for electricity were half that of the privately owned companies. In these towns common people gained access to the miracle of electric lights, while in other cities only the wealthy could afford to switch from traditional gas and kerosene lamps, or commercial businesses faced higher rates (Rudolph and Ridley 1986, 32).

The public power movement was spurred on by reform mayors in San Francisco, Toledo, Chicago, and Detroit, and by academicians such as Richard Ely from Johns Hopkins University and Frank Parsons from Boston University who connected political corruption with the rise of monopolies like electric companies. In Detroit, Hazen Pingree, a prosperous shoe manufacturer and municipal reformer, was elected in 1889 after a campaign that publicized the corruption of Detroit officials by utility companies. Pingree promised to create a city-owned power system, but General Electric balked at selling the necessary equipment to the city.

In April 1893, Detroit citizens voted 15,282 to 1,745 on an advisory ballot in favor of a municipal plant. DELP continued to woo city councilors who held authority over the creation of a city-owned power system, but with the weight of the voters behind him Pingree prevailed. He managed to establish a city-owned electric plant in 1895 to supply street lighting. A short time later, he urged the city council to extend services to the stores and homes of private citizens. "If this were done," he declared, "it will take electric lights out of the luxuries of life, only to be used by the wealthy, and place it within the reach of the humblest citizens" (Rudolph and Ridley 1986, 32–33). Municipal ownership brought with it the economy and improved service that Pingree had predicted.

The resistance that Pingree ran up against to provide the common people with electric power as a non-profit service also existed elsewhere. In Massachusetts, for example, a home rule petition from the town of Danvers, asking the state legislature for the right to sell electricity to local businesses and homes, led to a three-year legislative battle over the rights of municipally owned electric systems. The legislature also received petitions from Boston, Worcester, Lowell, Lawrence, and a number of smaller communities, requesting the right to produce and distribute gas or electricity to their residents. Opposed by a group of 61 private gas and electric companies, what finally emerged in 1891 was a highly restrictive version of the bill. It had a chilling effect on public power in Massachusetts and in other states where it was copied. A city or town could not develop a competing system, but had to buy out any existing private utility. To do this, a two-thirds vote of a town council was required in two consecutive years, followed by a majority approval of the town's residents. In the intervening period private companies could mount intensive publicity campaigns. The company could also stall for several years following a conclusive vote, while haggling over the fair market value of the system. During the next decade only 17 additional municipal systems were established in Massachusetts. Of these, seven were located in communities which had no previous electric service (Rudolph and Ridley 1986, 34).

As reformers pushed for public power systems, there were other forces at work which would hinder their development. By the early 1890s central power stations were no longer limited to generating power only for their immediate neighborhood. In 1886, George Westinghouse, the founder of Westinghouse manufacturing, began marketing a high-voltage alternating current that allowed transmission over longer distances. The development of large steam turbines to power the increased loads further accelerated consolidation under the private companies. This, of course, would spell trouble for town-owned systems. They were limited by law to operate within boundaries and, without the larger consumer market or access to capital to build huge generating stations, they would face growing pressure from private power (Rudolph and Ridley 1986, 36–37).

The issue over public power versus private power continued to rage through the 1890s, moving from the local level to the floor of state legislatures. Focused at the state and local levels, the movement for municipal ownership of power systems became part of an effort to eliminate rampant corruption in municipal government. During the fight over the Massachusetts public power proposal, Richard T. Ely, an economist from Johns Hopkins University, connected political corruption with the rise of private corporations in control of monopoly businesses like electricity. Other academicians, such as John R. Commons from the University of Wisconsin and Edward Bemis and Frank Parsons from Boston University, provided reams of statistics to show that publicly owned power systems were more efficient and cheaper. Popular movements for municipal reform and the desire for lower rates fostered a remarkable growth of public power systems.

Frightened by the surge in the growth of public systems, leaders of private companies adopted a bold new approach to stem the trend for public control of electricity. Samuel Insull, who would work his way up the corporate ladder, managing Commonwealth Edison, Public Service Company of Northern Illinois, Peoples Gas Light & Coke, and Commonwealth Edison of Chicago, was the first to recognize that the business of delivering electricity was in fact a natural monopoly and that state governmental agencies should fix rates, standards of service, and insure exclusive control of a territory for a single company. Along with stabilizing tumultuous competition between companies, Insull believed the plan for state regulation would head off the growth of public power systems by offering an alternative form of public control over the electric business. He argued that the public was really more interested in good service and reasonable rates than the form of ownership and control (Richardson and Kelly 2005; Rudolph and Ridley 1986, 39).

The 1920s were the golden years for the privately owned electric power industry. During the stock market boom of the decade, utility holding companies became the instrument of high finance. Insull and the other electric power barons restructured their companies through the establishment of holding companies which were used to buy up smaller utilities in an effort designed not to improve the company's operating efficiencies, but rather as a speculative attempt to maximize profits. The growing utility monopolies exploited this structure, pyramiding holding companies on top of holding companies, sometimes such that a holding company was as many as 10 times removed from the operating company. The resulting structure allowed holding companies to earn large profits on small increases in operating company profits.

Protected by state regulation, rising political influence, and access to nearly unlimited amounts of capital, these holding companies had smaller private companies and public power systems in a box. In the surge of mergers between 1922 and 1927, more than 300 small private companies were swallowed up each year by the holding companies. The growth of public power systems was brought to a standstill in 1923 when 3,066 public systems served one out of every eight electricity consumers. The drop in the next four years was precipitous, with a loss of 746 public systems. (Richardson and Kelly 2005; Rudolph and Ridley 1986, 41–42).

In response, public power advocates like Gifford Pinchot and Carl D. Thompson launched efforts during the decade to bring the small public power systems into a large integrated transmission system. They recognized that the public power systems were hopelessly handicapped by their confinement within city boundaries and were limited in their ability to raise money for new plant equipment. Pinchot tried to develop a "Giant Power" transmission system within Pennsylvania that was bitterly fought by private companies. Thompson promoted a nationwide "Superpower" transmission system linked to federal hydroelectric sites. Under his plan, the federal government would build new generating plants and lay out main trunk lines, and local systems would fill in the gaps so that electricity could be distributed to even remote rural areas all across the nation. His plan, which was brought to a National Public Ownership Conference, was endorsed by the attendees – labor leaders, representatives from farm organizations, national politicians, and public power advocates. They drafted a bill for a nationwide public power system based on Thompson's ideas. Although the effort for Thompson's Superpower failed, it sowed the seeds for similar ideas to emerge 10 years later in the form of the 1935 Rural Electrification Administration and calls for a "national grid" that would echo into the 1960s and 1970s.

Private power's answer to the growing revelation of power company abuses and Thompson's Superpower proposal was a massive propaganda assault. The campaign was launched by a network coordinated by the National Electric Light Association and backed with funds that were unmatched in the history of American industry. The purpose was virtually to reshape how the public conceived of electricity and the private companies that delivered it. When the more benign propaganda and biased academic studies failed, the private power companies resorted to political smear tactics. Power industry propagandists centered their criticism on the notion of public power as "un-American" and tied to "bolshevik" ideas. In a small prelude to the communist scares of the 1950s, the Illinois bureau went so far as to blacklist the United Society of Christian Endeavor, the American Farm Bureau Federation, the Religious Society of Friends, and the Women's Christian Temperance Union because of the organizations' support of public power systems. When the Teachers' Union of the AF of L objected to the committee's efforts to have certain books removed from schools and libraries, they were also blacklisted. A four-year Federal Trade Commission study completed in 1932 revealed a scandalous coordinated system of blacklisting of groups and individuals, propaganda disseminated in the schools, funding of political campaigns, and unbridled media influence. The industry spent $28 million of its $33 million publicity budget on advertising to gain favorable news coverage (Rudolph and Ridley 1986, 46–52; Hampton and Reno 2003, 88–90).

A turning point in the historic battle between public and private interests

The election of Franklin D. Roosevelt in 1932 marked a turning point in the historic battle between public and private interests for control of power resources and territory. He was a strong supporter of public power, believing communities dissatisfied with their services or rates had the "undeniable right" to set up a public utility. The opening salvo in what would be a decade-long battle for control of the industry was fired when Roosevelt called on Congress during the first 100 days of his administration to approve the Tennessee Valley Authority (TVA) Act which would transform the Tennessee Valley and its people from the poorest, most backward region of the nation into an area which would progress at a faster rate than the rest of the country. The remarkable enactment of this legislation came after more than 10 years of debate over what should be done with the partially constructed nitrate plant and dam at Muscle Shoals on the Tennessee River. The Muscle Shoals fight was over whether the government should own and operate the facilities or lease them to private owners. The issue pitted the defenders of public power against the private power interest and their allies in the Coolidge and Hoover administrations.

When the TVA act was considered by the full House, Republican congressmen predictably raised the well-worn cries of "bolshevism" and "communism." Despite this hostile testimony, the original bill would be left intact, chiefly owing to the efforts of Senator George Norris and the direct intervention of Roosevelt. Although the battle was finally over when Roosevelt signed the TVA Act on May 18, 1933, the new governing board of three directors would face stiff resistance as it attempted to carry out its mandate during the next few years.

During the New Deal, Roosevelt also promoted and signed legislation to break up electric holding companies. The Public Utility Holding Company Act (PUHCA) which was passed in 1935 was a response to the many holding company abuses of the 1920s and 1930s that subsequently resulted in the great Wall Street Crash of 1929. These abuses included defrauding investors, loose accounting practices, and carrying excessive debt. By 1932, three holding companies controlled almost half of the energy generated in the U.S.A. Along with Insull's utility empire, J.P. Morgan's United Corporation and the Electric Bond and Share Company were responsible for 45 percent of the electricity generated in the U.S.A. Despite Insull's belief that a disastrous "slump or calamity" of leveraged holding companies was "practically inconceivable," during the Great Depression the unbelievable happened. From 1929 to 1935, 53 holding companies went bankrupt, including 36 utilities with publicly held securities.

The PUHCA outlawed the pyramidal structure of interstate utility holding companies, determining that they could be no more than twice removed from their operating subsidiaries. It required holding companies which owned 10 percent or more of a public utility to register with the Securities and Exchange Commission and to provide detailed accounts of their financial transactions and holdings. Holding companies in a single state were exempt from the PUHCA. The legislation had a dramatic effect on the operations of holding companies. Between 1938 and 1958 the number of holding companies declined from 215 to 18. This forced divestiture led to a new paradigm for the electricity marketplace which lasted until the deregulation of the 1980s and 1990s: a single, vertically integrated system which served a circumscribed geographic area regulated by either the state or federal government (Thakar 2008, 908–909; Rudolph and Ridley 1986, 75–79; Hampton and Reno 2003, 90–91). In the course of the legislative fight over the PUHCA, Roosevelt issued an executive order establishing the Rural Electric Administration (REA). In 1935 only 11 percent of the nation's farms had electricity, and the costs for a private company to bring it in were enormous. Rural customers were usually required by private companies to pay between $2,000 and $3,000 per mile for line extensions. In addition, families could expect to pay between 10 and 12 cents per kilowatt hour, and in some regions as high as 25 and 40 cents. At a time when wheat sold for 80 cents a bushel and gross farm income averaged $1,800 a year, electricity was an undreamed-of luxury.

During its first year of operation, the REA furnished only a handful of farms with service. Surprisingly, the private power industry did not put up much of a fight against the Norris-Rayburn bill which established the REA on a more permanent basis in 1936. The private power industry was evidently confident that it would be another "New Deal Flop" and thus chose not to directly oppose the measure. They did not believe that farmers would be willing to go into debt for electricity; nor that they would be able to succeed given their lack of legal and financial skills. The prevailing attitude was best expressed by a utility executive who said, "Let the farmers build the electric cooperatives, then when they fail, we will buy them up at ten cents on the dollar" (Hampton and Reno 2003, 90–91).

Other strategies were used to obstruct the formation of cooperatives. Squads of canvassers were sent out in automobiles, driving from farm to farm to discourage farmers and their wives from joining the co-ops. Rural people were told "a thousand and one cooked up tales to bewilder and terrify them." They were assured that when a farmer signed for membership in a REA cooperative, he was putting a mortgage on his property. Farmers were told that they would be individually liable for construction costs and for any damage that might arise out of the construction or operation of the system. And if the cooperative failed, they would lose their farms to the government. But despite these and other tactics, the REA was a huge success. By 1941 there were 8,000 borrowers in the program. Among them were the names of 741 new cooperatives, 54 municipal or public utility district agencies, and 25 private companies. By 1944, 43 percent of the nation's farms had electrical service (Rudolph and Ridley 1986, 79–84).

REA's success was largely attributed to the policies that enabled farmers to obtain low-cost service without having to pay for construction costs for individual line extensions. Under its area coverage policy, the REA constructed a backbone electrical distribution system adequate for providing service to everyone in an area. The determination for a loan was based on the resources of the entire system, rather than on individual line extensions. For farmers who could not afford to make a financial commitment of an extra $1.50 a month to finance the line, the REA staff devised a plan of self-help under which a cooperative's members could work off a portion of the expense through labor line construction and home wiring. The cost of line construction was also drastically reduced. The success of the program not only fed into the growth of the TVA, but also in the establishment of other federal projects that Roosevelt envisioned as "yardsticks" against which the private companies would be measured. Federally assisted projects, such as the financing of the Santee-Cooper hydro project in South Carolina and the Loop River Public Power District in Nebraska and the Bonneville Project Act of 1937, would provide a broad base to the yardstick.

Reacting to the growing number of publicly owned utilities, the private power industry in the mid- and late 1940s sought to stop the growth of federal projects which would feed new public systems. With the backing of a Republican Congress, the private power companies sought consciously to cut off funding and construction for federal transmission lines and generating plants. One key fight erupted over a new coal-fired plant that the TVA planned to build in New Johnsonville, Tennessee. When Republicans in the House succeeded in blocking this and other federal projects, President Truman called their actions "bad, foolish, reckless, irresponsible and a capitulation to special interest groups." During the 1948 presidential campaign Truman spoke out about Republicans in words that echoed Franklin Roosevelt. "The Republicans don't like to sell cheap public power," he told an audience in El Paso in September 1948, "because it means that the big power monopolies cannot get their rake-off at the expense of the public" (Rudolph and Ridley 1986, 95–96). He warned that if the Republicans maintained control of Congress they would scrap the clause which provided public and cooperative systems to federally generated power. Truman's surprise election victory and the Democrats' return to power in 1948 would provide a temporary respite from the attack on the federal power system. But it would not be long before the issue would be raised again.

The setback in the post-World War II era

In the post-World War II era, private power companies regained their strength and embarked on an unprecedented building campaign. They promoted the use of electricity through artificially low rates and "Live Better Electrically" campaigns. As demand increased, more generating stations were built. They also carried out active advertising campaigns against public power and rural electric cooperatives as "the step to socialism." The election of General Dwight D. Eisenhower, the Republican candidate for president, in 1952 would send shock waves through the public power industry. He not only attempted to dismantle federal power programs, but he also supported the effort to rewrite the Atomic

Energy Act of 1946 which opened the doors for private development of nuclear energy (Rudolph and Ridley 1986, 103–109).

In the 1970s private power companies began to gain control of the public and cooperative systems by incorporating them into power pools which they dominated. They also used nuclear power as a strategy to increase their concentration and consolidate their power. Their influence could be seen in their massive expansion, which went unchecked by state regulators, despite public protest and intervention by consumer groups and environmentalists.

A number of publicly owned systems also began to participate in capacity-building programs of their own. Under the leadership of the Washington Public Power Supply System (WPPSS), 118 public and rural cooperatives along with three private utilities agreed to finance three nuclear power projects, while 88 public and cooperative systems pledged future rate hikes to build two more. In New England, the Massachusetts Municipal Wholesale Electric Company, the bulk-buying agency for 31 municipally owned utilities, would offer to buy 13.8 percent of the Seabrook nuclear project from the Public Service Company of New Hampshire. This proposed investment in addition to shares already purchased would have made the municipal utility system the second largest owner of Seabrook with a 19.5 percent share. The TVA also embarked upon a massive program of planning and constructing 17 nuclear plants (Radin 2003, 366–367).

Both the TVA and the Washington Power Supply System would be harmed by changing conditions that called into question the viability of their large-scale projects. TVA's nuclear program received its first jolt in March 1975 when a fire in the cable room of the Browns Ferry Nuclear Plant shut down units 1 and 2. Subsequently, falling demand for electricity, sharply escalating construction costs, rising interest rates, and construction delays would prompt the TVA to reconsider its nuclear power efforts. In 1979, the TVA deferred construction of four of its 17 units and in March 1982, the TVA Board of Directors voted to defer construction of three more units. Cancellation of four additional units would leave the TVA with five operating units (Radin 2003, 366–369). Faced with skyrocketing rates and high unemployment, ratepayers in a number of communities threatened widespread refusal to pay for the canceled plants. The new citizen organizations that sprang up in response to ever increasing utility bills and staged blackouts launched campaigns to demand that Wall Street "eat the debt."

In response to the Iranian oil crisis of 1979, President Jimmy Carter would ask for the most massive peacetime commitment of funds and resources in the nation's history to develop America's own alternatives sources of fuel. Carter called the drive for energy independence "the moral equivalent of war." In the previous year, Carter signed the Public Utility Regulatory Policies Act (PURPA) which was designed to promote fuel conservation through co-generation and greater use of alternative sources of power. The PURPA established a class of non-utility, non-oil generators called "Qualifying Facilities" (QFs). Utilities were required to buy electricity from QFs that produced solar, wind, biomass, and geothermal power. While QFs helped reduce oil-fired generation, they also produced power at significantly higher average cost than coal or hydroelectric power already in place. The extra cost, however, would pale in comparison to the cost of nuclear power plants being brought on line in the late 1970s and 1980s. These reactors experienced tremendous cost overruns due to significant construction costs, expensive compliance with safety regulations, and significant waste disposal expenses (Richardson and Kelly 2005; Hampton and Reno 2003, 165–166).

Although primarily intended to be an environmental statute, a primary effect of the PURPA was to introduce competition into the generation sector of the electricity marketplace, thus challenging the claim that the electricity market encouraged a "natural monopoly." The free market mania of the 1980s and 1990s would further challenge this notion. President Carter set the stage when he deregulated the commercial airline industry, the railroads, oil prices, and interest rates, as well as partially deregulating the interstate trucking industry. Carter also set up much of the deregulation machinery which his successors used to sweep away or sharply reduce regulation in the saving and loan banking, telecommunications, media, cable TV, and other sectors (Slocum 2008, 2; PBS n.d.).

As the last major act of his presidency, George H.W. Bush, in November 1992, signed the Energy Policy Act of 1992 (EP Act) which expanded the Federal Regulatory Commission's (FERC) authority to order utilities to allow independent power producers equal access to the utilities' transmission systems. Enron and other independent power producers of electricity lobbied heavily in favor of this legislation. So did large industrial customers who were seeking to escape the high costs of power in various parts of the country where utility companies had built expensive nuclear power plants.

The EP Act also partially repealed the PUHCA. The repeal exempted independent power generation facilities that produced and sold power wholesale, specifically exempt wholesale generators (EWGs), from the provisions of the 1935 Public Utility Holding Company Act. The exemption applied to EWGs regardless of whether they were owned by operating companies, utility holding companies, or parties not involved in the electric business.

To assist in the implementation of the PURPA and EP Act, the FERC would issue Order Nos 888 and 889 in April 1996 which further defined the terms of the industry's transition – mandating open access to transmission lines, establishing a "real-time" information system on transmission availability and rates. These orders also set out a process for utilities to recover their stranded costs.

The Energy Policy Act of 1992 and subsequent FERC orders providing for more competition in wholesale markets resulted in a wave of mergers and acquisitions in the 1990s. Electric utilities were part of 42 mergers completed between 1997 and 2000.

The passage of the EP Act also led states which had historically high electricity rates, such as California, to investigate whether competitive deregulated markets would benefit consumers. In 1996, both California and Rhode Island became the first states to pass deregulation legislation giving consumers the right to choose their electricity supplier. By 2000, 24 states had passed laws ordering or allowing their investor-owned utilities to sell their power plants to other companies or transfer them to their own unregulated affiliates (Slocum 2008, 3–5; Richardson and Kelly 2005).

A series of traumatic shocks would deal a major blow to public confidence in electricity deregulation. Besides fraudulent behavior by corporate executives which culminated in Enron's bankruptcy and prison sentences, there was a dramatic increase in electricity prices in the first states that deregulated. California was especially hard hit when the average price went up from $30 a megawatt hour to $2,400 per megawatt hour in December 2002. There was considerable evidence in California and other deregulated states that power traders and deregulated generators were withholding low-cost power during peak periods and manipulating the bidding process to drive prices up. The most significant factor affecting public confidence in deregulation was the extraordinary increase in deregulated electric prices once temporary price caps were removed. Between 2002 and 2007 electricity prices in regulated states increased 19.4 percent, but for eight deregulated states the expiration of price caps brought about a price increase of 39.7 percent (Trebing 2008, 470–471; Wasserman 2001).

Despite the abuses and related problems that resulted from the partial appeal of the PUHCA, President George W. Bush signed into law the Energy Policy Act of 2005, which completely repealed the Public Utility Holding Company Act of 1935. The repeal removed the Securities and Exchange Commission as the main overseer of holding companies and in its place allowed FERC and state regulators greater access to the companies' books. Repeal also removed limitations on the types of combinations and ownership structures allowed. Companies are now free to propose mergers of geographically remote utilities and can pursue diversification strategies beyond those businesses related to the electric industry.

The American Public Power Association which represents the interest of the publicly owned utilities urged caution regarding PUHCA repeal. Providing regulators with increased access to holding company information, it believed, was a crucial step in mitigating the effects of PUHCA repeal, but it was by no means sufficient to guarantee effective consumer protection. Both state and federal regulators, it maintained, must develop the expertise to interpret the new, more complex company structures, and impose "ring-fencing requirements" and other protections for consumers where necessary. In addition, regulators must be more diligent in evaluating the costs and benefits of mergers and pay particular attention to the potential for increased market power.

As predicted, the repeal of this law has led to a new wave of mergers and consolidations in the U.S. utility industry, further concentrating ownership, and providing more opportunities to exercise market power and increasing the potential for market manipulation. The increasing numbers of affiliate relationships and large and complex corporate structures have also made it more difficult to monitor financial transactions between affiliates. More than 50 companies have merged in the past decade. In July 2012, Duke Energy completed its $32 billion merger with Progress Energy, creating the largest electric utility in the U.S.with

7.1 million customers in six states in the Southeast and Midwest (Thakar 2008, 916–920; Wald 2012; American Public Power Association 2013).

The American Public Power Association (APPA) continues to question whether wholesale market restructuring has met the intended goal of promoting competition in order to produce efficiencies and reduce costs to consumers. A comprehensive review by this agency and the Consumer Federation of America of the data and studies of the wholesale electricity market revealed that price disparities between restructured and traditionally regulated regions of the country have increased since restructuring started. Merchant generators have earned higher profits than their regulated counterparts. The APPA believes the electric industry needs to work together to develop a regulatory regime for the electricity market in RTO (Regional Transmission Organizations) regions that will benefit consumers, businesses, and the environment. The FERC first established RTOs to coordinate transmission systems and wholesale markets on a voluntary basis in 2000. Today, there are six ISOs (Independent System Operators) regulated by the FERC that meet its criteria laid out in Order No. 888. These cover 28 states. According to the APPA and other critics, the four fully functioning RTOs which are utilizing "single clearing price" auctions are driving prices up. The clearing price model pays the single highest price accepted to all suppliers regardless of their bids. This price is often set by high-priced, natural gas-fired generation. Plants that burn oil, coal, or use nuclear fuel get the same price and reap a windfall. A market-based "clearing price" may also include opportunity costs or be driven up as a result of wholesale suppliers having undue market power.

In 2009, the APPA developed a plan to reform the RTO-operated wholesale electricity market, called the Competitive Market Plan, which was updated in 2011. It recommends that the core beneficial RTO operations be continued, including centralized least-cost dispatch, transmission planning, and ensuring open access. The plan calls for the use of bilateral contracts for the procurement of energy and capacity. RTO energy and ancillary service markets would become residual markets used primarily to balance electricity supply and demand rather as the primary market for the procurement of energy (Ridley 2007, 18–23).

Benefits of public power and its challenges today

Today, there are 2,010 municipally owned utilities and public utility districts ranging in size from the City of Los Angeles to the tiny hamlet of Readesboro, Vermont, delivering electricity to 46 million U.S. consumers. They are run by elected or appointed boards of commissioners and serve as a "yardstick" for consumers and regulators to measure the performance and rates of private power companies. Historically, they have offered rates that were at least 30 percent lower than investor own utilities. Despite changes in the industry, they are still able to provide rates that average 14 percent less than those of private companies. Public systems can keep rates low, since they are not bound by the profit motive. Instead, they provide electricity as a non-profit service, emphasizing efficiency and minimizing growth. For private power companies, conservation and least-cost efforts are pursued to a small degree, but they are anathema to a business whose purpose is to grow, build, and maximize profits (Wasserman 2001; Richardson and Kelly 2005; American Public Power Association 2013).

In contrast to private utility systems, public power systems can give a community some democratic control over the kinds of growth and technologies it may want to pursue. In the best public systems local voters can approve or deny major investments. For example, ratepayers in Seattle, Washington turned down the request of the city's light department in 1975 to participate in several nuclear construction projects. The following year, the Energy 1990 study put together by a citizen oversight committee provided the plan for meeting future energy demand through energy efficiency and other least-cost initiatives. This plan which was adopted by the full Board of Directors put Seattle in the forefront in pursuing least-cost resource options. Since 1977, Seattle City Light has developed and implemented an array of conservation programs and policies to increase the efficiency of electricity use in homes and businesses. These programs have provided information and financial incentives to encourage customers to insulate their homes, and to install energy-efficient hot water tanks and energy efficient lights in commercial and industrial establishments. From 1977 through 2006, Seattle's residential conservation programs alone saved more than 7,410 GWh (Seattle City Light 2008).

Stiff citizen opposition in Austin, Texas was also behind that city council's vote to sell off its 16 percent ownership share of the South Texas Nuclear Project. This municipal utility is committed to meeting its future electrical needs through a Conservation Power Plan. It has used a portion of the money that was slated for a new coal-fired plant to hire and train teams of inspectors to evaluate energy usage in businesses, schools, apartment units, and homes. The energy inspectors found and repaired a wide variety of energy problems, including leaking duct work, inefficient lighting and appliances, poor insulation, and much more. Austin Energy provided rebates to its customers who upgraded their inefficient technologies (refrigerators, lighting, etc). Today, the City of Austin saves more than 700 megawatts of power each day, more than the output of one power plant. This exceeds the original power plant which would have provided 500 megawatts daily. Austin Energy is also a leader in promoting green energy sales. Ranked by renewable energy sales (KWh)/year), this municipal utility sold the largest amount of renewable energy in the nation through its voluntary green power program. The Sacramento Municipal Utility District has also made energy conservation and efficiency central to its mission. The National Energy Resource Organization presented its Energy Conservation Award to SMUD in 2004. SMUD has teamed up with its customers in an effort to offset 20 percent of the anticipated growth in energy demand over the next 10 years. It is also among the top five sellers of green energy in the U.S.A. (Richardson and Kelly 2005; National Renewable Energy Laboratory 2011; Seattle City Light 2008).

Vermont's largest city, Burlington, located on the eastern shore of Lake Champlain, has also been long recognized as a leader in energy efficiency. While

Burlington Electric (BED), the city's Municipal Light Department, first set up a water heater energy conservation program in early 1983, the idea of promoting energy efficiency really didn't take off until local citizens spoke out against BED buying hydro power from Canada. In the early 1990s Burlington became the first city in the nation to use municipal bonds to capitalize a comprehensive program in energy efficiency. Although BED is focused on its two largest customers, the University of Vermont and Fletcher-Allen, the largest medical center in the state, it has established a comprehensive program targeting opportunities for commercial customers of all sizes. BED has also been successful in incorporating energy efficiency into the heart of the city's development process. Historically, one of the most significant headaches for BED was its electrical heating load. The utility has finally decided to exit the market. At one time about 22 percent of its residential customers were using electric heat; now they are down to just 2 percent. This not only helped reduce peak load costs, but also worked in conjunction with other measures to curtail load growth. Electricity consumption in Burlington in 2011 was 4.7 percent lower than in 1989. During the same period, statewide use of electricity increased by 8.3 percent. BED is also focused on reducing the summer peak demand caused by air conditioning. Over the 2009 to 2011 program cycle, BED reduced summer coincident peak demand by 3,203 kW, about 4 percent greater than the utility's target (Barker 2013).

Publicly owned electric utilities have also invested in wind generation. One of the first projects was developed in Princeton, Massachusetts. The Princeton Municipal Light Department used public land near the town to build a 320 kW wind farm. The Municipal Light Department in Hull, Massachusetts has also been a leader in promoting wind power in this south shore community. According to the American Public Power Association, the public power community as a whole is well poised to increase its wind capacity in the coming years. As technology improvements drive down the cost of wind-generating equipment, any public power utilities will gain inexpensive access to wind resources. Depending on location, wind may become a valuable option for reducing publicly owned utility costs while providing reliable electricity supply to customers.

Overall, publicly owned electric utilities have a solid performance record with their focus on resource adequacy, lower prices, high reliability, and public accountability. But making the switch isn't easy and many attempts have failed under intense opposition from private power utilities. San Francisco tried to municipalize in 2002, but a $2 million campaign by Pacific Gas and Electric helped defeat the ballot initiative. Creating a new utility is a complicated, expensive endeavor that requires a city to buy the electric poles and wires, and often haggle over costs in drawn-out legal fights. In 2000, Las Cruces, N.M. gave up when the amount it owned its corporate utility for already-made local investments ballooned (American Public Power Association 2009; Rice 2011).

Still, over the past 30 years 72 new publicly owned utilities have been formed and over one million additional customers have been added. High rates, poor service, and lack of attention on the part of the private electric service providers have tended to be the most important motivating factors. The present trend began when residents of Massena, New York finally won their seven-year battle for economic independence from one of New York State's utility monopolies, Niagara Mohawk. Although local residents approved a referendum authorizing a municipal takeover in 1974, it was not until 1981 that they finally began receiving low-cost public power. Fearing that a positive vote would have a domino effect on nearby communities, Niagara Mohawk would spend over $2 million during the campaign to prevent the takeover. Numerous court battles ensued, first over the price to be paid, then over the private company's refusal to transmit the power that the town needed. The struggle waged by the residents of Massena, New York to take over part of Niagara Mohawk's distribution system and to acquire low-cost hydro power from the New York Power Authority has more than paid off. The municipal utility cut rates by 20 percent when it began operating in 1981. Today, customers of National Grid, the British company that acquired Niagara Mohawk Power Corporation in 2002, pay 10 to 14 cents per kWh for electricity. Massena customers pay just over 5 cents per kWh. Looking forward to the future, Massena hopes to win a federal license to build its own 2,500 kW hydroelectric project in the center of town. The 18-foot-high dam would replace an old dam that was breached 17 years ago (La Bella 2006).

Massena's success story has encouraged other communities to take control. In 1987, 10,000 customers in three California counties started receiving electric power from the new Lassen Municipal Utility District. This public system which was created after a November 1986 vote started off with a 50 percent rate reduction. In 1998 the Long Island Power Authority (LIPA) replaced the investor-owned Long Island Lighting Company in Nassau and Suffox Counties in New York. It reduced rates in one year by an average of 20 percent. Since then LIPA's customers have saved more than $2 billion and it is estimated that the rate cut has expanded the region's economy by some $12 billion. Even more important, it has built a strong base for the future by making Long Island competitive once again (La Bella 2006).

Today, the struggle to create public power systems continues. Pacific Gas and Electric Company (PG&E) stands to lose 40,000 customers to a public power district which says it can deliver electric service that's cheaper, more reliable, and more accountable to ratepayers than what the private utility currently offers. By a unanimous vote, the South San Joaquin Irrigation District Board (SSJID), a public utility agency, voted in September 2009 to approve an application to the San Joaquin Local Agency Formation Commission to provide electrical service to customers who are currently served by PG&E. The move came after years of careful planning and extensive studies. An economic study that was completed for SSJID concluded that switching from PG&E service to public power would save ratepayers $11.6 million annually, cash that would stay in the community rather than lining "the pockets of a private monopolistic utility" (Bowe 2009).

Citizens in Thurston County Washington State have also recently voted to establish a PUD. Their electricity is currently being supplied by Puget Sound Energy (PSE), a for-profit energy corporation, owned by the Australian investment firm Macquarie Group. PSE's rates are the highest in the State of Washington –

much more expensive than the surrounding counties which are getting their energy from PUDS. While PSE has already spent hundreds of thousands in a PR campaign to crush the initiative, the organizers remain optimistic that their efforts will pay off in the long run, since the PUD will not only mean lower electric rates and good jobs for local workers, but will also provide citizen control over local energy policy and keep millions of dollars of utility revenue locally, rather than leaving for a foreign-owned corporation (Thurston Public Power Initiative Executive Board 2012).

Other communities are using a softer approach to take control of their power supply. Community Choice Aggregation (CCA) lets communities buy energy from where they choose, while the privately owed utility continues to own and manage the power lines, removing much of the up-front costs of municipalization. The founders of the Cape Light Compact in Cape Cod, Massachusetts led the way in 1997 when they convinced the state legislature to include language in the Massachusetts Restructuring Act allowing community choice aggregation. The Compact was initially created in response to Cape Cod customers paying among the highest electricity rates in New England. Barnstable County Commissioners were concerned about the flow of energy-efficiency dollars collected by power companies. A 1994 study found that energy efficiency dollars collected from local ratepayers were leaving the area and being distributed elsewhere in the state. The study prompted the Commissioners to organize an energy committee with representatives from the county's 15 towns. Ultimately, all 15 towns directly lobbied the Department of Public Utilities to include language in the bill to allow community aggregation. It offered a way for Barnstable County to exercise more local control and allocate energy efficiency funds in ways that made sense for the county. The goals of founders which established the Cape Light Compact in 1997 included advancing the competitive power supply, improving energy-efficiency programs locally, and providing consumer advocacy. These goals are still part of the organization's mission with the pursuit of renewable energy and local generation becoming increasingly important in recent years (Smith *et al.* 2011, 3–6).

At least five other states have passed legislation allowing community choice aggregation: Ohio in 1999, Rhode Island and California in 2002, and New Jersey passed legislation in 2003. Illinois passed enabling legislation in 2009 and more than 200 communities in Illinois have approved electric aggregation. Chicago voters added the city to those ranks last November when they approved a ballot referendum authorizing the City Council to move forward with aggregation. The Chicago electric aggregation program focuses primarily on lowering electric rates for customers. It also banned coal from its generation mix under the contract with Integrys, recognizing that it could do so in the process of lowering prices.

In contrast, San Francisco is promoting renewable energy as its primary goal. The San Francisco program, called Clean PowerSF, has the potential to spur hundreds of megawatts of new renewable energy project development. It will offer customers 100 percent green power with an opt-out choice for customers who do not want to pay more for renewable energy (Seligman 2013; Peters and Smith 2012).

Looking ahead, it is not clear how many other states will pass enabling legislation to allow community choice aggregation. Aggregating electric loads could fall out of favor as investor-owned utilities face declining load growth and cheap natural gas, which is driving down wholesale and retail electricity rates.

In November 2011, the citizens of Boulder, Colorado took the critical first step on the path to creating a municipally owned utility for environmental reasons. The impetus is the climate action plan the city passed committing it to reducing its emissions in line with the Kyoto Protocol that the city signed in 2002. The city has made great strides in reducing energy consumption over the past decade, but is still falling short of its targets, in large part because it gets its electricity from Xcel which gets 60 percent of its power from coal and brought a new 700MW coal plant on line three years ago.

Extensive engineering and legal work will need to be done to determine how much it will cost to purchase the distribution system. A preliminary Boulder analysis put the cost of buying Xcel's assets and creating a new municipal utility at about $223 million. An Xcel consultant, Utilpoint, placed the cost at more than $1.2 billion. While it is far too soon to predict an outcome, Boulder is keeping its options open. A month after the election the city began exploring other paths to local control such as legalizing community choice aggregation in Colorado – and discussed using the support for public power as leverage to bring Xcel behind the effort (Barker 2012; Roberts 2013).

Closing thoughts

Public power is a system that carries its own set of problems. State-wide public power agencies such as the Washington Public Power Supply System and the Massachusetts Municipal Wholesale Electric Company had insulated themselves from public opinion and the democratic process. Many had investment portfolios, which with few exceptions consisted of huge shares in troubled nuclear plants such as Seabrook in New Hampshire or the four partially built reactors that were cancelled in Washington State.

The reform of existing public power systems and the creation of new ones, however, can provide the missing political and economic bridge for a transition to least-cost policies and use of decentralized, solar, wind, and other alternative technologies. It could also provide a model for democratization and reform in other countries where public power systems are run by national governments and are often unresponsive to local residents. The best options are local non-profit municipal systems and rural cooperatives run by elected officials and employee representatives with an open-door policy on information and voter control over investment in major programs and projects. To ensure greater democratic control, annual neighborhood assemblies should be held to allow local residents an opportunity to meet their light commissioners, learn about policies, and bring new initiatives and suggestions. In larger cities, an ombudsperson should be appointed to collect and convey concerns of electric users.

Consumer control establishes the essential economic cornerstone upon which everything rests – electricity as a non-profit service. The political and business structure that rises from this foundation allows a process in which debate over development options can occur, with local people weighing social, economic, and environmental costs against the need for new power plants, conservation, or other alternatives.

The battles currently being waged to create new public power systems reveal how surprisingly little has changed over the past 125 years in the development of the power industry and how the ruthlessness for the control of electricity by private companies is still at the heart of the issue.

References

American Public Power Association. 2005. "The Electric Utility Industry after PUHCA Repeal: What Happens Next?" Washington, DC: American Public Power Association. Available online at: www.publicpower.org/files/PDFs/APPAreportAfterPUHCA-Repeal.pdf.

American Public Power Association. 2009. *2009 Wind Power Annual Report*. Washington, DC: American Public Power Association. Available online at: www.publicpower.org/files/PDFs/APPA2009WindAnnualReport.pdf.

American Public Power Association. 2013a. "Compilation of Investor-owned Utility Transactions – Mergers and Major Acquisitions." American Public Power Association website. Available online at: www.publicpower.org/About/content.cfm?Item Number=2729.

American Public Power Association. 2013b. "Q & A for Communities Considering the PublicPower Option." American Public Power Association website. Available online at: www.publicpower.org/files/PDFs/Forming%5FQA%5F2013.pdf.

Barker, Brent. 2012. "Boulder Explores the Path to Municipalization." *Public Power* 70(4): 14–21. Available online at: www.publicpower.org/Media/magazine/Article-Detail.cfm?ItemNumber=35176.

Barker, Brent. 2013. "Efficiency Infrastructure." *Public Power* 71(2): 24–27. Available online at: www.publicpower.org/Media/magazine/ArticleDetail.cfm?ItemNumber =36466.

Bowe, Rebecca. 2009. "Public Power Fights Back." *San Francisco Bay Guardian Online*, September 9. Available online at: www.sfbg.com/politics/2009/09/04/public-power-fights-back.

Hampton, Howard, and Bill Reno. 2003. *Public Power: The Fight for Publicly Owned Electricity*. Toronto, ONT: Insomniac Press.

La Bella, Jeanne. 2006. "New York Anniversaries." *Public Power* 64(November–December). Available online at: www.publicpower.org/Media/magazine/ArticleDetail.cfm?ItemNumber=17876.

National Renewable Energy Laboratory. 2011. "NREL Highlights 2010 Utility Green Power Leaders: New, Innovative Community Programs Support Local Power Generation." News release on National Renewable Energy Laboratory website, May 9. Available online at: www.nrel.gov/news/press/2011/1367.html.

PBS. n.d. "Regulation: Public vs. Private Power: From FDR to Today." *Frontline*. Available online at: www.pbs.org/wgbh/pages/frontline/shows/blackout/regulation/timeline.html.

Peters, Mark, and Rebecca Smith. 2012. "U.S. News: Cities Take on Utility Role: Chicago and Other Communities Buy Cheaper, Often Cleaner Energy for Residents." *Wall Street Journal*, November 11. Available online at: http://online.wsj.com/news/articles/SB10001424052970204707104578095323990799636.

Radin, A. 2003. *Public Power – Private Life: A Memoir and History of Public Power in the Twentieth Century*. Washington, DC: American Public Power Association.

Rice, Nathan. 2011. "Boulder, Colo., Votes for Energy Independence – from its Utility." *High Country News*, December 26. Available online at: www.hcn.org/issues/43.22/boulder-colo-votes-for-energy-independence-from-its-corporate-utility.

Richardson, Alan, and John Kelly. 2005. "Relevance and Importance of Public Power in the United States." *Natural Resources and Environment* 19(3): 54–59. Available online at: www.publicpower.org/files/PDFs/bararticle.pdf.

Ridley, Scott. 2007. *Decade of Upheaval: U.S. Electricity Markets in Transition, 1997–2006.* Washington, DC: American Public Power Association.

Roberts, David. 2013. "Energy Localism Update: Boulder, Colo., Wants to Take Control of its Own Power." Grist website, January 8. Available online at: http://grist.org/climate-energy/energy-localism-update-boulder-colo-wants-to-take-control-of-its-own-power/.

Rudolph, Richard, and Scott Ridley. 1986. *Power Struggle: The Hundred-year War over Electricity*. New York: Harper & Row.

Seattle City Light. 2008. "2008–2012 Action Plan: Building a World-class Conservation Power Plant: One Customer at a Time." Seattle: Conservation Resources Division, Seattle City Government. Available online at: www.seattle.gov/light/conserve/docs/Conservation_5_Year_Action_Plan.pdf.

Seligman, Jake. 2013. "Electric Aggregation: The Next Boost for Renewables?" *Lexology*, February 1. Available online at: www.lexology.com/library/detail.aspx?g=a4f51b5b-3000-44e5-95ee-1f666723990b.

Slocum, Tyson. 2008. "The Failure of Electricity Deregulation: History, Status and Needed Reforms." Public Citizen's Energy Program. Available online at: www.citizen.org/documents/USdereg.pdf.

Smith, Lisa, Madaleine Sorkin, and Ryder Reddick. 2011. "Cape Light Compact: A Case Study of Energy Transition." Case Paper. Available online at: University of Colorado-Denver. http://cudenverenergystudio.weebly.com/uploads/7/3/1/3/7313776/clc_final_paper.pdf.

Thakar, Nidhi. 2008. "The Urge to Merge: A Look at the Repeal of the Public Utility Holding Company Act of 1935." *Lewis and Clark Law Review* 12(3): 903–942. Available online at: http://law.lclark.edu/live/files/9522-lcb123art11thakar.pdf.

Thurston Public Power Initiative Executive Board. 2012. "Thanks Thurston County, We Appreciate Your Support! – A Message from our Executive Board." Thurston Public Power Initiative Facebook Page, November 16. Available online at: www.facebook.com/notes/thurston-public-power-initiative/thanks-thurston-county-we-appreciate-your-support-a-message-from-our-executive-b/496532603713726.

Trebing, Harry M. 2008. "A Critical Assessment of Electricity and Natural Gas Deregulation." *Journal of Economic Issues* 42(2): 469–477. Available online at: www.jstor.org/stable/25511332.

Wald, Matthew L. 2012. "Duke and Progress Energy Become Largest U.S. Utility." *New York Times*, July 3. Available online at: www.nytimes.com/2012/07/04/business/energy-environment/duke-energy-merger-creates-largest-us-utility.html?_r=0.

Wasserman, Harvey. 2001. "Power Struggle: California's Engineered Energy Crisis and the Potential of Public Power." *Multinational Monitor* 22(6): 9–20. Available online at: www.multinationalmonitor.org/mm2001/062001/wasserman.html.

8 Workers' cooperatives in Italy

Between solidarity and autocratic centralism

Devi Sacchetto and Marco Semenzin

Prologue

On March 22, 2013 a strike paralyzed several logistical hubs in northern Italy. It was only one of many episodes in the continual struggle of the transport and warehouse workers. Most of these workers were immigrants, employed through work cooperatives: a situation that has developed over the past 10 years or so. One of the most important protests in recent years was the one that took place in the logistical hub of Piacenza, in the middle in the northern Italy, an area where a large part of the Italian industrial production system is based. The city has a population of around 100,000 inhabitants and is part of the Emilia Romagna region, which up until 1989 was governed by the Communist Party and subsequently by the Party's successors.[1] It is precisely in this region where an important part of the Italian Cooperative movement developed (Earle 1986; Corcoran and Wilson 2010). On the outskirts of Piacenza, since 2000, a logistical center for transport and storage companies has developed: a real nerve center for the flow of goods to and from Northern Europe. Contrary to the claim of mainstream economic theories, this area is important, as multinationals need somewhere to produce and distribute their products (Sassen 2001). In total, around 1,400 companies (and cooperatives), both Italian and foreign multinationals, operate in this area, including DHL, TNT, General Logistics Systems (GLS),[2] Bartolini, Ikea, Amazon, and Whirpool. These companies are mainly involved in the transport and shipment of goods and employ around 3,000 people in total.

The first significant protest at Piacenza started in the summer of 2011 when the workers, almost all immigrants employed in cooperatives subcontracted to TNT, downed tools due to low wages, high pace of work, and a lack of rights.[3] The traditional trade union with its policies and attitudes kept them on hold. But the strike of the TNT cooperatives actually succeeded, as the workers managed to obtain a national labor contract, wage increases, and holiday and sick pay. This strike also inspired other protests, by those who worked for the cooperatives subcontracting to GLS, Antonio Ferrari, Bartolini, and Ikea. The most important protest took place at the Ikea warehouse in 2012. Cooperative workers, mostly North African migrants, asked for better wages, a lower pace of work, and a regular labor contract. Workers went on strike and sat down in front of the Ikea warehouse, but the police beat them and broke up their picket-line. After some months of struggle and demonstrations in front of Ikea shopping centers in other parts of Italy, workers managed to obtain better working conditions.[4] This successful protest was also made possible due to it spreading through internal communication channels, mainly in North African immigrant communities, strengthened by their own background of ongoing political change in their countries of origin.

At the same time the migrant workers were also very familiar with the production cycle, and therefore were able to strike or to put in place action in a way that wage losses were minimized while losses to the company were maximized. They met rank-and-file trade unionists, the so called SI Cobas, and other groups of activists that supported their protests. Cooperative migrant workers had to face the fact that all cooperatives, companies, and institutions operate hand in glove with the subcontractual system. Companies usually subcontract large parts of the production cycle to cooperatives, while public institutions look for "social harmony" to manage the growth of the local economy. In some cases institutions, cooperatives, and trade unions are strongly linked to each other due to similar political and ideological positions.

Migrant workers are looking for a new type of trade union because they consider that traditional unions are acting only as a "service agency" for migrant needs, such as the renewal of the permits to stay and family reunion. In fact, traditional trade unions are often engaged with the negotiation and protection of jobs, while trying to reach a consensus in management decisions. It is not surprising that workers want to get rid of the system of cooperatives and subcontracting because they think that "It's better to deal directly with the company."[5] However, it does not seem that these events have provoked any particular repercussions or second thoughts within the Italian cooperative movement as a whole, as these cooperatives were considered to not fully embrace the fundamental principles of traditional cooperation. In actual fact, the Italian cooperative movement has diverged considerably from its initial ideals. In this chapter the history of the Italian cooperative movement is discussed and the main characteristics of the present-day movement are analyzed.

The expansion of the cooperative movement (1854–1945)

The Italian cooperative movement started in the mid-1800s during a period when the working class suffered from terrible conditions, such as low wages, long working hours, and wide regional differences. The first cooperatives came about as instruments of self-defense by the working class, not only against the individual entrepreneurs, but also to avoid emigration. The success of the cooperatives was measured by the low rate of emigration in some areas, particularly in Emilia Romagna, while in southern Italy the expansion of cooperatives was limited, mainly due to the retention of land and public resources by landowners (Merli 1984).

The worker cooperative movement was interwoven with the mutual aid societies that were present mainly in northwest Italy. A worker cooperative is a firm membership where each member holds equal rights. The cooperatives are controlled by its members, who are the workers. This form of self-help gave rise to the first cooperatives that aimed to help workers to gain greater purchasing power for their own benefit (Zangheri 1987, 14).[6] By the end of the nineteenth century production and credit cooperatives were also formed by artisans and small independent farmers. Some, particularly the production cooperatives, came about as a result of worker's strikes, while others were established to help stop small-scale farmers finishing up in the hands of money lenders and loan sharks, and others were established by sectors of the Italian ruling classes. However, all these cooperatives were rather small with only tens or at the most hundreds of members, and had a strong local basis.

Toward the end of the 1800s, cooperatives of farm laborers and construction workers became established, particularly in northeast Italy, and were made up of day workers. If in some areas the working class emigrated *en masse* (Gabaccia 2003), in other areas they organized themselves into cooperatives, and with the support of left-leaning political parties tendered for public works. The members of these cooperatives were often "casual workers subject to chronic unemployment" who tried through the cooperatives, but also through unionistic strategies, to further their own interests and well-being. Some cooperatives which had won contracts far from their area of influence employed non-member workers, but paid them above the national average wage (Zangheri 1987, 113). Bank credit was given to cooperatives within local communities on the basis of mutual trust.

From the beginning of the mid-nineteenth century until at least World War II (1939–1945), the Italian cooperative movement embraced three different political ideologies. The first one considered the cooperatives as a way of developing an "association of free producers" in order to overcome, as preached by republican and anti-Marxist Giuseppe Mazzini, the contradictions between capital and labor. The second one was of a socialist leaning and saw cooperatives as a way of defending and organizing the working class. The third involved a section of the liberal upper classes who tried to support some forms of cooperatives in order to reaffirm their position in Italian society (Degl'Innocenti 1981, 5).

In 1886 the mutual society movement was legally recognized (Verruccoli 1979) and the first Conference of Italian Cooperatives was held. Almost all those who participated were from northern Italy and the discussions revolved around practical issues and future direction, while keeping the aforementioned different political viewpoints well in the background. The first conference decided to establish a National Federation (later renamed Lega co-op) which was initially held "in the hands of liberal bourgeoisies, democrats, and to a small degree, republicans" (Zangheri 1987, 75, 83). It had to deal immediately with the Italian workers' movement, since to overcome political divisions any connotation of class had to be avoided (Fabbri 1979, 33).[7]

The contribution of socialists to the development of Lega co-op became significant in the last decades of the nineteenth century, even though many of the Socialist Party leaders took on board the critical ideas of Karl Kautsky (1978) which shed light on how the cooperatives had a tendency to become capitalist enterprises (Fabbri 1979, 28). On the other hand, particularly following the publication in 1891 by Pope Leo XIII of the encyclical "Rerum Novarum," which the Catholics consider to be the Church's modern cornerstone of their social doctrine, promoted a strong cooperative movement in areas where they were strongly rooted.

The early years of the twentieth century up until World War I marked a revival of the cooperatives due to political changes wrought by the Italian political powers seeking to bring the proletariat back to a conciliatory attitude to the reigning monarchy and its government. During the Giolitti period (1904–1912) legislative proposals appeared to be favorable to cooperatives: the minimum number of members was set at nine and the principle of an "open door" was established, so that anyone could join a cooperative. The number of cooperatives started to expand as worker movements began to win government contracts.

In 1902 the cooperative movement embraced a total of 2,199 companies and 567,450 employees (Fabbri 1979, 45; Galasso 1987, 282). This dramatic increase was due to a change in leadership of the Socialist Party, which began to advocate reform and to take on board ideas promoted by the German social democrat Eduard Bernstein (1968) regarding the strengthening of the relationship between labor and capital.

The gap that had developed between the Socialist and Catholic cooperatives deepened. The objective of the Catholic cooperatives was to spread throughout the rural areas by creating banks and small farm owners' cooperatives. This move led to the creation of the Federation of Catholic agricultural cooperatives in 1898 (Zamagni and Zamagni 2008). In any case, the cooperative movement had gained the approval of the trade unions and could rely both on the banks to obtain loans and on the government to obtain subcontracts in order to build infrastructure. On the other hand, in 1910, the Second International and the Italian Socialist Party stated that the cooperative, now boasting more than a million members, was an indispensable means of defense and organization of the working class.

The radicalization of the Italian workers' struggles in the years immediately preceding World War I forced the Lega co-op to pull back. The emergence of Catholic cooperatives and tensions related to World War I changed the attitude of the movement from a neutral position to that of supporting openly the warmongering government and the monarchy who had the intention to intervene in World War I (Colarizi 2000, 66–69; Galasso 1987, 362). During the War, the cooperatives were strengthened due to military production and consumer cooperatives. Cooperatives were also used by the government to moderate prices and avoid speculation. The war economy was strongly supported by a section of the cooperatives, which also colluded with forms of speculation and profiteering by some cooperative managers (Fabbri 1979, 78).

Soon after World War I, the Socialist Party and the trade unions gave their support to the Lega co-op and brought about a "social" turning point. In 1919, the Confcooperative of a Catholic orientation was re-founded. But the workers' struggles that developed in particular throughout the so-called red biennium (1919–1920) frightened even the leaders of the cooperative movement who preferred to maintain a line of cooperation between capital and labor. In addition, Antonio Gramsci in the 1920s criticized the cooperative movement for holding back the struggle of the labor movement (1971, 145–149).

After hitting its highest point in 1922 with 8,000 associated cooperatives and two million members, the spread of violent fascist offensives, with the support of landowners, greatly imperilled the cooperative movement, while the authorities ignored fascist aggressions. The weight gained by the cooperatives was then directly attacked by the fascists and, after an initial destructive phase that particularly hit those inclined toward the Left, they were all absorbed into the so-called National Fascist Cooperative Body (1926). In fact, the aim of the fascists was not annihilation: the control of the cooperatives enabled them to bend even more to the fascist corporative system (Galasso 1987, 463). The period of fascism (1922–1943) saw a sharp slowdown in the spheres of production and consumption while the agro-industrial cooperatives expanded as they were required by the autarchic policy of the regime.

Fascism attempted to expel the Socialistic and Catholic social traits from the cooperatives (Ianes 2011), while some of the most prestigious leaders of the cooperatives immediately offered their technical experience to the dictatorship. Fascism used the "association instrument" to build "an ideological continuity with the past cooperation" and to enhance those elements designed to unite the interests of workers and employers (Fabbri 1979, 109). The fascist cooperatives would become fervent supporters, even in the wars that Italy was to launch against Ethiopia (1935) and Republican Spain (1936–1939). The continuity of management of cooperatives during fascism was an influential factor in the rapid reorganization of the movement after World War II, due to the fact that in 1945 at the fall of fascism there were 12,000 cooperatives with three million members (Zamagni and Zamagni 2008). Therefore, at the fall of fascism in 1943 to 1945 the cooperative movement was made up of a huge apparatus variously articulated throughout Italy. In fact, during the war of national liberation against fascism, some cooperatives provided a basis for the Italian partisan movement.

From the economic reconstruction to the workers' struggle (1945–1980)

After World War II the cooperative movement became an ideological arena in which both the left-wing parties (socialist and communist) and the Catholic political party sought to control and influence politically. The attempt to unite the two major cooperatives failed miserably due to the beginning of the Cold War. In 1945 the two bodies were re-established as the *Lega nazionale delle Cooperative e mutue* (National League of cooperatives, renamed Legacoop) which was of a socialist and communist leaning and the *Confedera zione Cooperativa italiana* (Italian Confederation of cooperative, renamed Confcooperative) supported by the Catholic movement.[8] Those political parties linked to cooperatives asked them to act as a “driving force.” In a euphoric spirit new cooperatives started operating (Ianes 2011) and new memberships at national level spread due to an internal reorganization of production.

The 20 years following World War II (1951–1971) were a time of rapid economic development for the Italian economy, but of stagnation for the cooperatives. Economic growth was based on capital-intensive sectors and cooperatives remained anchored to a defense of the working class with scarce funds (Battilani 2009). During these years the cooperatives, particularly those related to the Socialist Party (PSI) and the Communist Party (PCI), were an expression of the solidarity of the day laborers, construction workers, and more generally of the workers against the uncertainties of unemployment and the misbehavior of the owners, and social isolation. The outlook of these workers was bleak and the idea of a radical political change progressively disappeared (Fornasari and Zamagni 1997, 148). Catholic cooperatives instead developed, particularly among smallholding farmers, artisans, and some segments of the middle class, thanks to the rural and artisan banks.

As early as the mid-1950s, the Communist Party Congress (1956) and later the Congress of Legacoop (1958) marked a turning point in the cooperative movement. The centrality of working-class ideas decreased in favor of an alliance with the middle class through a reformism that could embrace the so-called “enterprise culture.” The aim of the Communist Party leaders was to promote cooperation as the “third sector” of the Italian economy, after the public and private enterprises, through a coordinated system of cooperatives. This purpose had to face, with the lack of preparation of the managers, an absence of coordination between economic sectors and a strong localism (Fabbri 2011). The priority of the Communist Party from the 1950s to 1970s was to develop a trade union subordinate to their directives and a cooperative movement that could also support the Party economically (Zamagni and Felice 2006). A strong link to the parties still characterizes the cooperatives, although, as will be seen below, the balance of power has gradually tipped toward large cooperatives.

The workers’ struggle that characterized the late 1960s and which continued in Italy into the 1970s, on the one hand, limited the forms of cooperative that were a mere exploitation of the workforce, but, on the other, ensured that the cooperative movement took an upturn and grew strongly in the wake of more parliamentary votes of the left-wing parties. Cooperation proposed itself as a “valuable resource” and a “real force” in order to overcome the economic crisis: Legacoop increased from two million members and 7,500 companies in 1973 to four million members and 15,000 companies in 1987 (Fabbri 2011).[9] The defeat of the working class in the late 1970s substantially modified the cooperative system that sought to enter the market and open up to meritocracy in order to express their constituent values in a non-punitive way regarding private enterprise. Many cooperatives in the service sector created in these years lacked a background of struggle and political militancy, and some trade unionists believed that "Cooperatives were masters who exploited the workers democratically" (Menzani 2008, 388).

During the 1980s, the expansion of the cooperative movement occurred in retail but above all in providing labor to the private and public sector services through the practice of contracts and subcontracts where the "lowest bid" was accepted. The system of outsourcing supported by private companies and public administration aimed to reduce the core of direct workers, but also to cut costs by subcontracting in order to reduce wages, while lowering the quality of services. The subcontracting system has produced both the expansion and a significant turnover in the cooperatives that had won the subcontracts. These elements accelerate the detachment of values between members and managers of cooperatives. The relationship between the member and the cooperative, in which the former is the owner of the latter, is deteriorating, and in some communist-oriented cooperatives the word "comrade" is no longer heard. As Vittorio Rieser (2006) reminds us, in the early 1980s in areas of Emilia Romagna, where the presence of cooperatives had been most prolific, workers feared that by voting for the Communist Party the model of cooperatives would spread. Meanwhile, the organization of the cooperative movement occurred through three processes: (1) training and self-training of managers thanks to courses related to their work; (2) hiring experts that could compensate for the lack of internal know-how; (3) use of external consultants to optimize business mechanisms in order to gain greater efficiency.

In the following two sections of this chapter, the development of the cooperative movement in the past two decades will be analyzed. First, light will be shed on how cooperatives have been involved in an ideological renewal that led them to change their structure in favor of both increasing in size and the construction of large cooperative groups, and the subsequent expansion of the movement into other fields, such as the health and care sectors. Second, the changes in the internal management of cooperatives will be considered, namely in terms of labor relations and social and working conditions.

Growing inside and outside national borders

The fall of the communist regimes linked to the Soviet Union caused a profound change both in the Italian political system and in the Italian cooperative movement. From the early 1990s the role of the cooperative as a "driving force" in favor of the political parties ended. The cooperatives turned from any political ideology and started a seemingly unstoppable process of growth in terms of assets and size.[10] Some cooperatives became joint stock companies in order to gain access to both the capital and the stock market, adopting a more businesslike approach. In the early 1990s the corruption scandal involving certain Italian left-wing politicians accepting bribes (the so-called Tangentopoli) accelerated this process of large-scale change in the relationship between cooperatives and political parties. In 1992 Giancarlo Pasquini, President of Legacoop, stated that "the mechanism of "driving force, as well as any type of relationship between the cooperatives and the [Communist] Party was well and truly dead and buried" (Fabbri 2011, 253). This break allowed the definitive transformation of cooperatives into "businesses," in accordance with Pasquini's words: "Enough with ideologies. Last century Mazzini [the anti-Marxist republican] stated that labor and capital must be in the same hands. We have the same policy" (Biondi and Campesato 2002, 20). The cooperative movement then moved toward a more liberal footing, making the benefits of a cooperative available also to non-members. The concept of external mutual aid, already present in the past, was thus restored.[11]

In the 1990s (1991–2001), the advantages of generous tax breaks for cooperatives and the favorable attitude of the unions led to further growth in the cooperative movement: the number of cooperatives grew by about 50 percent, while employment increased by 41 percent compared to a national average of 7.8 percent (Zamagni and Zamagni 2008). In 2001, the cooperatives represented 1.2 percent of active companies and employed 5 percent of the total Italian workforce (Ianes 2011, 73–74). The expansion in size of both Catholic and left-wing cooperatives brought about a change in the relationship with political parties and the trade unions, which at the same time were affected by a severe crisis of legitimacy. The relationship between the unions, the cooperative movement, and political parties has never been smooth or peaceful. While, up until the 1970s the cooperative movement funded and supported the parties in order to obtain favorable legislation, in the following period the interdependence and mutual conditioning became restricted to the leaders. This system of alliances, in fact, created a protected market in favor of those cooperatives that managed to enjoy a close relationship with local administrators or, better, with politicians of the government. On the other hand, it is not surprising that the unions often found themselves under pressure from the large cooperatives in the non-conflictual management of a workforce that enjoyed less and less the fruits of cooperative work and participated only passively in meetings. It is no coincidence that the unrest among the cooperative workers has increased in the past 15 years. An important component of these conflicts has been supported by migrant workers with the help of certain rank-and-file trade unions.

The increase in the business-style management of cooperatives has ensured a growth and transformation from small to medium- to large-sized structures. In 2010, cooperatives with more than 250 staff counted for 36.2 percent of the total amount employed in such organizations (Censis 2012, 11). The form of "cooperative groups," a mix of cooperatives and traditional enterprises, has become increasingly important. This creates "group structures in which a cooperative controls different companies" even to the point where limited companies are included (Bentivogli and Viviano 2012, 514–521). This large-scale form of cooperative has become an aggregate and acts as a coordinator of small and medium-sized enterprises and cooperatives, particularly in the sectors of logistics, large retail, construction, and agriculture (Menzani and Zamagni 2010). The complex financial and social structure has transformed cooperatives into companies that control other businesses.[12] The aim of mutual aid disappears in the face of business reasoning because the relationship is more binding and hierarchical in a cooperative group, and the relationship between co-members and non-co-members is often difficult (Battilani 2009). The increased organizational complexity, differentiation in the legal forms of organization members, and, finally, the increased weight of the business style of management, highlight problems for democratic governance.

In the past 20 years, cooperatives have grown due to the progressive involvement in other companies in order to both dominate certain sectors (i.e., logistics, social services, large retail) and to develop a more articulate presence in the market. The rhetoric which accompanied this important transformation was that only big cooperatives could survive in the global market.[13] The setting up of cooperative groups would be driven by: the need for growth and export to foreign markets; the management of the risk involved in innovation; the entry into an economic sector in which the cooperative has little experience, and the strengthening of the financial viewpoint (Legacoop 2009).

The consortia of cooperatives has become progressively multinational, even though they are relatively small, compared to the international level. They have developed stable and permanent relationships with the institutions which impact Italian politics, though not always to the benefit of their members, but more for the expansion of the business. One of the noteworthy factors of this transformation was undoubtedly the creation, by Legacoop and Confcooperative, of the company Obiettivo Lavoro, a temporary work agency (TWA). Obiettivo Lavoro started only one month after the approval of the law (June 24, 1997, no. 196) that permitted private work agencies to enter the Italian labor market. Obiettivo Lavoro is the third largest temporary work agency in Italy after Manpower and Adecco, and in 2010 it had a turnover of 357 million euro, nearly 700 direct employees, and a total of 90,000 temporary workers. It also has a presence in Romania (three branches), Poland (two branches), Brazil (one branch), and Peru and Bolivia (six branches in total).[14]

From 2000 to 2010 the size of the cooperative companies was on average significantly higher than that of other companies, while productivity was lower. Neverthless, thanks to the low cost of labor the profit margins did not significantly were affected (Bentivogli and Viviano 2012). The Italian cooperatives are concentrated in the labor-intensive sectors, where the skills of workers, members, or just the waged are essential. They are characterized by a specialization in the Italian market with very little inclination to export.

The structure of the Italian cooperative movement allows it to not only stand up to the international economic crisis, but it seems actually to benefit from it. From this point of view, Giuliano Poletti, President of Legacoop, could easily state that cooperation in fact "represents a resource to overcome the crisis and a business model to be copied in order to re-launch the country's economy."[15] In fact, between 2001 and 2011, the number of cooperatives increased by more than 14 percent, giving a total of nearly 80,000, with an increase of 7.8 percent even during the most recent economic crisis years (2007–2011). Cooperatives have thus guaranteed the maintenance of employment levels: between 2007 and 2011 the workforce of cooperatives increased by 8 per cent to 1.3 million and currently represents 7.2 percent of all employees in Italy (Censis 2012, 7–9).

The distribution of cooperatives throughout Italy is not uniform, reflecting a typical economic dualism. In the south, the cooperatives were mainly established in the period 1970 to 1980, as they took advantage of the aid provided by the government to this area with funds for the development of the south (Cuomo 2010). In this part of Italy the cooperatives' members have a lower turnover than in the north, mainly due to their small size and family-based recruitment.[16] In any case, it is in the more industrialized northern Italy that employment in cooperatives is at its highest, particularly in Emilia Romagna, Lombardy, and Veneto: areas that together count for 44 percent of all employees (Censis 2012).

The expansion of the cooperative movement in the course of recent years is due to several factors, including the cost of labor and the tax breaks provided for non-profit companies. In contrast to the stagnation of the Italian economy, the setting up of new cooperatives seems unstoppable: more than half of the existing cooperatives were created between 1998 and 2007, while 5,000 new cooperatives were founded in 2008. The increase in the number of cooperatives and employees has occurred in sectors where the workforce is a strategic factor (Borzaga 2011, 12–15). In fact, cooperatives, while representing a small part of the Italian productive system, prevail in areas such as logistics, large retail, construction, and personal and company services.[17] As many as 49.7 percent of all those employed in the health and social care sector in Italy work in cooperatives: 24 percent in transportation and storage, and 15.7 percent in business services (Censis 2012: 15). These three sectors, which count for almost two-thirds of the total number of cooperative employees, have developed efficiently, although with heavy human costs, over the past 20 years due to a substantial fragmentation of the production cycle and the expansion of large cooperatives.

The Italian cooperatives were established both in areas in which other capitalistic businesses operated, and where welfare services had been contracted out (Napolitano 2010). The left-wing cooperative businesses tend to be more prolific in the construction, transport, and industrial sectors, whereas the Catholic sector has its monopoly in health care, due to its winning subcontracts from public administration.

In 2011, the cooperatives searched for a new synthesis, perhaps also due to changes in the political system. The three pillars of the cooperative movement, the Social Communist-inspired Legacoop, the Catholic-inspired Confcooperative, and the Agci of liberal and republican ideas came together in the "Alliance of the Italian cooperatives." The aim was to unite the three main cooperatives: in 2010 the Alliance had a collective turnover of 140 billion Euros (equivalent to 7 percent of the Italian GDP) from 43,000 companies with more than 12 million members and about 1.3 million employees in total. The "Alliance of the Italian cooperatives" represents about 90 percent of the Italian cooperatives.[18]

Management models and working conditions in the enterprise cooperative

The transformations that have taken place during the past two decades seem to have produced two major segments in the cooperative movement. The first segment is that of larger cooperatives that work in accordance with a relatively convergent model with respect to capitalist companies, and that increasingly use networks where strong elements of rationalization and efficiency are promoted (Menzani and Zamagni 2010). The second segment consists of small cooperatives that show unrelated working practices: cooperatives with high solidarity values[19] as well as cooperatives where workers are working in what amounts to sweatshops.

In the 2000s, the need for trust, transparency, and good management prompted the cooperative movement to adopt regulations in which the concept of ethics and corporate social responsibility was well developed: something that was also happening in the private companies. The leaning toward the company-oriented model became established, in the large groups in particular, requiring the cooperative movement to exchange its good name regarding mutualism and direct participation for management strategies in order to fit into the market.[20]

While cooperatives are characterized by the strong ideology of "participation," the control of the decisions and strategic choices remains in the hands of the top managers. The broadening of cooperatives caused their members to be estranged and a severing of the strong ties with the cooperative managers (Holmström 1989).[21] The experiences of managers and employees of cooperatives differ, particularly in the large cooperatives, regarding the ways in which participation and solidarity are built and internal democracy is established. On the other hand, in small and medium-sized cooperatives that are not directly connected to the world of illegal hiring and to the mere exploitation of the workforce, top managers and workers often share the same experience.

The relationship between the member and the cooperative has changed, thus penalizing the elements of solidarity and participation in favor of a businesslike approach. The number of workers who believe that they lack information regarding decision-making within the cooperative is not insignificant. The space for participation in the cooperative is progressively reduced and transformed into simple communication of information without any real debate.[22] In many cooperatives the "social life" is limited to only one annual meeting, when the budget is approved, and when the profits (giveback) to be distributed among the members and the remuneration of the executives are set out. The meeting is usually of a formal nature: little information is given, decisions are taken, and the election of the board of cooperative which will manage the company for the next period is elected (Censis 2012, 95–96).

During such meetings the members, especially those of cooperatives with hundreds or thousands of partners, realize their own powerlessness against the executives who manage all the operations by laying down the tasks for everyone, selecting the personnel and deciding on their own remuneration. The development of an internal functional hierarchy causes an estrangement of members from the decision-making process that is actually the prerogative of a few managers, thus resulting in the development of a way of thinking similar to that of private companies; also because in large cooperatives there is a huge difference in the wage between workers and managers. In the large cooperatives the worker members struggle to rebuild less autocratic hierarchical levels.[23]

On the other hand, the cooperative movement is no longer based only on its members, as cooperatives also hire workers who are not members. External workers now constitute a substantial part of all employees: 42 percent of workers in cooperatives are not in fact members but only waged.[24] In large cooperatives workers have extremely diversified contracts, while the selection of workforce is carried out through specialized companies that aim to exclude those who are unionized (Frau 2010, 154).

In the cooperatives some workers do experience extreme frustration, as it is impossible for them to discuss their work situation. In some "old" cooperatives industrial relations are often better than in private companies, but workers have decreased collective bargaining power and are unable to contrast the segmentation of workforce inside the place of work. In fact, a significant proportion of workers in cooperatives are effectively excluded from becoming members, as admission can be very expensive: up to €15,000 (i.e., the wage for one year), a figure which creates disparity and which excludes migrant workers in particular.

The member worker of the cooperative is one of the most ambiguous employees in Italian employment, as he or she remains formally unrelated to what is distinctive of the typical workers and therefore, at least in part, is outside any legislation regarding unemployment benefits. Italian and migrant workers often try to find a job in a cooperative because it is usually easier than in a firm or in a public body. In the past 10 years some cooperatives have become a sort of intermediary for companies. At the same time, for migrant workers, working in a cooperative allows them to obtain or renew their permit to stay: in fact the legislation for migrants in Italy links the permit to a regular labor contract. On the other hand, for Italian workers, cooperatives present the easiest way to gain employment in the health and social services sector, because public bodies often prefer not to hire directly.

In a time of Italian workers' movement crisis, the member worker becomes a tool to weaken the bargaining power of the workforce. It is a situation that becomes extreme in the cooperatives of convenience, in which public inspection bodies do not exercise excessive control. The member worker, Italian or migrant, often develops an approach as a subordinate to managers, although in the historical cooperatives hierarchy is less pressing than in private companies. The mechanisms of task differentiation are not only functional to the strictly hierarchical organization of work, but also correspond to specific hierarchies that are often similar to those of private companies on the basis of factors such as nationality, race, and gender: "In an increasing number of cooperatives separation between workers and management is on similar lines as racial separation" (Brentel *et al.* 1999, 80). These changes are related to what has occurred in Italian society, where an attitude of selfish individualism is prevalent.

The condition of membership in some of the service cooperatives is reduced to a mere "technical function." Membership guarantees the legal continuity of the cooperative, but it is sometimes connected to tendering: the current Italian legislation provides that the member worker who works in cooperative A may become a member of cooperative B if the latter wins the new contract. This form of protection in terms of continuity of work does not provide member workers with more favorable treatment than the other external workers. In contrast, the member workers, propelled by their responsibility for the smooth running of the cooperative to ensure the continuity of the organization and ultimately of their work, are subject to a more stringent control over their work, which translates into more intensive labor, unpaid working hours, and an imbalance between the responsibilities of their jobs and their wage. In fact, for those working in the health and social care sector as well as in logistics, competitions between cooperatives becomes ferocious as new cooperatives are created that operate below cost, to the detriment of worker conditions.

Consumer cooperatives and social cooperatives: I am not the co-op![25]

The general transformation that has just been discussed above gives rise to profound repercussions within the individual cooperatives and in particular in the fields of services to business and to individuals and retail. It is a deterioration in both levels of internal democracy in the daily management, accentuated by the lack of attention to gender and migrants, and of the working conditions of members and employees of cooperatives. In particular, in this section two emblematic examples are discussed: workers of consumer cooperatives in the retail sector, and cooperatives in social and health care services.

In January 2011, the main Italian trade union CGIL, which can claim a socialist and communist tradition and which is usually linked to cooperatives, publicly denounced that in the chain of subcontractors of Coop Adriatica, in the supermarket industry, 80 Chinese people were working as member workers of a cooperative called the Coop Work Group of Rimini, which does not apply the National Collective Labor Agreement.[26] Coop Adriatica is part of the Coop, a leading retail group with many Italian giant hypermarkets belonging to a strong mother group called Coop Italy (Menzani and Zamagni 2010, 114–115). In fact, in the large-scale retail sector, among the top 10 groups (for turnover) that operate in the domestic market, three cooperatives cover a market share of approximately 34 percent (Censis 2012, 14). The peculiarity of consumer cooperatives is that workers are not members: they are consumer members, but being external workers makes the working identity of the subjects more complex. In consumer cooperatives such as Coop Adriatica and Coop North East, one can pinpoint a strong ambiguity between measures in favor of flexibility, managed by the same workers, as well as a general worsening of working conditions. Employment contracts are, for the vast majority, permanent, although they are almost all part-time, many of them up to 30 flexible week hours (average hours distributed over the year). Since 2002, the cashier work shifts have been managed through the "island" model that would, according to management, build self-managed working hours. However, the opening hours of shops and the shifts of the staff are decided on the basis of the needs of the company, which constrains the flow of goods and customers, rather than on the needs of the workers, something that in recent years the workers have repeatedly pointed out.[27]

The primary interest of consumer cooperatives is to create social wealth and promote its redistribution, particularly among consumer members. The interests of these members do not always coincide with those of the workers and this makes the dialogue difficult between the management and the workers of the cooperative. It seems that the social wealth for the benefit of consumers and members of the community is not so much created from acting cooperatively; rather it is transferred from one category (workers) to another (the consumer and the community) through the exploitation of the workforce that is strong with regard to invisible production segments, as in the case of the warehouse and logistics sector subcontracted by true or false cooperatives.

Social cooperatives have undergone a significant increase in recent years (Thomas 2004). They almost all operate as contractors on behalf of the public administration: in hospitals, nursing homes, and schools. In the cooperatives of the social and health sector, member and external workers describe their jobs as "hard work" with shifts at the weekend, physically exhausting, emotionally challenging, and badly paid.[28] The wage levels of external members and member workers are the same and they are 20 to 25 percent lower than in the public sector. In the case of cooperatives in the educational sector, some of the workers agree that their work has a "social mission," although they notice the lack of social recognition. The lengthening of the chain of contracts, often run by Catholic cooperatives, fragments the production cycle and further divides the workers, sometimes even between different cooperatives. The workforce is predominantly female with a rather distinct division of labor: while some of the Italian women are employed in jobs of high professionalism, the migrants, regardless of their educational level, are employed as unskilled workers. Italian women assigned intellectual tasks can generally be satisfied with the work performed, but they are paid much less than those who hold the same job and are employed directly by the public administration.

The double track, both regarding the payroll and the regulation between workers for cooperatives and public sector workers, has an impact on the identity of "the formers," but also creates friction among the workers themselves. In fact, even the cooperatives that maintain a good spirit of solidarity are used both by public and private companies for cutting down on labor costs. In these social services, the workers of the cooperative must obey a double command at work: one from the cooperative leaders and one from the leaders of the public administration managers. The hierarchical power of public administration managers is stronger than that of their cooperative which is bent, for convenience and complacency, to the willingness of local government. The entrance of cooperative workers into private companies and public administration often ends up in producing a split in the labor force because the cooperative worker "is completely separate from the rest of the workers and so ends up in being discriminated against" (Brentel *et al.* 1999, 78).

Conclusions

In its early days the cooperative movement advocated an alliance between capital and labor that was set up in favor of labor and was made up mainly of workers. The main aim of cooperatives was to ensure that members' working conditions and consumption would be better than those offered by the external market. Since the end of World War II a gradual shift of focus has been seen toward capitalism, with the transformation of cooperatives into more businesslike companies that still maintain the main feature of "social responsibility."

In particular, we suggest that the transformation into a more businesslike company is linked to the crisis of the Italian labor movement. In fact, since the end of the 1970s, the cooperative movement has become more and more permeable to the influences of the market and the government. The abandonment of mutual and solidarity practices in favor of an entrepreneurial workforce goes hand in hand with the construction of a discourse of solidarity addressed outside of the cooperatives which should increase their legitimacy. Cooperatives not only affect the market by spreading the values of solidarity and democracy, but they can also be overwhelmed by market rules. The laws approved by the Italian Parliament make cooperatives analogous to other business companies. Institutions, in fact, structure the actual relationships within cooperatives. The cooperative movement has been transformed from an economic-political movement that supported a model of industrial relations in favor of the employees, into an economic-entrepreneurial movement that has a significant degree of uniformity which is found among others in the merger of the three main central cooperatives into the Italian Cooperative Alliance.

The recognition of the legitimacy of the role of cooperatives is a process supported by several interlinked factors: economic, institutional, and academic. On the economic side the results in terms of employment implicitly confirm the advantage of the model; from the institutional side, cooperatives seem to be a tool used to support an ever smaller welfare state and the needs of increasingly strong competition; and finally, on the academic side, a significant number of studies on cooperatives have been produced but with little analysis of the social relationships and working conditions of employees. In fact, the leading scholars of the movement are often more careful regarding the cooperatives' role within the overall economic system, which affects the ability to significantly influence the social relationships and working conditions. It is perhaps no coincidence that only on rare occasions is there an awareness regarding the type of social and labor relationship and working conditions in cooperatives, particularly regarding women and migrant workers. And it is thus clear that the ideological apparatus and political support of the cooperative movement is broad because it represents a way to "socially govern" both the Catholics and the Italian left wing. The support, however, contains gray areas with short-circuits between historical observations and propaganda.

The increase in cooperative size seems to be, therefore, one of the key elements in the distancing of the cooperatives from their original principles: breaking the internal relationships of solidarity. It is true, however, that the presence of small and sporadic cooperatives which operate according to the original values and practices keep alive the idea that cooperatives could also act as a form of self-defense of the workforce against the worst aspects of the power of capitalist exploitation.

Notes

1 Piacenza itself, however, is an exception, as it has traditionally leant toward socialist and social democrat parties.

2 General Logistics Systems (GLS) is an European Holding owned by the British postal service. In Europe GLS has 32 store centres and 13,000 employees. GLS operates through subsidiaries in franchising.

3 One strike leader, a migrant worker, explained:

> Initially there were four cooperatives. Two of them folded up; now only two are in operation. The system of cooperatives is a huge problem: every two years they change name so as to not pay tax and cheat the workers. For 10–15 years the consortium of cooperatives at TNT has been the same. However, they change the names of people sitting in their boardrooms. For instance, they find owners who are 80 years old and can be prosecuted but cannot be jailed because of their old age. If they change the cooperative, we are at risk of losing the job.
>
> (Curcio and Roggero 2012)

4 Ikea maintained that the strikers were not actual Ikea employees, but workers of the CGS Consortium (Cristall, Euroservizi and San Martino Cooperatives): "We asked the CGS Consortium, as well as our suppliers, to comply with the national labour contract" (Anonymous 2012).

5 Interview with Mohamed Arafat (Curcio and Roggero 2012).

6 The first cooperative was established in Turin in 1854 and was aimed toward purchasing.

7 In 1887 the newspaper *La cooperazione italiana* [The Italian Cooperation] started publication. It was the newspaper of the Federation of Italian cooperatives in which numerous articles by English cooperatives, from which ideally the Italian movement was inspired, were published.

8 The hegemony on Legacoop by the Communist Party produced the more liberal and social democrat partners who would give rise in 1952 to the AGCI (General Association of Italian Cooperatives). Other two smaller peak organizations were added later: Unci in 1975 and Unicoop in 2004.
9 The so-called Pandolfi law (December 16, 1977 n.904) helps the capitalization of cooperatives through self-financing by providing for the non-taxability of profits under reserve indivisible and not distributed among the partners. The tax rate of cooperatives currently ranges from 16 to 28 percent, while a non-cooperative pays tax at 35 percent (Biondi and Campesato 2002).
10 The law no. 72 (1983) had already enabled cooperatives to form or be a partner of a limited company.
11 The law no. 59 (1992) introduced two new financial tools: (1) the financing partner that participates in the business risk, but not in the mutual exchange, and his or her goal is gaining from the invested capital; and (2) the joint stock of cooperative participation: they are bearer bonds, freely transferable to other people (Ianes 2011). In 1996, the law no. 30 aimed to assist cleaning, transport, and logistic cooperatives, thus supporting the process of outsourcing in the medium- to low-skilled labor market.
12 In the large cooperatives, participation and labor relations can become ambiguous. The 600 to 700 members of the Manutencoop, for example, may decide on the future of over 16,000 employees of a limited company controlled by the same cooperative.
13 In this respect, in the summer of 2005, Unipol, a major insurance cooperative, through unclear procedures, sought to acquire the Banca Nazionale del Lavoro (National Bank of Work), one of the largest Italian banks. In a telephone conversation, Pietro Fassino, then secretary of the main party of the Italian left (Left Democrats), asked Giovanni Consorte, a manager of Unipol: "And so do we own a bank?"
14 http://eng.obiettivolavoro.it/node.
15 Introductory report to the National Assembly of Delegates Legacoop, Rome, April 23, 2009.
16 On the other hand, in some cooperatives in northern Italy, the turnover of partners can reach even 50 percent per annum due to unskilled labor, low wages, and poor participation in decision-making and meetings within the cooperative itself (Menzani 2008, 383).
17 In 2009, Coop Italy, which brings together several cooperatives, became the Italian leader in the wholesale sector; CMB is the third largest Italian company in the building sector; Sacmi is in tenth place among the mechanical sector; Manutencoop is the seventh largest company in the service sector. Manutencoop controls a temporary work agency (TWA), a private equity fund, and owns shares in some of the largest Italian banks (www.manutencoopfm.it/eng/mercati_overview.asp) (see Bentivogli and Viviano 2012).
18 Legacoop and Confcooperative are the two main associations of cooperatives in Italy: respectively 8.5 and 3 million partners with 480,000 and 540,000 employees. The turnover of these associations in 2012 was about 60 billion Euros each (Ianes 2011, 113; Censis 2012, 35).
19 With regard to cooperatives with strong values, a supportive example is from Mag (mutual self-management): a network of financial service cooperatives whose fundamental objective is to create a financial network that is in contrast to the traditional rules of finance and speculative investment while at the same time trying to overturn the hierarchy. In May 2012 it had 1,200 members throughout Italy. (www.mag6.it/).
20 Some large federations of cooperatives in collaboration with universities created Master's and graduate degree programs for training managers for cooperative enterprises.
21 It should be remembered that in the 1980s several cooperatives, particularly those involved in distribution, started a social marketing campaign, supported also by actors and film directors including Woody Allen.

22 A female partner worker stated:

> When a cooperative is so big, and has such large investments beyond our limited experience, it is obvious we vote on the basis of what is presented by the management. How can you begin to understand what an investment of 300 million of euros means: we have to trust them. But we can decide formally … the bigger the cooperatives become the more difficult it is keep up to date with all the social aspects.
>
> (Garibaldo 2011)

23 A notable difference between the wages of workers and managers has developed over the past 20 years. In this respect, considering the experience of a manager of a major cooperative in Piedmont, Frau (2010) argues that managers of cooperatives in large retail earn a similar amount to those in capitalistic companies, from €500,000 to one million per year, compared to an annual pay of a worker in the order of €30,000 gross (see Bartlett *et al.* 1992, 110).

24 The non-partner workers are more common in cooperatives with sales of more than one million Euros and in the newer cooperatives that operate in the agricultural and fishing sectors. In the area of retail and distribution all employees are non-members (Censis 2012, 46–47).

25 The advertising slogan "The Coop is you. Who can give you more than you?" as a marketing strategy for the largest retail group in the cooperative movement in Italy, Coop, was invented in 1982 by Maria Carla Elvetico.

26 Chinese workers pack fresh vegetables for €4.5 per hour, a very low wage in Italy (Ponziano 2011).

27 Coop Northwest has unilaterally canceled wage increases for holiday days of its 4,300 employees (Garibaldo 2011; Polo 2012; Savelli 2012).

28 As a female member worker stated: "It's a joke. My wage is €1,000 per month, sometimes making €1,100, while working on average 165 hours per month. Of course, the night shifts range from 6/7 hours and when I do morning and night shifts I work 15 hours. What I get is a pittance" (Garibaldo 2011, 13).

References

Anonymous. 2012. "Scontri all'Ikea: Feriti 10 facchini e 2 agenti [Clashes at Ikea: Injured 10 Porters and 2 Agents]." *L'Unità*, November 2. Available online at: www.unita.it/italia/lavoro-rivolta-all-ikea-br-cinque-facchini-feriti-1.461231.

Bartlett, W., J. Cable, S. Estrin, D.C. Jones, and S.C. Smith. 1992. "Labor-managed Cooperatives and Private Firms in North Central Italy: An Empirical Comparison." *Industrial and Labor Relations Review* 46(1), 103–118. doi: 10.2307/2524741.

Battilani, P. 2009. "L'impresa cooperativa in Italia nella seconda metà del Novecento: istituzione marginale o fattore di modernizzazione economica? [The Cooperative Enterprise in Italy in the Second Half of the Twentieth Century: A Marginal Institution or a Factor of Economic Modernization?]." *Imprese e storia* 37, 9–57.

Bentivogli, C., and E. Viviano. 2012. "Le trasformazioni del sistema produttivo italiano: le cooperative [Changes in the Italian Economy: The Cooperatives]." *L'industria* 113(3), 497–528. doi: 10.1430/37816.

Bernstein, E. 1968. *I presupposti del socialismo ei compiti della socialdemocrazia* [The Preconditions of Socialism and the Tasks of Social Democracy]. Bari: Laterza.

Biondi, S., and G. Campesato. 2002. *1992–2002: Dieci anni che sconvolsero … il mondo cooperativo* [1992–2002: Ten Years That Shocked … the Cooperative World]. Rome: Edizioni cooperativa.

Borzaga, C. 2011. "Introduzione [Introduction]." In *La cooperazione in Italia: 1° Rappor to Euricse* [Cooperation in Italy: 1st Report Euricse], edited by Euricse, 1st Report, 4–19. Trento: Euricse. Available online at: http://euricse.eu/sites/euricse.eu/files/db_uploads/documents/1322838549_n1868.pdf.

Brentel, A., L. Enzo, G. Merotto, and S. Mestriner. 1999. "La subordinazione invisibile: lavorare nelle cooperative nel trevigiano [The Invisible Subordination: Working in Treviso Cooperatives']." *Altreragioni* 8: 63–85.

Censis, ed. 2012. *Primo rapporto sulla cooperazione in Italia* [First Report on Cooperation in Italy]. Rome: Censis.

Colarizi, S. 2000. *Storia del Novecento italiano: Cent'anni di entusiasmo, di paure, di speranza* [History of the Italian Novecento: One Hundred Years of Enthusiasm, Fear, Hope]. Milan: Rizzoli.

Corcoran, H., and D. Wilson. 2010.*The Worker Cooperative Movements in Italy, Mondragon and France: Context, Success Factors and Lessons*. Canadian Worker Cooperative Federation. Avaiable online at: www.canadianworker.coop/sites/canadianworker.coop/files/CWCF_Research_Paper_International_16-6-2010_fnl[1].pdf.

Cuomo, G., ed. 2010. *Le imprese cooperative* [The Enterprise Cooperatives]. Rome: Carocci.

Curcio, A., and G. Roggero. 2012. "The Revolution in Logistics: Interview with Mohamed Arafat." Translation by Arianna Bove and Wildcat. *Il Manifesto*, December 11. Available online at: www.uninomade.org/the-revolution-in-logistics (last accessed March 21, 2013).

Degl'Innocenti, M. 1981. "Geografia e strutture della cooperazione in Italia [Geography and Cooperation Structures in Italy]." In *Il movimento cooperativo in Italia: Storia e problemi* [The Cooperative Movement in Italy: History and Problems], edited by G. Sapelli and G. Bonfante (3–88). Turin, Italy: Einaudi.

Earle, J. 1986. *The Italian Cooperative Movement: A Portrait of the Lega Nazionale delle Cooperative e Mutue*. London: Routledge.

Fabbri, F. 1979. "Per una storia del movimento cooperativo italiano [For a History of the Italian Cooperative Movement]." In *Il movimento cooperativo nella storia d'Italia (1854–1975)* [The Cooperative Movement in the History of Italy (1854–1975)], edited by F. Fabbri (pp. 21–116). Milan: Feltrinelli.

Fabbri, F. 2011. *L'Italia cooperativa: Centocinquant'anni di storia e di memoria, 1861–2011* [Italy Cooperative: One Hundred and Fifty Years of History and Memory, 1861–2011]. Rome: Ediesse.

Fornasari, M., and V. Zamagni. 1997. *Il movimento cooperativo in Italia. Un profilo storico-economico (1854–1992)* [The Cooperative Movement in Italy. An Historical-Economic Profile (1854–1992)]. Florence: Vallecchi Editore.

Frau, M. 2010.*La coop non sei tu. La mutazione genetica delle coop: Dal solidarismo alle scalate bancarie* [The Co-op is Not You. The Genetic Mutation of the Co-op: From Solidarity to Climbing Banking]. Rome: EditoriRiuniti.

Gabaccia, Donna R. 2003. *Italy's Many Diasporas*. London and New York: Routledge.

Galasso, G. 1987. "Gli anni della grande espansione e la crisi del sistema [The Years of Great Expansion and the Crisis of the System]." In *Storia del movimento cooperativo in Italia* [History of the Cooperative Movement in Italy], edited by R. Zangheri, G. Galasso, and V. Castronovo (pp. 219–496). Turin: Einaudi.

Garibaldo, F., ed. 2011. *Ricerca sul movimento cooperativo di Reggio Emilia* [Research on Cooperative Movement of Reggio Emilia]. Available online at: www.francescogaribaldo.it/documenti.

Gramsci, A. 1971. *La costruzione del Partito comunista (1923–1926)* [The Construction of the Communist Party (1923–1926)]. Turin: Einaudi.
Holmström, M. 1989. *Industrial Democracy in Italy: Workers Co-ops and the Self-management Debate*. Aldershot: Avebury.
Ianes, A. 2011. *Le cooperative* [The Cooperatives].Rome: Carocci.
Kautsky, K. 1978. *The Agrarian Question*, 2 vols. Boston, MA: Unwin Hyman.
Legacoop. 2009. *Aspetti quantitativi e qualitativi della cooperazione italiana* [Quantitative and Qualitative Aspects of the Italian Cooperation]. Milan: Centro studi Legacoop. Avaiable online at: www.cslegacoop.coop/allegati/Documenti/Documenti/Cooperative/rapportocentrostudi.pdf.
Menzani, T. 2008. "Temi e problemi della rete [Subjects and Problems of the Networks]." In *Competizione e valorizzazione del lavoro* [Competition and Enhancement of Work], edited by P. Battilani and G. Bertagnoni (pp. 377–450). Bologna: Il Mulino.
Menzani, T., and V. Zamagni. 2010. "Cooperative Networks in the Italian Economy." *Enterprise and Society* 11(1): 98–127. doi: 10.1093/es/khp029.
Merli, S. 1984. *Proletariato di fabbrica e capitalismo industriale: il caso italiano 1880–1900. Vol. 1* [Factory Proletariat and Industrial Capitalism: The Italian Case 1880–1900. Vol. 1]. Florence: La Nuova Italia.
Napolitano, G. 2010. "I modelli cooperativi per la produzione e per il consumo di servizi pubblici [The Cooperative Models for the Production and the Consumption of Public Services]." Fondazione Ivano Barberini. Available online at: www.fondazionebarberini.it/allegati/nota_preliminare_napolitano_110524072228.pdf.
Polo, G. 2012. "La coop non sei più tu [The Co-op is No Longer You]." *Il Manifesto*, November 14. Available online at: www.resistenze.org/sito/te/pr/la/prlacm14-011878.htm.
Ponziano, G. 2011. "Coop, arrivano i precari cinesi: Sindacati contro la cooperativa sulla manodopera a basso costo [Coop, the precarious Chinese come: Trade Unions against the Cooperative on Cheap Labor]." *Italia Oggi*, January 11. Available online at: www.italiaoggi.it/giornali/dettaglio_giornali.asp?preview=false&accessMode=FA&id=1694938&codiciTestate=1&sez=giornali.
Rieser, V. 2006. "*Purché una volta al governo non si imponga il modello della Coop* [Provided That Once at the Government Co-ops model will not widespread]". Liberazione, January 10.
Sassen, S. 2001. *The Global City: New York, London, Tokyo* (2nd edn). Princeton, NJ: Princeton University Press.
Savelli, F. 2012. " 'Cara Littizzetto, no la Coop non sei tu'. La lettera-denuncia delle lavoratrici Usb [" 'Dear Littizzetto, No Coop's Not You'. The Letter-complaint of Workers Usb]." *Il Corriere della Sera*, November 26. Available online at: www.corriere.it/economia/12_novembre_26/usb-lavoratrici-coop-litizzetto_74be05f4-37d5-11e2-94e7-603de4c26bba.shtml.
Thomas, A. 2004. "The Rise of Social Cooperatives in Italy." *International Journal of Voluntary and Nonprofit Organizations* 15(3): 243–263. doi: 10.1023/B:VOLU.0000046280.06580.d8.
Verruccoli, P. 1979. "La società cooperativa nella legislazione italiana: dal Codice di commercio del 1882 al Codice civile del 1942 [The Cooperative Society in the Italian Legislation: The Commercial Code of 1882 to the Civil Code of 1942]." In *Il movimento cooperativo nella storia d'Italia (1854–1975)* [The Cooperative Movement in the History of Italy (1854–1975)], edited by F. Fabbri (pp. 797–805). Milan: Feltrinelli.
Worldwatch Institute, ed. 2007. *State of the World: Our Urban Future*. New York: W.W. Norton.

Zamagni, S. and Zamagni, V. 2008. *La cooperazione* [The Cooperation]. Bologna: Il Mulino.

Zamagni, V. and Felice, E. 2006, *Oltre il secolo. Le trasformazioni del sistema cooperativo Legacoop alla fine del secondo millennio* [Beyond the Centuries. The Transformations of the Cooperative System of Legacoop at the End of the Second Millennium]. Bologna: Il Mulino.

Zangheri, R. 1987. "Nascita e primi sviluppi [Birth and Early Development]." In *Storia del movimento cooperativo in Italia* [History of the Cooperative Movement in Italy], edited by R. Zangheri, G. Galasso, and V. Castronovo (pp. 5–216). Turin: Einaudi.

9 Developing solidarity economy in Asia

Innovations in policy and practice

Denison Jayasooria

Introduction

In the context of the recent global economic crisis, alternative economic arrangements are being sought worldwide. The crisis has resulted in a loss of confidence toward state-driven and market-driven economic models and initiatives, whereas free market models continue to dominate the global business environment. These free market economic models have demonstrated that despite wealth creation, the poor continue to be poor and greed dominates economic arrangements. Furthermore, inequalities continue to widen in market-driven economies. Consequently, alternatives are being sought to enable ordinary people, particularly grassroots communities, to experience economic liberation and increased livelihood control. These new initiatives are emerging in concurrence with the adoption of the "triple bottom-line" approach in which a balance among profits, people, and the planet is emphasized.

Distinct terms are used to define this process in various contexts, but the basic principle of this approach is that business principles are used to fulfill social needs and to solve social problems in a sustainable manner. Several differences exist regarding the emphases and approaches used, but the bottom line is typically a balance between wealth creation and sustainability. The Social Solidarity Movement in Asia is a recent movement with roots in traditional community development and self-help initiatives involving cooperatives, micro-credit and micro-finance institutions, and fair trade initiatives. The related models and approaches are exhibited in most Asian societies, but they may not have been presented in this manner until recent years.

Two key studies from Asia have been recently published by the Asian Solidarity Economy Council (ASEC). The first is "Sowing the Seeds of Solidarity Economy: Asian Experiences," which was written by Benjamin R. Quiñones (2012). The second is "Developments in the Solidarity Economy in Asia," edited by Denison Jayasooria (2013). The work by Ben Quiñones (2012) is unique in that it documents the 2007 gathering of 700 people from 26 countries at the University of the Philippines in Diliman, Quezon City, the Philippines. This was the most recent gathering in which social solidarity economy in Asia was advocated. Grassroots movements that are recognized worldwide have developed innovative approaches to wealth creation and distribution. These may be considered small-scale revolutions for social justice in which ordinary people at the grassroots level are challenging the dominant approaches to economics. Their critique is based on the recognition that conventional economic models are creating substantial inequalities in society because the economic models of economic growth are rendered unsustainable by the consumption model.

In a similar way, Denison Jayasooria (2013) documented the 2011 gathering of grassroots workers, academics, and policy-makers in Kuala Lumpur. The participants comprised 351 people from 33 countries, and 17 Asian countries were represented. During the gathering, a memorandum of agreement for 18 Asian countries to institute an Asian Solidarity Council was created. Prior regional cooperation was informal, but was institutionalized at the gathering in Kuala Lumpur. The 2007 and 2011 gatherings were part of national, regional, and global movements toward socio-economic transformation, resulting in grassroots movements for creating alternative economies. This was observed by both Quiñones (2012) and Jayasooria (2013).

The work by Rosa Mercado (2009) of the Philippines and the Center for Labor and Grassroots Initiatives provides a strong link between the solidarity economy and cooperative experiences, including the link between the solidarity economy and trade union movements. This link and comparison is helpful because both movements aspire toward collectivism, cooperation, and empowerment. These writings establish the roots of the movements and articulate the alternatives.

Other writers have also described these developments in the social solidarity movement worldwide. Marcos Arruda's publications (2008, 2009) provide a global social economy framework. In these works, the writer conceptually explains the economic critique of conventional models and documents alternative economic experiences across various continents. In addition, Emily Kawano, Thomas Neal Masterson, and Jonathan Teller-Elsberg (2009) have comprehensively documented the concepts and development processes involved in building alternative economies with a focus on people and the environment in the United States. They have provided a full overview of existing and plausible alternatives to not being blinded by economic growth and profit maximization.

Understanding the Asian context

In seeking to understand the social solidarity movement in Asia, understanding the context of Asia and recognizing its vast potential and possibilities is crucial. The diversity of people and economic models in Asia is based on several social indicators.

First, Asia is the most populated region of the world. This demographic indicator suggests that Asia is a unique area that contains a multicultural and religiously diverse society.

Second, the geographical area of Asia is vast, stretching from South Asia to the Far East and spanning the Association of Southeast Asian Nations (ASEAN) countries.

Third, Asia contains several of the fastest growing economies in the world, such as the economies of Japan, South Korea, Singapore, Taiwan, and Hong Kong. Other rapidly growing countries include Malaysia, Indonesia, Thailand, and the Philippines. However, the most prominent among these countries are the two emerging economic giants, China and India, which are characterized by diverse political and economic models. China is based on the authoritarian capitalism model and India is based on democratic capitalism.

Fourth, Asia has recently experienced massive rural–urban migration. The largest cities in the world are now located in Asia, as are several of the tallest buildings in the world. This phenomenon has affected the urban infrastructure and local communities in Asia. At the micro-level, families and communities are divided through divorce, social dislocation, and displacement.

Fifth, although increasing wealth and prosperity may be observed in Asia, socio-economic inequalities are simultaneously increasing; for example, Asia exhibits the largest population of poor people worldwide. In addition, the poverty in Asia includes both income poverty and deprivations in other dimensions such as increasing digital technology and knowledge gaps.

Sixth, mass movements are occurring within Asia and involve both skilled workers owing to the brain-drain, and low-skilled workers, who comprise the majority of participants. These workers are primarily from Myanmar, Cambodia, and Vietnam, but are also present in other Asian countries such as Malaysia and Singapore.

Seventh, comprehensively documented cases of human trafficking for cheap, bonded labor and prostitution have been recently reported. In addition, trans-border crime, terrorist activities, and drug-trafficking activities are currently increasing.

Eighth, numerous Asian countries have adopted neoliberal economic policies that are primarily based on free market approaches. However, a shift toward democracy has occurred in Myanmar and Cambodia. In this context, the Asian approach toward development remains dominated by traditional Asian values in that economic and social development are strongly emphasized, whereas civil and political rights receive minimal attention. This is reflected in the frequent ASEAN human rights movements, indicating that a strong sense of political patronage still exists within a majority of Asian nations.

Asian thinkers in the field of alternative economics

The dominant economic philosophy in Asia is neoliberal economic philosophy. However, numerous Asian writers have undertaken creative thinking and writing to challenge the stereotypes perpetuated by the capitalistic framework toward radical alternatives. Among the four most widely recognized development thinkers, three are economists – Amartya Sen, Muhammad Yunus, and Benjamin Quiñones – and the other, Coimbatore Krishnarao (C.K.) Prahalad, is a management guru. All have their roots in Asia and have an academic background, and they are all rethinking the manner in which economics and business should be run with the ultimate focus being the common good.

Amartya Sen (1999) adopts a human rights focus in which human freedoms and democratic rights are fundamental to socio-economic development. Sen considers total human development to be more critical than growth or income levels, and that the participation and empowerment of the poor is central to development. Yunus (2007, 2010) challenges the capitalism framework of profit maximization to restore the true objective of wealth creation, which is the common good. He recognizes the positive aspects of capitalism, which are the efficiency and sustainability of wealth creation; however, he redirects the creativity of capitalism in the form of business solutions to reduce poverty and develop society. Providing a new perspective of considering the poor not as victims but as consumers is Prahalad's major contribution to the discussion on poverty and inequality. He argues that considering the poor as dynamic people with dignity and not as passive recipients of aid and assistance is fundamental. The poor are consumers and they must buy basic goods and services. Quiñones asserts that a strong communitarian and collective orientation should be implemented in enterprises through the bonds of solidarity. This approach dismisses the traditional view of individualism, greed, and self-centeredness, which is a component of the market-driven economy based on competition. Furthermore, the values underlying the proposed approach undergird economic and collective activity for the common good. His approach does not focus on the individual enterprise businesses. Instead, he focuses on the supply chain, which is a string of associated enterprises. This approach provides a comprehensive method of accessing the community economy on a large scale.

Philosophers influence practice and practice influences theoretical frameworks. This is a dynamic process. All four of these thinkers are practitioners because they have presented dynamic research and policy advocacy approaches, and are all still exploring their theories in practice. Furthermore, they are demonstrating, based on their grassroots work, that various alternative theories exist which challenge traditional neoliberal economic assumptions. Further examination of the four thinkers and three innovative practices are presented in the following section to elucidate the dynamic developments that have been observed, both at the theoretical and practical levels, in Asia.

Professor Amartya Sen

The Nobel Laureate in Economics, Amartya Sen is an Indian economist originally from West Bengal who is currently based at Harvard University, and has provided a valuable critique on the manner in which poverty is defined and measured. His arguments are comprehensively described in his book entitled *Development as Freedom*. He called for a departure from the narrow perspective of development (growth based on GNP or an increase in personal income) toward a more inclusive and integrated perspective of development (economic, social, and political). He also suggested a shift from the term "income poverty" to "capability deprivation." Furthermore, he advocated for a more effective human rights approach to poverty reduction, emphasizing social justice, equality, nondiscrimination, participation, and accountability. This prompts the question as to how this economic analysis is associated with social solidarity economy and social enterprise. The key link is the focus on development planning and priorities set at the national level.

According to Sen (1999), development does not mean economic growth at the expense of economic, social, civil, and political freedoms. He affirmed the importance and place of democracy and people's participation in development. In addition, Sen stated that "an adequate conception of development must go much beyond the accumulation of wealth and the growth of gross national product and other income-related variables" and "development has to be more concerned with enhancing the lives we lead and the freedoms we enjoy" (1999, 14). In the context of poverty reduction, Sen moved beyond "income poverty to a more inclusive idea of capability deprivation." He emphasized the consideration of "poverty as a deprivation of basic capabilities, rather than merely as low income" (Sen 1999, 20).

Professor Muhammad Yunus

Muhammad Yunus is the founder of the Grameen Bank. He is a Nobel Laureate for Peace and is from Bangladesh. He revolutionized the banking system through micro-credit and saving mobilization for the poor. As an economics professor at Chittagong University, he experimented using no collateral for borrowing except for the peer support of the group. He recognized that the poor are trustworthy and women were particularly interested in using small funds to generate additional income through micro-business. For his work at Grameen, he is globally known as the "banker to the poor" (Yunus and Jolis 1999).

After successfully innovating the collateral free loan, he began pioneering social business. His two publications on this topic focus on developing the new approach of using business solutions to solve social, economic, and environmental problems (Yunus 2007, 2010). In these works, he also develops a critique of capitalism, the purpose of which he considers as maximizing profit. One major criticism of the Yunus approach is that he does not provide strong structural criticism of the system based on injustice and inequality. Regardless, he has effectively used market capitalism by applying the potential for innovation and free enterprise to the social good of the people, community, and environment.

Professor Coimbatore Krishnarao Prahalad

C.K. Prahalad was born in Coimbatore, India and became a management guru. He worked as a management professor at the University of Michigan Business School. Among his publications, *Fortune at the Bottom of the Pyramid* provided a novel perspective on the poor. He stated that approximately four billion people lived on a wage of less than US$2 a day. However, he considered them a latent market for goods and services (Prahalad 2010).

His goal was to change the belief that the poor are victims or a burden, to the belief that the poor have immense entrepreneurial capability and purchasing and buying power. People must begin to recognize that the poor are resilient and creative entrepreneurs. They should also be regarded as value-conscious consumers. According to Prahalad, if people are committed to this change in perspective, "a whole new world of opportunity will open up" (Economia 2012). This approach challenges the perception of the poor as passive recipients waiting for cash hand-outs. This new paradigm enables people to review the task ahead by converting the poor into consumers through market development. This requires providing the poor with the capacity to consume on a sustainable basis.

Prahalad (2012) highlights four key dimensions, or the "4 As," in this context:

Awareness: know what is available and offered, and how to use it;
Affordability: pay the minimal amount without compromising quality or efficacy;
Access: to be ensured through geographically intensive distribution; and
Availability: to be ensured through distribution efficiency.

Prahalad (2010) recognized the markets and economic potential at the grassroots level. This is a new perspective on the poor that may be applied to take advantage of their potential, especially that of the informal sector, which is a major component of the Asian economy that comprises the bottom 40 percent of the socio-economic ladder. Asian governments must consider this seriously owing to the high percentage of poor people in both China and India.

Dr. Benjamin Quiñones

Benjamin. R. Quiñones Jr. is from Manila, the Philippines. He served as the host of the 2007 Solidarity Economy gathering in Manila, and is regarded as the prime advocate of solidarity economy in Asia. He coined the term "Bayanihan," which represents the compassionate economy of the Philippines. In 2011, he formally established the ASEC, which is the Asian representative in the Intercontinental Network for the Promotion of Social Solidarity Economy (RIPESS).

His early work focused on micro-finance and poverty alleviation, especially in the pioneering work he and others at the Asian Pacific Development Cooperation conducted to prove that "the poor are creditworthy, capable of utilising scarce capital efficiently in viable income-generating projects, and able to pay back their loans" (Getubig *et al.* 2000, 6).

Quiñones (2013) emphasized five major attributes of social and solidarity economy that could serve as the standard framework for measuring and evaluating solidarity economy performance. The five features are described as follows.

First, he refers to socially responsible governance, which means socially inclusive, participatory, democratic, just, and equitable, and promotes self-management and collective ownership.

Second, he looks at edifying values as essentially an ethical- and values-based approach to economic development as opposed to a solely growth- and profit-oriented focus. In addition, this approach is oriented toward justice, equality, and empowerment.

Third, he focuses primarily on people and has a social development orientation.

Fourth, he mentions the planet which involves ecological conservation measures.

Fifth, he states that profits entail economic sustainability.

Quiñones (2013) incorporated the widely recognized triple bottom-line approach, which focuses primarily on people and has a social development orientation. The secondary focus is on the planet, which involves ecological conservation measures, and the third focal concern is profits, which entails economic sustainability. In this method, the emphasis is not based on greed or disregard for the environment, but on sustainable profits.

Quiñones is currently using the five-dimensional framework to evaluate various community and social enterprises. A major contribution from Quiñones (2013) is the new way of assessing not just an individual enterprise but also the entire supply chain, including various social businesses (interconnected nature – supply chain analysis). In most scenarios, enterprises are considered as single units and, when they are evaluated, they are too micro. However, when these scenarios are approached from a supply chain perspective, the extent of outreach efforts increases and affects local economies.

According to Quiñones, in contrast to the market-oriented neoliberal economy that is devoted to the expansion of private profit regardless of ecological and human cost, solidarity economy is committed to achieving social, ecological, and economic justice. Finally, Quiñones (2013) recognizes that the current literature on social economics is descriptive and no performance standard has been established. Based on this context, the solidarity economy must be conceptualized, measured, and evaluated.

Asian innovations in practice

Innovative approaches are being applied in practice across Asia through concrete community-based actions for creating an alternative economy. However, although these actions are widespread, they have neither been adequately recognized nor documented. The mapping work being undertaken by academics and researchers indicates a growing number of alternative models of economic activities, such as micro-credit, fair trade, handcraft-based, or community-based agricultural activities. In addition, they are creating wealth and contributing to reducing poverty and hunger. Asians must be recognized as a part of the global movement of people at the grassroots level seeking new innovative approaches to wealth creation, distribution, sustainable development, and environmental protection. Over time, small-scale socio-economic revolutions for the purpose of achieving socio-economic transformation have resulted in a movement of people creating an alternative approach. This experience is empowering, sustainable, and produces effects at the level of local communities.

Three innovative examples of social economy are presented in this chapter. They are Asian examples from Indonesia, India, and the Philippines. All the organizations in these examples are partners with the ASEC. In all three models, the organizations were voluntarily formed by citizens and not by the government or private corporations. In addition, they were initiated by the people and involve a "bottom-up approach." They grew from small to large organizations by networking with other organizations nationally and globally. Furthermore, these organizations are neither state driven nor funded but community led and sustained.

The governments in these examples have created an enabling environment and do not obstruct these community innovations. In India, Indonesia, and the Philippines, rural development policies have been implemented for establishing a civil society and enabling community participation, especially through the strengthening of grassroots democracy. In addition, the hegemonic sphere of development dominated by a "political–bureaucratic–business" world must be broken by the majority of people for the common good.

Bina Swadaya Movement in Indonesia

Bina Swadaya (self-reliance development foundation)[1] is a sustainable citizen-led initiative based in Indonesia that was founded by Bambang Ismawan[2] in 1967. This was the period of the Suharto regime when a large proportion of Indonesians were in poverty and practicing subsistence agriculture. The primary approach adopted was building self-reliance among rural famers through self-help groups. Currently, more than 10,000 community leaders have been trained and approximately 12,000 grassroots self-help groups have been formed, serving 3.5 million people.

Bambang adopted an enterprise model for financial sustainability by establishing a series of revenue-generating companies. Sixteen socially oriented companies were established and they have a collective revenue of US$33 million and employ approximately 1,000 staff members. Three examples of these companies are a publishing company that has published 70,000 monthly copies of *Trubus*, an agricultural magazine, and other agriculture-related publications; a chain of agricultural shops that sell tools, seeds, fertilizers, and other farming products, 10 of which Bina Swadaya operates and has franchised; and a micro-credit savings and loans scheme. One-third of the proceeds generated by these profitable businesses is reinvested into Bina Swadaya (Ashoka n.d.).

At the heart of the Bina Swadaya initiative is community empowerment and economic independence. Early on in his life, Bambang was influenced by a Dutch priest named Father Dijkstra, who taught him that the "most effective way to help people was not simply to give them things, but to support them with the information and skills" (Ashoka n.d.). The work of Bambang and Bina Swadaya is comprehensively documented in the Malay/Indonesian language. These are listed in the reference section. Two of these books are tributes to Bambang that were given to him on his seventieth birthday, and contain many moving stories of the man and the contributions he made while working alongside the poor (Budianta 2008). Bambang is recognized for his modesty, and is known as a grassroots man for his dedication to the poor in the countryside. He won numerous awards including the "Indonesian social entrepreneur of the year" award in 2006.

Sarvodaya: the Association for Sarva Seva Farms movement in India

The Association for Sarva Seva Farms (ASSEFA) was established in Tamil Nadu, India in 1969 with the aim of enabling former landless families to cultivate the land they had received through the Gandhian Bhoodan or land gift movement in the 1950s and 1960s. The outreach program currently provides services to one million rural families in 10,000 villages across eight states in India. The primary focus is economic development among marginal farmers or the landless.[3]

The development of ASSEFA is documented in detail in the publication *Silent March of the Invisible Force* (Sarvodaya Action Research Centre 2008). The movement was built on the Gandhian vision of social justice and non-violence. The foundation of Gandhian thought is the concept of sardaya, which means "the welfare of all," and is oriented toward the landless poor. The man behind the movement was S. Loganathan, a young Gandhi-inspired development worker who was in contact with an elderly Italian activist and academic, Giovanni Ermiglia. Their vision was "to construct a society based on the availability of resources and the aspirations of the people." The idea was based on collective cultivation (Sarvodaya Action Research Centre 2008).

Tim Brodhead states that ASSEFA's goal is:

> to reduce economic inequalities in rural areas, to ensure people to have access to basic services like health and education, and to foster harmony amongst all elements of the community. The strategies it has evolved to achieve these goals are first, to create viable local institutions; second, to identify and develop local assets, including land, skills and resources; and third, to establish external linkages to break the isolations of many rural communities.
>
> (Sarvodaya Action Research Centre 2008, 30)

Yvon Poirier (2013) noted that a community development approach is used with a focus on self-help groups for women and they "have schools, cooperative milk plants, micro-finance institutions for their needs, technical training, micro-insurance for maternity, [and] peace activities."

The Alliance of Philippine Partners in Enterprise Development

The Alliance of Philippine Partners in Enterprise Development (APPEND) was established in 1991 as an umbrella coordinating body. Currently, it has 10 micro-finance non-governmental organizations (NGOs) and one thrift bank with a collective outreach of 2.9 million clients through 170 branches in 127 key cities and provinces in the Philippines. It has transformed its activities from providing simple micro-credit to community-based enterprise development (Juan 2013).[4]

APPEND is built on a strong spiritual basis, facilitating human transformation to achieve community transformation. Its vision is to build a transformed and progressive society in which people live in accordance with God's plan, with dignity, sufficiency, and responsibility toward others and toward all living things. APPEND is committed to helping eradicate poverty and promoting national transformation by contributing to the growth and development of God-fearing, socially responsible micro- and small entrepreneurs.

Virginia Juan (2013), in her article entitled "Solidarity Economy and Micro Credit," provided a comprehensive review of the APPEND experience. At its heart, the APPEND

> leadership strongly believed that human development is beyond money. Micro enterprise development could be used not only as a means of improving the material conditions of the poor but also as a means of bringing hope to people. Because the root cause of poverty is spiritual, MED organisations like APPEND continued to balance its organisational sustainability with the spiritual development and maturity of its people to ensure that greed and self-interest will not creep in.
>
> (Juan 2013, 171)

Asian innovations policy

The policy and legislative framework is an essential dimension. This framework reveals the extent to which social solidarity economy is the focus of public policy. All Asian countries have social development and poverty reduction agendas. In addition, laws governing cooperative development and micro-credit savings and lending will be established in these countries.

A number of countries have been creative and innovative, both at the policy and legislation levels, in making social economy the formal feature of their agenda. In this section, three case studies are described to illustrate this theme: the Japanese, South Korean, and Philippine experiences. Two of the three cases have a highly advanced economy and are democratic nations; however, in the Philippines, sizable portions of the population are living in poverty. Thus, they have an extremely active and dynamic informal sector.

Although similarities and differences exist among these cases, this section reveals that despite the aim of solidarity economy to depend minimally on the state and the markets, a strong supporting, enabling, and regulating public sector exists nonetheless. The implementation of public policies and social legislation focusing on social enterprise and community economy is possible and effectively demonstrated by these examples of developed (Japan and South Korea) and developing (Philippines) nations within Asian.

The Japanese experience

Following the change of government in 1993 and the collapse of the Liberal Democratic Party, the political space opened up for decentralization and the functioning of the non-profit and voluntary sector in Japan. Professor Jun Nishikawa recognized that in the late 1990s, two new laws directly affected the traditional development-oriented power structure: the Non-Profit Law (NPL) (1998) and the Decentralization Laws (1999). Nishikawa stated that this was the first time that importance had been given to the non-profit civil sector by recognizing it formally through legislation (Nishikawa 2013). The NPL, which was prompted by the government, was envisioned to promote the "new public commons." In addition, the shift from central government to decentralization facilitated increased local ownership of communities, which provided local community members with the space for participating in the government.

Prime Minister Yuko Hatoyama developed a new consensus document called the "Declaration of the New Public Commons." The Japanese government envisioned that "a vibrant community of mutual support can be created when people make their fair share of contributions" (Cabinet Office, Government of Japan 2010). Ishizuka (1999) estimated that by 1996, more than 85,000 non-profit organizations (NPOs) had been established in Japan, constituting approximately 2.5 percent of the total employment in Japan and contributing approximately 3.2 percent of the gross domestic product in 1990. Approximately 40 percent of NPOs were engaged in social welfare services. Under the NPL, the registered NPOs could be engaged in profit-making activities, provided that the proceeds were used to advance social and community objectives (Ishizuka 1999).

The introduction of the two new laws in 1990 facilitated the rise of associations and collectives, in addition to advocacy for increased corporate social responsibility. Nishikawa also stated that the March 11, 2011 earthquake tragedy had resulted in the creation of a more democratic public space and an increase in people's participation in alternative development (Nishikawa 2013, 187).

The South Korean experience

South Korea enacted the Social Enterprise Promotion Act (2006) on December 8, 2006 with the establishment of the Korea Social Enterprise Promotion Agency. The context for this major social policy innovation is rooted in civil society and citizens' movements, in addition to the liberal reformist political party in the government; this party promoted public policies that favored social justice and increased civil society involvement in addressing social problems (Bidget and Eum 2011).

The Act defines the term *social enterprise* as an enterprise that pursues a social objective. The social objective may be one of numerous topics, ranging from improving the quality of life of local residences, or considering the provision of social services or jobs. The assistance may be further linked to activities such as financial support and business advice (Bidget and Eum 2011). The state support is enhanced by this legislation, which provides a conducive policy environment and relevant resources, including financial support through the Ministry of Employment and Labor. In addition, a Korean Social Enterprise Promotion Agency has been established for fostering and promoting social enterprises.

Professor Lee Kwang Taek (Work Together Foundation, Korea) noted that Korea is one of few countries in which legislation measures were implemented to promote social enterprises. In this context, Lee also notes the danger of the state neglecting its obligation of providing services to emerging social enterprises (Lee 2013). Currently, more than 300 social enterprises have been officially recognized by the Korean government, and these enterprises collectively employ approximately 10,000 people.

The Philippine experience

In the Philippines, an estimated 30,000 social enterprises have been established under six categories: cooperatives, micro-finance institutions, fair trade organizations, NGO-initiated earned income enterprises, sector- or area-based enterprises serving specific poverty groups, and small entrepreneur-initiated enterprises that express a clear social agenda (Dacanay 2012).

Poverty and inequality are major concerns in this developing economy and, therefore, the vibrant voluntary and non-profit sector is dynamic in the absence of effective state or market solutions. Cooperatives play a major role in achieving collective action for addressing poverty through micro-finance institutions. In this context of poverty, state, and markets failures, the dynamism of the not-for-profit sector could be optimally harnessed through the enactment of the Social Enterprise Bill. This housed bill 6085 is currently in second reading in Congress, and was championed by Congressman Teodoro Casino. The bill involves the promotion and development of social enterprises for ensuring poverty reduction.

In an explanatory note pertaining to the bill, Representative Lorenzo Erin R. Tanada indicated that this bill is the Magna Carta for social enterprises. He also indicated that:

> social enterprises refer to organisations engaged in providing goods and services that are directly related to its mission of improving societal well-being. It generates profit or surplus with due regard to social and environmental costs, and makes a pro-active contribution to resolving social and environmental problems.
>
> (Congress of the Philippines 2012, 1)

Civil society activists are hopeful that Congress will pass this bill. They have established a Poverty Reduction through Social Entrepreneurship Coalition and continue to lobby and advocate for the bill. In this context, Dacanay (2012) envisioned the government playing a development role in partnership with a proactive and innovative social enterprise sector playing a substantive role in reducing poverty.

Solidarity economy and post-Rio+20

Asian countries, especially ASEAN countries, have the opportunity to respond to the recent global gathering at Rio de Janeiro, Brazil held from June 20 to 22, 2012, in which a global consensus was reached and described in the document entitled "The Future We Want." This event was the Rio+20 United Nations (UN) Conference on Sustainable Development. This UN document was adopted by member countries and can serve as a global consensus document, stating a specific time frame required for global action. Combining the social solidarity economy agenda with the global sustainable development agenda, and enabling the combined agendas to be recognized as a viable option is a challenge that will be addressed in the future.

The UN outcome document[5] is based on a number of core values that are shared by social solidarity economy. Central to these values is the theme of inclusive and equitable economic growth and distribution to all, which is reflected throughout the document. Paragraph 9 expounds on a commitment to human rights; Paragraph 10 promotes democracy, effective governance, and rule of law; and Paragraph 13 emphasizes participation, decision-making, and the voicing of concerns. In addition, Paragraph 1 emphasizes the key features of sustainable development, which are the economic, social, and environmental dimensions. These are similar to the features of the triple bottom-line approach.

Three specific references on themes related to alternative economies and arrangements were mentioned in the UN document (United Nations 2012a). The first is a reference to corporate social responsibility (CSR) in Paragraph 46 (p. 8), which focuses on public and private sector cooperation to attain sustainable development. This is a crucial reference and is specifically mentioned in the Rio+20 outcome document, which emphasizes responsible business practices. However, on numerous occasions, CSR approaches have been limited to a strong public relations and charity focus.

By contrast, social solidarity economy has a much stronger commitment toward community and people empowerment than does CSR. However, CSR has the potential for promoting a solidarity orientation, thereby contributing to the benefits of long-term socio-economic empowerment strategies.

The second reference focuses on the valuable contributions of NGOs, as noted in Paragraph 53 (p. 9), especially in promoting sustainable development. This is essential to note because the global community recognizes NGOs as the third major sector alongside the public and private sectors. However, the paragraph does not specifically define social solidarity economy as a concept or label.

The third reference is mentioned in Paragraph 70 (p. 12), in which the role of cooperatives and micro-enterprises in addressing poverty and enabling social inclusion is acknowledged. Both of these enterprises are components of the social solidarity economy. The cooperative movement is an old model of collective economic development and has been proven to be effective. This model has been applied repeatedly and, consequently, numerous dynamic innovations have been made worldwide in which businesses provide a favorable and equitable distribution of wealth by using effective methods.

The United Nations General Assembly declared 2012 as the International Year of Cooperatives,

> to raise public awareness of the invaluable contributions of cooperative enterprises to poverty reduction, employment generation and social integration. The Year will also highlight the strengths of the cooperative business model as an alternative means of doing business and furthering socio-economic development.
>
> (United Nations 2012b)

In the past, the micro-credit model of lending was rarely applied, but it underwent a process in which the unbankable situation was revolutionized. This model was once considered high risk, but is currently included in financial services. This is a radical departure from conventional banking in which non-collateral base lending made inroads into financial arrangements. However, the banking-for-the-poor initiative was not accepted as viable for a long period. Eventually, this model became globally appealing and received global approval through policy advocacy based on objective evidence, which was based on findings that included the results of social impact assessments conducted by researchers, academics, and activists.

Therefore, the major task of social solidarity economy advocates is determining how to apply relevant terms, concepts, and models to mainstream global public policy documents, forming a viable initiative for realizing the sustainable development agenda.

Strategies for future action

The UN Rio+20 outcome document describes several specific strategies to be implemented up until 2015, particularly in the context of the Millennium Development Goals (MDGs). These are crucial for developing social solidarity economy because they provide a formal endorsement by the UN. The UN has established an intergovernmental committee comprising 30 experts with the mandate to develop sustainable development goals (SDGs), which will replace the MDGs in 2015. This process will include extensive consultation with all stakeholders. In addition, this global process includes national consultations. Therefore, social solidarity economy networks worldwide must play a critical public policy advocacy role and ensure that, in the years prior to 2015, the social solidarity economy agenda is included in the SDGs.

In this context, the United Nations Research Institute for Social Development (UNRISD) hosted a conference on the Potential and Limits of Social and

Solidarity Economy from May 6 to 8, 2013 in Geneva. Over 40 researchers from 18 countries attended this gathering to address various topics. Both the UNRISD Director, Sarah Cook (2013), and International Labour Organization (ILO) Director General, Guy Ryder (2013), recognized the growing importance of SSE. They are hopeful that this conference will "raise the profile of discussions and debates about the SSE within the UN system and beyond." Therefore, SSE may be on the agenda for the post-2015 SDGs.

SSE partners in ASEAN are playing a key role in networking with the ASEAN Connectivity section through the ASEC to ensure that ASEAN member countries adopt the social business and solidarity economy as a key policy direction toward sustainable development and economic empowerment by using the triple bottom line as a primary target. In this context, SSE in Malaysia, the Philippines, and Indonesia has taken the lead.

At the global level, the ASEC will work with other continental partners through the RIPESS to influence both the national and regional bodies of both the public and NGO sectors to make this a key agenda in the 2015 global framework. The work of RIPESS[6] and its partners is extensively documented on the RIPESS website. In addition, the web-based portal Socioeco[7] serves as a depository of research, policies, articles, and case studies on SSE. One process that the ASEC has initiated is documenting grassroots examples through case studies by using a five-fold framework developed by Dr. Ben Quiñones. This documentation, based on case studies that use clear sets of indicators, will enable researchers to conduct comparisons and quantify how these initiatives affect and transform individual lives and communities. The ASEC, Asian Strategic and Leadership Institute, and the ASEAN Leadership Forum on Social and Solidarity Economy will present an alternative model for inclusive and sustainable development during the RIPESS global meeting from October 17 to 18, 2013 at the University of the Philippines. Therefore, SSE may be on the One ASEAN 2015 agenda.

Conclusion

As we reflect on the Asian trends, potential, and challenges, a number of key topics and concerns can be identified. The first is that the major public policy orientation is toward big businesses and multinationals. Most Asian countries are considering foreign direct investments. The agenda for small and micro-businesses on the domestic front seems to be a low priority of public policy. Consequently, development policies in Asian countries continue to marginalize the poor and disadvantaged.

Second, the definitions and use of related terms in Asia are complex. In certain countries, "solidarity" cannot be effectively expressed owing to the historical context and ideology associated with the term. For example, in Malaysia and Singapore, the term has pro-Marxist implications, and in Cambodia, the response to collectivization, which was enforced during the Khmer Rouge, is negative. Therefore, Malaysia prefers the term "community economy" and in

Cambodia, the term "social enterprise and social entrepreneurship" is preferred. However, at the formative stage, establishing inclusive terms that can define the characteristics of the triple bottom line or the Quiñones measurement of commitment to five dimensions is essential. Thus, in this context the need to work toward defining and measuring a social solidarity economy is imperative. The ASEC is currently documenting case studies and innovative approaches in preparation for the Global RIPESS Gathering in Manila that will be held from October 15 to 18, 2013. The purpose of this project is to include the topic of solidarity economy into the mainstream development agenda.

Third, the networking among national, regional, and global partners has been consistent and growing. The ASEC has hosted three Asian regional solidarity economy forums at Manila (2007), Tokyo (2009), and Kuala Lumpur (2011). Quiñones noted that the nine networks in the ASEC have outreach programs that involve a total of 13 million people through 394 independent organizations in 21 Asian countries (Jayasooria 2013). Three key features may be observed across the region: social motivation, people participation, and excellent governance. The ASEC is the Asian continental partner of RIPESS, which is an intercontinental network for the promotion of social solidarity economy. Since 1997, global gatherings have been held once every four years. In 1997, the gathering was in Lima, Peru; in 2002, it was in Quebec, Canada; in 2005, it was in Dakar, Senegal; in 2009, it was in Luxembourg; and in 2013, it was in Manila, the Philippines. Yvon Poirier (2013) provides a comprehensive historical overview of the RIPESS global network and the various innovations that have been made around the world.

The "breakthrough" of social solidarity models of alternative economy may be observed across Asia. Despite numerous challenges, they have emerged and are rapidly growing. Asian governments are noticing it and have fostered an enabling environment, providing the resources for the growth and institutionalization of this movement in Asia.

Notes

1 Refer to Bina Swadaya's English official site: http://binaswadaya.org/bs3/?lang=en. Please also read its working areas on this site: http://binaswadaya.org/bs3/?p=182. Note that Bambang Ismawan wrote an article, "Responding to the Nation's Problems with Entrepreneurship." This may be viewed at http://binaswadaya.org/bs3/?p=106.
2 A good reading on Bambang Ismawan is Budianta (2008).
3 Please refer to its official site: www.assefa-sss.org, and Action Village India (n.d.).
4 Please also refer to its official site: http://append.com.ph/.
5 Please refer to United Nations (2012a) in the paragraphs related to the conference.
6 Please refer to the RIPESS official site: www.ripess.org/category/feeds-en/?lang=en.
7 Please refer to the Socioeco official site: www.socioeco.org/index_en.html.

References

Arruda, Marcos, ed. 2008. *Exchanging Visions of a Responsible, Plural, Solidarity Economy RPSE*. Rio de Janeieo: ALOE.

Arruda, Marcos, ed. 2009. *A Non-patriarchal Economy is Possible: Looking at Solidarity Economy from Different Cultural Facets: Asia-Latin America-North America and Europe*. Rio de Janeiro: ALOE.

Ashoka. n.d. "Ismawan, Bambang." Ashoka Fellows. Available online at: www.ashoka.org/fellow/bambang-ismawan.

Bidget, Eric, and Hyung-Sik Eum. 2011. "Social Enterprise in South Korea: History and Diversity." *Social Enterprise Journal* 7(1), 69–85. doi: 10.1108/17508611111130167.

Budianta, Eka. 2008. *Bambang Ismawan bersama Wong Cilik* [Bambang Ismawan together with Wong Cilik]. Jakarta, Indonesia: Bina Swadaya.

Cabinet Office, Government of Japan. 2010. "Declaration of 'New Public Commons 2010.'" Cabinet Office. Available online at: www5.cao.go.jp/npc/pdf/declaration-english.pdf.

Congress of the Philippines. 2012. "An Act Ordaining the Promotion and Development of Social Enterprises in Order to Ensure Poverty Reduction, Providing the Mechanisms therefor, and for Other Purposes." Philippines Social Enterprise Bill 2012. Peace and Equality Foundation. Available online at: www.pef.ph/phocadownload/Social-Enterprise-Bill_HB-6085.pdf.

Cook, Sarah. 2013. "Opening and Introductory Remark." Speech at the "Potential and Limits of Social and Solidarity Economy," an UNRISD Conference co-hosted with the ILO, May 6–8. Available online at: www.unrisd.org/80256B42004CCC77/(httpInfoFiles)/2A7A8591884A99F5C1257B72004A9ABA/$file/SSE%20Opening%20Remarks%20Sarah%20Cook%20(for%20web).pdf.

Dacanay, Marie Lisa. 2012. "Perspectives on the Policy Environment Affecting Social Enterprises in the Philippines." Institute for Social Entrepreneurship in Asia. Available online at: http://isea-group.net/resources/SE_Policy_Environment_Philippines_for_ISEA _May_2012.pdf.

Economia. 2012. "The Big Idea: C.K. Prahalad." *Economia*, October 3. Available online at: http://economia.icaew.com/business/october-2012/the-big-idea-c-k-prahalad.

Getubig, Mike, David Gibbions, and Joe Remenyi. 2000. "Financing a Revolution: An Overview of the Microfinance Challenge." In *Microfinance and Poverty Alleviation: Case Studies from Asia and the Pacific*, edited by Joe Remenyi and Benjamin Quiñones Jr. (ch. 1). London: Pinter.

Ishizuka, Hideo. 1999. "Legislation Enacted for Nonprofit Organizations in Japan." World Volunteer Web. Available online at: www.worldvolunteerweb.org/fileadmin/docs/old/pdf/2002/JPN990901_legislation_npo.pdf.

Jayasooria, Denison, ed. 2013. *Developments in Solidarity Economy in Asia*. Kuala Lumpur: Asian Solidarity Economy Council (ASEC). Available online at: http://socio-eco.org/bdf/en/corpus_document/fiche-document-1873.html.

Juan, Virginia. 2013. "Solidarity Economy and Micro Credit: The Append-Philippines." In *Developments in Solidarity Economy in Asia*, edited by Denison Jayasooria (pp. 161–181). Kuala Lumpur: ASEC.

Kawano, Emily, Thomas Neal Masterson, and Jonathan Teller-Elsberg, eds. 2009. *Solidarity Economy 1: Building Alternatives for People and Planet: Papers and Reports from the 2009 U.S. Forum on the Solidarity Economy*. Amherst, USA: Center for Popular Economics.

Lee, Kwang Taek. 2013. "The Social Enterprise Promotion Act in South Korea." In *Developments in Solidarity Economy in Asia*, edited by Denison Jayasooria (pp. 139–151). Kuala Lumpur: ASEC.

Mercado, Rosa C., ed. 2009. *Solidarity Economy and the Cooperative Experience*.

Quezon City, The Philippines: Centre for Labor and Grassroots Initiatives, University of the Philippines Diliman.

Nishikawa, Jun. 2013. "The Development of Solidarity-based Economy in Japan." In *Developments in Solidarity Economy in Asia*, edited by Denison Jayasooria (pp. 182–188). Kuala Lumpur: ASEC.

Poirier, Yvon. 2013. "The International Forum on the Social and Solidarity Economy: Three Outstanding Examples to Know." Canadian CED Network. Available online at: http://ccednet-rcdec.ca/sites/ccednet-rcdec.ca/files/ccednet/pdfs/YPoirier-FIESS_examples.pdf.

Prahalad, C.K. 2010. *Fortune at the Bottom of the Pyramid: Eradicating Poverty through Profits*. Upper Saddle River, NJ: Pearson Education.

Prahalad, C.K. 2012. "Bottom of the Pyramid as a Source of Breakthrough Innovations." *Journal of Product Innovation Management* 29(1), 6–12. Available online at: http://onlinelibrary.wiley.com/doi/10.1111/j.1540-5885.2011.00874.x/pdf.

Quiñones Jr., Benjamin R. 2012. *Sowing the Seeds of Solidarity Economy: Asian Experiences*. Kuala Lumpur: Centre for Social Entrepreneurship, Binery University College.

Quiñones Jr., Benjamin R. 2013. "The Triple Bottom Line Social Solidarity Economy (SSE) Supply Chain: Its Role in Building a New Model of Development." Unpublished paper.

Ryder, Guy. 2013. "Opening Remarks to the UNRISD Conference on Social and Solidarity Economy." Speech at the "Potential and Limits of Social and Solidarity Economy," an UNRISD Conference co-hosted with the ILO, May 6–8. Available online at: www.ilo.org/global/about-the-ilo/who-we-are/ilo-director-general/statements-and-speeches/WCMS_212653/lang-en/index.htm.

Sarvodaya Action Research Centre. 2008. *Silent March of the Invisible Force*. Madurai, Tamil Nadu, India: Sarvodaya Action Research Centre.

Sen, Amartya. 1999. *Development as Freedom*. New York: Alfred A. Knopf.

United Nations. 2012a. "The Future We Want." *Outcome of the Conference*. Document presented at the Rio+20 United Nations Conference on Sustainable Development, Rio De Janeiro, Brazil, June 20–22. Available online at: www.uncsd2012.org/content/documents/774futurewewant_english.pdf.

United Nations. 2012b. "Homepage." International Year of Cooperatives 2012. Available online at: http://social.un.org/coopsyear/.

Yunus, Muhammad. 2007. *Creating a World without Poverty: Social Business and the Future of Capitalism*. New York: Public Affairs.

Yunus, Muhammad. 2010. *Building Social Business: The New Kind of Capitalism that Serves Humanity's Most Pressing Needs*. New York: Public Affairs.

Yunus, Muhammad, and Alan Jolis. 1999. *Banker to the Poor: Micro-lending and the Battle against World Poverty*. New York: Public Affairs.

Part III

Social economy in Chinese societies

10 Zhoujiazhuang village

A study of the heritage of the people's commune[1]

Ngai Pun, Lu Huilin and Li Changjiang

Reform and rural China

China's reform is a sublation and extension of the practice of socialist collective economy in the past 30 years. Prior to 1978 the Chinese socialist system was marked chiefly by the highly centralized planned command economy and public ownership. The government-led economy, policy, and social pattern have been established by denying a free market and condemning all forms of ownership other than public ownership. The reform instead centers on the establishment of market economy and privatization. The replacement of planned economy by market economy implies changes in the mode of production and resource allocation. In other words, the production mode dominated by state and collective ownership gives way to market-oriented private economy. Meanwhile, in the ideological sphere, it also means the transformation from denial of public ownership economy to high praise for the advantages of private economy, including foreign-funded and private companies. In terms of scale, the non-public ownership economy has now become the main body of China's economy.[2]

In rural areas, this reform is most obviously reflected in the widespread collapse of people's communes and implementation of the household contract responsibility system, which helped re-establish the dominance of the household-based peasant economy in rural China. The people's commune system, which lasted for over 20 years in China, faded out of history in a mere six years from late 1978 when Xiaogang village fired the opening shot in China's rural reform by announcing "fixing of farm output quotas for each household" (Ling 2011) to 1985, which saw the separation of government functions from commune management and the set-up of township governments.[3]

Criticism of the people's commune

As a special form of cooperative, the people's commune is an important institutional arrangement for the practice of socialism in China before its reform and opening up, and it has far-reaching impacts on rural China or even the whole country. At present, the people's commune has often been viewed negatively. In general, a few researches criticizing the commune have the following three characteristics (Lin 1994, 2000).

First, these researches are critical of the people's commune, holding that it is an inefficient institutional arrangement.

Second, with reference to the peasant economy under the household contract responsibility system, most of these researches argue through comparison that the peasant economy is a more efficient production mode with greater vitality.

Third, most of these researches blame the failure of the people's commune on high organization costs, (e.g., equalitarianism caused by work points, lack of incentives to the commune's members and management due to defective ownership, and extremely high supervisory costs owing to the complexity of agricultural production).

Besides equalitarianism caused by unreasonable methods for calculating work points, the emergence of "lay-up" workers was also a major reason for the stagnation and even decline of work point values every year (Cao *et al.* 1995). Lay-up workers are defined by Cao Jinqing and colleagues in their study as "the result of subtracting the total number of workers used from the total number of workers actually used by a production team in the whole year" (Cao *et al.* 1995, 172). A study of Chenjia village shows that the number of lay-up workers took up 50 percent of the total number of workers used by the production team, which means that half of the work points obtained by the members corresponded to ineffective labor input. This was due to the constant increase in labor force and labor input and insufficient arable areas. Therefore, there were actually huge numbers of redundant laborers in the people's communes.

This was in fact a result of inadequate land and large populations, and massive surplus laborers in China. To prevent surplus laborers from shifting toward cities and non-agricultural industries, the state set up the household registration system to control migration movements. Therefore, the countryside served as a labor force reservoir for an extended period of time. Under these conditions, a surplus of laborers is inevitable if the large-scale rural collective economy cannot be brought into full play to expand production and get the redundant population into work via reinvestment.

Influence of external factors

Apart from internal reasons, many researches have also pointed out the adverse impact of the external environment. For example, the excessive grain purchased by the state and price scissors between industrial and agricultural products represent an invisible deprivation of farmers, and the strict household registration system has restricted the flow of the rural population and their freedom of choice, etc. The commune system was also criticized as a totalizing entity which became mixed up with Party work and government work, and government administration with commune management (Zhang 2005). Such an external environment resulted in the rigidity of the commune system and ineffective labor in the commune (Zhang 2007). Government emphasis on heavy industry also increased deprivation in rural areas. Justin Yifu Lin's (2000) study indicates that the planned purchase price and the price for premium purchase offered by the state were lower than the substantive market price, reducing the income of farmers. Zheng Yougui (2007) pointed out in his study that from 1959 to 1978, the state took net accumulations of RMB407.5 billion away from the Ministry of Agriculture via "price scissors" between industrial and agricultural products.

Empirical research on Zhoujiazhuang Cooperative

Zhoujiazhuang village, a subordinate of Jinzhou City, Hebei Province, is just 50km away from Shijiazhuang, the provincial capital of Hebei. From 1952 when the first agricultural producers' cooperative at village level was built, to 1956 when the cooperative turned into a joint village cooperative and up until the present, Zhoujiazhuang village has had its name changed, for example, from the people's commune in the past to township government. However, its cooperative system has remained unchanged for more than 60 years. It is one of the very few villages which have maintained the practice of collective economy. Many members living in Zhoujiazhuang village today still rely on a collective planned economy. The primary labor form of recording work points, distributing rations, and centralized farming and unified distribution in Zhoujiazhuang village provides us with an opportunity to conduct close observation and research. It is indeed a miracle that Zhoujiazhuang Cooperative subsists up until the present day when the people's communes are widely criticized and the household contract responsibility system has obtained its leading position.

At the end of spring and the beginning of summer 2009, we came to Zhoujiazhuang Cooperative for the first time; the village occupied 15.73 km^2 in total and covered a land area of 21,046 mu. It had 4,495 households with 13,029 people in 2009. With a two-level management system, the cooperative had 10 subordinate production teams. During our short stay, we experienced the surprising development of Zhoujiazhuang village, the orderly villas which are not luxurious but neat. We often have negative impressions about people's communes, but Zhoujiazhuang village is an exception. Its existence challenges our "common sense" allow us to realize that "common sense" may be the mainstream structure of reform ideology. In March 2010, we visited Zhoujiazhuang Cooperative again. During our five-day stay, we visited two production teams and browsed abundant village archives and files.

"Nobody has worked outside and no girl has married out in Zhoujiazhuang Village. Some of us have opened shops and some have opened factories, but they are all around the village." We heard words like this repeatedly during our five-day visit. We asked them many times, "Why don't you divide up fields so that you will be more driving?" The most typical answer is, "It is worry-saving that we don't divide up fields!" In 2010, the rural labor force in the village generally comprised older people, who received an annual dividend income of RMB25,000 to RMB28,000, accounting for 25 percent of the total labor force in the village. Young people who worked in collective factories received an annual dividend income of RMB30,000 to RMB35,000. A woman who had recently given birth to a baby and stayed at home said, "Don't worry, I can return to work in the factory after the child grows up." There are no retirees in Zhoujiazhuang village. If he is willing, an 80-year-old man can serve as a doorkeeper and receive an annual income of over RMB10,000. At first glance, life in Zhoujiazhuang village is carefree. "Worry-saving" is a word we heard the most in the village. Sometimes there are complaints. A villager withdrew from the cooperative and opened a store in 2010 because he was not happy about the production team leader's unequal division of labor. He said, "If my business is good, I will stay outside [the cooperative] and if not, I will go back. We can make choices once a year."

If the cooperative's advantages are reflected in agricultural production and collective enterprises, how can Zhoujiazhuang village achieve effective labor management and reasonable distribution, and how can it lower the costs of supervision and management? On this basis, we probe into the practice of Zhoujiazhuang village, especially the reasons why the collective economy is superior to and more efficient than the small-scale peasant economy.

Brief history of Zhoujiazhuang Cooperative

In November 1951, three agricultural producers' mutual aid teams in Zhoujiazhuang village merged to form the first cooperative of the county – Cao Tongyi Agricultural Producers' Cooperative, which comprised 20 farming households with 194.6mu arable land. By July 1952, two cooperatives, 49 long-term mutual aid teams and 37 temporary mutual aid teams had been established in Zhoujiazhuang village, covering 369 farming households (77.7 percent of the total) who participated in mutual cooperation. After that, mutual cooperation among farmers kept developing and the mutual aid teams gradually changed into agricultural producers' cooperatives. On February 13, 1954, Zhoujiazhuang Agricultural Producers' Cooperative was formally established by merging 10 primary agricultural producers' cooperatives and 13 mutual aid teams in Zhoujiazhuang village on the basis of Cao Tongyi Agricultural Producers' Cooperative, consisting of 425 households (87.8 percent of the total in the village).

At the climax of the cooperative movement in China in 1955, the county committee of Jin County decided to focus on developing and expanding Zhoujiazhuang Agricultural Producers' Cooperative into the first socialist agricultural producers' cooperative In February 1956; cooperatives from six unincorporated villages in Zhoujiazhuang County merged to form Zhoujiazhuang's advanced joint village cooperative for agricultural production consisting of 1,509 farming households. Since then, the scale of cooperative was determined and continues today. In the climax of people's commune campaign in 1958, Zhoujiazhuang joint village cooperative developed into Zhoujiazhuang People's Commune. Following the reform and opening up, Zhoujiazhuang Agricultural, Industrial and Commercial Cooperative was established after Zhoujiazhuang People's Commune separated government administration from commune management.[4]

At present, the cooperative still keeps to collective production. As for agricultural production, the production team is still the basic calculation unit for field crops like wheat and corn; the orchards successively established after 2000 are contracted to individuals, but the revenues from sales and production are distributed by the production teams according to laborers' work; the collective enterprises including valve plants and printing houses are under unified operation and management of the cooperative, and their revenues are distributed by the cooperative according to work among production teams, which provides a strong subsidy to agricultural production.

Therefore, we will analyze Zhoujiazhuang Cooperative from three aspects. Generally speaking, the significance of "able persons" in the village is emphasized in researches on the cooperative, and we do not deny the functions of "able persons" in this research. However, we believe the social structures and production relations in the cooperative are more important, especially how the cooperative formulates the labor quota management system, how it settles the problem of "raising dawdlers" under collective economy, and how it distributes revenues among its members. Finally, we analyze the scale advantage of the cooperative.

Labor quota management system

The cooperative and people's communes are mainly criticized for their inefficiency. It is believed that the characteristics of agricultural cooperative production and difficulties in supervision have caused serious equalitarianism in distribution, frustrating members and reducing production efficiency.

If such criticism is reasonable, the exceptional Zhoujiazhuang Cooperative gives us different explanations. If collective production of the cooperative is inevitably insufficient, how can Zhoujiazhuang Cooperative survive and sustain development in the surging wave of "household farming"? Why did its members willingly insist on rather than oppose and abandon such a production mode?

The secret lies in the cooperative's labor management and distribution system.

Zhoujiazhuang Cooperative adopted a labor management and distribution system on the basis of labor quota management, unified calculation by the cooperative and distribution according to work, which effectively reduced the supervision and calculation costs and provided a reasonable evaluation of different members regarding their labor input so as to conduct fair distribution, avoiding free riding and equalitarianism in collective production to the greatest extent possible.

In 1961, the central government adjusted the people's commune system as "team-based ownership at three levels (commune, production brigade and production team)" and specified that the people's communes could also implement "team-based ownership at two levels," with the production brigade removed. Hence, Zhoujiazhuang People's Commune implemented the system of ownership at two levels, namely the commune (cooperative) and production teams. In

1980 when the household contract responsibility system was promoted across China, Zhoujiazhuang Cooperative denied "household farming," insisted on its original operation mode and management system, and adjusted it according to actual conditions so as to make it more efficient.

Moreover, this research shows that if the reasonable labor management and distribution system has prevented the cooperative from falling apart, the cooperative's scale advantage may have helped to constantly strengthen the collective economy and improve all members' welfare, which is also important to the cooperative's development.

Quota management and work point system

The work point system is criticized by many researchers as the chief culprit of equalitarianism and inefficiency of people's communes. However, in Zhoujiazhuang Cooperative, the work point system under the labor quota system was not canceled but made new progress under the new historical conditions to become the fundamental basis for the labor management and distribution system of the cooperative.

Labor quota in agricultural production

Quota management centers on labor quota, which is also called "work quota." Labor quota means "a certain amount of work that an average laborer should complete under certain conditions by exerting certain strength in a unit time and to a certain quality standard" (Liu *et al.* 2003, 22). Therefore, labor quota is actually a set of measurement criteria assessing the standard quantity and quality needed in a certain production activity, aiming to evaluate the labor input of members in a production activity as reasonably and fairly as possible, which serves as the basis for work points assessment and performance-based distribution.

Here, for example, we take the *Labor Quota Items and Remuneration Standard*, issued by Zhoujiazhuang Cooperative in 2004, to explain how quota management and work point systems work.

The quota management system divides the 372 labor quota items into 13 levels, with different levels corresponding to different work day remuneration standards:

1 The labor quota system is actually a type of piecework wage system. Take, for example, "machine ploughing": 1.1 work days will be recorded for one labor force (tractor driver) to finish the work of tilling 27.5 mu of land with the instruments of production such as Model 50 and 60 tractors and four-tooth plow. Each work day can be converted to 10 work points; thus the member gets 11 work points for finishing the task.
2 The labor quota system also shares certain features with the time wage system. Based on the amount of work that an average laborer can achieve in

one day, the above labor quotas usually specify the amount of labor to be achieved within one day.

3 The same working hours do not necessarily earn the same work points, as the labor intensity and skill entailed in different quota items are different. For example, machine plowing is classified as level-5 labor, where one can get 1.1 work days and 11 work points to finish the said amount of work; while the high-skilled labor of mechanized wheat sowing is classified as level-3 labor, where one can get 1.25 work days and 12.5 work points to finish the said amount of work.
4 There are also certain odd jobs or types of casual work, like gathering the loose ears of wheat along with the harvester. Odd or casual work is usually auxiliary, with the amount of work depending on the major production progress. For example, gleaning (sickling and collecting the remaining wheat that the large harvesters may have missed) is quite an easy job, so its working hours and amount of labor depend on the harvesting progress. Since it is hard to calculate the amount of work achieved, such work is measured by the time involved.
5 Labor quotas are set in consideration of the tools used, distance of farm land, labor intensity, technical requirements, as well as quantity and quality of work. For example, different quantity and quality standards are specified for machine plowing with Model 55 and 60 machines equipped with four-tooth plows and Model 18 to 20 tractors equipped with two-tooth plows, so as to make a distinction between the values of different labors.
6 Although most labor quota items each involve one laborer, there is also some work needing several people working together. In this case, the value of the work day is calculated by multiplying the number of work days under the level by the number of people.
7 The above labor quotas set out the amount of labor to be achieved per day based on the production progress of an average laborer involving normal labor intensity. However, laborers work at different speeds, and some highly efficient laborers may not need one day to accomplish the required task. For example, those who can pick 11 jin of cluster red pepper in half a day may feel frustrated as they have to waste half a day if the task is fixed. Therefore, the cooperative allows excess production and makes payments for the actual excess quantity.

The labor quota items and remuneration standard are formulated upon democratic discussion and based on rich agricultural production experience. The quota standard needs to be constantly adjusted in light of changes in production techniques and crop strains. In fact, Zhoujiazhuang Cooperative generally adjusts its labor quota every two years.

Zhoujiazhuang Cooperative sets the above labor quotas mainly for the cultivation of fields, as its field crops (mainly winter wheat and summer maize) are suited to mechanized cultivation. On the other hand, its orchards adopt another quota management system.

Labor quota management of production teams' orchards

In recent years, aside from field crop planting, the cooperative has also vigorously developed high value-added agriculture such as orchards. At present, production teams have established thousands of mu of fruit-planting bases including vineyards and pear gardens.

Different from field crops like wheat and corn, orchards are specially contracted and separately accounted for by production teams. The following are the main points:

1. To convert the entire process from trimming to harvesting of orchards of a certain size into a certain number of workdays according to the degree of difficulty of production,[5] and then contract it to a specialized team, which is responsible for the entire production process and is assigned the agreed number of work days.
2. By contracting out the whole labor process for a certain number of work days, the production team does not need to set labor quotas and work points for each part of fruit production. This is actually similar to the "labor contract system."
3. To account for orchard production separately from field production can better motivate orchard contractors, as they will have their work points linked to their fruit output: the better they harvest, the bigger dividends they get, and vice versa.
4. The production team, instead of the contractors, has the right to allot the area and number of people, thereby avoiding the possibility that orchards are monopolized by a handful of large contractors, which will trigger discontent and tensions among members.

INTERVIEWER: Are the orchards contracted by a team?
MEMBER: Three people appointed by the production team have contracted them.
. . .
INTERVIEWER: Will everyone scramble for the highly profitable orchards?
MEMBER: You cannot scramble for it. In fact, running orchards is hard work. We just obey the assignment of the production team. The ones who run orchards generally remain unchanged, as running orchards is quite skilled and requires years of experience.

This shows that the orchard contract system in Zhoujiazhuang Cooperative is different from the household contract responsibility system in the following aspects. First, although the entire process of orchard running is contracted out to specialized teams, unified sales by the cooperative will form a scale advantage, which is an attraction for customers and contributes to a higher price than the fruit of neighboring scattered farmers. Second, instead of being directly paid to contractors, the earnings of fruit sales will be accounted for and then distributed in a unified way by the cooperative and production teams with the income from orchards and fields moderately adjusted to avoid income disparity. Third, the number of contractors and area to be contracted are specified by production teams. Generally, orchard contractors will have a slightly better income but the work is harder than those running fields. This is intended to avoid the unfair situation in which only a minority can profit from the orchards, which means serving the minority with public interests. After all, orchard land is a collectively owned asset, and the investment in the orchards comes from public savings of production teams and the cooperative.

Labor quota management of collective enterprises

In playing the role of standardizing the labor process, the quota management system lays more emphasis on cooperation among its members compared with the family-based peasant economy. There is a trend of factory-like operation as the production process is increasingly mechanized, standardized, and normalized. In particular, labor quota and work point systems are applied not only to agricultural production, but also to the production of collective enterprises. More than 1,000 labor quotas were set for the Valve Plant in 2000, compared with 374 of its predecessor, Hardware & Thermos Factory, in 1990. The increase in quotas is associated with product varieties and technology complexity. Products are more and more varied and production becomes increasingly specialized and minutely divided; hence the increasing number of quota items.

Supervision of the labor process

As the basic production units of Zhoujiazhuang Cooperative, production teams have their team leaders and vice team leaders responsible for their production work, who need to assign tasks and supervise members' labor using evaluation criteria including the quantity and quality of the work achieved.

INTERVIEWER: Who examines and evaluates the work finished?

MEMBER: The team leader. If you don't do well, he will deduct your work points. As a result, you may get six points or eight points for a workday.

INTERVIEWER: The team leader just examines your work quality every day?

MEMBER: Yes, he examines our work. For example, I have done some work, he just examines it and reports it to the accountant if it is based on quota, or keeps account of the actual working hours if it is odd job.

To ensure progress, the team leader of a production team who has great power has to call up team members to start working and assign tasks every day, and urge them to speed up in the season of "harvesting and planting in a rush." As a result, he usually gets up earlier and sleeps later than members. In comparison, although not so free and having to follow instructions of team leaders, members basically have nothing to worry about.

INTERVIEWER: For example, running picking gardens is more lucrative than running fields, and then who will be assigned to run picking gardens and who the fields?

MEMBER: It's not of your choice. It's up to the team leader. Everyone just follows his assignment.

INTERVIEWER: Will he make assignment by household? I mean, will he assign different operation sites for members in the same family?

MEMBER: The officials have the final say.

...

MEMBER: If it happens that you are reluctant to do what you are assigned, then you just do other work you want to do or just have a rest. Now we are running out of labor forces as most of them have got employed in the plants. Now the population of 1,500-plus is mostly old people. Even the youngest laborer in the village is in his fifties. Anyway, no youngster is willing to do such work.

Each production team appoints several group leaders, who lead and urge their group members to finish their allotted tasks and may be criticized by the team leader if their groups perform poorly. This helps to decentralize the right of supervision and makes supervision more effective by reducing the scale of work groups.

MEMBER: Previously team leaders group their members on the field, now they just use the loudspeaker to broadcast the work assignment and group leaders.

INTERVIEWER: Then how to supervise the quality?

MEMBER: Group leaders are responsible for the quality and they will deduct your work points if you cannot pass muster.

INTERVIEWER: Will group leaders have their work points deducted if they performed poorly as supervisor?

MEMBER: Yes. Of course their work points will be deducted if they led badly.

It is interesting that no female acts as group leader. A male leader will be appointed even for a group consisting exclusively of women. Some members explain that such practice is conducive to the communication of group leaders with the team leader, as leaders of the village are all male.

Do team leaders commit fraud in their supervision? Our research found that, although not perfect, basically team leaders are objective and fair.

INTERVIEWER: What if someone disagrees when reporting work results? For instance, what if a member is displeased as the team leader evaluates his work as bad and deducts his work points?

MEMBER: Whatever he feels. Of course his points must be deducted if the quality is not up to standard.

INTERVIEWER: Is it the case that the team leader just lies that everyone did a good job for fear of hurting friendship?

MEMBER: No consideration for friendship.

...

INTERVIEWER: Is there anyone publicly recognized as lazy?

MEMBER: I cannot say no. Generally everyone does a good job as no one can cheat in the work.

Thus we see that, actually, supervision is a process of interaction between the supervisor and the supervised. The team leaders should fairly and objectively evaluate the labor of members, and allot tasks reasonably and fairly to get acknowledged among members; while members in turn can actively follow team leaders' arrangements, finish their tasks on time with quality assured without being indolent on duty or rejecting the assignment. Such a harmonious labor relationship is rooted in the acquaintances network in the rural society, which will impact heavily upon those members violating widely accepted arrangements.

Distribution system of "three guarantees and one reward system" of the cooperative

If the labor quota management system aims at solving problems of supervision and calculation of members' labor input during production, the "three guarantees and one reward system" established on a unified calculation and system of distribution according to the work is intended to solve distribution problems between the cooperative and production teams, and between production teams and members. On the one hand, distributing incomes is according to labor input of members on the principle of more pay for more work, so as to give positive incentives to members; on the other hand, before distribution, reasonable deduction at the collective level for public savings is calculated, so as to make reinvestments to expand production and give full play to scale advantage.

If the "three guarantees and one reward system" aims at adjusting the relationship between production teams and the cooperative in production and distribution, then the system of distribution according to work is the basic principle for the distribution of collective economy, and is a different method for the calculation and payment of remuneration different the wage labor pay system. This section will introduce the distribution system of Zhoujiazhuang from two aspects: (1) the cooperative and production teams; (2) the production teams and members.

Contents of unified calculation

- Revenues of production units (including production teams and collective enterprises, as below) are handed over to the cooperative, and the cooperative organizes the year-end distribution to members.
- Revenues and costs of each production unit are calculated separately at the cooperative, without financial consolidation.

- The cooperative purchases agricultural materials required by production teams for agricultural production and states the specific amount they used as their production costs.
- The cooperative deducts a certain proportion of the production cost, common reserve fund, public welfare fund, and to-be-distributed fund for making up a deficiency with the surplus from the total revenue of each production unit, and the remainder is the net income thereof.
- The net income of each team is distributed to its members according to the principle of more pay for more work, less pay for less work, and no pay for no work.

Distribution between the cooperative and production teams

Revenues of production teams comprise three parts: production cost, deduction of public savings by the cooperative, and net income to be distributed. The cost of agricultural production mainly includes agricultural production materials such as fertilizer, seed, pesticide, diesel, agricultural film, and electricity. As agricultural production materials required by production teams are purchased by the cooperative, relevant costs are deducted during the unified calculation by the cooperative from total revenues of each team.

Net income refers to the amount after deducting the production cost. After deducting from the net income the collective common reserve fund, public welfare fund and to-be-distributed fund for making up a deficiency with the surplus, the remainder is distributed to members as per their work points. In recent years, owing to the development of collective enterprises, the total value of industrial output has exceeded that of agricultural output. In addition, due to low agricultural output, more common reserve funds and public welfare funds are withdrawn from industrial enterprises rather than from agricultural enterprises, so as to "nurture agriculture by industry."

Distribution between the cooperative and collective enterprises

Statistics show that since 2001 the revenues of collective enterprises accounted for more than 90 percent of the total revenue of the collective operation of Zhoujiazhuang Cooperative, and no more than 10 percent contributed by agriculture. Obviously, collective enterprises have become the leading force in the cooperative economy, since they not only create many job opportunities and improved non-farming income, but they also provide considerable public savings.

After deducting production costs from the operating income, the remainder is the enterprise's net income. For early collective enterprises, the construction of plants and purchase of machinery equipment are invested by the cooperative, so the enterprises need to pay the cooperative the interest on investment, asset depreciation costs, and interest on circulating capital occupied. However, from the late 1990s, enterprises were allowed to prepare circulating capital for themselves and to purchase equipment invested by the cooperative, so that they no longer needed to pay the interest on investment and depreciation costs. However, collective enterprises still need to pay the common reserve fund, public welfare fund and management fee to the cooperative which serves as their contributor and owner.

It should be especially noted that in Zhoujiazhuang Cooperative, wages are stated as net income rather than as production cost, which is exactly the difference between the cooperative and privately owned enterprises. Privately owned enterprises include employees' wages into their production costs, and squeezing employees' wages as much as possible to maximize profits going to capitalists or owners. In Zhoujiazhuang Cooperative, there is a reciprocal relationship between profits and wages. Collective enterprises and their profits are collectively owned by the members. In these enterprises, the profits and incomes of members are interrelated rather than antithetic.

Distribution according to work

Distribution according to work has two meanings: first, the members' incomes reflect the value of their labor input rather than the mere wage income obtained by selling their labor; second, the income can give a true and fair view of quality and quantity of labor inputs of different laborers. According to the analysis above, the net income of the cooperative after deducting costs and public savings is distributed among all the members participating in collective productive labor, and there are no other profits beyond members' income.

The income is distributed once a year, usually at the end of the year before the Spring Festival. Given unified calculation, the distribution is carried out at the office of the cooperative, which is also a great annual event for the cooperative and its members. The one-time distribution amount is relatively large, so outsiders are forbidden to go near the place for distribution, which is usually supported by the police from the county public security bureau.

The formula for calculating dividend income of members is: dividend income = number of work points * value of work point. Value of work point = to-be-distributed net return of the production team (R) ÷ total work points of the production team; the former represents total return, the latter represents quantity of work. The higher the value of the work point, the better economic results of the production team, the higher output of unit labor, the more per capita dividend of members.

It may be seen that Zhoujiazhuang Cooperative implements the "three guarantees and one reward system" and system of distribution according to work for the purpose of increasing initiatives of production teams and giving full play to scale advantage with production efficiency guaranteed. Meanwhile, the two systems also help the cooperative make moderate adjustments in distribution among production units, so as to ensure that laborers can achieve incomes corresponding to their labor input and quality, rather than receive an equal share regardless of the work done and egalitarianism in distribution. All these systems also represent the advantages of the two systems.

Scale advantage of the cooperative

If a proper labor quota management and distribution system effectively avoids the influence of equalitarianism on initiatives of members, the cooperative exceeds the peasant economy in the scale advantage based on public savings. The "three guarantees and one reward system" mentioned above aims at increasing public savings with a sound protection to production autonomy of production teams and collective enterprises, which is vital for bringing into play the scale advantage of the cooperative. This section will further elaborate on the scale advantage of Zhoujiazhuang Cooperative from two respects: production and distribution.

Industrial structure of the cooperative: parallel development of multiple businesses

Zhoujiazhuang Cooperative has a long history of sidelines. However, agriculture has always been the leading industry and major source of income of the cooperative/people's communes prior to 1980.

Development of collective enterprises

Before the reform and opening up, the development of sidelines in Zhoujiazhuang Cooperative was frequently affected by the external environment. However, a preliminary foundation had been laid for sidelines from the 1970s, when measures were taken to encourage the development of commune- and brigade-run enterprises, to 1974 when the income of sidelines accounted for 24.94 percent of the total revenue of the cooperative.

The deepening of opening-up since the 1980s created larger development space for collective enterprises of Zhoujiazhuang Cooperative. There were 18 collective enterprises by 1992. Later this figure dropped due to adjustment, but collective enterprises contributed the lion's share to the total revenue of the cooperative (Liu *et al.* 2003, 57–62). In 2009, the total output value of industry and agriculture of the cooperative amounted to RMB564.93 million, with RMB495.05 million (accounting for 87.6 percent of the total output value) contributed by the industry, RMB52.52 million (accounting for a mere 9.3 percent of the total output value) by agriculture, and RMB17.36 million by the tertiary industry (Chronicles Office, Jinzhou City People's Government 2009).

Differing from private capital today, the development of collective enterprises of the cooperative relies mainly on public savings of the collective economy. As stated above, apart from costs of production units (production teams and collective enterprises) of the cooperative, public funds such as a common reserve fund and public welfare fund are also deducted from the net income before distribution to members. In particular, the common reserve fund is mainly used to expand reproduction. In the early 1980s, collective enterprises were still in the initial stages and required massive capital input, which could only be withdrawn from the common reserve fund from agricultural production. In 1980, RMB228,500 agricultural reserve was used for developing the collective industry (Liu *et al.* 2003, 27).

Characteristic scale agriculture

In addition to the industry, Zhoujiazhuang Cooperative also continued to transform agricultural production, and realized scale and specialized production with its own characteristics.

Jin County is a major cotton-producing area in China. After 1979, China increased the purchase price of cotton several times, which considerably mobilized the cotton planting initiative. Both the per unit and total yield of cotton of Zhoujiazhuang Cooperative repeatedly hit new highs and brought substantial cash returns to the cooperative.

After 2000, the cooperative started to promote diversified agricultural operations, especially the production of farm products with high added value. In 2009, Zhoujiazhuang Cooperative had a total land area of 21,046 mu, with 18,516 mu for planting field crops, including winter wheat, summer corn, millet, and beans. The planting of field crops was completely mechanized, which greatly improved the agricultural production efficiency. At present, the agricultural labor only accounts for less than 10 percent of the labor force, and most of the workers are middle- and old-aged men and women.

In recent years, the cooperative signed an agreement with seed companies in Jin County about turning all wheatland to seed-breeding field, except for grain-ration farmland. The purchase price of seeds is 10 to 20 percent higher than that of common wheat. Zhoujiazhuang village got orders of wheat planting thanks to its scale advantage of collective production. It not only provides adequate land, but also implements unified farming and management, so that the quality of seeds may be guaranteed.

Fruit tree planting mainly includes orchards and picking gardens. The 900 mu picking gardens were first built in 2005 and were mainly used for developing agricultural tourism and ecological breeding, and planting fruit trees, strawberries, and vegetables. Production teams determine their own agricultural production, but they usually consult with the cooperative in this regard. For example, the picking garden is invested by the cooperative and Team X, but the profits are owned by Team X. Different from the highly mechanized field-crop planting, orchards and vegetable farms involve considerable manpower, but enjoy higher returns.

Distribution pattern of mutual complementation between industry and agriculture

Zhoujiazhuang Cooperative derives its economy mainly from agricultural and industrial production, which are conducted by production teams and collective enterprises, respectively. As the investment of the cooperative's reproduction comes from their internal accumulation, revenues from agricultural production were used to invest in industry and to establish a number of collective enterprises in the early stages of industrial development.

In the 1990s, collective enterprises began to take shape and became more capable of providing public savings, which made it possible to nurture agriculture by industry. In 1990, thanks to the considerable profit from industry, RMB666,500 was exempted from being withdrawn from agricultural production, and RMB900,000 from industrial profit and other revenues was also withdrawn as a year-end bonus for agricultural producers (Liu *et al.* 2003, 27). In 2009, the cooperative even received a total subsidy of RMB2.16 million for agricultural production.

Since the mid-1990s, the cooperative has clearly specified that agriculture can use funds without paying interests and be exempted from depreciation charges and withdrawal of reserve. As agricultural production is affected by natural conditions, the labor force will inevitably flow into the high-yield industry if no subsidy is given to the fundamental and low-yield agriculture, which may affect agricultural development. As unified calculation was implemented, Zhoujiazhuang Cooperative could use revenues from the production of collective enterprises to subsidize agricultural production so as to narrow the income gap between the workers in production teams and the cooperative while maintaining healthy agricultural development. As the labor bonus in collective enterprises is higher than that for agricultural production, the Cooperative also specified that a family have workers in both production teams (for agricultural production and for production in collective enterprises) so as to avoid a family income gap between different members.

In addition, as production teams differ greatly in land areas, labor forces, and means of production, the fast-paced ones will assist the slow-paced ones in a busy farming season so as to give better pay-to-scale advantage in production.

The Cooperative's public welfare

Furthermore, the Cooperative's leveraged collective economy provides many public welfare services. For example, it began to award subsidies to the elderly and poor and lonely people, and to provide free nine-year compulsory education in the 1990s. Zhoujiazhuang Cooperative always talked delightedly about its 10 welfare undertakings, including:[6]

The elderly aged 65 and above received a pension of RMB30 per month.

The peasant cadres aged 65 and above who had worked for over 20 consecutive years enjoyed a retirement treatment of average living standards of incumbent cadres.

The childless elderly aged 65 and above were supported by the Cooperative for living expenses, medicare, and medical expenses, and granted a subsidy of RMB20 per month.

As for the elderly who only had a daughter, the Cooperative undertook their living expenses and issued them with a subsidy of RMB30 per month. The daughter bore the medical expenses if her parents become ill and she inherited the family property.

The family of each soldier was given special care funds of RMB5,000 per year.

The free nine-year compulsory education system covered the whole village.

The cooperative provided tap water to farmers for free.

Unified residential buildings were reasonably planned and established with support from the Cooperative.

Anyone who was hospitalized for a serious disease in the hospital above the county level, causing financial difficulties to his family, received financial aid from the Cooperative.

Seemingly ordinary today, these subsidies actually reflect the merits of the Cooperative as they were in place during 1980 to 2001. This was a crucial period for China when it was undergoing market economic reform, the former system was broken up, the social security system based on public ownership and collective economy disappeared, and the individual farmer had to undertake huge external risks concerning public services including medical insurance, free education, and social endowment. In this context, the overall welfare system established by the Zhoujiazhuang Cooperative was particularly valuable.

Conclusion: insights from Zhoujiazhuang Cooperative for social economy

As Zhoujiazhuang Cooperative stands out from hundreds of thousands of collapsed cooperatives, it is certainly not universal or even typical. Our description of Zhoujiazhuang Cooperative covers its steady development and practice and conditions from the commune days up until the present. We believe that by studying the Zhoujiazhuang case in detail will help us to impartially evaluate collective economy in history and pave the way for ideas about cooperative economy in the future.

Thus far, China has seen considerable development in industrialization and privatization, which means that many historical conditions that enabled collective economic development have disappeared. Given such altered historical conditions, Zhoujiazhuang's practice in collective economy is a especially enlightening for us in solving the significant issue of the agrarian crisis under the market economy.

With the acceleration of industrialization and urbanization in China, it is inevitable that agriculture will be operated on a large scale and that the small-scale peasant economy will fade out. The question is how to replace the small-scale peasant economy.

From the perspective of government policy and in reality, it is the general trend that land will be concentrated in minority hands. Although the development of new rural cooperatives is encouraged, they cannot achieve the broad and deep cooperation of Zhoujiazhuang Cooperative and, what is worse, they have become a tool of rich and influential people in seeking profits. Moreover, the state tends to focus its financial aid on large farming households, which actually implies that China is imitating the USA in agricultural development featuring large farms.

However, it is obviously not be the most appropriate developmental course for China which has less land and a large population. In this sense, social economy or cooperative economy is of great significance. As reproduction expansion and effective accumulation cannot be achieved under a small-scale economy, it is an approach worth exploring to conduct an alternative mode of production via scale operation and cooperative labor instead of capital-led wage labor. In this case, Zhoujiazhuang Cooperative stands out as a valuable example for us during the period of socialist transitional economy.

In sum, Zhoujiazhuang Cooperative is different from mainstrain state- or privately owned enterprises in the following two aspects: first, common property, which means that the manager of the cooperative is not the owner of the means of production, helps avoid exploitation based on private ownership; second, on this basis, the fruits of labor can be distributed among all the workers according to their performance.

Thanks to the collective economy of Zhoujiazhuang, its members are undoubtedly different and more secure in work and life as compared with the migrant workers who left their hometowns to work in the "world factory" as well as the farmers who scraped by on a few mu of land following the implementation of single production in separate fields. It is these characteristics that enable the Cooperative to become a possible trial of social economy which serves as a substitute for the capitalist mode of production.

Notes

1 This chapter is the partial result of the research subject "Forging New Trans-border Links: Social/Community Economies in Hong Kong and the Pearl River Delta," Strategic Public Policy Research, 2010 to 2012. We would like to thank Zhang Hexuan, Wang Wei, and Wang Dunmeng who participated in the field study, and Hairong Yan and Mr. Tian who introduced Zhoujiazhuang village to us.

2 According to the data from the National Bureau of Statistics, in 2007 non-public enterprises contributed 68 percent of the gross industrial output value, and absorbed 75.7 percent of the total employed population in urban areas. Please refer to http://money.163.com/08/1029/20/4PESDUN0002524SD.html.

3 According to the report by Xinhua News Agency dated June 4, 1985, the separation of government functions from commune management in China's rural areas and the set-up of township governments were completed, with a total of 92,000 townships (including ethnic townships) and town governments and over 820,000 village committees established.

4 An excerpt from *Zhoujiazhuang's Road* by Liu Zengyu, Du Rongshui, Wang Shengqiu, and Mu Xingzeng, and *Jin County Chronicles* by the Chorography Compilation Committee of Jinzhou City, Hebei Province.

5 Labor number, namely the number of work days, one work day per laborer, equal to 10 work points.

6 An excerpt from *Code of Conduct for Zhoujiazhuang Agricultural, Industrial and Commercial Cooperative* (Liu *et al.* 2003, 323).

References

Cao, Jinqing, Letian Zhang, and Zhongya Chen. 1995. *Dangdai zhe bei xiangcun de shehui wenhua bianqian* [Social and Cultural Change of Modern Rural Country in North Zhejiang]. Shanghai: Shanghai Far East Publishers.

Cheng, Shulan. 1999. *China's Rural Development: Theory and Practice*. Beijing: China Renmin University Press.

Chronicles Office, Jinzhou City People's Government, ed. 2009. *Jinzhou nianjian 2009* [Jinzhou Yearbook 2009]. Shenyang: Lianing Nationality Publishing House.

Du, Peng, Zhihong Ding, Quanmian Li, and Jiangfeng Gui. 2004. "Nongcun zinu waichu wugong dui liushou laoren de yingxiang [Impact on Aging Parents of their Children Leaving Home for Work Outside]." *Renkou yanjiu* [Population Research] 28(6), 44–52.

Guo, Hongdong. 2011. *Zhongguo nongmin zhuanye hezuoshe fszhsn: Lilun yu shizheng yanjiu* [The Development of Farmer Cooperative in China: Theory and Empirical Research]. Hangzhou: Zhejiang University Press.

Huang, Shengzhong. 2008. *Zhuǎnxíng shíqí nóngmín zhuānyè hézuòshè de zǔzhī xíngwéi yánjiū: Jīyú chéngyuán yì zhí xìng de shìjiǎo* [A Study on Farmer Specialized Cooperative's Organizational Behavior in Transitional Period: From Membership Heterogeneity Perspective]. Hangzhou: Zhejiang University Press.

Jiang, Junsong, Zongfan Xie, and Zijun Gui. 2009. "Renmin gongshe shiqi laodongli chanquan de zhidu jingji xue fenxi [Institutional Economics Analysis on the Labor Force Property Right during the Period of People's Commune]." *Journal of Xiangtan University* 33(4), 97–101.

Lin, Justin Yifu. 1994. *Zhidu, jishu yu zhongguu nungye fazhan* [System, Technology and China's Agricultural Development]. Shanghai: Shanghai Joint Publishing Company, Shanghai People's Publishing House.

Lin, Justin Yifu. 2000. *Zailun zhidu, jishu yu zhongguo nongye fazhan* [More on System, Technology and China's Agricultural Development]. Beijing: Peking University Press.

Lin, Zili. 1983. *Lian chan chengbao zeren zhi – shehui zhuyi nongye hezuo jingji zai zhongguo de xin mishi* [Contract Responsibility System – A New Mode of Socialistic Agricultural Cooperative Economy in China]. Shanghai: Shanghai People's Publishing House.

Ling, Zhijun. 2011. *Lishi bu zai paihuai: Renmin gongshe zai zhongguo de xingqi he shibai* [We Can't Turn History Back: The Rise and Failure of People's Commune in China]. Beijing: People's Daily Press.

Liu, Qingle. 2010. *Quanli, liyi yu xinnian-xin zhidu shijiao xia de renmin gongshe yanjiu* [Power, Benefits and Beliefs: A New Institutionalism Perspective on People's Commune in Rural China]. Beijing: China Social Sciences Press.

Liu, Wenge. 2007. *Jingji zhuangui yu zhidu bianqian fangshi bijiao: Yī zhōng é gǎigé zhànlüè yǎnbiàn wèi bèijǐng de fēnxī* [A Comparison Between Economic Transitions and Ways of Institutional Changes: Analysis Based on the Evolution of Reform Strategy of China and Russia]. Beijing: Economic Science Press.

Liu, Zengyu, Rongshui Du, Shengqiu Wang, and Xingzeng Mu. 2003. *Zhoujiazhuang zhi lu xuji: Zhongguo nongcun weiyi chuangban wushi zhounian de hezuoshe* [Sequel to Zhoujiazhuang's Road: The Only Rural Cooperative in China Finding its 50th Anniversary]. Baoding: Hebei University Press.

Lu, Yunhang. 2005. "Dui jianqing nongmin fudan wenti de yige gongxian: Tonggou tongxiao dui liangshi shengchan yingxiang de shizheng yanjiu: 1953–1982 [A Contribution to Lightening the Peasant's Burden: A Positive Study on the Influences of State Controlling Market on Grain Production During the Time 1953–1982]." *Nankai Economic Studies* 2005(4), 3–8.

Wang, Yongzuo. 2010. *Nongye yu nongcun zhidu chuangxin* [Agricultural and Rural System Innovation]. Beijing: China Agriculture Press.

Wright, Erik Olin. 2006. "Compass Points: Towards a Socialist Alternative." *New Left Review* 41, 93–124. Available online at: http://newleftreview.org/II/41/erik-olin-wright-compass-points.

Xin, Yi. 2005. *Nongcun renmin gongshe fenpei zhidu ysnjiu* [A Study on Distribution System of Rural People's Communes]. Beijing: CPC History Press.

Ye, Jingzhong, and Lu Pan. 2008. *Bie yang tongnian: Zhongguo nongcun liúshou ertong* [Differentiated Childhoods: Children Left Behind in Rural China]. Beijing: Social Science Academic Press.

Zeng, Yi. 2007. "Options for Fertility Policy Transition in China." *Population and Development Review* 33(2), 215–246. doi: 10.1111/j.1728-4457.2007.00168.x.

Zhang, Jianghua. 2007. "Gongfen zhi xia de laodong jiliyu jiti xingdong de xiaolu [Labor Incentive and Inefficiency of Collective Labor under the Work Point System]." *Sociological Studies* 22(5), 1–20.

Zhang, Letian. 2005. *Gaobie lixiang: renmin gongshe zhidu yanjiu* [Farewell to Ideals: Studies of People's Commune]. Shanghai: Shanghai People's Press.

Zhang, Xiaoshan, and Zhou Li. 2009. *Xin zhongguo nongcun 60 nian de fa zhan yu bianqian* [60-year Development and Change of Rural Areas of New China]. Beijing: People's Publishing House.

Zheng, Yougui. 2007. "Bijiao shijiao de nongchanpin tong pai gou zhidu [The System of Unified Purchasing of Farm Products by the State According to Fixed Quotas in a Comparative Perspective]." *Contemporary China History Studies* 14(5), 15–19.

Zhou, Qiren. 2002. *Chanquan yu zhidu bianqian: Zhongguo gaige de jingyan yanjiu* [Property Rights and Institutional Changes]. Beijing: Social Science Academic Press.

11 Debating the rural cooperative movement in China, the past and the present[1]

Hairong Yan and Chen Yi Yuan

Introduction

Rural cooperatives appear to be flourishing in China. With the Law on Specialized Farmer Cooperatives formally implemented in July 2007, rural cooperatives having industrial-commercial business registration stood at 100,000 in 2008. This number had increased to 689,000 by the end of 2012 and is expected to reach 900,000 by 2015 (China Review News 2013). For the purpose of such cooperatives, the law defines specialized farmers as "the producers and operators of the same kind of farm products or the providers or users of services for the same kind of agricultural production and operation" and allows agro enterprises to join as cooperative members. According to the law, specialized farmer cooperatives should "mainly serve their members, offering such services as purchasing the means of agricultural production, marketing, processing, transporting and storing farm products, and providing technologies and information related to agricultural production and operation."[2] In 2008 the central government encouraged a closer linkage between agro enterprises and rural producers (Zhang 2009, 14). A number of government or quasi-government organs are involved in promoting cooperatives, including the Ministry of Agriculture, the All China Federation of Supply and Marketing Cooperatives, China Association for Science and Technology, People's Bank, etc. At local levels, more government agencies are also involved in promoting cooperatives (Tong and Wen 2009, 16). Concerned intellectuals and student youth groups who adopt rural support positions are pioneer promoters of cooperatives.

Yet the development of cooperatives thus far has been rather controversial. Some contest the promotion of specialized farmer cooperatives and see the promotion as following a Euro-American model that promotes the interests of capitalist farmers. Many criticize that most of the cooperatives thus far developed are "fake" cooperatives. Some propose comprehensive peasant associations in Japan, South Korea, and Taiwan as a model for emulation. These contestations are about rural cooperatives, but also go way beyond them. For those who are passionately involved in the support and critique of rural cooperatives, what is at stake is both rural sustainability and the possibility of China pursuing a third-way development.

We should remember that this is not the first time that rural China saw a rising tide of the rural cooperative movement. Rural cooperatives first blossomed in the 1930s in the context of the Rural Reconstruction Movement (RRM) that enjoyed much official promotion and intellectual participation. At the same time, the flourishing of the movement then was accompanied by heated intellectual debates about the future of China, epitomized in the conversation between Liang Shuming (1893–1988) – one of the leading figures of the 1930s RRM – and Mao Zedong about the generality and particularity of Chinese society. The current growth of rural cooperatives also enjoyed much official promotion and intellectual engagement. Contemporary intellectuals in China who adopt rural support positions also see rural cooperatives as a key component of the new Rural Reconstruction Movement. Despite many differences between the 1930s and today, both the old and new RRM have been involved in the search for an alternative national development and both have seen a lack of organization among rural producers to be a fundamental problem for rural and even national reconstruction. Both old and new RRM have determined that rural cooperative organization is the way to get small rural producers organized. For today's leading rural advocates,[3] such as Wen Tiejun, the earlier movement is an inspiration and a legacy. The cooperative movements in the 1930s and today have both experienced conundrums whose conditions are intractably structural.

In our view, the debate surrounding the 1930s RRM and its cooperative movement is highly relevant today, for two reasons. First, there some remarkable intellectual parallels between the two RRMs and it is from the earlier RRM that some promoters of the RRM today by and large draw their inspiration (Li *et al.* 2008). The factors contributing to the contemporary significance of the earlier movement will be examined later in this chapter. Second, both movements have their own structural difficulties. The old debate on the nature of agrarian China, particularly between Liang Shuming and Mao Zedong, is little heeded today, but it is – as will be argued – worth revisiting for our own critical reflection on the problems of the contemporary rural cooperative movement. This chapter will thus examine intellectual perspectives and debates both in the past and in the present about rural cooperative development in China. In the face of the rapid agrarian change in China, the 1930s debate may still shed some light on today's conundrum.

The debate in the 1930s: the commonality or particularity of Chinese society

Chinese peasants have long had traditional practices of mutual help on an ad hoc basis, typically involving no more than a few families.[4] It was in the early twentieth century's context of intellectual fermentation that some Chinese intellectuals became attracted to the idea of the cooperative (Du 2002).[5] One of the earliest promoters of cooperatives, Tang Cangyuan, was fairly representative in embracing cooperativism as an alternative. In his view,

> Cooperation is opposed to capitalism. Its impact will more than undermine economic imperialism. But its approach is different from that of Marxism. Cooperativism does not emphasize revolution, but emphasizes construction. It does not rely on the state, but is based on organizations. Its approach is gradual and its action is far-reaching.
>
> (Chen 1983, 97, quoted in Bo 1994, 122)

This view was considered by Yu Shude, an early communist and secretary of Sun Yat-Sen, himself also an important proponent of cooperatives, to be a misconception of cooperative organization. Yu unambiguously pointed out in 1927 that cooperative organization is not socialism, but belongs in the realm of social policy (Yu 1929, Foreword). This insight was borne out in the reality of the first half of the twentieth century when different political forces – the Nationalist Party (KMT), the CCP, non-partisan intellectuals of different political positions, and even Japanese colonial forces in northeast China – all promoted cooperatives as a matter of social policy, but in different contexts and for different ends.

CCP's promotion of cooperatives was part of its larger class-based political mobilization. It first began with workers, but was soon extended to the peasantry, when the peasant movement rose in the 1920s. In 1922, while organizing a famously successful strike among mine workers in Anyuan, Jiangxi province, Mao and his colleagues also organized workers to form a consumer cooperative. The cooperative's rapid growth was met with a warlord military crackdown in 1925. Similar worker-centered cooperatives were also organized in parts of Hunan and Guangdong (Du 2002, 35–36). In 1925, the CCP's "Letter to Peasants" (*zhongguo gongchandang gao nongmin shu*) encouraged the emerging peasant associations to be active in forming cooperatives. In 1926 and 1927, cooperatives was one of the topics taught at the Guangzhou Institute of Peasant Movement that was jointly run by both the CCP and KMT (Du 2002, 37). From 1925 to 1927, peasant associations in Guangdong, Hunan, Hubei, and Jiangxi, where peasant movements were strongest, all issued resolutions on cooperatives (Shi 1957, 73–78).

Organizing cooperatives was part of the overall class-based peasant movement in the 1920s that included the suppression of landlord political and military power, rent reduction, anti-imperialist mobilization, literacy movements, etc.[6] These resolutions on cooperatives stated that they were for "poor peasants" or "small peasants," to avoid extortion by "landlords," "rich people" (*fuweng*), or rich households (*fuhu*) (Shi 1957, 74). These resolutions promoted cooperation in marketing, supply, and credit. After the KMT broke away from the two-party coalition in 1927, the CCP began to build its own rural bases where land reform was carried out. In the context of land reform and the need for men to join the Red Army and the local militia to defend these bases, initiative existed among peasants both to use traditional cooperation and to invent new forms of cooperation in sharing tools and animal power, and mobilizing women in production.[7] The CCP promoted cooperatives, particularly in production. In 1933, the CCP produced a policy outline on the organization of labor cooperatives, which was based on the principle of "relying on poor peasants and uniting middle peasants," as well as keeping landlords, rich households, and capitalists out of cooperatives (Shi 1957, 35–36; Mei 2004a, 105). In the 1940s when the CCP was in the midst of organizing national resistance against Japanese invasion, it enthusiastically promoted cooperatives in its Jin-Cha-Ji bases (Mao 1943). By this time, CCP-led class-based mobilization had achieved land reform in one half of these bases and rent reduction in the other half (Mao 1943). In this context, cooperatives served the purpose of not only stimulating cooperation and productivity, but also organizing a united front of all those who resisted Japanese invasion, including anti-Japanese rich peasants, landlords, and capitalists (Q.L. Liu 2010, 14).

The KMT began to organize rural credit cooperatives in 1928 (Bo 1994, 127).[8] Cooperatives grew in the 1930s in KMT-controlled areas. In 1932, the KMT government issued its first policy to support cooperatives in areas where it was combating the communist presence. In the ensuing years, the KMT government continued to support cooperatives with policies and funds. The number of cooperatives grew, with a great many being credit cooperatives. The presence of credit cooperatives could not help poor peasants with their production. Nor did it relieve them from predation by loan sharks. Instead, it made them vulnerable to extortion by landlords and merchants who took control of credit cooperatives and acted as their guarantors for credit (Mei 2004b, 87).

In the context of the widespread agrarian crisis in China in 1932 and the imminent national crisis brought on by the Japanese occupation of China's northeast, some non-partisan intellectuals dedicated themselves to the RRM and promoted cooperatives as the RRM's key component.[9] These intellectuals saw the cooperative movement as a way of people's self-organization and a key to national salvation. They also saw it as an alternative to the cropping up of Soviet bases in rural counties (1930–1934) founded by the Chinese Communist Party (Bo 1994, 129). The cooperative movement grew quickly, owing in part to the endorsement by the Nationalist government. The year 1933 saw the establishment of the first national network of rural reform organizations. By its third convention, in 1935, the network had recruited 99 organizations from 10 provinces, including civil associations, universities, and government departments, as well as some major newspapers (Xin Jiang and Xiaoyan Jiang 2008, 76, 80). At its peak, the end of 1936, there were over 1,000 rural experiment sites (Yan Yangchu 1989, 305 quoted in Jiang Xin and Jiang Xiaoyan 2008, 79), 37,318 cooperatives in 16 provinces that covered over 1.6 million members (Bo 1994, 127).[10] These experiments were financed either by the KMT government or by foreign funders (Liang 1989, vol. 2, 580). Renowned sociologist Fei Hsiao-tung (Fei Xiaotong) proposed in 1939 that cooperative rural workshops and rural industry could play a very important role in reconstructing rural China (Fei 2002, 238–239).

Despite the fact that both the CCP and the KMT promoted cooperatives for different ends, intellectual proponents of the 1930s cooperative movement continued the earliest proponents' vision for it to be a "third way" alternative to both

Western capitalism and communism. Liang Shuming's experiment in Zouping of Shandong province, running from 1931 to 1936, was the largest, having 307 cooperatives that involved 8,828 members in its peak year of 1936 (Qiu 2002, 101–102). It became one of the KMT government-endorsed experimental counties in 1933 and Liang himself was briefly head of the county in 1935 (Bo 1994, 129). An established neo-Confucian thinker and social reformer,[11] Liang Shuming gave his experiment a wide significance by clearly linking it with nation reconstruction. Due to Liang's influence both in the past and in the present, I focus on his view as the most important in the 1930s RRM.

A variety of socialisms became popular in China around the May 4th Movement in 1919 and attracted a large number of Chinese intellectuals. Influenced by Peter Kropotkin's writing on mutual aid, cooperation, and guild socialism (Yang 1999), Liang believed that RRM could build a new social structure with which China could embark on a path that was neither capitalist nor communist (Liang 1989, vol. 2, 151). Like many of his contemporaries, Liang saw China experiencing deterioration in the political (harassment by soldiers, banditry, severe taxations, etc.), the economic (economic invasion by foreign countries, etc.), and the cultural dimensions (social disorder). The demise of China in the past century, in his view, is "a history of rural destruction" (Liang 1989, vol. 2, 150). Not unlike Mao, he held that the countryside was the key to solving China's problem (Liang 1989, vol. 2, 161; vol. 5. 374), but these two figures differed in their diagnosis, as will be shown below. Disappointed with political-military powers that had been socially destructive since the fall of the last dynasty, Liang turned to a social-cultural structure for diagnosis and cure. (Alitto 1986, 280; Liang 1989, vol. 2, 162–163, 164). He stated, "China's problem today is that the social organization and structure, which had lasted for thousands of years, has collapsed, but the new one has not yet been established. RRM is a movement that reconstructs China's social organization and structure" (Liang 1989, vol. 5, 375).

Liang based his RRM on two major assumptions. First, rural reconstruction in itself is a self-adequate foundation for the reconstruction of the entire Chinese society. On the one hand, Liang emphasized that China's problems were ignited from outside and were not autogenic (Liang 1989, vol. 2, 233–234, 577). On the other hand, he believed that the solution to China's problems lies in the RRM, which "naturally contains solutions to all problems," as it includes progress in productive technologies, the development of cooperative organizations, improved levels of education, and a growth in peasant power (Liang 1989, vol. 5, 374). Liang envisioned "rural school programs" (*xiangnong xuexiao*) to provide two things that he saw were sorely lacking in rural China: knowledge of science and techniques, and a new form of social organization (Liang 1989, vol. 2, 191). The schools treated all villagers as students (*xue zhong*) and taught cooperation, agriculture skills and knowledge, literacy, etc. It also organized more than 300 cooperatives in production, sales, credit, procurement, etc. More than educational functions, Liang's rural schools interfaced with the political, economic, and military defense functions of the locality. Liang believed that this experiment served to develop a model for the political system of the entire state. The presumed self-adequacy of the RRM is based on the assumption that it could be autonomous from the dominant imperialist and local warlord political-economic powers. Liang's confidence in this assumption was to be devastated in 1938 (Yang 2001, 216, 221).

Liang's assumption of rural self-adequacy also includes his vision that China's agriculture production could serve as a foundation for its industrialization (Liang 1989, vol 2, 496). Liang reasoned that compared with China's feeble industry which was oppressed by Western industrial interests, agriculture was China's comparative advantage (508). Liang envisioned that China's path of development would have to be an agricultural one, based on cooperation, needs-based non-profit industrialization could be developed with enterprises owned not by individuals, but by cooperatives, social organizations, and the state (509). It would be a new civilization, different from both the old agrarian civilization and Western urban civilization. Liang planned a route to national construction: "inland rural areas can make use of surplus funds from elsewhere to restore and increase [agricultural] production, [rural folks'] increased purchasing power can then spur the development of national industry. Then industry and all other sectors can in turn prosper" (Liang 1989, vol. 5, 367–368). As discussed below, this vision of a positive circularity between agriculture and industry and its promise to bring about national reconstruction was criticized for ignoring the predominance of imperialism in China.

The RRM was unfolding alongside a series of heated intellectual debates, between the late 1920s and first half of the 1930s, about the nature of Chinese society. These debates covered the nature of Chinese society (1927–1928), Chinese social history (1932–1933), and rural society (1934–1935), with the last debate being the most important.[12] This series of debates was driven by grave concern for the future of China. As observed by a prominent editor at the time, "The question about the nature of the Chinese economy now demands an answer from scholars of all classes. Intellectuals of any class, for the sake of their class's future, will have to address this question" (Guo 2003, 50–51). These debates – in the wake of the 1927 violent split between the KMT and the CCP – also dovetailed with the debates within international and Chinese communist movements about aims and strategies of Chinese revolution. The outcome of the debates was a much wider intellectual reception of the characterization that China was not a capitalist, but a semi-colonial, semi-feudal society.

The China Agrarian Group (Zhongguo nongcun pai), a network of Marxist and left-wing intellectuals, which had earlier engaged in the debate about the nature of China's rural society, launched critiques of RRM, including experiments led by Liang Shuming and James Yan, another leading figure known for his reformist experiment in rural education. In their 1936 publication, *A Critique of China's Rural Reconstruction* [Zhongguo xiangcun jianshe pipan] (Qian and Li 1982), the editors challenged the assumed autonomy or self-adequacy of RRM: "Can the RRM or the construction of Chinese national economy be accomplished independently of the political task of national liberation?" (Qian and Li 1982, 64). More specifically, they asked, "can development of agriculture bring about industrialization and salvage the cities?" While Liang intended a non-capitalistic development, the actual situation was indeed that these "funds" (*zijin*) – as he referred to them – from commercial banks or government-owned financial institutions – behaved in stereotypically capitalistic manner; when going to the countryside, they concentrated in localities that had easy transportation, benefitted the rich and middle peasants, and excluded poor peasants (Bo 1994, 132–133).[13] Citing cases of how cotton grown by rural cooperatives in Hebei and Shandong fed imperialist enterprises in China, the editors questioned the relationship between rural reconstruction and imperialist expansion in China. A few years later, an influential study by Chen Hansheng [Chen Han-seng], the leading figure of the China Agrarian Group, published his findings on how the British–American Tobacco Company, through comprador merchants, local gentry, and rural cooperatives, trapped tens of thousands of Chinese peasants in Anhui, Henan, and Shandong provinces in unfavorable terms of production and sales of tobacco leaf to the company (Chen *et al.* 1980 [1939]).

Liang's second major assumption about rural construction is his basic outlook on Chinese social particularity, which became the core of his 1938 debate with Mao. In Liang's view, Chinese society was unlike Western society in two respects. Chinese society had a division of labor, but no division of class, and Chinese society was held together by ethics – duties and obligations toward each other, not based on individualism. Liang argued that China lacked class dynamics for revolution, as none of the classes – peasants, workers, and capitalists – could serve as a class base for revolution. On the one hand, Liang recognized disparity in landownership in China, due to the system of private ownership, and believed that equality in land could be achieved either by public ownership or by equalization of landownership. Yet he dismissed the possibility of either, as he saw China lacking the necessary political conditions (Xu and Zhao 2011). On the other hand, Liang particularly refuted the relevance of class for rural China and saw rural China as lacking a radical separation between land and rural producers. Liang's evidence was that landholding could both concentrate and disperse, as land could be freely bought and sold and family assets be equally divided among all sons (Liang 1989, vol. 3, 146; Xu and Zhao 2011). In a similar vein, Liang denied the existence of a ruling class in China and argued that there was social mobility, and rulers and the ruled could exchange places in China. He thus famously stated, "Chinese society has rulers, but no ruling class" (Liang 1989, vol. 3, 155). As opposing classes could not be formed in China, Chinese society had no class struggle, a condition Liang thought conducive to cooperation. Liang once advocated avoiding words such as "*nongmin*" (peasantry) and "*bei yapo de minzu*" (the oppressed nation) because of their class connotations, and instead using "*xiangcun jumin*" (rural residents) to create inclusiveness (Liang 1992 [1933], 215).

Although often regarded as conservative (Webb 2008) or Confucianist (Alitto 1986), Liang Shuming's RRM was nevertheless about finding a new social organization beyond the age-old institutions such as family, lineage, or village.

As Liang explained, the mission of the RRM is "to build a *normal* (*zhengchang xingtai de*) human civilization so that economic 'wealth' and political 'power' are in the hands of the society and shared by everyone" (Liang 1989, vol. 2, 76). This "social movement" – as Liang called it – should be led by intellectuals and should be based on the villagers themselves (Liang 1989, vol. 2, 377). Regarding villagers as an undifferentiated group, what Liang wanted to construct might be called a rural civil society that would be jointly headed by the old/rural and new/urban elites. Rural schools in the RRM became the "public sphere" where social reformers from the outside mobilized villagers (Thogersen 1998, 147). Schools were overseen by school boards whose members were always drawn from among rural elites, while teaching was led by social reformers. Liang and his followers considered their organization to represent an autonomous society independent from the state, but in reality it functioned as "a mediator between the Chinese state and a rural hinterland which had so far been almost inaccessible to state officials" (159). Liang was more a prototype modernizer in practice than what he appeared to be from his writing (158).

In their critique of the RRM, the China Agrarian Group also took on Liang's RRM philosophy and practice for failing to address the ownership of means of production. They questioned rhetorically whether the movement could alleviate the pains of Chinese peasants if it focused only on agricultural skills, transportation, marketing, and finance, but left the problem with the ownership of means of production, particularly land, untouched (Qian and Li 1982, 64). In 1935, Liang himself admitted that the RRM could neither relieve peasants of their burden of taxes, nor help them with land redistribution (Liang 1989, vol. 2, 581). Moreover, Li Zixiang, a member of the China Agrarian Group, indicated in his critique that cooperatives based on small producers not only do not contradict large enterprises, but are actually dominated by large enterprises and banks (Li 1982, 69). Li predicted that Liang's "socialization of production" and "socialization of distribution" would thus be blank checks that would never be cashed. As to what Liang touted as a positive cycle between production and consumption, it would end up facilitating the expansion of imperialist industry and commodity markets in China. In practice, the RRM also depended almost solely on intellectuals, even though Liang thought it should be otherwise (70). While Liang in his RRM methodology emphasized objective conditions, Li pointed out that the objective conditions in Liang's eyes are immutable and thus his theory and methodology is inevitably a form of conservatism which succumbed to these "objective conditions" (70). Liang's philosophy of RRM was therefore idealist, his methodology was conservative, and his "new civilization" was only to be a semi-colonial civilization (69). Li Zixiang sharply concluded that the movements (including the one led by James Yan) "intended to use 'cultural work' to mend the fundamental contradictions of the entirety of China's social-political-economic problems" and that these efforts, like pushing a cart uphill, would collapse one day (74).

The RRM ended with Japan's invasion of China in 1937. In 1938, searching for hope to defeat the Japanese invasion and intrigued by the CCP's united front policy, Liang made a trip to Yan'an where he had some lengthy exchanges with Mao.

These candid and friendly talks allowed them to find some common ground in national liberation and in their disapproval of Western-style constitutional democracy, but they also made most apparent their different views on Chinese peasantry and society. When Mao asked Liang what he found difficult in his RRM, Liang frankly stated, "The biggest difficulty is that peasants prefer passivity to action (*hao jing Bo hao dong*)" (Alitto 1986, 289). This had been Liang's consistent view, as he wrote about peasants that "Their character is deeply conservative. Therefore, to talk to peasants about revolution is banging your head against the wall" (1992 [1933], 176). In 1935 Liang reflected on one of the difficulties of the RRM:

> In the so-called "village movement," the village does not move [*hao cheng "xiangcun yundong," xiangcun Bo dong*].... Villagers were indifferent and it was only outsiders making a big noise.... The most ideal RRM is when villagers move and we cheer them on. Or it at least ought to be like this, they want to move, and we lead them. But it's now completely the opposite, we move, but they don't, not only do they not move, but also because we move, our relationship with them has become such that it's almost difficult for us to continue our work.... We thought our work beneficial to the villages, but villagers do not welcome it.
>
> (Liang 1989, vol. 2, 575)

Even regarding the modestly successful program of compulsory adult education, Liang remarked in 1935 with disappointment that the peasants were still the object of the transformation, while intellectuals were the subject and it was not uncommon for the RRM activists to compare passive villagers to "stones" (Thogersen 1998, 152).

With the CCP's experience in peasant mobilization not only for land reform but also for vibrant rural cooperatives in their rural bases, Mao instantly disagreed with Liang's characterization of the peasantry, "You are wrong! Peasants want action. How can you say that they want to be passive?" (Alitto 1986, 289) After reading Liang's *Theories of Rural Reconstruction* and listening to Liang expounding his cultural theory and RRM for a week, it became apparent to Mao that their differences lie in whether China needed a reform or a revolution and whether class analysis is relevant to Chinese society. Mao summed up their differences:

> Chinese society has its own particularities, its own cultural tradition, and its own ethics, which is not wrong for you to emphasize. Chinese society also has qualities in common with Western societies, which include class opposition, contradiction and struggle. These are its most fundamental attributes, which determine social progress. You overemphasize its special nature and neglect its universal nature.

Liang answered resolutely: "The reason why China is China lies in these special features. You overemphasize its common qualities and neglect its special qualities" (Alitto 1986, 289; 2003, 208).

Many of Liang's admirers and followers today lament the unfortunate disruption of Liang's rural reconstruction by the Japanese invasion or some argue that the merit of the RRM should not be measured in terms of success or failure (Pan 2012). Liang himself was more reflective and forthright about the grave structural difficulties his RRM faced. First was the contradiction between the RRM's social reform position and its dependence on local warlord political power. The local power upon which Liang's RRM depended was headed by an old warlord, Han Fuqu, who murdered CCP members and their supporters, suppressed peasants' armed uprisings, and promoted the KMT's "new life movement," which was a combination of Chinese traditions and European fascism. The second and, in Liang's view, most painful contradiction has already been mentioned above: "in the so-called 'village movement,' the village does not move." Liang was also aware that because of the RRM's inability to respond to peasant problems of taxation and land, it had not been able to address issues that really matter to villagers and "therefore cannot win them over" (Liang 1989, vol. 2, 581). Although Liang admitted that the problem was unavoidable, he believed it would gradually ease. However, up until 1949, Liang had been confident about his assessment that China lacked a class base for revolution. After witnessing the CCP's success in the land reform, Liang acknowledged that he had a static view of Chinese society and had failed to see that disparity could develop into class-based conflicts. He reflected that he had made a mistake by overemphasizing the particularity of China's problems (Liang 1989, vol. 6, 866, 950–951; Wang 2004, 157).

Contemporary rural advocacy and the debates about cooperatives

The post-Mao rural reform disbanded the rural communes and instituted two-tiered land rights: landownership rights belong to the village collective while land use rights were equally divided and leased to families for family contract farming. Within this land institution, a rural household can further lease part or whole of their land use right to others within or beyond the village. To this day, farmland in China has not been treated as a full commodity.[14] However, the reform over the years has solidified de facto privatization of land use right while at the same time hollowing out the collective ownership right to the extent that the collective is left with little ability to coordinate village public infrastructure.[15]

Three decades of reform and a continuous process of marketization has brought about the commodification of agricultural inputs, labor, public goods, and technical services, a steady exodus of educated rural youth as migrants to cities, the aging and feminization of rural producers, fragmentation of familial life, estrangement of social relations within villages, growing rural disparity,[16] etc. This complex of interrelated problems has been termed "*san nong* problems"; that is, rural sustainability has been threatened in three dimensions: rural livelihood and its reproduction (literally *nongmin* or peasants), the coherence of rural society (literally *nongcun* or the countryside), and the sustainability of agricultural production (literally *nongye*, agriculture). The new RRM is a response to "san nong problems" (Day and Hale 2007; Day 2008, 2013). The beginning of the new RRM was marked by the first New Rural Reconstruction convergence in Beijing in 2002,[17] the founding of the James Yan Rural Reconstruction Institute in 2003, and the Liang Shuming Rural Reconstruction Center in 2004 by some university-affiliated intellectuals and students and non-governmental or para-governmental rural support organizations. The New RRM includes mobilizing and training student volunteers for rural support, incubating rural advocate student groups on university campuses, policy critique and advocacy at public forums, articulating alternative ideas of rural development, etc. Since then, other intellectuals have rural advocacy each in his or her own way.

Intellectual advocacy and promotion of rural cooperatives, including training rural cooperative leaders, had been a key component of the new RRM since its beginning,[18] although since the return to family-based farming three decades ago, informal mutual aid practices and cooperative associations have existed in rural China.[19] Following the new RRM, the Chinese central government in 2005 initiated "constructing a new socialist countryside" in its eleventh five-year plan, which, while different from the new RRM, aimed mainly to divert investment to and stimulate demand in the countryside.[20]

The intellectuals' concern for rural sustainability and their promotion of a new RRM and cooperatives place them as critics of the mainstream modernization trope that has been prevalent in the process of reform. With 200 million or so rural households as individuated producers, mainstream policy-makers and economists have hoped that agro enterprises will play a leadership role like "dragon-heads" in streamlining and scaling up production and bringing rural producers into the process. The Chinese government has been supporting "dragon-head enterprises" (*longtou qiye*) with preferential policies since the mid-1990s. "Company+households," with a company being the integrator through which households are connected with the market, has been promoted as a win-win formula for both companies and rural producers. Since the formal implementation of the Law on Specialized Farmer Cooperatives, government agricultural bureaus and some para-governmental agencies have been active in promoting cooperatives and training cooperative leaders. Cooperatives have mushroomed. However, the nature of cooperatives is highly controversial, which will be discussed below. The remarkable development of cooperatives has not really lessened the above-mentioned agrarian problems. The mainstream vision for dealing with the "*san nong*" problem remains urbanization of much of the rural population and capital-led vertical integration of agriculture (*chan ye hua*).[21]

Sharing a normative "rural support" stance, intellectual proponents of cooperatives not only organize training workshops for farmers and rural support students, but also engage in on-the-ground experiments. They also debate about what kind of cooperation should be promoted and to what end. Some see cooperatives as a welcome revision of the "company + households" model, because the reformed "company+cooperative+households" operation supposedly allows farmers more collective power in their relationship with the company. Others advocate that a displacement of the dragon-head company by cooperatives can offer a more direct and rural–beneficial link to the market. Li Zhonghua, head of the Institute for Cooperatives in Qingdao Agriculture University, draws on his experience in Japan to push cooperatives to directly supply supermarkets (*nongchao duijie*) (2008). Yuan Peng, a scholar at the Chinese Academy of Social Science (CASS), argues that the cooperative organization is both a product of the market and has an anti-market quality (2001). A more critical approach, taken by anti-corporate intellectuals and students, tries to forge an alternative linkage between rural producers and urban consumers, bypassing corporations (He *et al.* 2009, 6–8).

For some intellectual proponents of rural cooperation, the form and purpose of cooperation goes to the heart of the larger issue of China's path of development. Their advocacy is based on resituating and reassessing China's national conditions and experiences in a global comparative context. Indeed, their advocacy involves a change of reference, contrary to the mainstream elite discourse in China, where the USA or the West has been the dominant reference point for envisioning development, these intellectuals are very clear in their rejection of the US/Western model as relevant for China. Steering away from ideological debate, they support their rejection by frequently emphasizing the conditions of rural China development. Even with urbanization, rural China will continue to host a large population – about 900 million – with dwindling farm land and resources. On this constrained premise, rural China has to achieve the goal of a prosperity and sustainability that is shared by most, not a few (Yang 2011, 36–37).

What is becoming shared knowledge among many rural support intellectuals is clearly stated by Yang Tuan, a scholar at CASS, the US/Western model, associated with de-peasantization (*qu nongmin hua*), industrialization, and urbanization,[22] is a model that works for a small number of capitalist farmers and corporations who enjoy big government subsidies, while China needs to find a way to sustain a large rural population (Yang 2011, 38). Wen Tiejun, Dean of the School of Agriculture and Rural Development at Renmin University, discusses three types of agriculture around the world: the large-scale plantation agriculture found in America is a product of colonialism, the medium-scale agriculture in EU is mainly run by middle-class, part-time farmers; the small-scale agriculture in Japan and South Korea, operating under a tight population–land resource condition, is the only useful reference for China (Wen 2011, 29). A consensus exists among rural advocates that neither the US nor the European model of agriculture can be useful examples for China. Rural advocates also take warning from the modernization experiences of other developing countries, particularly in South Asia and Latin America (Wen 2004, 8–12; 2007). In what he calls "the Philippines Path," well-known rural advocate Li Changping sees how the American model of agrarian capitalism has damaged rural livelihoods in the Philippines and how the "company+households" model there has only hastened the bankruptcy of rural households (Li 2009, 85–89). Both Yang and Li point out that the application of the "company+households" model in China has only benefitted a few.[23] Li argues most forthrightly that companies and households have an unequal relationship that involves exploitation, only resulting in companies squeezing rural producers out of processing, transportation, circulation, rural finance, etc. (76–78, 85). Zhang Xiaoshan, another scholar at CASS, remarks that determining who benefits from cooperatives is a serious question of principle and directionality (Zhang 2009).

Going against the thrust of the mainstream that promotes rural cooperation as singularly centered on commodity production, Wen Tiejun, Yang Tuan, and Li Changping envision empowerment through a cooperation that encompasses village and farmers and conjoins production and reproduction, economy and culture. They see such a "comprehensive cooperation" practiced in Japan, South Korea, and Taiwan. In the Japan-South Korea-Taiwan (JKT) model, sometimes referred to as "the East Asia model," the state supports the national farmers' union to coordinate and integrate production, transportation, finance, etc. and provides laws that limit the presence of corporate capital in agriculture. Arguing that the path of "comprehensive cooperation" fits with China's own six decades of rural development, Yang proposes the township to be the building block of comprehensive farmers' association (Yang 2011, 38). Li proposes a community-based collective economy that has finance cooperation at its core and farm land cooperation as the foundation (2009, 75). Contrary to mainstream silence and aversion, Li further lauds the "new collective economy" embodied by the existing few thousand collective villages that have survived de-collectivization (81). He Huili, a faculty member at the Chinese Agricultural University who experiments with rural cooperatives in Henan province, advocates the local state to be a key agent in organizing community-based comprehensive cooperation (He 2007, 28).

While agreeing with the rejection of the US–European models of agriculture, He Xuefeng, Director of China Rural Governance Research Center at Huazhong University of Science and Technology, questions whether JKT's rural conditions are actually sufficiently comparable to those in China for the JKT model to be relevant (He 2012, 125). Similarly, Philip Huang and his co-authors also see a significant divergence between Chinese agriculture and the so-called East Asia model, because unlike in China, Japan's rural population is less than 10 percent of the national total and its family farming is greatly overshadowed by the expansion of wage-labor-based capitalist agriculture (Huang *et al.* 2012, 141). He Xuefeng's discussion provides a different assessment of the major problem faced by rural China and asks what problems cooperation is able to address. Estimating that 70 percent of Chinese farmers have to grow staple grains, He asserts that there is little room for staple grains to increase in price within the existing macro-structure. He thus argues that the pressing need for most farmers – hence the purpose of cooperation – is not about their empowerment vis-à-vis the market, but about improving socio-cultural and infrastructural public goods provision in villages. Villagers suffer not so much from the current level of income as from the corrosive effect of modernity penetrating the rural space and subjectivity, atomization, the problem of old age, left-behind children, the community deterioration that becomes the push factor for migration, etc. Hence He and his team focus on the potential agency of rural governance in creating such public goods or creating conditions for such public goods. The provision of socio-cultural public good can help rebuild the rural social fabric and remake the meaning of rural life. The provision of infrastructural public goods can improve conditions of production for fragmented and individuated rural producers.

While other rural advocates mentioned above see in cooperation a way for small farmers to be organized so as to collectively wrestle with the market and capital as external forces, He argues that rural sustainability can be achieved via re-socialization within the village. Rather than looking elsewhere for inspiration, He suggests that the PRC's own history could serve a useful reference for rural organization. In his proposal, the existing rural governance structure – which was rooted in Mao-era collectivization, but played a notorious role in 1990s predatory taxation (see Day's elaboration of state involution in this special issue) – can be reformed in the post-taxation era to better mediate between the now-increased state subsidy and the actual needs of villagers, and bring about improved socio-cultural and economic public goods provision (He 2012, 124–130).

Wen Tiejun, the leading intellectual in the new RRM and the most scathing critic of modernization, interprets China's fin-de-siècle rural decline as an outcome of a relentless drain of rural resources that include money, labor, and land. In the past three decades, the city has gained the benefit of marketization and capitalization of these resources, while the countryside is left with the negative social and economic cost of such capitalization, manifested as the *san nong* crisis. The new RRM is necessary both because small rural producers will continue to have a large and long-term presence in China and because its preservation will shelter China from the sharp impact of periodic capitalist crises. Contrary to the mainstream view that attributes the *san nong* crisis to rural backwardness and deficiency in modernization, Wen argues that the crisis is not sui generis, but has its roots in the very dynamics of modernization. The rural hinterland, whose resources escape complete monetization and capitalization, rather than being a drag on modernization, is modernization's potential rescuer. It has the practical capacity to buffer the country against the worst impacts of modernization's crisis (Wen 2012a). For example, rural China cushioned the social impact of the large lay-off of 20 million labor migrants during the 2008 to 2009 financial crisis.

Wen's critique of modernization is not limited to the post-Mao period or to China. His deconstruction of modernization as a false universalism exposes the historical and particular kinds of violence and resource expropriation that have made modernization attainable in only a small number of countries (Wen 2004, 3–22; 2007). His deconstruction of modernization in China stretches across the entire twentieth century. The defining characteristic of rural China, in Wen's view, is having a large population of scattered (*fensan de*) small producers who have scarce resources and accumulate little surplus. The constant challenge for modernization in twentieth-century China was how surplus can be extracted from such numerous and meager producers for the sake of industrialization. Thus Wen is interested in explaining how the contradiction between rural China and modernization has played out through various waves and crises of modernization that included the KMT's industrialization in the 1930s, as well as the industrialization blunder in the Mao era (Wen 2012a). Going against the mainstream discourse that continues to push China along the path of modernization, Wen believes that deconstruction and disenchantment of modernization is the necessary condition to win public understanding of the new RRM (Wen 2010a).

In the face of the *san nong* problems, Wen observes both "market failure" and "government failure." As the outflow of rural resources has been through marketization, Wen argues that the conventional market is unable to address the *san nong* problems. He terms this inability "market failure." As small producers' farming yields too little surplus itself, a superstructure of conventional modern governance in rural China is beyond rural affordability and therefore has to be supported via large subsidies and fiscal transfers. This only results in reinforcing ponderous and compartmentalized bureaucratic self-interests. This is demonstrated by how government bureaucracies and rural elites in the post-taxation era have intercepted much of the subsidy for rural producers, leading to the failed implementation of rural support policies ("Jianshe" 2009; Wen 2001a, 25). This "government failure" manifests itself as a negative relationship: the more modern the political governance superstructure, the less it is able to treat the decline of the rural economic sector (Wen 2012b).

Based on the thesis of deconstructing modernization, Wen and his team propose "comprehensive cooperation" as a way to organize rural producers into larger subjects that can negotiate and transact with the state and market (Yang and Wen 2011). Cultural reconstruction, referring to creating village-based cultural activities, will help rebuild the social capital lost in the fragmentation of village social relationships and facilitate cooperation in other dimensions. Wen and his team envision "comprehensive cooperation" to cover finance, marketing, and production, and call on the state to grant new organizations preferential policies and exclusive rights in fields that involve agriculture. He Huili argues that the new RRM is about building a post-capitalist new civilization that respects farming traditions and values ecological agriculture. In her experiment with comprehensive cooperation, villagers pool land resources together and cooperate in production, marketing, and building ecological houses (He *et al.* 2009, 5–6).

Rural advocates differ from the liberal mainstream on the question of rural self-organization. Liberal scholars such as Qin Hui denounce China's Mao-era experience of rural collectivization on the basis that it involved a top-down state coercion. In contrast, rural support intellectuals urge the state to support the cooperative movement and acknowledge that it is very difficult for farmers to self-organize (Yang and Wen 2011). Li Changping avers that while it is now fashionable to promote voluntary self-organization in rural China, even well-endowed urban middle-class home owners have not achieved much self-organization against real estate developers, let alone rural producers, who since the 1990s have been exploited by policy-supported dragon-head enterprises in all four fields – finance, processing, circulation, and agricultural inputs – and cannot afford the cost of self-organizing. With the relationship between the state and rural producers shifting from extraction through taxation to compensation through subsidy, Li opines that the state should have no cause to fear, but to have reason to support rural organization (Li 2009, 82). Although not particularly associated with *san nong* studies, Lao Tian analyzes the historical difficulty of peasant self-organization by examining William Hinton's documentation of complex dynamics and tendencies among peasantry in the land reform processes (Lao 2009).

Similarly, Wen and his team argue that the capacity and mechanism for cooperation has been weakened by industrial and commercial capital expansion into the rural sector, which has reduced the benefit – or organizational rent – of cooperation. Hence a vicious cycle, lesser cooperative capacity leads to deficient village governance, which makes it less effective in mobilizing for external subsidy and support (Wen and Dong 2010, 22–23). Wen and his team point to the Japanese state's role in the formation of Japan's national farmers' union and argue that "cooperatives that ensure fairness and protect the disadvantaged ... will have to result from strategic support by the state that represents integrative and long-term social interests" (Yang and Wen 2011, 45).

If one of Liang's predicaments was "in the so-called 'village movement', the village does not move," then contemporary support for the cooperative movement is confronted with the predominance of "fake cooperatives," in which small producers barely participate. Liang lamented that villagers had a very indifferent attitude toward the presence of his RRM institute. Indifference has also been observed today: " 'cooperation' becomes an activity that concerns government officials and elites and ordinary farmers are indifferent" (Zhang 2011, 59). Among the 272,000 cooperatives formally registered by 2010 in China, it is estimated by many observers that 80 to 95 percent of them are fake (L.S. Liu 2010, 54). Such cooperatives are fake in several different and overlapping ways: they are empty shells that exist only in name, they are actually controlled by "large households" (rich farmers) that rarely involve small producers' cooperation, they are actually dragon-head enterprises or "company + households" putting on a new hat as cooperatives, and they are organized by government departments (Zhang 2011). Among the 136 registered cooperatives in a county in Anhui, 125 are set up by large households, four by government departments, five by dragon-head enterprises, and two by village committees (Zhang 2009, 14). In Hubei Province, only 10 percent of the 4,375 cooperatives are found to be economically active and 95 percent are dominated respectively by village "big men" (*neng ren*) who specialize in farming, processing, and trading (55%), agro-technology associations and government agro-technology departments, etc. (30%), and dragon-head enterprises (10%) (Zhang and Zhang 2007, 62–63). In these cooperatives, small producers are "being cooperativized" (*bei hezuo*) (Zhang 2011), meaning that their "cooperation" is orchestrated and managed by a dominant minority without their actual participation. With the introduction of the cooperative law in 2007, the situation of "fake cooperatives" has only worsened ("Jianshe" 2009, 11; Zhao 2010, iii). These pretenders have mushroomed in recent years in order to benefit from central and local governments' preferential policies and subsidies for cooperatives (Li 2010). In the face of this adverse situation, some concerned scholars have called for a crackdown on the fakes (Liu 2010, 54).

How to account for this phenomenon is an issue for debate. Many attributed it at least in part to farmers' deficiency in cooperative consciousness, cooperative culture, or cooperative capacity, or to the problem of an insufficient legal framework (Tong and Wen 2009, 21–22; Yuan 2010, 17). Yuan Peng also suggests that the heterogeneity of cooperative membership – referring to the varied endowment of resources among members – accounts for a lack of democratic participation within cooperatives. Yuan argues that the problem can eventually be solved when members complete their own transformation into homogeneous entrepreneurial commercial farmers (Yuan 2010, 17).

Liu Laoshi, the late leader of Liang Shuming Rural Reconstruction Center, who dedicated his life to the rural support cause, argued that the seeming predominance of fake cooperatives is a problem of criteria (Liu 2010). He figured that 1 percent of rural cooperatives in China would meet the seven principles adopted by the International Co-operative Alliance in 1995, no more than 10 percent would reach the criteria set out in the 2007 Chinese law on cooperatives, most importantly both "one member one vote" and patronage refund (income in excess of expenses generated by the cooperative members' use of their business that is refunded to them), and no more than 20 percent institute patronage refund. Yet, in Liu's view the problem is not whether cooperatives are fake, but whether these external criteria, particularly Western criteria, would fit China's complex situation. Liu instead proposed "one member, one share of power" as a more flexible "autochthonous" (*bentu zizhi de*) criteria and believed that this would enable farmers' control of cooperatives (59). He argued that as long as farmers have the right to control cooperatives, they can choose to allow major shareholders to gain more at an early phase of a cooperative development. So long as farmers are in control, then farmers control capital, and such capital, regardless of where it is sourced, is people's capital (59–60). The political logic here eerily resembles what is applied to the Chinese state that, by its own self-identity as the helmsman of national economy, is believed to be in control of capital and thus qualifies as socialist.

By Liu's reckoning, cooperatives fall into three groups. Fewer than 20 percent run smoothly and may be considered "genuine" cooperatives. Most of these are not strictly local, but have external – NGOs or universities – involvement. Fewer than 30 percent are fakes, empty shells without actual members controlled by large households or companies. More than 40 percent are between genuine and fake and between cooperative and company. They include those initiated by large households, those having "company+households" arrangements and those initiated by local governments. Cooperatives in the latter category have members and rule books, but the actual operations do not follow rules; rather, they follow the decisions of a few. Liu believed that the ambiguous 40 percent are nevertheless local initiatives and their problems are not their own, but derive from the larger context. Liu thus argued that these 40 percent should be regulated and guided, rather than be denounced as fakes. Liu warned that talk of crackdown on the fakes would discourage these 40 percent, resulting in stifling and even destroying the development of cooperatives (62). Pan Jiaen similarly dismisses the categorization of true and fake cooperatives as an "artificial binary" (Pan 2012, 145) and shares Liu's prioritization of the movement. This logic resonates in the words of a cadre in Heilongjiang who went all out to encourage local cooperatives: "let hair grow first before having a haircut."[24]

A rare in-depth ethnographic study of one cooperative by Christopher Lammer finds that it lacks active involvement by average members and is dominated by a few (Lammer 2012, 166). Yet it is usually considered "genuine" within the rural support circle. Like most cooperatives, its management is also dominated by men (ibid.).[25] Lammer argues that the new rural reconstruction effort in this case has actually led to "the development of capitalist class relations *within* the village" (Lammer 2012, 153, emphasis in original). Some villagers who contest social relations and practices within the cooperative have labeled it "a fake cooperative" (160–163). Wary that the term "fake cooperative" invokes intention on the part of the cooperative founders, Lammer differentiates this kind of cooperative from those that are no more than empty shells and terms it "an imagined cooperative" in order to mark the tension, as well as the possible potential of transformation between the reality and the representation: "they are nominal cooperatives and imagined as cooperatives by those who dominate them and who support them. They are non cooperatives in the sense that patron–client and class relations exist between those involved in the organizations" (169). Transformation of this kind of imagined cooperative would face challenges that are both internal and external. Matthew Hale's study of four cases of cooperative experiments in China points to a structural contradiction: their success in commercial projects requires a deeper integration with capitalist dynamics and thus the "internal" social-community principles cannot be neatly separated from "external" market dynamics (Hale 2013).[26]

Liu's prioritizing of the movement and his attribution of fake cooperatives to external factors is not shared by all rural advocates in China. Tong and Wen argue that the fast growth of cooperatives dominated by relatively wealthy households, characterized as "big farmers exploiting small farmers" (*danong chi xiaonong*), present only a fake blossoming of cooperatives (*xujia fanrong*) (Tong and Wen 2009). The fast growth of cooperatives is not only due to the need of scattered producers in linking up with the market, as many have hoped to see, but is also propelled by the interest of capital and government departments (Tong and Wen 2009, 15). The formation of fake cooperatives, rather than being due solely to exogenous factors, results from three dynamics in the past three decades: the process of rural differentiation into large and small producers produces rural capital and agricultural wage labor, rural capital is joined by urban capital and together they expand from marketing to processing, and now, in agriculture, government departments not only play a leading role in facilitating the capitalization of agriculture, but also seek to increase their own revenue and subsidize their operations by providing fee-based services.

These dynamics feed on each other and produce three further dynamics: government capital is converted into bureaucratic capital and even private capital, rural differentiation, serving the necessary condition of capital expansion in agriculture, becomes intensified, and fake cooperatives, dominated by large producers who are favored by capital, government departments, are instrumental in furthering rural differentiation. Such cooperatives play the role of middle-men between capital and small producers and cannot be expected to empower small producers on the market (Tong and Wen 2009, 13–18). In fact, it is found that "the key economic goals of co-operatives are also successfully filtered by elites to allow and even reinforce the existence of monopolies and retain inequalities between farmers and business" (Zhao 2010, 168). Tong and Wen propose as an alternative a community-based multiple cooperation and call on the state – "the most authoritative public power" – to intervene. Their proposed interventions include preventing government departments from engaging in for-profit operations, restraining capital, supporting small producers, and encouraging mutual benefit and cooperation between large and small producers (Tong and Wen 2009, 23).[27]

The past and the present: resonances

The new RRM shares with the 1930s RRM a similar self-positioning as a social reform that explores within the dominant political-economic structure an alternative to the ongoing agrarian change perceived to threaten rural sustainability. Not unlike the early RRM intellectuals, rural advocates today also look for a third way for rural China and attempt to "go beyond" both the Left and the Right (Pan 2012, 6). Philip Huang's proposition more or less represents this shared vision:

> An alternative perspective is that agriculture remains mainly based on the peasant family and not on capitalist farming, and its ideal direction of development should be toward neither capitalism nor socialism, but something different, along the lines of marketized cooperatives, in the manner originally envisioned by Chayanov.
>
> (Huang *et al.* 2012, 140)[28]

Deng Xiaoping's market reform, launched in 1978 for what is called the primary stage of socialism, is based on an assumption which he already held in 1956, namely that Chinese society has eliminated class divisions and has only a division of labor (Meisner 1999, 453). Deng's post-revolutionary assumption about Chinese society in a way resonated with Liang Shuming's reformist thesis. In the post-Mao trend of de-radicalization and "farewell to revolution" (Li and Liu 1995), the social reformist position of the 1930s RRM – including its assumption of rural society as an undifferentiated whole – although a target of political critique by leftist intellectuals then and later in the Mao-period – has again appeared respectable and progressive.[29] In fact, one might say that the political evaluation of RRM is in an inverse relationship with that of revolution in contemporary Chinese discourse. To be sure, the contemporary search for the third way in China is certainly not limited to rural support scholars. Cui Zhiyuan, for example, makes use of the idea of rural producer cooperatives in his well-known manifesto of "petty bourgeois socialism" which proposes to make the petty bourgeoisie the social foundation for market socialism (Cui 2003).[30]

"Radical" has become a negative signifier in the post-Cultural Revolution liberal discourse, whose signification has been expanded to include the twentieth-century Chinese revolution. In this context, Wen Tiejun makes his own re-signification of "radical" by calling the twentieth-century efforts at modernization radical, thereby making modernization – particularly the current thrust of urbanization and capitalization – an object for deconstruction and rejection (2010b). Pan Jiaen, a key member of Wen's team, includes in the category of radical the following: the May the 4th movement, communist revolution, the Cultural Revolution, neoliberalism, as well as fast urbanization, modern governance for rural society, and developmentalism (Pan 2012, 11). Wen argues that neither yesterday's Soviet model nor today's American model should be the reference for Chinese emulation. In Wen's view, the link between the two RRMs lies in the persistent need to disengage from modernization, which is even more urgent with today's more severe resource stress (2010a, 17). Pan (2012) and Day (2008) frame the historical and current RRM as Polanyi's social protectionism.

Rural advocates today also share with their 1930s forerunners some basic assumptions and conceptualizations about rural China. Their rural support position is based on taking rural society as a whole and assuming that the threat to rural sustainability is primarily external. The "wholeness" is an epistemological assumption embedded in the very term *san nong* – *nongmin*, *nongcun*, and *nongye*. While the policy concept of *san nong* – embraced by government planners, general academia, as well as rural advocates – succeeds in making social subjects, place, and production an interrelated set of problems, it makes differentiation within rural society invisible or insignificant.[31] This outlook resonates with the early RRM conceptualization of rural society as largely undifferentiated and fits in with the post-Mao dominant ideology that admits stratification, but disavows class analysis.[32]

To be sure, recently some rural support intellectuals, particularly He Xuefeng's team, have begun to incorporate rural stratification into their case studies, by examining the diverse compositions of rural household incomes.[33] Having been concerned about troubles in public goods provision, rural social disorder, and governability, and particularly worried about the accelerating trend of the rich dominating rural governance (He 2012, 290–307),[34] they find "the middle stratum" – particularly the medium-sized commercial farmers (who they call *zhongnong* or middle farmers) – to be the guardians of rural social order and the stabilizing force for rural production and governance. This unwittingly mirrors the growing liberal normative assumption about the urban middle class as good for China's future.

Yet, whether this rural stabilizing force can maintain its own stability remains an open question. Perhaps recognizing that the middle farmers are not inherently stable, He and his team call for the state to support this particular stratum. In addition to the differentiating tendency inherent in market conditions, the middle farmer stratum also depend on a number of factors for their own reproduction. One of these factors is the uncertainty of keeping the land-use rights they have accrued from rural-to-urban migrants, who often constitute about one-third of village laborers (see, e.g., Lin 2012, 61) and whose labor employment in the city is contingent on global and regional economic dynamics. What He and his team termed "middle farmers" reproduce themselves in the context in which agro-business has been gaining increasing control of means of production (Zhang and Donaldson 2008, 26) and has demonstrated a significant tendency to reap growing gains in the value chain (Wu 2012).

Wen makes a similar but more sweeping generalization about rural society as an autonomous social body. Referencing Liang Shuming, Wen is convinced that a combination of ethics (culture), rural elites, and village commons constitutes what he calls "internality" (Wen 2009, 7), or a form of local institutional arrangement that is conducive to low-cost governance and development (Wen and Dong 2010, 21). Within this institutional arrangement, the traditional elite are said to have their interests integrated with those of the rural body as a whole. Similar to Liang Shuming, Wen argues that landownership was dispersing instead of concentrating in pre-revolutionary China. Thus Wen reinterprets the cause of Chinese revolution: rather than the dual social contradictions created by imperialist oppression and land-based class conflicts, the real cause of revolution was the extortion of agriculture and rural society by industrial and commercial capital, brought on by the KMT's decade-long modernization (1927–1936) (Wen 2001b, 7; 2009, chs 4 and 5). In Wen's view, the outcome of both Chinese revolution and the post-Mao rural reform was the making of rural producers into petty bourgeoisie. In the overall context of excessive extortions during the KMT modernization, benevolent rural gentry became displaced by malevolent ones, exacerbating the tension. Wen sees a similar replay of the displacement of the benevolent "community elites" by malevolent elites in China's 1990s predatory taxation practices, which resulted in elite interest diverging from the overall community interest. In most rural areas these elites now intercept and appropriate for themselves most opportunities and government subsidies, described by Wen as "elite capture" (Yang and Wen 2011, 44).

How rural support intellectuals understand the current status of rural society impinges upon their advocacy of the rural cooperative movement. Wen's perception of the external threat to the rural social body resonates with one of Philip Huang's characterizations, namely that the main threat for rural producers in China today is commercial capital and thus it is relations of circulation, rather than relations of production, that matter most (Huang 2012, 95). In conjunction with this, Huang and his co-authors also argue that Chinese agriculture is undergoing capitalization – referring to increased capital input – without proletarianization, with wage labor calculated to be about 3 percent of the total labor input in agriculture, in contrast to India's 45 percent (Huang *et al.* 2012). Due to evenness in the value addition of agricultural products, Huang and his co-authors also find that in 2009 wage labor was 8.5 percent of the total labor input for vegetable farming, 6.7 percent for cotton farming, 40 percent for apple farming, 28 percent for dairy farming, and 27 percent for chicken egg farming.

Yet, while Huang *et al.* argue that China's land institution puts a brake on proletarianization and enhances the viability of family farming, they do not rule out the possibility of Chinese agriculture developing into "capitalization with proletarinization." Wu Guanghan's examination of rural producers' shrinking share in the value chain of agriculture products reaches a similar view of the threat of commercial capital to rural households, but suggests that rural producers' subjection to merchants is such that rural producers experience semi-proletarianization. Rural producers in Wu's conceptualization are both petty bourgeoisie and proletarians, but their apparent autonomy in production elides their subsumption to capital in circulation. Rather than manifesting a viability of family farming, this dual nature in Wu's view is not a stable condition but a transitional one. For there is a detectable trend that rural producers' subsumption to capital will expand from circulation to production (Wu 2012, 108). On the basis that rural producers as a whole are under an external threat, Huang explicitly (Huang 2010) and Wu implicitly (Wu 2012) advocate support for rural cooperatives to integrate production, processing, and marketing in order to counterbalance the power of commercial capital. Yet, capital interests are no longer external to the village, but are part of the forces that are remaking rural society. This is demonstrated in a report by a rural cooperative organizer:

> In today's countryside, businesses that have scale and profit are in the hands of dragon-head enterprises, businesses that have small scale and profit are in the hands of rich villagers, [any] business that have profit are in the hands of all-pervasive small merchants, 70–80% of households in the village make money only by selling primary products or labor.... There are already monopolistic interests in the village that treat some businesses as food on their plate. If a cooperative touches on their interests, the organizers will face harassment and even reprisal.
>
> (quoted in Pan 2012, 143)

To conclude, rural support intellectuals increasingly understand China's agrarian problem in a global context that is furnished by a set of references different from those of modernization theory. They form a critical mass which challenges the ongoing dominant neoliberal vision that promotes the urbanization and capitalization of agriculture as a viable future for China. While differences and contradictions exist among rural support intellectuals, many have questioned or disagreed that specialized farmer cooperatives would benefit the majority of rural producers. Cooperatives dominated by "large households" are certainly not unique to China. Interestingly, many rural support intellectuals in China would not hesitate to include such cooperatives among "fake cooperatives" and denounce them as such. Even as many dismiss the Mao-era rural commune system, this recent past experience has perhaps sharpened their practical – though not always theoretical – egalitarian sensibility on the one hand and has, on the other hand, made it easier for them to project a communal coherence that they hope to revive in the future.

It is not difficult to see parallels between the 1930s RRM and the contemporary RRM. Like their forerunners, rural support intellectuals today politically look for a third way, intellectually adopt the rural support position in their policy/social advocacy, and practically use community as the building block for rural reconstruction. For these political, intellectual, and practical reasons, they conceive rural society as a largely undifferentiated whole. Class analysis of agrarian change has little place in the study or advocacy of cooperatives or in rural study in general. In that, rural support intellectuals do not depart from the mainstream intellectuals in China who disavow class analysis. Yet, as Tong and Wen (2009) suggest, the dominant presence of rich farmers in rural cooperatives is the very product of rural differentiation, which is an open dynamics that involves local and translocal interests. Also similar to Liang Shuming for whom "China's problems are externally induced, not internally derived" (Liang 1989, vol. 2, 577), leading rural support intellectuals today apply the same perspective to rural China. The rural support stance which rural producers adopt as a whole is logically connected with the perception of the externality of threat.

Since the introduction of the "company+households" to China in the mid-1990s (Lin 1994), dragon-head enterprises now perhaps already involve about a quarter of rural producers in China (Huang *et al.* 2012, 165). Even with the land institution in China that puts a break on land concentration and the complete commodification of land, in the fast advance of agrarian capitalization, rural producers are found to be differentiating into commercial farmers, contract farmers, semi-proletarian producers, and proletarian farm workers (Zhang and Donaldson 2008, 32; Chen 2013). While Philip Huang argues that the current characteristic of Chinese agriculture is "capitalization without proletarianization," he acknowledges that producers in contractual relationships with enterprises are in effect "semi-proletarianized" (Huang *et al.* 2012, 166). Among rural support intellectuals, Tong and Wen (2009) provide a rare in-depth understanding of the mutually reinforcing dynamics that are producing rural differentiation, capitalization of agriculture, and the large presence of fake cooperatives. Their finding and its implications have yet to be widely discussed and debated.

In addition to taking rural society as a whole, contemporary rural support intellectuals also resemble their forerunner Liang Shuming in having a strategic assumption about the state. Whether rural support intellectuals pin their hopes for rural sustainability on the middle farmers or on community-based comprehensive cooperation, they reason with and appeal to the state to restrain capital as the necessary condition for rural sustainability. The state is assumed – not naively, but strategically – as the public power that rises above various interests. Yet it is clear that the state (both the central and local governments) has provided much stronger support to dragon-head enterprises than to cooperatives (Huang 2010, 25). In 1935 Liang Shuming reflected on two difficulties faced by the RRM. First, the RRM positioned itself as a "social movement" (Liang 1989, vol. 2, 377), but it depended on political power for its social reform. Second, in the so-called village movement, the village does not move. Liang's candid reflection and the 1930s debate about RRM can still serve as a useful reference point for our reflection on the contemporary rural cooperative movement.

Acknowledgment

This chapter was first published in the *Journal of Peasant Studies*, Volume 40, Issue 6, 955–981, by Taylor & Francis Ltd., written by Hairong Yan and Chen Yiyuan. Available online at: http://dx.doi.org/10.1080/03066150.2013.866555.

Notes

1 The authors wish to acknowledge the support of the project "Co-production of Quasi Public Goods: Community and Collective Action in Villages of Three Provinces, China" (1-ZV93). We would like to thank Alex Day, Matt Hale, Burak Gurel, as well as two anonymous reviewers for their valuable comments and suggestions.
2 For an English translation of the law, see http://bk.mylegist.com/bilingual/4394.html.
3 The rural advocates discussed in this chapter are rural support intellectuals who show concerns for the well-being of the rural population and who often declare their pro-rural positions and their appreciation of rural values in their intellectual works and policy proposals.
4 Shi Jingtang (1957, 3–69) has a wonderful collection of investigative reports produced in the 1940s and 1950s on traditional forms of mutual help found in China's different rural regions.
5 Some Chinese intellectuals, who studied in or visited Japan, Germany, France, and the USA, introduced the idea of cooperative economy to the Chinese reading public via publications and university teaching. The earliest promoters include Qin Shougong (1877–1938), Xue Xianzhou (1878–1927), Xu Changshui (1895–1925), Dai Jitao (1891–1949), Tang Cangyuan (1881–1931), Zhu Jinzhi (1888–1923), and Yu Shude (1894–1981). See Du (2002, 11–14) for a description of their publications and activities.
6 Mao's well-known 1927 investigative report in Hunan detailed the kinds of struggles engaged in by the peasant movement at the time (1991, Vol. 1, 12–44).
7 Mao's 1933 rural investigation reports on Changgang in Jiangxi and Caixi in Fujian detailed post-land reform rural cooperative initiatives (Mao 1982). In 1932, the Communist government issued a guideline for cooperative organization (Wei and Zeng 2010, 34). See Selden (1971) for cooperative economy promoted by the CCP in the Yan'an period.
8 Chen Guofu, a KMT leader, established a "Zhongguo hezuo yundong xiehui" (Chinese association for the cooperative movement) in 1924 and the KMT passed a resolution on "the peasant movement" in 1926, in which promotion of peasant cooperatives was mentioned. In 1928, Jiang Jieshi and Chen Guofu again called for a resolution on the cooperative movement. in 1931, the KMT government issued "A preliminary regulation on rural cooperatives" and in 1934 it formally issued a "Law on Cooperatives" (Bo

1994, 130). Bo Guoqun argues that without the KMT government's promotion, rural cooperatives would not have been possible (ibid.).

9 It was widely believed that rural China was facing collapse or bankruptcy. It was partly impacted by the world economic crisis from 1929 to 1931 and partly brought on by the 1931 flooding of the Yangtze River and Japanese invasion (Bo 1994, 129).

10 Of all the organizations facilitating and overseeing cooperatives, 87 percent were governmental and 12.7 percent were social (He 2007, 20).

11 Alitto (1986) and Lynch (1989) provide the most comprehensive scholarly works in English on Liang Shuming.

12 For summaries of these debates in the English language, see Chiang (2001, chs 6–8) and Han (2005, ch. 4). For a comprehensive summary in Chinese, see He (1937).

13 Two monographs published in the 1990s about Liang or his experiment in Shandong take the view that the cooperative members were mostly landlords and rich peasants (Ma 1992, 205–206; Zhu 1996, 147, 150). Guy Alitto [Ai Kai] argued that the cooperative mainly included the middle peasants, even though there was a tendency toward rich peasant domination (Alitto 1996, 262, 260). Yang Feirong re-examined the cooperative records and argued that most cooperative members were likely to be middle and poor peasants (Yang 2001, 201–204). Although, at the time, cooperative records had information on the size of land held by member households, they had no information on the size of each household, thus making it difficult to estimate the class status of the member households based on per capita landownership. However, even if cooperative members were mostly middle and poor peasants, available cooperative records cannot tell us the decision-making process within cooperatives and who benefitted most from them.

14 For a good examination of rural households and farm land distribution, see Unger (2009). There is a considerable force within and beyond China that pushes for land privatization. Liu (2008) for a special issue of *China Left Review* on this topic (http://chinaleftreview.org/?page_id=98).

15 Hu Jing, a professor at Huanan Normal University, makes a searing critique of the increasing marginalization of the collective Right in Chinese central government's rural policies (2011). Forrest Zhang (2012) argues that the current land institution still provides some protection for rural producers when they contract with companies.

16 While this is the general trend, there are also regional differences in rural social connectedness, due to the varying levels of local kinship and clan relations (see He 2009).

17 We thank Matt Hale for this information.

18 As an exception, Wen Tiejun began to advocate rural financial cooperation as early as 1994 (Wen 1994).

19 In the 1980s such cooperation often existed in the form of associations of agricultural technology, but the content of cooperation often went beyond technologies. For example, according to my field research in Hejian county (in Hebei in 2009), the county had over 100 such associations in 1980s, organized by rural cash crop producers. Over the years, most had dissipated and disappeared. One cotton research association has grown into a prominent shareholding cooperative company (Nongye jingji hezuo zuzhi yanjiu ketizu 2005).

20 According to Wen Tiejun (2012b), it was economist Justin Yifu Lin who in 1999 first proposed to the central government the idea of the construction of a new countryside. In the wake of the Asian financial crisis, Lin proposed the idea as a solution to the problem of the dual surplus that China was already facing: over-capacity and over-capitalization. Lin estimated that many industries in China already had 30 percent over-capacity in 1999 (Lin 1999).

21 *Chan ye hua* is sometimes translated as agricultural industrialization. It typically refers to a process of integrating agricultural production, processing, and marketing in a value chain – which is often led by dragon-head enterprises – in order to create greater economic efficiency and profit.

22 Yang Tuan used the term "de-peasantization" (*qu nongmin hua*) in her original text, although this reference is a little odd in the US context.

23 Wen Tiejun and his team observe that "company+households" enjoyed an unstable relationship in China and 80 percent of such contract relations are undermined by farmers opting out ("Jianshe" 2009, 6).

24 Field research in Nehe county, Heilongjiang, July 2012.

25 See He and Zheng (2013), and Ku (2013) for notable exceptions.

26 The existing collective villages in China also face a similar contradiction. The famous Nanjie village articulates a spatial separation between the internal (vis-à-vis collective members) and external (vis-à-vis the market) principles as "*wai yuan nei fang*" (round on the outside, square on the inside). While members of these villages do enjoy much better collective welfare and egalitarian treatment, collective enterprises do build its accumulation based on the exploitation of non-members who are migrant workers and the main workforce in these enterprises. See Liu (2008).

27 The interventions proposed by Tong and Wen resemble the vision of Sun Yat-Sen (1866–1925), the founding father of KMT and the Republic of China. Sun and the progressive force with the KMT were unable to realize his vision.

28 Most rural support intellectuals do not reference Chayanov. Wen Tiejun in his dissertation-turned-book argues that both Alexander Chayanov's vitality of family farming and Theodor Schultz's rational peasant farmer encounter challenges in contemporary rural China. With labor migration becoming a key economic activity among rural laborers, the emergence of labor price has played the role of a "shadow wage" for those engaged in agriculture such that households now make labor input decisions in the context of comparative gains. Within China's larger political-institutional context, farm land – not a commodity – serves the triple function of production, guarantee of subsistence, and social stability. Thus Schultz's presumed market-based peasant rationality does not quite work either in the Chinese context (Wen 2009, 27–29).

29 As is observed, "The political evaluation of the RRM was mostly negative before the 1990s, but has turned much more positive since then" (Qiu 2002, 100). In the words of Catherine Lynch, Liang's intention for a non-capitalist industrialization represented "fresh possibilities of a progressive modernity" (2010, 161).

30 During the workshop, where Cui's paper was presented, Wen Tiejun pointed out that rural households' land entitlement was an outcome of twentieth-century revolutions, not of petty bourgeoisie sentiment and agency (Cao 2003, 224). Lin Chun reminded Cui that the petty bourgeoisie as a class is not inclined toward socialism (Cao 2003, 225). For a fuller critique, see Cao (2004).

31 Even in the Mao era's rural commune system, known for its high-level egalitarianism, there was notable differentiation. See Huaiyin Li's summary of research findings on this topic: the top 10 percent of households took 28 percent of the total income; while the bottom 40 percent took 16 percent, per capita income of the top 25 percent of households was two to three times that of the bottom 25 percent. As landholdings were collective and collective labor contributed toward 20 to 30 percent of total household income, Li convincingly made demographic differentiations the primary factor in such differentiation (Li 2009, 208).

32 For disavowals of class in post-Mao ideology and intellectual discourse, see Pun and Chan (2008) and Yan (2008, ch. 5). Philip Huang complains that class categories have largely disappeared from official statistical practices (Huang *et al.* 2012, 141).

33 See He (2011). For a collection of their case studies that makes this argument, see the special issue of *Kaifang shidai* (Open Times) in 2012, which includes articles by Chen Baifeng, Lin Huihuang, and Yang Hua. See Day and Hale (2008) for an introduction and collection of essays by scholars in He Xuefeng's team.

34 He maps different kinds of rich people and views their wealth generation as external to rural place and agriculture (He 2012, 290–307).

References

Alitto, G. [Ai, K.] 1986. *The Last Confucian: Liang Shu-ming and Chinese Dilemma of Modernity*. Berkeley, CA: University of California Press.

Alitto, G. [Ai, K.] 1996. *Zhege shijie hui hao ma? Liang Shuming wannian koushu* [Has Man a Future? Liang Shuming's Narration in His Late Years]. Shanghai: Oriental Publishing Center.

Alitto, G. [Ai, K.] 2003. *Zuihou de ru jia* [The Last Confucian]. Translated by Wang Zongyu and Ji Jianzhong. Nanjing: Jiangsu People's Publishing.

Bo, G.Q. 1994. Zhongguo sanshiniandai de hezuo yundong ji xiangcun gailiang chao. [Co-operative Movements and Rural Reform in China in the 1930s]. *Zhongguo jingji shi yanjiu* [Researches in Chinese Economic History] 4, 122–134.

Cao, T.Y., ed. 2003. *Xiandaihua, quanqiuhua yu zhongguo daolu* [Modernization, Globalization and China's Path]. Beijing: Social Sciences Academic Press (China).

Cao, T.Y., ed. 2004. Xiaokang, xiaozi yu shichang shehuizhuyi [Modest Affluence, Petty Bourgeoisie and Market Socialism]. *Dushu* [Reading] 3, 10–15.

Chen, H.S., Y.S. Wong, H.C. Chang, K.K. Huang, and K.A. Wittfogel. 1980 [1939]. *Industrial Capital and Chinese Peasants: A Study of the Livelihood of Chinese Tobacco Cultivators.* New York: Garland Publishing.

Chen, Y.S. 1983. *Zhonghua hezuo shiye fazhan shi* [The History of Co-operatives Development in China]. Taibei: Taiwan Commercial Press.

Chen, Y.Y. 2013. Ziben zhuyi shi jiating nongchang de xingqi yu nongye jingying zhuti fenhua de zai sikao [The Rise of Capitalist Family Farms and a Reflection on the Differentiation of Agricultural Subjects]. *Kaifang shidai* [Open Times] 4, 137–156.

Chiang, Y.C. 2001. *Social Engineering and the Social Sciences in China 1919–1949.* Cambridge: Cambridge University Press.

China Review News. 2013. Gongshang zongju: nongmin zhuanye hezuoshe yi da 68.9 wan jia [State Administration of Industry and Commerce: Specialized Farmer Cooperatives Have Reached 689,000]. *Zhongguo pinglun* [China Review], January. Available online at: www.chinareviewnews.com/doc/1023/9/6/8/102396817.html?coluid=123&kindid=0&docid=102396817 (last accessed on February 10, 2013).

Christof, L. 2012. "Imagined Cooperatives: An Ethnography of Cooperation and Conflict in New Rural Reconstruction Projects in a Chinese Village." MA thesis, University of Vienna. Available online at: http://othes.univie.ac.at/21503/1/2012-07-19_0400999.pdf.

Cui, Z.Y. 2003. "Ziyou shehui zhuyi yu zhongguo de weilai [Liberal Socialism and the Future of China]." In *Xiandaihua, quanqiuhua yu zhongguo daolu* [Modernization, Globalization and China's Path), edited by T.Y. Cao (pp. 192–228). Beijing: Social Sciences Academic Press (China).

Day, A. 2008. "The End of the Peasant? New Rural Reconstruction in China." *Boundary 2* 35(2), 49–73. doi: 10.1215/01903659-2008-003.

Day, A. 2013. *The Peasant in Postsocialist China: History, Politics, and Capitalism.* Cambridge: Cambridge University Press.

Day, A., and M. Hale. 2007. Special issue on "New Rural Reconstruction." *Chinese Sociology and Anthropology: A Journal of Translations* 39(4).

Day, A., and M. Hale. 2008. Special issue on "The Central China School of Rural Studies." *Chinese Sociology and Anthropology: A Journal of Translations* 41(1).

Du, R.S., ed. 2002. *Dangdai Zhongguo de nongye hezuozhi* [Contemporary China: Agricultural Cooperative System]. Beijing: Contemporary China Publishing House.

Fei, X.T. 2002. *Jiangcun jingji: Zhongguo nongmin de shenghuo* [Peasant Life in China: A Field Study of Country Life in the Yangtze Valley]. Beijing: Commercial Press.
Guo, R.P. 2003. Xinminzhuzhuyi Lilun de Xueli Tanyuan [An Exploration of the Theory of New Democracy]. *Zhonggong dangshi yanjiu* [Researches of the History of Communist Party of China] 4, 50–56.
Hale, M.A. 2013. "Tilling Sand: Contradictions of 'Social Economy' in a Chinese Movement for Alternative Rural Development." *Dialectical Anthropology* 37(1), 51–82. doi: 10.1007/s10624–013–9294–1.
Han, X.R. 2005. *Chinese Discourses on the Peasant, 1900–1949*. Albany: State University of New York Press.
He, G.Z. 1937. *Zhongguo shehui xingzhi wenti lunzhan* [Debate on the Character of the Chinese Society]. Shanghai: Shenghuo shudian.
He, H.L. 2007. "Nongmin hezuo de jiegou yu guocheng [The Structure and Process of Farmers Cooperation]." PhD thesis, Peking University.
He, H.L., H.B. Ku, Z.H. Tong, L.S. Liu, X.F. He, L.W. Tian, and Y. Pan. 2009. "Chengxiang lianjie yu nongmin hezuo [Urban–Rural Links and Farmers' Cooperation]." *Kaifang Shidai* [Open Times] 9, 5–28.
He, J.H. 2007. Liang Shuming de nongye hezuohua sixiang yu shijian [Liang Shuming's Thought and Practice on Rural Cooperatives]. *Dongnan xueshu* [Southeast Academic Research] 1, 17–24.
He, X.F. 2009. *Cunzhi moshi* [Modes of Rural Governance]. Jinan: Shandong People's Publishing House.
He, X.F. 2011. Quxiao nongye shui hou nongcun de jieceng ji fenxi [An Analysis of Rural Stratification after the Abolishment of Agricultural Taxes]. *Shehui kexue* [Journal of Social Sciences] 3, 70–79.
He, X.F. 2012. *Zuzhi qilai* [Get Organized]. Jinan: Shandong People's Publishing House.
He, Y.F., and J. Zheng. 2013. "Neifaxing shequ fazhan: Shanxi Yongji shehui jingji anli [An Endogenous Development: A Case of Social Economy in Yongji, Shanxi)." *Taiwan: A Radical Quarterly in Social Studies* 91, 261–280.
Hu, J. 2011. "Jiating chengbao jingying zao yi mingcunshiwang [Family-based Contract System Has Long Ceased to Exist Except in Name]." Available online at: www.snsnsn.net/article/article.asp?typeId=17&id=1454.
Huang, C.C.P. 2010. "Longtou qiye hai shi hezuo zuzhi? [Dragon-head Enterprises or Cooperative Organizations]?" *Zhongguo laoqu jianshe* [China's Construction of Old Revolutionary Base Area] 4, 25–26.
Huang, C.C.P., Y. Gao, and Y. Peng. 2012. "Capitalization without Proletarianization in China's Agricultural Development." *Modern China* 38(2), 139–173. doi: 10.1177/0097700411435620.
Huang, Z. 2012. "Xiao nonghu yu da shangye ziben de Bo pingdeng jiaoyi: Zhongguo xiandai nongye de tese [An Unequal Transaction between Small Rural Households and Big Commercial Capital: A Distinctive Feature of China's Contemporary Agriculture]." *Kaifang shidai* [Open Times] 3, 88–99.
Jiang, X., and X.Y. Jiang. 2008. "Minguo xiangcun gongzuo taolunhui pingyi [On Symposium of Countryside Works in the Period of Republic of China]." *Xuzhou shifan daxue xuebao* [Journal of Xuzhou Normal University] 34(3), 76–81.
"Jianshe shehuizhuyi xin nongcun mubiao, zhongdian yu zhengce yanjiu ketizu" ["Target, Focus, and Policy Research of New Socialist Rural Areas Construction Group]." 2009. "Bumen he ziben xiaxiang yu nongmin zhuanye hezuo jingji zuzhi de fazhan [Governments and Capital Entering Rural Areas and (the Impact On) the Development of

Specialized Cooperative Economic Organizations of Farmers].” *Jingji lilun yu jingji guanli* [Economic Theory and Business Management] 7, 5–12.

Ku, H.B. 2013. “Funu, shouyi yu hezuo jingji [Women, Skills and Cooperative Economy].” *Taiwan: A Radical Quarterly in Social Studies* 91, 241–260.

Lammer, C. 2012. “Imagined Cooperatives: An Ethnography of Cooperative and Conflict in New Rural Reconstruction Projects in a Chinese Village.” MA thesis, University of Vienna.

Lao, Tian. 2009. “Han ding bixia de zhang zhuang: Zhongguo xiangcun biange zhong de zi zuzhi kunjing [Hinton pen Zhangzhuang: The Dilemma of Self-organizing in the Transformation of the Chinese Rural].” Renwen yu shehui [Humanities and Society] website. Available online at: http://wen.org.cn/modules/article/view.article.php/article=838 (last accessed on October 5, 2012).

Li, C.P. 2009. *Da qi hou* [The Great Climate]. Xi’an: Shaanxi People’s Publishing House.

Li, C.P. 2010. “You zheyang yige hezuoshe [There is Such a Cooperative].” *Shanxi nongye: Cun wei zhuren* [Shanxi Agriculture: The Village Cadre] 5. Available online at: www.caogen.com/blog/Infor_detail.aspx?ID=38&articleId=20515.

Li, H.Y. 2009. *Village China under Socialism and Reform: A Micro History, 1948–2008*. Stanford, CA: Stanford University Press.

Li, Z.X. 1982. “Zhongguo nongcun yundong de lilun yu shiji [Theory and Practice of China’s Rural Movement].” Vol. 8, Series 2 of *Zhongguo xiandai zhexue shi ziliao huibian: cunzhi pai pipan* [A Collection of Works about Chinese Modern Philosophy: A Critique of the Village Governance School], edited by L.M. Zhong and F.L. Yang (pp. 65–74). Shenyang: Liaoning University Publishing House.

Li, Z.H., and Z.F. Liu. 1995. *Gaobie geming: Ershi shiji zhongguo duihua lu* [Farewell to Revolution: Dialogues about Twentieth Century China]. Hong Kong: Cosmos Books.

Li, Z.H., Q. Gao, and C.Y. Cao. 2008. “Xiangcun jianshe yu xiangcun hezuo yundong jujiang: Liang Shuming [The Great Master of Rural Construction and Rural Cooperative Movement: Liang Shuming].” *Zhongguo hezuo jingji* [China Cooperation Economy] 5, 46–49.

Liang, S.M. 1989. *Liang Shuming quanji* [Complete Works of Liang Shuming], vols 2, 3, 5, and 6. Jinan: Shandong People’s Publishing House.

Liang, S.M. 1992 [1933]. *Zhongguo minzu zijiu yundong zhi zuihou juewu: xiangcun jianshe lilun* [The Final Social Awareness of the Chinese National Salvation Movement: Theories on Rural Construction]. Shanghai: Shanghai shu.

Lin, H.H. 2012. “Jianghan pingyuan de nongmin liudong yu jieceng fenhua: 1981–2010 [Peasant Mobility and Stratification on the Jiang-Han Plain, 1981–2010].” *Kaifang shidai* [Open Times] 3, 47–70.

Lin, Q.P. 1994. “Gongsi jia nonghu: Yindao nongmin zou xiang shichang de youxiao xingshi [Company Plus Household: An Effective Way to Direct Farmers Toward the Market].” *Nongye jingji wenti* [Issues in Agricultural Economy] 5, 6–9.

Lin, Y.F. (Justin). 1999. “Xin nongun yundong yu qidong neixu [New Rural Movement and Boosting Internal Demand].” *Zhongguo wuzi liutong* [Materials Circulation in China] 10, 8–12.

Liu, L.S. 2010. “Hezuoshe shijian yu bentu pingjia biaozhun [Social Practice of Rural Cooperatives and Local Evaluation Criterion].” *Kaifang shidai* [Open Times] 12, 53–67.

Liu, Q.L. 2010. “Kangzhan shiqi Jin-cha-ji bianqu de hezuoshe lunshu [Policies on Cooperatives in Jin-Cha-Ji Border Region during the Anti-Japanese Period].” *Dangshi wenyuan* [Culture and History of Chinese Communist Party] 4, 13–15.

Liu, Y.J. 2008. “Yi Nanjiecun wei li dui reng baochi de jitizhi jinxing hezuozhi gaige

[Nanjie Village as a Case: Transforming the Existing Collective System into a Cooperative One].” *China Left Review* 1. Available online at: http://chinaleftreview.org/?p=17 (last accessed on July 20, 2013).

Lynch, C. 1989. “Liang Shuming and the Populist Alternative in China.” PhD thesis, University of Wisconsin-Madison.

Lynch, C. 2010. “The Country, the City, and Vision of Modernity in 1930s China.” *Rural History* 21(2), 151–163. doi: 10.1017/S0956793310000075.

Ma, Y. 1992. *Liang Shuming pizhuan* [Biography and Commentary on Liang Shuming]. Hefei: Anhui People’s Publishing House.

Mao, Z.D. 1943. “Lun hezuoshe [On Cooperatives].” China Co-op website. Available online at: http://gxs.changyang.gov.cn/art/2012/5/11/art_3172_79829.html (last accessed on July 18 2013).

Mao, Z.D. 1982. *Mao Zedong nongcun diaocha wenji* [Collected Works of Mao Zedong on Rural Investigation]. Beijing: People’s Printing House.

Mao, Z.D. 1991. *Mao Zedong xuanji* [Collected Works of Mao Zedong]. Beijing: People’s Printing House.

Mei, D.P. 2004a. “Gongheguo chengli qian geming genjudi huzhu hezuo zuzhi bianqian de lishi kaocha [Case Investigation of the Transformation of Cooperative Organizations in the Revolutionary Base before the Foundation of PRC].” *Zhongguo nongshi* [Agricultural History of China] 2, 102–107.

Mei, D.P. 2004b. “Guomindang zhengfu shiqi nongcun hezuoshe zuzhi bianqian de zhidu fenxi [An Institutional Analysis of Rural Cooperative Organization during the Rule of Kuomintang].” *Minguo dangan* [Republican Archives] 2, 84–87.

Meisner, M. 1999. *Mao’s China and After: A History of the People’s Republic* (3rd edn). New York: The Free Press.

Nongyebu [Ministry of Agriculture]. 2012. “2011 nian nongmin zhuanye hezuoshe fazhan qingkuang [The Situation of the Development of Farmers’ Specialized Cooperative in 2011].” Available online at: www.ccfc.zju.edu.cn/a/shujucaiji/20120701/11515.html (last accessed on January 7, 2013).

Pan, J.E. 2012. “Ziwo baohu yu linglei shijian: Shuangxiang yundong shiye xia de zhongguo xiangcun jianshe [Self-protection and Alternative Practice: China’s Rural Construction Seen as a Double Movement].” PhD thesis, Lingnan University.

Pun, N., and C.K.C. Chan. 2008. “The Subsumption of Class Discourse in China.” *Boundary 2* 35(2), 75–91. doi: 110.1215/01903659–2008–004.

Qian, J., and Z. Li. 1982. “ ‘Zhongguo xiangcun jianshe pipan’ bianzhe xu [Editors’ Introduction to ‘A Critique of China’s Rural Construction’].” Vol. 8, Series 2 of *Zhongguo xiandai zhexue shi ziliao huibian: cunzhi pai pipan* [A Collection of Works about Chinese Modern Philosophy: A Critique of the Village Governance School], edited by L.M. Zhong and F.L. Yang (pp. 63–64). Shenyang: Liaoning University Publishing House.

Qiu, Z.Q. 2002. “Dui Liang Shuming xiangcun hezuo yundong de fansi [Reflections on the Rural Co-operative Movements Led by Liang Shuming].” *Zhongguo shehui jingjishi yanjiu* [The Journal of Chinese Social and Economic History] 2, 100–104.

Selden, M. 1971. *The Yenan Way in Revolutionary China*. Cambridge, MA: Harvard University Press.

Shi, J.T. 1957. *Zhongguo nongye hezuohua yundong shi liao* [Historical Documents on China’s Agricultural Cooperative Movement]. Beijing: Sanlian shudian.

Thogersen, S. 1998. “Reconstructing Society: Liang Shuming and the Rural Reconstruction Movement in Shandong.” In *Reconstructing Twentieth-century China: State*

Control, Civil Society, and National Identity, edited by K.E. Brødsgaard and D. Strand (pp. 139–162). Oxford: Clarendon Press.

Tong, Z.H., and T.J. Wen. 2009. "Ziben he bumen xiaxiang yu xiao nonghu jingji de zuzhi hua daolu: jian dui zhuanye hezuoshe daolu tichu zhiyi [The Transference of Capital and Departmental Capital to Rural Areas and the Organization of the Farming Household Economy: Questioning the Path of Specialized Cooperatives]." *Kaifang shidai* [Open Times] 4, 5–26.

Unger, J. 2009. "Families and Farmland in Chinese Villages: Unexpected Findings." In *Twenty-first Century China: Views from Australia*, edited by M. Farquhar (pp. 138–155). Newcastle upon Tyne: Cambridge Scholars Publishing.

Wang, D.L. 2004. *Liang Shuming wenda lu* [Dialogue with Liang Shuming]. Wuhan: Hubei People's Press.

Webb, A.K. 2008. "The Countermodern Movement: A World-historical Perspective on the Thought of Rabindranath Tagore, Muhammad Iqbal, and Liang Shuming." *Journal of World History* 19(2), 189–212. doi: 10.1353/jwh.0.0015.

Wei, B., and Y. Zeng. 2010. "Minjian huzhu, hezuo yundong, geming celue: Zhongyang suqu nongye huzhu hezuo yundong zai yanjiu [Folk Mutual Aid, Cooperative Movement, Revolutionary Strategies: Restudying Mutual Aid and Cooperative Movement of Agriculture in Central Soviet Area]." *Gannan shifan xueyuan xuebao* [Journal of Gannan Normal University] 2, 32–38.

Wen, T.J. 1994. "Nongcun hezuo jinrong yanjiu yu fazhan de jiben silu [The Basic Idea for Research and Development of Rural Cooperative Finance]." *Nongcun hezuo jingji he jingying guanli* [Management and Administration on Rural Cooperative Economy] 1, 27.

Wen, T.J. 2001a. "Shichang shilling+zhengfu shiling: Shuangchong kunjing xia de 'sannong' wenti [Market Failure+Government Failure: The 'Three Agricultural' Problems under Double Predicaments]." *Dushu* [Reading] 10, 22–29.

Wen, T.J. 2001b. "Bainian zhongguo, yi bo si zhe [Twists and Turns in Twentieth-century China]." *Dushu* [Reading] 3, 3–11.

Wen, T.J. 2004. *Jiegou xiandaihua* [Deconstructing Modernization]. Guangzhou: Guangdong People's Publishing House.

Wen, T.J. 2007. "Deconstructing Modernization." *Chinese Sociology and Anthropology* 39(4), 10–25.

Wen, T.J. 2009. *Sannong wenti yu zhidu bianqian* [Rural Issues and Institutional Evolution]. Beijing: Economic Press, China.

Wen, T.J. 2010a. "Weishenme women hai xuyao xiangcun jianshe [Why We Still Need Rural Construction]." *Zhongguo laoqu jianshe* [China's Construction of Old Revolutionary Base Area] 3, 17–18.

Wen, T.J. 2010b. "Gaobie bainian jijin [Farewell to a Radical Century]." Renmin luantan wang [People's Tribune website]. Available online at: http://politics.rmlt.com.cn/2010/1231/13320.shtml.

Wen, T.J. 2011. "Zonghexing hezuo jingji zuzhi shi yi zhong fazhan qushi [Comprehensive Cooperative Economic Organization is the Development Trend]." *Zhongguo hezuo jingji* [China Co-operation Economy] 1, 29 30.

Wen, T.J. 2012a. "Ba ci weiji yu ruan zhuolu [Eight Crises and Soft Landing]." Renwen yu shehui wang [Humanities and society website]. Available online at: http://wen.org.cn/modules/article/view.article.php/3485 (last accessed on November 15, 2012).

Wen, T.J. 2012b. "Xiandaihua weiji yu zhongguo xin nongcun jianshe [Crisis of Modernization and New Countryside Construction in China]." Zhongguo xiangcun faxian wang [China rural discovery website]. Available online at: www.zgxcfx.com/Article/51702.html (last accessed on November 30, 2012).

Wen, T.J., and X.D. Dong. 2010. "Cunshe lixing: pojie 'sannong' yu 'sanzhi' kunjing de yige xin shijiao [Village-community Rationality: A New Perspective to Solve the Predicaments of 'Sannong' and 'Sanzhi']." *Zhonggong zhongyang dangxiao xuebao* [Journal of the Party School of the Central Committee of the C.P.C] 14(4), 20–23.

Wu, G.H. 2012. "'Zhongjian shang+nongmin' moshi yu nongmin de ban wuchanhua [The Model of 'Intermediary Merchants plus Peasants' and the Semi-proletarianization of the Peasants]." *Kaifang shidai* [Open Times] 3, 100–111.

Xu, L.M., and J. Zhao. 2011. Liang Shuming de tudi lilun [Land Theories of Liang Shuming]. *Lianhe shibao*, July 5. Available online at: http://shszx.eastday.com/node2/node4810/node4851/node4864/userobject1ai47610.html.

Yan, H.R. 2008. *New Masters, New Servants: Migration, Development and Women Workers in China*. Durham, NC: Duke University Press.

Yan, Y.C. 1989. "Xiangcun yundong chenggong de jiben tiaojian [Basic Conditions for the Success of Rural Movements]." In *Yan Yangchu quanji* [Complete Works of Yan Yangchu], edited by E.R. Song, Vol. 1. Changsha: Hunan jiaoyu chubanshe.

Yang, F.R. 1999. "Liang Shuming yu shehuizhuyi [Liang Shuming and Socialism]." *Shehui zhuyi yanjiu* [Socialism Studies] 5, 37–39.

Yang, F.R. 2001. *Liang Shuming hezuo lilun yu Zouping hezuo yundong* [Liang Shuming's Cooperative Theory and Zouping's Cooperative Movement]. Chongqing: Chongqing Publishing House.

Yang, S., and T.J. Wen. 2011. "Nongmin zuzhihua de kunjing yu pojie: Hou nongyeshui shidai de xiangcun zhili yu nongcun fazhan [The Predicament of and Solution to Farmers' Organization: Rural Governance and Development of the Post Agricultural Tax Era]." *Renmin luntan* [People's Forum] 29, 44–45.

Yang, T. 2011. "Zonghe nongxie: xin nongcun jianshe lujing xuanze [Comprehensive Agricultural Cooperatives: The Path for New Rural Construction]." *Jinri guancha* [Observation Today] 10, 36–39.

Yu, S.D. 1929. *Hezuoshe zhi lilun yu jingyin* [Theory and Practice of Cooperatives]. Shanghai: Zhonghua shuju.

Yuan, P. 2001. "Zhongguo nongcun shichanghua jincheng zhong de nongmin hezuo zuzhi yanjiu [A Study of Farmer Cooperative Organization in the Process of Rural China's Marketization]." *Zhongguo shehui kexue* [Social Sciences in China] 6, 63–73.

Yuan, P. 2010. "Hezuoshe minzhu guanli de yiyi he mianlin de tiaozhan [The Significance of Democratic Management for Cooperatives and the Challenge they Face]." *Zhongguo nongmin hezuoshe* [China Farmers Cooperatives] 6, 16–17.

Zhang, D. 2011. "'Pibao hezuoshe' zheshe chu de jiceng guanmin guanxi: dui nongmin hezuoshe de suo jian suo si diaocha ganwu [The Government–People Relationship Reflected by 'Brief-case' Cooperatives: Reflection on Study of Rural Cooperatives]." *Renmin luantan* [People's Tribune] 25, 58–59.

Zhang, F.Q. 2012. "The Political Economy of Contract Farming in China's Agrarian Transition." *Journal of Agrarian Change* 12(4), 460–483. doi: 10.1111/j.1471–0366.2012.00352.x.

Zhang, F.Q., and J.A. Donaldson. 2008. "The Rise of Agrarian Capitalism with Chinese Characteristics: Agricultural Modernization, Agribusiness and Collective Land Rights." *The China Journal* 60, 25–47. Available online at: www.jstor.org/stable/20647987.

Zhang, K.H., and Q.L. Zhang. 2007. "Nongmin zhuanye hezuoshe chengzhang de kunhuo he sikao [Puzzles and Thoughts about the Growth of Farmers' Professional Cooperatives]." *Nongye jingji wenti* [Agricultural Economic Issues] 5, 62–66.

Zhang, X.S. 2009. "Nongmin zhuanye hezuoshe ying chao shenme fangxiang fazhan [To What Direction Should Peasant Specialized Cooperatives Develop]." *Zhongguo laoqu jianshe* [China's Construction of Old Revolutionary Base Area] 2, 13–14.

Zhao, J. 2010. "The Political Economy of Farmer Cooperative Development in China." PhD thesis, University of Saskatchewan.

Zhu, H.G. 1996. *Liang Shuming xiangcun jianshe yanjiu* [A Study of Liang Shuming's Rural Construction]. Taiyuan: Shanxi Education Press.

12 "Yingxiu mother" as agent of community development

Case study of a practice of community economy in Sichuan post-disaster rebuilding in China

Ben Hok-bun Ku and Ma Yuna

Introduction

Natural disasters have become a normal feature of China, even of the world. On May 12, 2008, an 8.0 magnitude earthquake struck Sichuan province, a mountainous region in western China, in which nearly 70,000 people died, 18,000 went missing, and which affected over 15 million people. Where physical infrastructures were concerned, 21 million buildings were damaged and 7,000 schools destroyed.

By that time, different earthquake relief teams had already arrived in the most serious stricken town – Yingxiu. Most were from Guangdong Province. Guangdong was designated as the supporting partner and was, therefore, responsible for earthquake relief and rebuilding in Wenchuan County. Guangzhou was assigned to help Yingxiu Township. As Hong Kong Polytechnic University was the partner university with the Sun Yat-sen University in Guangzhou, we got the chance to enter Yingxiu town.

However, because social work, a relatively new profession, was not recognized by Sichuan and the local government, we were not allowed to work in earthquake-stricken areas. When we arrived in the town, we did not have any connections with the local government and other organizations at first. The local people and other relief teams did not know what social work was or who we were. When we began our work, we had to find ways not only to meet enormous needs but also to overcome the survivors' distrust. The situation was embarrassing, but it stimulated our agency and creativity. In the first 60 days we spent in Yingxiu town, we cooperated with four other social work departments from the universities in Guangzhou and the Guangzhou Civil Affairs Bureau. In total, more than 50 teachers, students, and volunteers from Guangzhou came to work in Yingxiu Township. Our services covered more than 10 administrative villages in the towns of Yingxiu, Xuankou, and Shuimuo, and extended into the five other areas of the Wenchuan prefecture. We gradually became familiar to the local governments and people, and our beliefs and methods were finally accepted. The media referred to our collective work model as the "Guangzhou Model" (Yu 2008; Pei *et al.* 2009).

Although we were highly appreciated by the local people and government for our efforts, we clearly understood that the critical factor in making the project successful was the participation of the local people. We discovered the power of the local people in this catastrophe. They did not passively receive assistance from the outside as the mass media claimed, but participated actively in the community rebuilding process in response to the extremely difficult situation. In this chapter, by using the case of Yingxiu Mother Embroidery Project, we will illustrate how the rural social workers facilitate a community economy project by invigorating female participation not only in healing the post-disaster trauma, but also in improving their livelihoods.

Social work and disaster intervention

As a helping profession, social work in Western societies has a long history in dealing with the aftermath of natural disasters such as hurricanes, tsunamis, earthquakes, and snow storms. It has been well documented that social work is most effective in traumatic stress management, and delivery of resources and services to vulnerable populations (Galambos 2005; Mitchell 1983; Van den Eynde and Veno 1999; Zakour 1997), the formulation and implementation of different service plans (Banerjee and Gillespie 1994; Dodds and Nuehring 1997), and community organization and advocacy (Pyles 2007). As Yanay and Benjamin (2005, 263, 271) rightly concluded, responding to disasters is "part of social work practice and profession" and "social workers are the professionals best prepared to deal with complex situations resulting from an emergency."

In the past, social work interventions in disasters have largely focused on the work of relief and recovery for the affected individuals, families, communities, and organizations, and meeting the special needs of vulnerable groups (Cherry and Cherry 1996; Shahar 1993; Zakour 1997). However, some researchers believe that the provision of relief and services is far too limiting a role for social work as a profession. Certainly, disaster causes destruction, traumas, and tragedies, but emerging from them are also opportunities for social change and development. As the UN Disaster Relief Organization (1992, 202) rightly commented, "disasters often create a political and economic atmosphere wherein extensive changes can be made more rapidly than under normal circumstance."

Nonetheless, some have argued that in order for a disaster-affected area to overcome the devastation it has experienced and to embark on a sustainable pathway to reconstruction, the empowerment and participation of local community organizations and residents are critical (Harrell and Zakour 2000; Ozerdem 2003; Pyles 2007; Vandeventer 2004; Zedlewski 2006). In this context, Dominelli (2009, 141–142) was correct to highlight that the role for social workers in disaster intervention is indeed multifarious – as facilitator, coordinator, community mobilizer, negotiator, broker, and educator.

Taiwanese scholar Zhou (1999) summarized the services provided by social workers at both the micro and macro level based on Taiwan experience. At the micro level, social workers provide psychotherapy and psychological counseling for survivors and their families, and help individuals and families access resources, facilities, temporary housing, and relief services. At the macro level, social workers facilitate access to resources, recruit workforces, coordinate relief teams, establish volunteer services, promote community welfare, and advocate changes in systems and policies, speak out on behalf of the marginalized, empower the local community, and improve institutional mechanisms.

Zhou and his colleagues (2001) note that Taiwanese social workers undertook many functions in the "September 21" earthquake relief in 1998. Their undertakings included crisis intervention, emotional support, needs assessment, public education, community empowerment, information provision, community mobilization and organization, and policy advocacy. During reconstruction, social workers continued to fulfill these vital functions. Another Taiwanese scholar argues that social workers working in disaster areas must adhere to the core values of social work: the profession can serve in community recovery, rebuilding, and disaster prevention (Feng 2008).

However, if these are the roles that social workers can play in disaster relief, it seems that they can do anything. But in the specific political and social context, is this actually the case for social workers in the Chinese mainland? What conditions are created by the specific context of the Chinese mainland? Are there any universal experiences of social work intervention in disaster-affected areas? What are the true needs of people whom we served in Yingxiu township?

Our perspective

Staying in Yingxiu town for about a month, we found that the function of social workers was limited and not all the perspectives could be applied in working with the disaster-affected community. Like swimming in the sea, we were slowly searching for a suitable approach in the literatures for our work. Finally we identified that community-based social work was the right direction for Chinese social work in disaster intervention. As Taiwanese scholar Wang (2001) argues, a people-centered approach is important when working in a disaster-affected community. Based on his experience in Taiwan, Wang observes that the original spirit of community work is to accompany the people in the process of reconstruction. The aim is not to help them go back to their normal lives, but to make use of the challenges to redraw a much more beautiful picture of their future lives. Post-disaster rebuilding provides an opportunity to reconstruct social justice and to improve social welfare. The community social work fulfills many functions: a basic unit of the social administrative system, establishing social welfare policies for the county government; the bridge between the people and social resources, providing a link between policies and services; a service center, responding to the needs of disadvantaged people with casework and case management; a community platform, promoting solidarity, encouraging cooperation, and enhancing the community's capacity to solve its own problems; and a source of information, communicating people's needs to policy-makers.

The community approach to disaster intervention challenges the mainstream individualist approach of psychotherapy, which focuses on the individual problems of a victim. As Wang (2001) points out, the work of psychological recovery, which focuses on the individual's mental state, is not sufficiently encompassing to address the devastation created by an earthquake. The problems confronted during post-disaster reconstruction are ones where individual, community, and societal states are inextricably mixed and, therefore, cannot be resolved at the individual level. Many survivors of the earthquake in Taiwan became suicidal because of the economic pressures exerted by house loans, personal difficulties, and unemployment. Psychological intervention alone could not solve their problems.

Social work has a long tradition of practice focused on strengths and assets. We believe that the local poor and the marginalized always have many capacities, which may not be obvious to outsiders and which even they themselves may not recognize (Saleebey 1997; Sherraden 1991; Green and Haines 2002; Tice 2005; Templeman 2005). The assets and capacity-building framework help us to see that local communities contain a wide range of assets and strengths, rather than focusing on their deficiencies, problems, or disabilities. The practice models that keep us focused on the strengths, assets, and capacities of people are critical for social work practice in rural communities (Ginsberg 2005; Lohmann and Lohmann 2005; Collier 2006). As Scales and Streeter state, the role of the rural social worker is to "seek to uncover and reaffirm people's abilities, talents, survival strategies, and aspiration, and community's assets and resources" (Scales and Streeter 2003, 2). We have a commitment to empower rural communities to use their resources in innovative ways to create new assets as well as to help them determine their own direction, set their own priorities, and leverage both internal and external resources.

Therefore, holding onto this belief in Yingxiu, we endeavored to make efforts in understanding the need of the local community, discovering local capacities and developing these potentialities in order to promote individual and communal change. We also understood that capacity building implies long-term investments in people and their organizations, and a commitment to changing the various processes and forces which are affecting people's lives in the community.

Field site

Yingxiu town is one of the most developed areas in Wenchuan County. It provides access to the famous tourist resorts Jiuzhaigou and Wolong, and is called "the southern gate of Aba Prefecture." The area of the town is 115.12 square kilometers. The population of 12,000 was divided into seven administrative villages and 31 villager groups before the earthquake. Han, Zang, Qiang, and Hui people lived together harmoniously. Following the earthquake, there were only 3,000 survivors. Almost every family lost at least one member, and everyone witnessed the destruction of their families and neighborhoods. When we arrived, most of the residents were living in tents, a few lived in temporary housing which the locals called boarding rooms (banfang), and a small group remained in the destroyed village trying to fix their ruined houses.

Schools suffered the greatest devastation. About 322 of the 473 students in the primary and high schools were killed, and 26 of 46 teachers. Many teachers' relatives who also lived near the campuses were killed as well.

In addition to the psychological trauma of losing family members and friends, the residents had to deal with the destruction of their community and way of life. As a local government official said, "We in Wenchuan used to be the gate of Aba Prefecture, but now we have lost everything." One resident told us sadly, "Before the earthquake, every house had electricity. We owned every kind of household appliance and motorcycles. However, after the earthquake, we have nothing. Our living standard is now what it was in the days before liberation [1949]." A villager observed, "We don't have any field land or even land to build houses."

The situations told us that we had to respond to both psychological trauma of the people and their economic needs. The survivors started to return from the temporary settlements in Dujiangyan and Shuangliu, and the homes of their relatives. They could not come back to their homes as the town had been destroyed. Instead, they stayed in tents that were erected on a patch of land no larger than two square kilometers, near the Minjiang River. More than 5,000 people were crowded together in this small space, including 2,000 relief workers. More than 1,700 boarding rooms were constructed on the site. The resources were extremely limited. Trucks that transferred drinking water from a distant mountain spring were the only water supply; oil engines generated electricity, sometimes only enough for a few tents; relief workers sprayed disinfectant into the temporary toilets every day; and shower trucks could only provide a limited service for the residents and relief teams. As far as the locals were concerned, we came to "create trouble and chaos."

That was our situation upon our arrival in Yingxiu. We still remember how difficult it was to find a place to live. Temporary shelters were under construction and there were not enough tents or even spaces to set up a tent. The only person we knew in the town was an official from the Guangzhou Civil Affair Bureau who was helping the locals build a cemetery. He advised us to go back to Chengdu before sunset because he did not think we could endure the privations, let alone carry out social work services. We refused to go back and kept on searching for people who could help us. After several hours, we learned that the members of the Guangzhou Urban Construction Committee were in charge of the construction of shelter rooms. At the recommendation of the Guangzhou Civil Affairs Bureau, they agreed to lend us two rooms for three days. The temporary compartment rooms had just been completed: the concrete floors were still wet, and the doors and windows were still to be fitted. But we moved in immediately and lived there for more than 40 days until we were "formally allocated" three other rooms in a temporary housing area by the local government.

Although we found temporary housing, what could we do in this extremely difficult situation?

Discovering women's needs and strengths in an extremely difficult situation

Strongly holding the strengths perspective, we were encouraged to see the positive side of the people who had begun work in the fields a few days after the earthquake, planting vegetables and feeding pigs to recover their livelihoods. We would never forget the villagers who did not wait for relief from the outside but built simple shanties on the ruins of their homes. The most moving thing was that the mothers who had lost their children in the quake were very strong. Their perseverance educated and encouraged us. Their actions told the world that it was wrong to stigmatize them as "waiting, depending, and demanding" (*deng, kao, yao*).

Working in extremely difficult conditions, we knew that one ray of light would be the entire sun in such dire circumstances. The strength of social workers was to discover the needs and determine the potential strengths of the local people and connect them with outside resources. During our three-month sojourn, we devoted ourselves to local capacity building and discovered the creativity of the local people.

In order to reach our goal of long-term community rebuilding, it was necessary to perform a needs assessment. Bypassing the conventional types of social work needs assessment, we took an ethnographic approach, which involved developing a holistic understanding of people's lives through long-term participant observation. We decided to stay with the local people for as long as we could, at least for a period of three years. We began to participate in the community and to establish good relationships with the residents. On the day we arrived, while looking for a place to pass the night, we walked into the area where the tents were set up, visited the residents individually, and found out about their needs, emotions, and thoughts in informal conversations. In the following days, we accompanied the villagers who went back home to feed their pigs or salvage possessions from ruined houses, walked across the broken landscape, and investigated all seven administrative villages in Yingxiu. Against the backdrop of their destroyed homeland, the villagers told us about the changes in their lives and their feelings, difficulties, and expectations.

Adopting an anthropological approach helped us to build a close relationship with the community. Then it was time to begin asset mapping, needs assessment, and formulating plans. We adopted an action research method, which aims to strengthen and support the ability of communities to grow and change (Moyer *et al.* 1999; Plummer 2000). Like the strengths perspective, the objective of action research is to empower the local community and build up its capacity. We strongly believe that strengthening people's capacity to determine their own values and priorities, and to act on these, should be the basis of post-disaster community rebuilding (Small 1995; Park 1993; Eade 1997; Plummer 2000; Chambers 1992). Our action research allowed us to collect data and adjust our methods according to people's needs. This made our intervention more effective than that of ordinary volunteers or psychologists.

While performing the needs assessment and asset mapping, we found that, though the earthquake had shattered the physical manifestations and infrastructure of the community, it could not destroy its culture and history. We found that after the disaster, the women stayed in their tents most days. They did not farm or work elsewhere because their land and nearby factories were severely damaged. The women made embroidery to fill their empty time. Sometimes they gathered at the Yingxiu social work station and made embroideries there. In our interaction with the local women, their ideas inspired us that economic need was extremely important for them and a female embroidery project could be an attempt at community economy in Yingxiu town. The following fieldnote shows how we got the idea of forming a women's embroidery project:

> On June 23 of 2008, with the support of Guangzhou Civil Service, we went into the town of Yingxiu and established a work station on the day [of] arrival. On the second day while we visited the village of Zhangjiaping, the "center of the epicenter," where a group of women had lost their children or close family members in the earthquake, we met Sister Dong, a young divorcee who lost her two daughters in the earthquake. She was eager to tell us how bright and lovely her daughters were when they were all alive. She showed us the photos of the daughters which were kept in a small bag hanging around her chest. She led us to her half destroyed house and showed us the clothes and hairs of her daughters and kept telling the stories of the two angels. On one stand wall of the house, we saw a colorful picture of a lovely little girl. Dong said the picture was made by her elder daughter, a girl who was talented in drawing and was very docile both at home and at school, but she died in the school at 13 years old, her young sister, 11 years old, died at school the same day, May 12, the darkest day to the mother.
>
> Sister Dong was deeply sad and angry in the early days when we met her, but she volunteered to accompany us to visit the community as she couldn't get rid of thinking of the daughters all day and night, she knew she must find something to do to save herself, or she couldn't survive emotionally. We were new audiences of her stories of the daughters, and that was our biggest virtue to the sad mothers as Dong. Sister Dong told us that she wanted to embroider her daughters' drawing for keeping the memory. She also mentioned that many women there knew how to do traditional Qiang embroidery. Sister Dong inspired us that the women's handicrafts and embroidery were assets that could be developed as long-term projects for community rebuilding.

When we learned that Qiang and Zang ethnic minority women all knew how to do traditional embroidery before the earthquake, we had several questions in our minds: Could we take advantage of these women's specialty and develop an embroidery group? We thought that the women could get together to do embroidery and support each other during this critical period. Clearly, doing embroidery work would shift their attention from the past to the present and relieve their sadness and enrich their lives. In order to involve more women, the social workers suggested that they form an embroidery group. The women expressed great readiness for the idea. One woman said, "My husband is working now, but I could not find any job. Actually, I do not want to work. I am lonely at the relief tent. It is great if we can embroider together." Another woman also said,

> After the earthquake, we got a lot of support from the government and volunteers. That was very touching. But we must rely on ourselves in the future. We need to take care of our families and children. Many people can't manage to work outside. If embroidery could bring us some income, even if it is only a little money, we would like to do it.

After assessing the feasibility of the project and determining the availability of tools and materials in the village, we decided to form a women's handicraft group. We established the "Yingxiu mothers' embroidery self-help group," an economic program that combined the functions of providing bereavement relief and psychological support, nurturing grassroots cultural organizations, and rebuilding livelihoods. This group has benefitted more than 100 women in 10 villages in the area.

"Yingxiu mother" as agent of community development

The "Yingxiu mother" project, as a community economic initiative, aimed at forming the women into a mutual help group. In the group, they could do embroidery together and chat all about their lives. The reason why we chose doing embroidery as a way to organize them was based on the following considerations.

First, we found that the women used to do embroidery before the earthquake. While the earthquake destroyed the houses, industry, and field lands, embroidery became the most convenient work women could do, as it required very limited work space and tools.

Second, doing embroidery, especially in the traditional Qiang style, required tighter attention than ordinary work. Women had to be very focused on the way to apply the needles; otherwise the picture would not be balanced and the women would have to unknit it and redo it. As Sister Dong said, the time when she did embroidery was the only time when she stopped missing her daughters. She did not know how to embroider before the earthquake; however, we found her trying to learn in late June. While we proposed that the women be organized and do embroidery together, Sister Dong responded quickly and said that she would make all the drawings of her elder daughter into embroidery, so that people would know how talented the girl was. There were other women who encouraged their children to draw pictures and they did embroidery based on these pictures, which could make the children, who had been frightened by the disaster and who seemed in low spirits, cheerful and confident. This kind of embroidery was called by us "children drawing embroidery" and had never been heard of before in this area. Both traditional embroidery and the new kind of embroidery functioned as emotional work and therapy.

Third, and more and more importantly later, the embroidery project became the main channel for the women to pursue economic independence. Following the earthquake, the women no longer wanted to work in the cities, which were far away from their families. They lived on social and state relief, and most of them did not know what they could do in the future. As they said, "we dared not think of it." The embroidery project provided small hope for the women, the family, and the community. One woman said, "We want to take care of our children. If we can sell embroidery work again and earn some money, even just a little money, we are glad to do it!"

Forming the women group

In encouraging them to start the project, we promised to purchase all their products from the day the group formed. We still remember the date: on July 8, 2008, 56 days after the earthquake, the first women's embroidery group was founded in Yingxiu and involved about 20 members whose ages ranged from 19 to 45. Due to the earthquake, most of the needles and thread were buried in the rubble, and the women did not have enough money to purchase these materials. We provided them with RMB500 from project funds as start-up capital. Then the group of women purchased materials and made embroidery works collectively in their relief tents and next to the ruins of their homes.

Although we only promised to purchase their products for a very short time, for example, in the month of July and/or August, 10 women acted to do embroidery, including Sister Dong. Meanwhile, we actively tried to search out a potential supporter for the project, including potential markets for women's products. The first funds we received were RMB60,000 from Chengdu YWCA (Young Women's Christian Association), which was very encouraging for the women and for us. We held the first purchase bazaar in an unfinished boardroom on August 19, 2008. The women sat together and discussed how to set prices collectively. The bazaar marked the first time that women received incomes from their own hands, not from social or state relief. It was extremely important as, after the disaster, like other local villagers, the women had passively received outside help for nearly two months. This small amount of money allowed them to be proud of themselves. The first thing the women did after the purchase was to return the money we had lent to them to buy needles, thread, and clothes when the group newly formed. A woman also told the social workers, "Now our products have been sold. We will work hard and make better works." The purchasing meeting not only enhanced women's enthusiasm for doing embroidery, it also attracted more community women in nearby villages to join the embroidery projects.

Expanding the group

Before the bazaar, in order to benefit more women and families, we tried to mobilize more new members from two other villages to join the group. However, these women were all reluctant to do anything, using the excuse of "no spirit." After the first bazaar, women from other villages told us they hoped to form such a group too. In order to involve more women, the social workers encouraged the Yingxiu embroidery group women to mobilize their relatives and friends in nearby villages. With the Yingxiu women's help, the embroidery projects were expanded from Yingxiu Township to surrounding villages (such as Zhong and Feng villages) and involved more women in the embroidery groups. The women's embroidery group in Jinbo village was a good example. Lin Mei, a woman from Jinbo village, learned about the embroidery project from her friend Yang Wen, who was a member of the Yingxiu group. Yang introduced Lin to the social workers. According to Lin, the social workers knew that Jinbo village was the most remote mountain village in nearby areas, and which faced severe economic hardship. As Lin said, "It was very hard for us to go outside and find livelihood because of the increased landslides and debris after the earthquake. We have no way to make money and only stay in the village. I really don't know what I can do."

Because of its remote location and bad traffic conditions, Jinbo village was the last place to access outside help after the earthquake and also attracted less public attention in disaster relief. Lin proposed joining in embroidery projects with other Jinbo women. However, it was hard for the social workers to get into Jinbo because the road there was damaged and blocked; furthermore, there were only five full-time social workers who provided services for Yingxiu people and also undertook the Yingxiu women's group organization; therefore, the social workers were unable to organize the Jinbo women. In this situation, Lin volunteered to assist in organizing the women's embroidery group in Jinbo village. She also helped to transport the products to Yingxiu because she had a car. Before the earthquake, Lin and her husband had operated a small business in the township, which was exceptional in the context of Jinbo's widespread poverty. Lin started to organize the women in the community after she left the Yingxiu social work station. Finally, 20 Jinbo women were gathered by Lin to produce embroidery products. Lin regularly collected the women's finished products and brought them to the Yingxiu social work station. When she collected the products, Lin and the female producers set the prices. Then Lin transported the products to the social workers in Yingxiu. Based on the prices set by the Jinbo women's group, the social workers gave money to Lin, who then passed on this money to other women in Jinbo village.

In addition to the women's embroidery groups in Jinbo and Yingxiu, the social workers also successfully organized three other women's embroidery groups in nearby villages. By January 2009, 100 women from five villages in three townships had joined the embroidery projects. In the following months, the five women's groups made more than 400 products. All of the products were purchased by the social workers with nearly RMB100,000[1] funded by the Chengdu YWCA. At least 100 families benefitted from the embroidery livelihood projects.

During the development of the groups and the project, women not only received emotional support from each other and financial support from their own work; their collective capability has been developed in many aspects, such as product design, group organization, and public welfare participation. The women creatively embroider children's drawings which have become a new type of traditional Qiang embroidery; they have also tried to embroider their own names and some characters such as "Wenchuan," "Guangzhou," and "512" into the products, which required them to study more the techniques of embroidery and basic characters, since some of them were illiterate and had never tried to write their own names before, but now they knew how to protect their author rights. Some women showed capability in organizing the groups, such as how to set prices collectively, how to display their products in the bazaars, and how to interact with us and with people from outside, as there were always people visiting. Female cadres appeared during the development of the groups, and we tried to provide opportunities for them in capability building.

Between January 2 and January 6, 2009, we invited embroidery experts and women cadres from other projects in rural areas of Yunnan and Guizhou provinces to Yingxiu to share their experiences with our female cadres. We called it the "three provinces women's conference." Women learned a lot from each other at this conference. From April 8 to April 13, we arranged for 10 women to visit an embroidery school and museum in Guizhou province; they were very excited and cheerful on the tour and felt touched by the products and organization of Guizhou women's embroidery groups.

The most impressive aspect of the women's capacity building was their participation in public welfare. In late August, there was a heavy traffic jam in Yingxiu. More than 100 vehicles had been stuck on the damaged highway of Yingxiu for three days. Some people started to sell food to the hungry drivers and asked for unreasonable prices. Women in the embroidery groups felt ashamed of these people; they put down their embroidery, volunteered to provide cooked food for the drivers, and did not ask for any payment. They said: "We Yingxiu people got so many help by kind people after the earthquake, now we should offer our help to the others."

The project of the Yingxiu mothers continued. On the first anniversary of the Earthquake (May 12, 2009), we held an embroidery charity auction, the Qiang and Zang Embroidery Auction of Yingxiu Mothers, which was jointly sponsored by the Guangzhou government, the Chengdu YWCA, and other NGOs. The auction, held in Guangzhou City, lasted for three days and more than 400 embroidery works were exhibited in the Art Center of Yuexiu District in Guangzhou. In the three days of the auction, more than 200 people participated in the bidding, thousands of people were invited to the exhibition, and about 400 volunteers joined in. Seven women from the project also came to Guangzhou to join the exhibition and auction meeting. The audiences and purchasers were able to communicate with these women directly. Participants also listened to the stories of the producers (women) of the products. We also attached a cultural card with women's pictures and names on each piece of embroidery. A work embroidered with a panda attracted some bidders' attention. It was made by Dong according to a drawing by her daughter and sold at a good price. She had mixed feelings because she was sad at losing her children but happy, for "she felt that they [had] become a painter now."

The charity auction meeting was a success. Totally we raised about RMB250,000. All the income from the bazaar would be returned to the area of Yingxiu to help more women in their pursuit of sustainable development. Following the discussion, in order to help more people in Yingxiu, the women decided to use this money to set up a collective development fund for their long-term development. The development of the women's groups helped us to clarify our roles as supporters, facilitators, and capacity builders. It also taught the women the importance of collective action. No matter how small or big a decision, it should be made collectively; then, everyone is responsible. Gradually the team spirit of the group of women grew. Group leaders emerged, and there was a clear division of labor. Each woman had a job according to her particular talents and abilities (e.g. pattern and product design, material acquisition, marketing, quality control, paper cutting, or book-keeping).

From charity to long-term community economy

The charitable funds were unsustainable. The social workers and the women needed to find a long-term method for livelihood recovery. The funds raised from the charity auction were for the long-term livelihood development of the women's group and other community members. When they discussed the idea with the women, they were happy with that. One of the members, Yu, said, "After the earthquake, we were helped little by little, like sprinkling pepper. It could not resolve the practical difficulties like house reconstruction. If you [the social workers] help us to generate long-term livelihood, we can overcome the difficulties by ourselves" (Zhang *et al.* 2011, 30). Finally, we and the women decided to use the Yingxiu Mothers' Fund to support micro-credit which enabled the women to establish livelihood initiatives.

Before the earthquake, Yingxiu Township enjoyed economic prosperity and an advantageous location. Most villagers farmed for a living, such as planting corn and vegetables. They also raised pigs and made preserved ham, which was the staple meat in their diet. As the villagers said, "We can feed ourselves by farming." Furthermore, Yingxiu and the surrounding areas were rich in hydropower and mineral resources, and many related enterprises were established nearby. Therefore, the villagers could work in enterprises close to their homes. Yingxiu was also a necessary road through which outside visitors traveled to Jiuzhai and Wolong, famous tourist attractions in Sichuan province, by bus or by car. Therefore, it developed service industries, especially catering and entertainment businesses, which not only created prosperity but also provided employment opportunities for the villagers.

After the earthquake, the prosperous days in Yingxiu were over. As a local official said, "Before the earthquake we had the most advantageous conditions, but now we have nothing." All the homesteads and farm land in four villages of the township (seven villages in total) were destroyed, and those lands in the other three villages were almost destroyed. Places of public entertainment and industrial enterprises were also ruined. Therefore, the villagers could live neither on farming nor on working in nearby enterprises. Official food relief and relief funds (RMB10 per day) were provided in the first three months following the earthquake. Three months later, the relief resources were sharply reduced. The villagers had to buy food in the market and needed more money than before.

In response to their economic hardships, some villagers turned to work in the cities far away from their home towns. For example, villager Wei was always ready to work in the city. His parents were over 80 years old and his niece was disabled. Over the previous three months, he spent only RMB10 to buy vegetables and twice cooked cured meat, which had been salvaged from the ruins. The whole family lived on instant noodles and biscuits distributed by the government in the first month and sometimes had rice with chili sauce. His homestead and farm land were totally ruined, and he also lost his job in the ironworks, which were submerged by the mud-rock flow after the earthquake. He told the social workers, "I cannot spend all the relief money. I have to save some for transportation in case I need to go to the city to work."

However, working in the cities at a distance was only a last resort for the villagers. Most of the villagers tended to earn money close to their communities. At that time, they were busy rebuilding their houses and taking care of the elderly and children. More importantly, they expected to be together with their families because of frequent secondary disasters such as aftershocks, landslides, and debris flow. In this situation, a local livelihood could reduce their economic pressures and enable them to take care of family members. Furthermore, they hoped to find jobs that they were interested in or skilled at, and which would be easier for them to succeed in.

In May 2009, post-disaster, Yingxiu became a scenic spot, and many people travelled there to appreciate the landscape affected by the earthquake. They visited Yingxiu also because they were concerned about the affected people's situation in disaster recovery. At that time, the road to the epicenter became a busy shopping street where local villagers sold stones excavated from the epicenter, photos of the 5.12 Earthquake, and traditional ornaments. Visitors usually bought souvenirs on the streets before they left. On a given day, a woman could sell more than 10 pairs of embroidered insoles and another woman selling ivory combs would earn several hundred Yuan.

When the embroidery group women discussed their work plan with us after the auction, the women suggested that they work together to open a Yingxiu Mothers' Restaurant and a Yingxiu Mothers' Embroidery Shop in their neighborhood, which they were more familiar with because they had previously done work there and would be able to look after their families. Given the tourism environment in post-disaster Yingxiu, the business plans for a restaurant and embroidery display shop were feasible. At first, the women could not find places to open their shops. The social workers offered two rooms, which had been their working and living space, and stayed with the villagers. One room was for the restaurant and the other was for the embroidery shop. The group of women collectively borrowed RMB10,000 from the Yingxiu Mothers' Foundation and bought dinnerware for the restaurant. Yang, who had once run a restaurant, worked as a leader in charge of financial management and daily operation of the restaurant. Dong, who was good at cooking, worked as the chef. The embroidery shop was mainly managed by Yu, who was experienced in embroidery. In order to organize the group, the women also made rules for their group and posted them on the wall of the restaurant and the embroidery shop. They were enthusiastic about their careers and new lives.

During these five years, we explored the alternative urban market together with the women. At the beginning of the project, to further assist them to test the market and strengthen their confidence, as well as to promote what we believe as fair trade, we decided to introduce their work to some NGOs (non-governmental organizations) and fair trade shops. In the fair trade shops in Guangzhou City and Hong Kong, their handicrafts were displayed in a special booth along with a brief introduction to the project, highlighting what fair trade could do to help the people's livelihoods in disaster areas as well as to revive their cultural tradition and pride. Their works were much admired by the delegates and sold well at the beginning. More importantly, many were interested in knowing how the works were achieved and wanted to find out the meanings of their embroidery designs as well as how they were organized. We also found an opportunity to present the women's project at different academic conferences. Women had a chance to share their experiences in setting up the women's group following disaster, and entertained questions from conference participants. In the process, it was evident that they had been empowered and found their strength.

However, people's concern about Sichuan 5.12 Earthquake gradually faded. We faced a lot of difficulties in the year after the first anniversary of the 5.12 Earthquake. A breakdown in order and some women moving away for resettlement were the main problems. We worked very hard to market their products in the city and the situation improved. Finally, we obtained an order from an international conference. About 20 women from the Jinpo villages joined together to produce embroidery for the conference souvenirs. From the winter of 2010 to May of 2011, their income totaled about RMB30,000.

We also endeavored to create opportunities for the women to promote their products in cities. In November 2010, the women's group attended a conference in Beijing. The theme was "Mother and Daughter: Women, Culture and Development Forum." The women danced at the conference's opening and closing ceremony of the forum and also introduced their embroidery at the conference. Audiences' feedback was very encouraging. Therefore, their morale and confidence was strengthened again. The solidarity of their group was also enhanced. In May 2011, the women designed a pendant and used it as a souvenir at an international conference on Sichuan Earthquake Redevelopment and Social

Work. These souvenirs were admired by participants from all around the world. The positive feedback gave the women high confidence in future development.

All the women have returned to their permanent homes now that the Yingxiu town has been rebuilt. They had a long-term development plan. They not only continue to do embroidery, but also plan to set up a Yingxiu mothers' community kitchen, eco-tourism, and organic farming.

Conclusion

In the perspective of social economy, economic development must return to society and gradually shift from a market economy to a community economy. Disaster opens the door for capital to intrude into rural society, commodifying farm land and peasants subsequently disposed from their means of production and livelihood in the process of post-disaster rebuilding. What we have done in disaster-affected communities is not only to offer disaster relief, but also to resist the invasion of capital and promote an alternative community initiative that is people-centered, community-based, cooperative, democratic, as well as defined by harmony between people and the environment.

The "Yingxiu mother" experience shows us that, in order to achieve long-term sustainable community economic development, it is important to understand the local economic situation before a disaster, which influences developing people's economic expectations, their economic consciousness, and their ways to restart their livelihoods in the current context. It is also important to adopt a strength perspective to rediscover local capacity and assets. Strength perspective kindles "Hope" in a community. In the first three years, we accessed the strength, courage, and capacity of the local community. From experiences such as the establishment of the Yingxiu mothers' embroidery group, we learned that disaster community redevelopment can be more than economic; it can represent advances in peace, justice, human rights, health, education, and the environment. We believe that the restoration of cultural identity and self-confidence to the survivors is critical, and they must be encouraged to work toward this restoration. Improving people's lot is only possible when there is vigorous community participation. The creation of the Yingxiu mothers' embroidery group was proof of the success of our integrated approach. We may conclude that cooperation is the key to capacity building and empowerment.

After three years of effort, what changes did the Yingxiu mothers make in their lives and community in post-disaster rebuilding? Most apparent was the emergence of a core group who were both strongly motivated and committed to transform their life chances and restore the identity of their community. With a newfound sense of solidarity and cohesiveness, they seemed less hesitant about their own abilities and had become more confident about themselves, and had more pride in their traditional culture. It was also evident that they had matured rapidly in the participative and empowering processes, and began to feel that they had regained control over their own destiny and developed a stronger identity about themselves and what their heritage represented.

In short, our approach challenged the mainstream model of development, which champions individualism and competition; instead, we promoted a new form of collectivism based on mutual help, the pooling of resources, and the active participation of women.

Acknowledgment

The authors wish to acknowledge the GRF [project code: PolyU 5491/09H] of the University Grants Council of Hong Kong and Zeshan Foundation in support of this research project.

Note

1 The Chengdu YWCA manager initially promised to donate RMB60,000, which was later increased to RMB100,000.

References

Banerjee, M.M., and D.F. Gillespie. 1994. "Linking Disaster Preparedness and Organizational Response Effectiveness." *Journal of Community Practice* 1(3), 129–142. doi: 10.1300/j125v01n03_09.

Chambers, R. 1992. *Rural Appraisal: Rapid, Relaxed and Participatory*. Brighton: Institute of Development Studies.

Cherry, A.L., and M.E. Cherry. 1996. "Research as Social Action in the Aftermath of Hurricane Andrew." *Journal of Social Service Research* 22(1–2), 71–87. doi: 10.1300/j079v22n01_05.

Collier, K. 2006. *Social Work With Rural Peoples*. Vancouver: New Star Books.

Dodds, S., and E. Nuehring. 1997. "A Primer for Social Work Research on Disaster." *Journal of Social Service Research* 22(1–2), 27–56. doi: 10.1300/j079v22n01_03.

Dominelli, L. 2009. *Introducing Social Work*. Cambridge: Polity Press.

Eade, D. 1997. *Capacity-building: An Approach to People-centred Development*. Oxford: Oxfam.

Feng, Y. 2008. "Zaibian shehui gongzuo gongneng yu juese—yi taiwan 921 dizhen wei li [The Functions and Roles of Disaster Social Work: The Experience of Social Work in Taiwan 921 Huge Earthquake]." Available online at: www.chinaswedu.com/news/yxjj/yxjj.html/www.docin.com/p-338470724.html (last accessed on December 1, 2008).

Galambos, C.M. 2005. "Natural Disasters: Health and Mental Health Considerations." *Health and Social Work* 30(2), 83–86. doi: 10.1093/hsw/30.2.83.

Ginsberg, L.H., ed. 2005. *Social Work in Rural Communities*. Alexandria, VA: CSWE Press.

Green, G.P., and A. Haines. 2002. *Asset Building and Community Development*. Thousand Oaks, CA: Sage.

Harrell, E.B., and M.J. Zakour. 2000. "Including Informal Organizations in Disaster Planning: Development of a Range-of-type Measure." *Tulane Studies in Social Welfare* 21(2), 61–83.

Lohmann, N., and R.A. Lohmann. 2005. *Rural Social Work Practice*. New York: Columbia University Press.

Mitchell, J.T. 1983. "When Disaster Strikes: The Critical Incident Stress Debriefing Procedure." *Journal of Emergency Medical Service* 8(1), 36–39.

Moyer, A., M. Coristine, L. Maclean, and M. Meyer. 1999. "A Model for Building Collective Capacity in Community-based Programs: The Elderly in Need Project." *Public Health Nursing* 16(3), 205–214. doi: 10.1046/j.1525–1446.1999.00205.x.

Ozerdem, A. 2003. "Disaster as Manifestation of Unresolved Development Challenges: The Marmara Earthquake, Turkey." In *Natural Disasters and Development in a Globalizing World*, edited by M. Pelling (pp. 199–213). London: Routledge.

Park, P. 1993. "What is Participatory Research? A Theoretical and Methodological Perspective." In *Voices of Change: Participatory Research in the United States and Canada*, edited by P. Park, M. Brydon-Miller, B. Hall, and T. Jackson (pp. 1–20). Westport, CT: Bergin & Garvey.

Pei, Y.X., H.Q. Zhang, and H.B. Ku. 2009. "Guangzhou Social Workers in Yingxiu: A Case Study of Social Work Intervention in the Aftermath of the Sichuan 5.12 Earthquake in China." *China Journal of Social Work* 2(3), 151–163. doi: 10.1080/1752509 0903211705.

Plummer, J. 2000. *Municipalities and Community Participation: A Sourcebook for Capacity Building*. London: Earthscan.

Pyles, L. 2007. "Community Organizing for Post-disaster Social Development: Locating Social Work." *International Social Work* 50(3), 321–333. doi: 10.1177/0020872807 076044.

Saleebey, D., ed. 1997. *The Strengths Perspective in Social Work Practice* (2nd edn). New York: Longman.

Scales, T.L., and C.L. Streeter. 2003. *Rural Social Work: Building and Sustaining Community Assets*. Belmont, CA: Brooks/Cole/Thomson Learning.

Shahar, I.B. 1993. "Disaster Preparation and the Functioning of a Hospital Social Work Department during the Gulf War." *Social Work in Health Care* 18(3/4), 147–159. doi: 10.1300/j010v18n03_14.

Sherraden, M. 1991. *Assets and the Poor: A New American Welfare Policy*. Armonk, NY: M.E. Sharpe.

Small, S.A. 1995. "Action-oriented Research: Models and Methods." *Journal of Marriage and Family* 57(4), 941–955. Available online at: www.jstor.org/stable/353414.

Templeman, S.B. 2005. "Building Assets in Rural Communities through Service Learning." In *Social Work in Rural Communities*, edited by L.H. Ginsberg (pp. 123–138). Alexandria, VA: CSWE Press.

Tice, C.J. 2005. "Celebrating Rural Communities: A Strengths Assessment." In *Social Work in Rural Communities*, edited by L.H. Ginsberg (pp. 95–108). Alexandria, VA: CSWE Press.

Van den Eynde, J., and A. Veno. 1999. "Coping with Disastrous Events: An Empowerment Model of Community Healing." In *Responses to Disaster: Psychosocial, Community and Ecological Approaches*, edited by R. Gist and B. Lubin (167–192). Philadelphia, PA: Brunner/Mazel.

Vandeventer, P. 2004. *From Chaos to Community: A Guide to Helping Friends and Neighbours Recover and Rebuild after a Major Disaster*. Los Angeles, CA: Community Partners.

Wang, Z.Y. 2001. "Yi shequ wei danwei de xinli fu jian shiwu shuoming yu jiantao-nantou xian shenghuo chongjian zhongxin jingyan [Examining the Experience of Nantou Life Reconstruction Centre through the Practice of Community-based Psychological Counseling]." Paper presented at a conference on 9.21 post-disaster psychological rehabilitation policy and practice organized by the Ministry of Health and China Association of Psychology (currently Taiwanese Psychological Association), Taipei, December 7–8.

Yanay, U., and S. Benjamin. 2005. "The Role of Social Workers in Disasters: The Jerusalem Experience." *International Social Work* 48(3), 263–276. doi: 10.1177/0020872805051704.

Yu, X.X. 2008. "Zainan jiuzhu zhong de 'guangzhou moshi' ['Guangzhou Model' in Disaster Relief]." *Zhongguo shehui dao kan* [China Society Periodical] 16, 14–15.

Zakour, M.J. 1997. "Disaster Research in Social Work." *Journal of Social Service Research* 22(1–2), 7–25. doi: 10.1300/j079v22n01_02.

Zedlewski, S.R. 2006. "Building a Better Safety Net for the New New Orleans." In *After Katrina: Rebuilding Opportunity and Equity into the New New Orleans*, edited by M.A. Turner and S.R. Zedlewski (pp. 63–72). Washington, DC: Urban Institute. Available online at: www.urban.org/UploadedPDF/311406_after_katrina.pdf.

Zhang, H.Q., Y.X. Pei, H.B. Ku, and X.C. Yang, eds. 2011. *Zaihai shehui gongzuo: Zhongguo de shijian yu fansi* [Disaster Social Work in China: Practice and Reflection]. Beijing: Social Sciences Academic Press (China).

Zhou, Y.Q. 1999. "Shehui gongzuo zhe zaibian fuwu de juese ji qita xiangguan yiti zhi wanxian tantao [Exploring the Role of Social Work in Disaster Service and its Related Issues]." *Fuli shehui* [Welfare Society] 74, 23–27.

Zhou, Y.Q., T.Y. Wang, F.Y. Tao, and D.Y. Xie. 2001. "Jiu'eryi dizhen shehui gongzuo zhe zaibian fuwu juese yu gongneng tansuo [Exploring the Roles and Functions of Social Work in 9.21 Earthquakes]." Paper presented at a conference on the 9.21 earthquake and social cultural reconstruction. Organized by the Academia Sinica of Taiwan, September, Nangang, Taipei.

13 Local economy growing at a steady pace

The case of the peasant farming project by the Taiwan Rural Front[1]

Pei-hui Tsai and Chi-wei Liu

Introduction

On August 8, 2009, Typhoon Morakot brought heavy rain to Taiwan and caused catastrophic damage to southern Taiwan with record-breaking rainfall of 2,900 millimeters (114 inches) in three days. Rainstorms, mudslides, and floods destroyed some towns, and a mountain village, Xiaolin, was buried by the mudslide. Reports indicate that 693 people died, 97 people were missing, and decades of aboriginal villagers were forced to move. It was estimated that economic losses reached NT$90.4 billion (US$31.2 billion), about 0.75 percent of GDP.

As a matter of fact, Taiwan's economic development and people's way of life could be regarded as the trigger for such a disaster. On the one hand, we have been used to a very convenient life and cheap consumption, which are underpinned by the chain stores and supermarkets. On the other hand, such a lifestyle compels involvement in the capitalist system which advocates free trade and competition for corporate profit. The capitalist system exhausts the earth's resources while its influence continues to expand across national boundaries. In the meantime, the earth takes its revenge by causing natural disasters.

Actually, we do not have too many choices when facing this situation. But we ponder, to a certain extent, how to free ourselves from the existing economic system. We need to develop the so-called "local economy," which intends to meet the demands of local community and local people instead of the world market. As Polanyi (1957) hints, the local economy is an economy embedded in the socio-cultural context.

Back to reality in Taiwan, this chapter focuses on "community economy reconstruction." We will show how diversified regional activities reconstruct the relationship between people and the land through the production, processing, consumption, and exchange of local agricultural goods, enabling people to cut down on food miles and avoid oil-based agriculture.

Beginning in October 2009, Fen-Yu Chen of the Taiwan Rural Front (TRF) and the authors asked our friends affected by Typhoon Morakot about the possibility of initiating community economy reconstruction. Subsequently, the TRF reached agreement with the communities in Gauzhong village and Qinhe village in the Taoyuan District of Kaohsiung City, and Liqiu village in Jinfeng Township of Taitung County. The project "Peasant Farming Rehabilitation" aims to: (1) promote land-friendly farming through cultivation of public farm land; (2) assist villagers in establishing a simple agricultural process system; (3) create a self-owned brand for their agricultural products, and connect external consumers with the local economy; (4) encourage villagers to manage external resources collectively.

This chapter presents our reflections on the process of implementation. The following illustrates our concept of the local economy and its reconstruction. It then describes the cases of plum processing in Qinhe and millet farming in Liqiu. Finally, we attempt to explore how environmentally friendly farming ignites the local economy, cooperation among villagers in their daily lives and labor, and how the local economy is embedded in the social structure.

Reconstruction of the local economy

Taiwan has been regarded as the development model for other industrializing countries. The average economic growth rate was 8.2 percent between 1952 and 1982. Rapid industrialization and successful economic development led Taiwan to become one of the four Asian tigers, alongside Hong Kong, Singapore, and South Korea. However, to a large extent, the urban–rural gap has become increasingly wider since the 1990s due to economic globalization. People in remote areas not only suffer from the economic inequality, but also bear the social cost resulting from rapid industrialization. Accordingly, they are much weaker than those who live in urban areas when facing natural disasters. It is also much more difficult to reconstruct the communities in which they live.

However, "community economy reconstruction" is constrained by the dual structures. On the one hand, the existing community economy had been involved in the global world system. Everything was under the control of the commoditized world, dominated by monopoly capitalism. On the other hand, it inevitably caused numerous natural disasters. Therefore, it is necessary for the reconstruction of the community economy to move from the dual structures mentioned above.

However, how can these aspirations be realized? First, we will discuss the so-called "local economy." The word "local" is a relative concept which needs to be socially contextualized. As Shuman points out:

> Going local does not mean walling off the outside world. It means nurturing locally owned businesses which use local resources sustainably, employ local workers at decent wages, and serve primarily local consumers. It means becoming more self-sufficient, and less dependent on imports. Control moves from the boardrooms of distant corporations and back to the community, where it belongs.
>
> (Shuman 1998, 6)

In other words,

> it means rebuilding the very engine of public service – the healing and educative relationship between doctor and patient, teacher and pupil. It means re-discovering that ordinary users of services have something to offer which society needs. It means re-writing the software the distant institutions use to manage us. And it means rebuilding the possibility of local enterprise and energy to breathe life into our local economies.
>
> (Boyle 2009, 19)

To put it simply, the local economy establishes connections within regions, and maintains plural and autonomous patterns of livelihood. It does not necessarily relate to efficiency seeking, cost reduction, or profit maximization. The local economy emphasizes that people live and share with each other in their community and society. Therefore, they can construct cooperative relationships and the social basis for material exchange.

Patterns of the local economy include micro-finance, community democracy, community supported agriculture (CSA), and so forth. As for agricultural consumption, CSA participants look for safe food and share the risks and harvest with the producers. The local economy is a set of sustainable social relationships that remove exchange from capital accumulation and embed it in social actions. Producers and their community will engage in a stable exchange relationship, in which they can practice environmentally friendly farming and provide safe and fresh food. Through participating in CSA, farmers can connect labor and production and the network of cooperation (Henderson and Van En 2007). The local economic pattern of peasant farming can reconstruct the connection of humankind and land through reconstructing the relationship between humankind and food. Significantly,

> a focus on sustainable food is particularly attractive because it provides a basis for a holistic approach to the challenge of re-making the food system. Issues around well-being, social justice, stewardship and system resilience arise throughout the food system – in production, processing, manufacture, transportation, retail, preparation and waste disposal – and for producers, workers and consumers, whether they are located in the UK or abroad.
>
> (Sumberg 2009, 2)

The postwar land reform accomplished in Taiwan in 1953 consolidated and constructed smallholding agriculture in Taiwan. The Taiwanese state exploited rural surplus via two systems – "exchanging fertilizer with rice" and "collecting agricultural tax in kind."[2] Due to the trend of neoliberalism, the agriculture market in Taiwan was forced to open. Farmers had to confront severe market challenges. Some of them gave up farming, and some tried to make a transition or struggled to survive (Tsai 2009). Many farmers who had shifted to produce cash crops were unable to resist the dumping of foreign agriculture products.

Some of them even moved to mountain areas to grow fruit and vegetables, which caused the emergence of commercial monoculture. However, this badly damaged the environment, and the farmers lost the means of subsistence for the aboriginal community.

It was the very commercial monoculture that constrained the reconstruction of community economy after Morakot. This culture had driven mountain villagers to seek monetary accumulation via commodity exchange. It also limited their possibilities of obtaining a livelihood. When facing the huge disaster caused by Morakot, they became confused about how to change and what to do. Therefore, the TRF attempted to cooperate with the aboriginal communities and to explore collaborative and environmentally friendly ways of farming.

Here, peasant farming refers to the way a peasant cultivates and labors to eliminate his or her economic disadvantage, improve the agricultural market channels, and regenerate the environment. Currently, two areas are supported by the TRF. Due to different production conditions, support patterns for them also differ. In Liqiu, the retrieval of traditional agriculture wisdom, the development of farming methods accommodating the local social context and environment, and improvements in the quality of agriculture products were emphasized in the first year. Meanwhile, in Gauzhong and Qinhe, in which large-scale production of cash crops prevailed, we attempted to develop the plum-processing industry and to establish market channels free from the wholesalers, and to promote the product. We encouraged cooperation among the farmers. For the past year, we organized discussions with farmers, focusing on the choice of crops, the pattern of cultivation, the use of funds, the visualization and revision of brand and logo, product pricing, packaging, and the market prospects for the following year., The process might be complicated, but we truly hoped that it would enhance our experience of sharing and learning. Ultimately, people would generate consensus, and therefore unite together (Hao Ran Foundation 2010).

Peasant farming may be seen as the synthesis of the community economy and eco-agriculture. The TRF initiated discussions in the local communities through specific cases. In addition, together with community residents, the TRF explored the practice of eco-agriculture.

Plum processing in Qinhe village of Taoyuan

The main agri-products in Taoyuan are plums, mango, Japanese plums, and peaches. Plums account for the largest area under cultivation: 938 hectares. Taoyuan is the second largest plum production area in Taiwan after Xinyi Township, Nantou County, which has 1,224 hectares under cultivation. The price of plums in season around April is NDT$5 to NDT$10 per kilogram.

Farmers in Taoyuan used to sell fresh plums direct to consumers. They did not have any processing skills such as pickling and brewing, nor a brand name for their plums, unlike the farmers in Xinyi. This situation made farmers in Taoyuan suffer insufficient and unstable income. Farmers have to sell fresh plums immediately due to the very short harvest period; otherwise the ripe plums will rot on the trees. Under this constraint of not being able to store the fresh plums for a long time, the farmers have to sell the plums immediately; otherwise they are controlled by wholesalers and cannot achieve a reasonable price.

If farmers have the skill to process plums, they will be able to break the restriction, add more value to the plums, and make more money. In addition, if farmers could create a local brand for their plum products, they will find a market niche, and even help enhance the identity of their community. Moreover, discussion among them about community public affairs would be prompted through the process of cooperation in their daily processing work.

Compared with the similar processing workshops and small plants in Xinyi, there was only one small processing plant in Taoyuan. Most farmers in Taoyuan had no experience of processing plums. In order to solve the problem, 20 farmers from Taoyuan visited family processing workshops in Xinyi in February 2010. The concept of plum processing was further consolidated during this visit. However, some expressed concerns about the transition. For example, would the plums appear less attractive without the use of fertilizers and pesticides? Would sufficient labor be available for weeding and care of the crops (Hsu 2010a)?

The anxiety of farmers is precisely the key point for environmentally friendly agriculture. Shifting from conventional farming dependent on chemical fertilizers and pesticides to environmentally friendly farming is a challenge to farmers' labor and skills. Undoubtedly, farmers need to learn a new way of farming, reallocate their family labor, and be prepared to take the risk of such a shift for their produce. Therefore, they selected a small area as public farm land to grow plums without pesticides and herbicides, and to initiate plum processing.

In March 2010, a series of courses was arranged to provide the opportunity for farmers to learn how to make additive-free processed plum products, such as pickled plum, plum essence, and plum sauce. In April, 900 bottles of pickled plum, 420 bottles of plum essence, 245 bottles of plum sauce, and 800 kilograms of soft plums were produced.

During the moon festival of 2010, the brand "Mi Ru Hu Plum" was introduced to consumers and generated high market response through e-mail networks: 100 gift baskets were sold out in a very short time. The women of Taoyuan organized a production and marketing group. They also learned to process jelly figs and other kinds of fruit. In 2011, 1,000 gift baskets were produced. In addition to promotion via the Internet and farmers' markets, the community has been cooperating with the "Homemakers Union Consumers Co-op," the most important consumer organization in Taiwan, in order to penetrate the market of green consumption.

However, the shift seems very slow and difficult. Numerous issues and problems emerged during the transition, including organization of the division of labor, whether the products manufactured by individual farmers can join cooperative marketing, how the public fund is managed, and identification of the market.

Division of labor and the heavy labor input generated complaints from farmers. As for products made by individual farmers, after a long discussion, the villagers decided to reject this proposal because of the uncertainty of quality and sanitation. Third, currently the public fund is managed by women in Qinhe village. All the sales revenue is invested in the fund for future research and development, and operation. Some NT$500,000 has been invested in this project, most of which has been used to purchase equipment. The public fund, generated from the sale revenue, reached NT$360,000 in April 2011.

The hardest challenge for the local economy is market development. Farmers are always worried about finding the market, and whether they have produced too many processed products. Such a situation raises two significant questions. The first is that "production" and "exchange" in the local economy cannot be separated and need to be treated equally. "Exchange" practiced within social networks can bring about meaningful values, including the production of reports for the public media, application of the Internet, and participation in the farmers' market. These extended discussions expanded the market, but we have to recognize that there is a dilemma when we advocate the embedding of exchange in social relationships. Marketing channels for plum products depend heavily on the social capital of partners and participants. Usually they share the same social networks, so that they often receive the same marketing e-mails from friends. Therefore, it is difficult to find new customers and to expand the reach of the products. In response to this constraint, we have sought to expand our customer base through participation in farmers' markets and Internet marketing.

Second, it was revealed that our thinking is still constrained by the market economy. We still use the numbers as the only criteria to evaluate our efforts; meanwhile the values of the reconstruction of relationships among people are overlooked.

One partner in plum processing questioned via e-mail how "community team work" could be established:

> We all worked very hard today. I am more curious about how you interact while waiting or working. I think it is the very key to form a team, and might influence our future discussion, compromise among us, and even cause the potential conflicts. For example, some of you work very hard, but some don't. Some come very often, but some don't. We also see some new faces occasionally. So, how many people do we really have in this team? If we decide not to allocate the earnings, okay, fine, there will be no problem. But, if we want to distribute the earnings, then, how will we do?
>
> It's not the free will which causes people to cooperate with each other. On the contrary, we do it after struggling and compromising. Yes, it is so real! A real fight! Everyone thinks it more important to improve their lives. We need to understand it with sympathy. I responded immediately.

Apparently, everyone experienced these challenges and conflicts, but meanwhile they recognized the necessity of cooperation and publicity. The community had accumulated the power to keep on moving forward.

Work division and mutual learning during the labor process are worth a mention as well. Obvious improvements in Qinhe's work group may be seen in a few aspects: work division, yearly yield plans, and quality control. Fen-Yu Chen said,

> In the first year, people who came and joined us were those with interests and curiosity, and we couldn't tell exactly who would come....
>
> In the second year, one of the core members, Savi, started to estimate the labor they needed and assigned leaders for each work item. Thus, quarrels happening while making plum essence in the first year did not appear again in the second year. This time, three couples were assigned to make plum essence with a clear work shift schedule.
>
> ...Besides, based on the market response, Qinhe's farmer group started to discuss 2012's production plan, heading toward planning production.

On one occasion of a gathering of farmer groups, one of the core members, Umav, said, "Although farming is really hard-working, every day is a brand new day with challenges." Another core member, Savi, often says, "Give yourself a whole new beginning; keep confidence and courage, make efforts and success is always there." Qinhe's farmer group also rewards community youth, including arranging classes and allocating scholarships. The group encourages children to develop their community recognition and take immediate action, from handing in reports to doing community clean-up works. Members' concrete belief and positive attitudes toward the future are probably the motivation to strengthen their minds during difficulties and struggles, so that they can maintain the quality and cleanliness of their plum products and connect their efforts to community life and the local economy.

Growing millet in Liqiu indigenous community

Liqiu is located in the Taimali River Valley. The main crops are drought tolerant, including millet, taro, cajan, ginger, and roselle. A few farmers grow seasonal vegetables, and one or two farmers grow tomatoes under protected cultivation. During the first visit, the author was puzzled about the way of farming in this district. The farmers there were conducting extensive farming rather than intensive farming that we often found in Taiwan.

In October 2009, discussions were held for the youth and farmers in Liqiu. Initially, they had no idea about our project at all. Therefore, an orientation was held before Christmas. We promoted environmentally friendly farming, and broadcast a documentary film *The Power of Community*, which features community-based organic agriculture. During the orientation, participants talked about the scenery they saw in the film. One mentioned that, when he was a child, he had to take care of buffalo, and the buffalo chips could be used as manure.

Although everyone exchanged their ideas and thoughts on different occasions, the realization of real cooperation could not be guaranteed. After showing the documentary, it was decided that peasant farming in Liqiu would be extensive and environmentally friendly. In addition to continuing to grow their existing crops they decided to plant soy bean, which is adaptable to extensive farming.

In order to create possibilities for a plural local economy and to keep the surplus value, the TRF suggested that they develop a local processing plant on a small scale. The TRF also suggested that the decision-making and management should be transparent. However, the project was postponed due to disagreements among the villagers. One night when everyone was talking about the division of labor, one of the local women said in a straightforward way: "If we all work for the public lands, then, how about our own lands?" Her question soon initiated a lot of debate and discussion. The author suddenly realized that most people imagined that every project should have its own agenda and "external resources." To them, "external resources" meant that a certain amount of money would be brought into the community. There was also a pre-set rule and procedure to carry out the project and the way to arrange the resources. This misconception of "project" limits the actions and future plans of the participants.

Therefore, in the "small peasant farming project" promoted by the TRF, we tried to use different ways of doing projects. At the outset we expected the farmer participants to discuss how to use the resources from the TRF collectively. In the meantime, they were also expected to enhance their abilities to organize and manage all the available resources. The question raised above reminded us to notice different perspectives on external resources. Farmer participants in the project were confused about the way to use the fund. We then recognized that the project-oriented thinking restricted our actions. Therefore, we told the participants that they could use the fund to purchase cultivating machines, rent farm lands, and even pay wages if consensus was reached. Hence, the challenge for self-management represented not just the superficial issue about "whether they should get the pay if they work on the public farm land," but it forced people to think carefully about the essence and value of labor. Because of the self-management of the fund from the project, farmer participants watched every cent spent. Only one-fifth of the total budget was spent at the end of the first year of the project.

Besides the challenge of co-management, the shift from conventional farming to environmentally friendly farming is also very challenging. A youth who participated in the project shared his doubts about whether chicken feces or lime should be used as an organic fertilizer. He said:

> Two voices, then, began to appear in my mind. On the one hand, I was so happy, just like a toddler starting to walk on his own path. However, on the other, I was worried about that the peasants might withdraw if they knew the process was so complicated and troublesome. Although I felt very depressed, I still didn't want to retreat.
>
> (Xie 2010)

In 2010, millet was grown in the first season, and soy beans and roselle in the second season. The cultivation area in the first season was about 0.7 hectares, but one-third of the harvest was devoured by birds. The harvested millet was used to produce millet wine, which was sold in a farmers' market during the same year. In the following year, local youth were hired to act as field managers. They were expected to participate in the agricultural labor force and learn about Liqiu's traditional farming methods under the guidance of the elders. In 2011, soy beans were grown again but the soy beans died of rust disease due to the ceaseless rain in April. Afterwards, they grew the millet again and tried to develop eco-tourism in order to diversify the local economy.

The peasant farming rehabilitation project implemented in Liqiu has shown two valuable outcomes. One is the formation of the farmers' organization, and the other is the participation of village youth in the workforce.

Strong solidarity developed during the promotion of the peasant farming project. Their learning, working, and co-managing of resources took place continuously in frequent discussions. When learning agricultural knowledge and skills, they formed a certain kind of autonomous organization through their involvement in decision-making. They also integrated their production and marketing on a small scale. Although "co-work" may seem to be a modern term, the elders in Liqiu often mentioned their experiences of "labor exchange" in the past. This lost experience seems to have been rediscovered via our project.

The labor participation of youth was beyond our expectation. Students from National Taiwan University and National Tsing Hua University joined the post-disaster reconstruction after Typhoon Morakot. Working together with the TRF, they assisted in conducting the survey to gather basic information about local farming. These youth became an important labor force for environmentally friendly agriculture. They helped in thinning and cleaning during the millet-planting process. The hard and continuous labor led them to realize what "labor" and "pragmatic" mean. They appreciated the local knowledge and tacit wisdom as well. As Hsu said, "Laboring themselves to the land for all their lives," the elderly in Liqiu naturally have deep emotions tied to the land (Hsu 2010b).

Conclusion: local economy growing at a steady pace

Since the project "Peasant Farming and Green Consumption" has been implemented for only two years, it is a little difficult for us to evaluate its influences, but some findings from our cases contain heuristic value.

First, in regard to community participation, an active "leader" is very critical in both Kaohsiung and Taitung. The leaders play an important role in organizing social resources and community human resources. One of the leaders was an art designer, who moved back to his home town and worked as the village director, the lowest officer in the government administration system. He organized the tribal youth club, developed an after-school tutoring program, and promoted the Peasant Farming Rehabilitation project by contacting outside organizations after Typhoon Morakot. Not only did he organize the cultivation team, he also created the blog "Life in the Tribe," and a Facebook fan page "Peasant Farming in Liqiu." This attracted social media attention and received media coverage.

There is also an active leader in Kaohsiung, a piano teacher working in a children's home. After Morakot she quit her job, began to devote herself to community rehabilitation, and worked as chief director of the community development association. In Qinhe village she is in charge of plum processing, establishment of the workshop, and designing and positioning the plum brand.

The importance of active leaders is apparent in both the Li-Qiu and Qinhe cases. It goes without saying that team work is important. However, as these examples aptly illustrate, outside specialists or volunteers can never replace the activists within the community. Thus, we need to re-evaluate the role of outside organizations. In the past, we assigned community workers to play the role of the "leader." This usually led the villagers to become dependent on outside assistance, and made them unable to be self-independent.

Second, with regard to economic benefits, about NT$500,000 has been pumped into Liqiu by outside organization through the project, and the public fund has currently accumulated to NT$120,000. In addition, they also own two medium-sized power tillers (about NT$100,000). In Qinhe, about NT$2 million has been spent. The public fund has grown to NT$1.1 million, and they own a factory covering a workshop area of 66 square meters, including some plum-processing machines (about NT$700,000). The money spent was used for public farm rents, machines, learning courses, brand designing, and wages. The public fund was generated from the sale of agricultural goods and processed foods. The public fund is to be used as "capital" for the continuous operation as the project ends. It is worthy to noted that the management of the public fund is determined by all the community participants. As mentioned above, discussion on the use of the money is necessary. Only through this process can villagers come to value their labor. Thus, the project may have its own way in both Li-Qiu and Qinhe from an economic perspective, but if we look at it from the perspective of community cooperation, more time is needed to figure out whether the villagers can be independent.

It is hazardous to look at the globalized world system only through local eyes. Similarly, optimism without being aware of the structural constraints is dangerous as well. Here we should emphasize again that, in order to take action in response to the structural constraints derived from the market economy, the state should assume more responsibilities and allocate more resources to rehabilitation. However, we are not always able to wait quietly for the ideal world. The chance of change is always created through action. The examples discussed in this chapter show the possibilities for a diversified local economy. This chapter has discussed our reflections on these experiences and efforts. More examination will be needed after more experience has been accumulated.

The notion of peasant farming seems ideal. It deals with the environment, sustainable development, and peasant livelihood problems. However, a lot of questions still remain: What to do? How to start? And how long will the transition period be? Ultimately, the answers to these questions can only be provided through continued practice.

At present, the scale of farming in both locations is small. Neither does it create enough jobs. However, it is necessary to revitalize the local economy through agriculture at the present time. It is not good for the rehabilitation of the community to jump too far in too short a time. We observe several perspectives. First, collaborative cooperation should be rooted in our daily lives. Second, differences between human-based labor and alienated labor lie in whether laborers themselves are able to control the output and process of labor, create person-to-person relations via labor, and recognize the value of such labor. With the experiences in Qinhe and Liqiu outlined above, we see the possibility of realizing human-based labor through peasant farming. Third, as a field of labor learning, the "small peasant farming" project also becomes the platform for youth to learn the value of agriculture, raising their inner aspirations for farming. The project has already shifted concern from the economic dimension to the social dimension. We observe that four dimensions of social connection are involved: a local economy initiated by eco-friendly farming, collaborative cooperation in daily labor, human-based labor experiences, and embedding of exchange in social relationships.

"Peasant farming" is not only the reflection of productive forces, but also the reallocation of the relations of production. Moreover, it is our attempt to establish a diversified livelihood. In practice, the farmers in Taitung are still struggling with the humid climate and prolific insect life, and plum processing in Kaohsiung is still at the phase of taste and packing testing. Even so, we also see that people are getting stronger internally through their learning via public farm lands, managing their resources collectively, and all the details of their actual labor. This creates a new opportunity for the rehabilitation of the community.

Acknowledgment

This chapter was first published in the *China Journal of Social Work*, Volume 5, Issue 1, by Taylor & Francis Ltd., written by Pei-hui Tsai and Chi-wei Lui.

Notes

1 This chapter was originally presented at the International Conference, "A Year After: Taiwan Indigenous People's Post-disaster Reconstruction and Sustainable Development," held at the National Taiwan Normal University on November 12, 2010. The authors wish to thank Professor Wei-Chi Chang for her comments and suggestions, and Yi-Ting Chung for translating this paper into English. The "Peasant Farming and Green Consumption" project has been funded by the Hao Ran Foundation. We would also like to thank Fen-Yu Chen for conducting this project.

2 This system did not allow the farmers to buy their fertilizers in the market for cash. They could only exchange the fertilizers with rice. This implied that the farmers had lost their autonomy in production. The exchange rate is 1:1, which means that one kilogram of rice can only be exchanged for one kilogram of chemical fertilizer. As the price of rice is much higher than fertilizer, that is why we say it is the exploitation of rural surplus.

References

Boyle, D. 2009. *Localism: Unravelling the Supplicant State*. London: New Economics Foundation.

Hao Ran Foundation. 2010. "Xuyan: Xiaonong fu geng zhichi jihua [Preface: Support Project for Small Farm Rehabilitation]." *Xiaonong fu geng: 2010 Wan yao shenghuo jie* [Small Farm Rehabilitation: 2010 Land Nature Farmers] 4–5. Taipei: Hao Ran Foundation. Available online at: http://issuu.com/bowtoland/docs/1 (last accessed on May 9, 2014).

Henderson, E., and R. Van En. 2007. *Sharing the Harvest: A Citizen's Guide to Community Supported Agriculture*. White River Junction: Chelsea Green Publishing.

Hsu, Peiran. 2010a. "Nong zhen tuidong xiaonong fu geng Taoyuan xiang nongmin cong 'mei' chufa [Peasant Alliances Called for Recovery of Peasant Economy: Farmers of Taoyuan Township Start with 'Plums']." April 6. Coolloud website. Available online at: www.coolloud.org.tw/node/51354.

Hsu, Chao-wei. 2010b. "Canyu (guancha) li qiu xiaonong fu geng de xueshengmen [Students Participated (Observed) the Small Farm Rehabilitation in Liqu]." *Xiaonong fu geng: 2010 Wan yao shenghuo jie* [Small Farm Rehabilitation: 2010 Land Nature Farmers], 42–55. Taipei: Hao Ran Foundation. Available online at: http://issuu.com/bowtoland/docs/1 (last accessed on May 9, 2014).

Polanyi, K. 1957. *The Great Transformation: The Political and Economic Origins of our Time*. Boston, MA: Beacon Press.

Shuman, M. 1998. *Going Local: Creating Self-reliant Communities in a Global Age*. New York: Free Press.

Sumberg, J. 2009. *Re-framing the Great Food Debate: The Case for Sustainable Food*. London: New Economics Foundation.

Tsai, Pei-hui. 2009. *Nongye jiegou zhuanxing xia de nongmin fenhua (1980–2005)* [Peasant Differentiation under the Agrarian Structural Transformation, 1980–2005]. PhD dissertation, National Taiwan University.

Xie, Shenhua. 2010. "Kaigongle [Going to Work]." Available online at: www.wretch.cc/blog/evin1210/13713082.

14 In the struggle over urban space

The solidarity economy movement and urban utopianism in Hong Kong

Terence Yuen and Pauline F.Y. Chan

Introduction

As in many other metropolises, alternative economic practices in Hong Kong have grown out of contradictions of advanced capitalism, and they take a variety of forms, including producer and consumer cooperatives, local exchange and trading systems (LETS), community-supported agriculture (CSA), the fair trade movement, and so on. There is no question that the small city-state, dominated by hegemonic market forces and the heinous power of property and finance capital, leaves very little space for the continued survival of these alternative economic practices. Yet, the very existence of highly resilient projects devoid of mainstream market logic manifests rich and diverse political imaginations, and they are in effect heterotopias occupying urban spaces coexisting with those dominated by capital.

To social economy practitioners, a utopian vision is embodied in the political and economic praxis they endeavor to promote and realize. Yet, absent of any well-traveled paths for practitioners and economic participants to follow through, there is no guarantee that the heterotopias of alternative economic praxis could live up to their utopian vision and resist cooptation or elimination by capitalist market forces; indeed, the movement could lose its vibrancy and emancipatory potential and degenerate into localized, reactionary practices. It is telling that the solidarity economy is mostly ignored by "serious" economists as a realistic, tenable movement in altering the course of neoliberal economic development, let alone fulfilling the overarching ambition to remake the capitalist market system.

In his 2000 book *Spaces of Hope*, geographer David Harvey, by way of elucidating the inherent defects and difficulties of utopian imaginaries anchoring either spatial form or social process, advocates that building a utopianism that is "explicitly spatiotemporal" is the only way to rescue "any pretense at utopianism whatsoever" (Harvey 2000, 182). Calling it spatiotemporal utopianism or dialectical utopianism, Harvey suggests that the production of space and time must be incorporated into the formulation of any utopian vision, and it implies that any political project bearing utopian vision must contemplate the question of spatiotemporality as an integral part of the movement's internal dynamics that contributes to and provides for the "conditions of possibility" for instigating political translation and transcendence.

Of course, following our experiences of the past decade, this "utopianism" has to be linked to the explosive development in social media-based forms of relationality (with its potentials and pitfalls) and with the growing opposition to the globalized corporate system of political-economic globalization. There are growing signs of its fragility and impending collapse, as we witness thc rapidly spreading protest movements and their sometimes violent suppression on the one hand, and the global financial tsunami and the various permutations of states' crisis management, on the other.

Both sides offer a sense of what Harvey's spatiotemporal possibilities are up against and a sound contextualizing of his socio-geographical contribution. Adding some of its earlier origins and contemporaries, including Henri Lefèbvre, Gilles Deleuze, and Felix Guatarri, Ursula Heise (2008) describes the growing deterritorialization of the human experience and suggests the need for *eco-cosmopolitanism* as a necessary complement to re-localization. The multiple World Social Forums in different locations have also clearly shown the need for the acceptance of the specificity of the diverse local "spatialities" and their potential for the anchoring of instances of the social economy (Ramos 2012).

As a movement of movements, the social and solidarity economy[1] has a clear vision "to put the economy at the service of human beings, rather than putting human beings at the service of the economy" (Neamtan 2010, 241). Participants in solidarity economy movements would certainly embrace utopian visions in the sense that they all believe "another world" is possible. Against this formulation, this chapter aims to serve two purposes. First, in the following section, the core values and key attributes of the social and solidarity economy as a pluralistic and yet cohesive social movement are examined, and its potential in building a sustained spatiotemporal utopianism is explored. In the third section, the Social Economy Action Research Project initiated in Hong Kong since the middle of 2010 is introduced, with a brief analysis of early case findings that offers insights into the potency and practicability of the urban utopian vision it carries.

The utopian vision in social and solidarity economy

In his paper delivered to the 2009 U.S. Forum on the Solidarity Economy, practitioner and organizer Ethan Miller offers the following statements in summarizing his vision for the solidarity economy movement:

> [S]olidarity economy is *a way of thinking about the economy* that opens up spaces of hope and possibility for building a more just, sustainable and democratic economy. It is an *emerging language* for building a movement to transform economic life. It is a *framework for strategizing* about how to create this other economy, building on our strengths and connecting our practices from the ground-up. And finally, solidarity economy is *a space in*

which to imagine, debate and create visions for another economy based on shared values.

(Miller 2010, 40–41; emphasis in original)

While most narratives and definitions of the social and solidarity economy typically draw attention to the nature of economic activities, the basis of organizing, or the shared values of economic subjects in their attempts to characterize the broad-based social movement (see, e.g., Fonteneau *et al.* 2010; Myers 2009; Tremblay 2009), Miller takes a somewhat different route in making the above statements and instead gives emphasis to the temporal dynamics of the social movement (*an emerging language* and *a framework for strategizing*) and to the production of space for propagating the struggle (*a space in which to imagine, debate and create vision*). Similar important discussion is also found in David Featherstone's (2012) *Solidarity: Hidden Histories and the Geographies of Internationalism*; he describes the nature of integration as a "*transformative political relation*."

It is apparent that Miller is paying attention to both space and process which are intermingled in his imaginary of a prospective solidarity economy movement, and it echoes the call made by Harvey in that the production of space and time be incorporated into the formulation of utopian visions. While Miller has not explicitly addressed questions of utopianism his formulation is intriguing, as it offers hopes and insights into developing a spatiotemporal utopianism for guiding the solidarity economy movement. It would thus be interesting to survey the social, spatial, and processual dimensions of social and solidarity economy as a unique movement of movements, in order that we may better grasp its utopian vision.

The social dimension: shared values and common attributes

With the joint efforts of numerous organizers, practitioners, and academics across the globe, we have gradually gained a better understanding of the social and solidarity economy both theoretically and empirically. On the empirical front, diversity and plurality are the trademarks of social economy initiatives, which may be grouped according to the following five activity spheres:

1 Production: examples include worker cooperatives, producer cooperatives (local example in Hong Kong: women workers' co-ops).
2 Exchange/transfer: for example, community currencies, fair trade operators (local examples: Project COME (a LETS project); fair trade groups).
3 Consumption/use: for example, consumer cooperatives, ethical purchasing (local examples: group purchasing; the ethical consumption movement).
4 Surplus allocation: for example, cooperative loan funds, social investing (local examples: community reinvestment programs; the Social Investors' Club).
5 Creation: for example, creation of the commons, collective landownership (local example: community shared farming in Tsoi Yuen new village, the first "intentional community" in Hong Kong).

The clustering of activities in five activity spheres is, of course, somewhat misleading, given that any alternative economic practice has to navigate all five spheres (which are to be conceived in *both* social *and* material terms) and they eventually form a full cycle of activities.[2] As they travel along the five activity spheres, different social economy groups would place different emphasis on value propositions that are linked to the well-being of different economic subjects (e.g., producers, consumers, inhabitants of a local community, etc.) and to humankind (e.g., impacts on cultural or environmental commons).

Much recent work has been published on the emergence of a new sense of the *commons* through a diverse plethora of initiatives across most continents. *The Wealth of the Commons: A World beyond Market and State* (Bollier and Helfrich 2012) assembles over 70 contributions, while Charles Eisenstein's (2011) *Sacred Economics* usefully attempts to re-cast local economics and its relational components into a *gift economic* paradigm. Thus, despite their necessary differences, clear commonalities may be found between the diverse economic practices and the shared values, as neatly summarized by Miller:

> Cooperation and mutuality are emphasized above unfettered competition. Individual and collective well being – defined by people and communities rather than distant "experts" – are prioritized over profit and financial accumulation. Economic and social justice (or equity) – struggles to end social and economic oppression in its many forms – are seen as key priorities. The responsibility to work towards ecological health – developing respectful and sustainable relationships with our ecosystems and their other inhabitants – is a core focus. Robust democracy at all levels of society and of organizations, placing people and communities as the active agents of their own lives and development, runs like a thread weaving other values together. And finally, these values are articulated with a strong emphasis on diversity and pluralism – the belief that there can be no "one way"; that people, working together, must forge their own unique paths toward freedom.
>
> (Miller 2010, 33; emphasis in original)

The diverse intents and potentially conflicting program objectives would necessarily require those involved to make trade-offs and to engage in reiterated decision-making via "ethical debate and learning." Yet they are united in a shared identity in that "despite their differences, these practices share characteristics that allow for parallels: they all attempt *to introduce the notion of solidarity into economic activities*, thus advocating a solidarity economy" (Jean-Louis Laville, quoted in Miller 2010, 33; emphasis added).

Miller further notes that:

> while all economic relationships are social in one form or another, solidarity names a specific mode of relationship: it begins with a recognition of interdependency … [and solidarity is enacted] when we recognize these connections, take active responsibility for our own participation in them, and work

> to simultaneously transform those relationships that are destructive or exploitative and to cultivate those relationships that embody care and mutual respect for those with whom we are connected.
>
> (Miller 2010, 33)

In other words, an important shared purpose for all practitioners of and participants in solidarity economy to work on is to restore and do justice to the multitudes of social relations in economic life that have been hidden, erased, or utterly destroyed by the capitalist economic system (see also Boulet 2009). The movement participants would all share a *committed aspiration* toward enacting the broad range of program objectives and values, as they all carry the "commitment to both self-transformation and to the transformation of the world in the service of these shared values" (Miller 2010, 34). Often, making trade-offs is necessary and unavoidable, but a shared commitment to the notion of solidarity would dictate that ethical decision-making emphasizing participation and economic democracy will be practiced on an ongoing basis, which would become in itself an integral part of the solidarity movement's dialectics of self-transformation and the transformation of circumstances. We can refer directly to the cooperative movement already existing for 170 years.

The spatial dimension: the politics of economic space

The discussion thus far has highlighted two important aspects of the solidarity economy movement; borrowing from the feminist economic geographers Gibson-Graham and colleagues, it focuses on:

> rethinking economy as a social space of interdependence … [with economic subjects] turn their attention away from the so called structural dynamics of a capitalist system, and emphasize instead the ethical dynamics of decision making involved in constructing community economies.
>
> (Gibson-Graham and Roelvink 2009, 35)

The focus on *social relations and interdependence* and the *shared commitment in solidarity* thus characterizes the "social" dimension of the movement, but still leaves the question open as to how a place-based politics can be brought into the narratives, so as to fill the abstract "social space of interdependence" as referenced in the above statement. This leads us to the spatial dimension of the movement with regard to the production of urban space, namely the creation of alternative economic spaces to be materialized geographically in the urban landscape.

The question of place-based politics and the spatial perspective of the movement may appear redundant at one level, as all alternative economic practices are rooted in certain locations on earth. The true question, then, is not (merely) about claiming (and reclaiming) urban space to allow experimentation with and development of alternative economies. In the opening section of this chapter, we suggested that many alternative economic practices are, in effect, heterotopias coexisting in urban space with capital-dominated endeavors. Given the hegemonic capitalist market, it is nothing short of a fierce local struggle to try and create, or even just defend, the space for alternative economies, as exemplified by the Tsoi Yuen village residents during the past two years opposing the construction of the US$8.6 billion Express Rail in Hong Kong. It is indeed a huge triumph for the people to be able to pressure the government into making concessions and to allow the villagers to build a new eco-village on another site which will certainly turn into a heterotopian space in the territory and perhaps the first-ever intentional community in town featuring collective ownership of land and community-supported agricultural initiatives. For the activists and social economy practitioners, the follow-up question is the emancipatory potential of this particular piece of heterotopian space for future social movements (particularly since the "Anti-Express Rail Link" struggle has now become an iconic social movement in Hong Kong following the political handover).

In his more recent work elucidating the politics of place-making, Harvey again reminds us that "[place] is always a crucial basis for progressive and emancipatory movements" (2009, 195). He regards place (and the production of space) as "a crucial mediating factor in the movement from the foundational moment in which the personal is political through the organization of local solidarities in particular places to a more universal politics of rights and justice" (2009, 195; see our previous references to the global/local interpenetrations (Heise 2008) and the peer-to-peer approach). The solidarity economy movement, as a collection of place-based alternative economic initiatives originating from the grassroots, necessarily manifests a strong dose of place-based politics. The more relevant question, then, is: What do we mean by terms like "place-making" and "the production of space" when it is the task of the solidarity movement to build "another economy" and to produce "economic spaces" within which progressive and emancipatory dynamics will have a better chance to thrive, while tendencies toward exclusionary and reactionary politics could be eliminated?

In our own discussions with local practitioners on the current state of social economy development in Hong Kong, the question of space has been mentioned repeatedly in the conversations. It is noteworthy that the conceptions of space as expressed by practitioners would go beyond *absolute space* and move into the realms of *relative space* and *relational space*.[3] In fact, we are able to establish parallels between the three kinds of "economic spaces" as referred to by local practitioners, and the three conceptions of space long emphasized by critical geographers. The parallels to the three kinds of economic spaces (namely *physical space*, *policy space*, and *market space*) as recorded in our research inquiry are given in Table 14.1.

The broad message we gathered from local practitioners is that it is very difficult to find and expand their activity space in their ongoing efforts to disseminate alternative economic praxis, and the hurdles they face simply go beyond physical space (even if the lack of physical space is a critical issue which they are constantly facing). The practitioners we talked to readily made the suggestion

Table 14.1 Different conceptions of space affecting alternative economies

Conceptions of space	*Local struggles*	*Examples*
Absolute space	Physical space	Difficulties in gaining access to vacant space in public housing estates and the denial in the use of "public space" for running alternative economic activities
Relative space	Policy space	In the name of maintaining a "level playing field," the terms of government outsourcing service contracts are made unfavorable to alternative economic practices
Relational space	Market space	Substantial efforts needed to change people's "market imaginaries" in order to open up alternative market space (e.g., via ethical consumption and fair trade movements)

that "policy space" and "market space" are two other frontiers where they encountered significant hindrances. To achieve political transcendence, it is imperative that the imaginaries of "alternative economic spaces" be opened up to allow economic subjects to conceive and experience them, or else common citizens would have no choice but to continue and make their everyday economic decisions subservient to the logic of the dominant economic praxis.

In the end, the emancipatory potential of alternative economic praxis rests upon the struggle over the contested relationalities of "economic space." Yet, at the same time, the constraints in relation to physical space and relative space will always present real difficulties. These are, however, being overcome in a great many local endeavors, as is being documented in the previously mentioned Bollier and Helfrich reader as well as in *The Localization Reader* (De Young and Princen 2012), and theoretically underpinned in a much earlier work by Daniel Kemmis (1990) entitled *Community and the Politics of Place*, in which he talks about *Reclaiming the Marketplace (the Economics of Re-Inhabitation) and The Art of the Possible in the Home of Hope (*the two final chapters of *The Politics of Re-inhabitation).*

Therefore we will not lose sight of the politics and the dialectics of space creation and place-making, and, as Harvey has reminded us, we will delineate and pay attention to different spatiotemporal dynamics linking up absolute, relative, and relational space (Harvey 2009). To build a politics of transcendence, we need to find out how the "social" and the "spatial" could join up with the "temporal" so as to create a utopian vision for the solidarity economy movement through setting in motion and sustaining the necessary spatiotemporal dynamics (see Clark and Teachout 2012; Kemmis 1990; Bollier and Helfrich 2012).

This takes us finally to the temporal/processual perspective of the solidarity economy movement, which has already been touched upon in the above discussions as we examined the social and the spatial; indeed, the temporal/processual dimension may be the most strategic of all, given the solidarity economy movement's vision to build a politics of transcendence.

The processual dimension: setting in motion the spatiotemporal dynamics

Miller, in his paper delivered to the U.S. Forum on the Solidarity Economy, is explicit in describing it as process-based politics, noting in his opening remarks:

> Solidarity economy is an open process, an invitation. The concept does not arise from a single political tradition or body of ideas. Its very nature and definition are in continual development, discussed and debated among its advocates. Seeking to "make the road by walking" rather than to push a closed or finalized ideology, solidarity economy is a "movement of movements" continually seeking connections and possibilities while holding on to the transformative commitment of shared values.
>
> (Miller 2010, 26)

In seeing solidarity economy as process-based politics, Miller attempts to address two potential problems that are commonly associated with place-based politics, namely:

1 As an open process, solidarity economy could eliminate the tendencies toward exclusionary and reactionary politics, i.e., "to move beyond the factionalism that has so often weakened historical efforts to imagine and build other economies."
2 The problem of closure is evaded: "solidarity economy is not so much a *model of economic organization* as it is a *process of economic organizing*; it is not a *vision*, but an active process of collective *visioning*" (Miller 2010, 28; emphases in original).

The latter point concerning the process of *collective visioning* by economic subjects is particularly relevant to building a politics of transcendence. In order to achieve the ultimate goal to transcend and reclaim the economic space captured by the capitalist system, the solidarity economy movement has to display a distinct dynamism that has to be strong enough to outlast the accumulation process of capitalism. It requires the economic participants to effect self-transformation and in the process also change the everyday reality of the world around us. It is thus very important to regard solidarity economy as an open process, a critical element of which is "to recognize the ways that conventional economics has described reality so as to *make invisible* a whole host of practices, initiatives, human relationships and motivations, and thus to limit our abilities to imagine economic alternatives" (Miller 2010, 29; see also Gibson-Graham 2006; Ramos 2012). In other words, solidarity economy – as a transformative politics – should be regarded as an ongoing process of debate, discovery, and collective visioning.

In this vision, political transcendence would come about through the instigation of spatiotemporal dynamics that would guide economic participants – as economic citizens – to become enlightened as they engage in collective visioning for a better economy, and to get themselves immersed in the "ethical dynamics of decision making" while negotiating and debating economic alternatives for a better world. And once the necessary spatiotemporal dynamics are set in motion, they would transcend what Henri Lefèbvre describes as *material space*, *conceived space*, and *lived space*.[4] It is hence important for the utopian vision of solidarity economy to be able to transcend the space/time of these different space dimensions. Table 14.2 is our attempt to depict the utopian vision as embedded in solidarity economy across the different space conceptions.

In his inquiry into the different dimensions of space, Harvey makes a strong case for the identification of these various conceptions as central to our understanding of the relationality of place and space:

> Political spaces facilitate change by creating a distinctive place to develop new identities and practices. The political power of place comes from its ability to link the social, symbolic, and experiential dimensions of space. Transformative politics comes from separating, juxtaposing, and recombining these dimensions.
>
> (Kohn 2003, cited in Harvey 2009, 158)

Of the three space concepts shown in Table 14.2, the material space of heterotopias may be readily identified in most societies, but their emancipatory potential may be easily compromised in the face of the dominant economic praxis. After all, it is an all too familiar strategy for the capitalist class to take over and transform heterotopian spaces according to its own image. This is why it is important to refer to the social, symbolic, and experiential dimensions of space, i.e., moving from material space and toward conceived and lived space. It is in the domains of the latter two that a politics of transcendence (and an explicitly spatiotemporal utopianism) can be built (see also the contributions to the "peer-to-peer economy" at www.ctheory.net/articles.aspx?id=499).

Earlier, it was argued that the solidarity economy movement has to display a distinct dynamism, and if this analysis is correct, the source of the dynamism would have to be originated from the social and symbolic dimensions of space (the conceived space and the lived space). The emancipatory potential of heterotopian spaces could only be realized when social economy advocates manage to transcend the material space and create a sustained metaphorical space within which practitioners can get themselves fully immersed in alternative economic praxis and henceforth make their everyday economic decisions according to new identities and practices. This demands that actual (alternative) economies be built at multiple scales in order that participating in alternative economic practices could become a serious endeavor and not something that could be easily coopted into the mainstream economic praxis. New identities and practices would be built along the way.

Table 14.2 Space/time analysis of utopian vision of social and solidarity economy

Dimensions of space	*Utopian vision of social and solidarity economy (SSE)*	*Examples/implications on economic life*
Spaces of material practice (experienced)	Absolute material space of alternative economic practices – heterotopias	Local examples include tuck-shops run by women's co-ops in college campuses and social enterprises in public hospitals (discussed in the text) and the new Tsoi Yuen village featuring community-supported agricultural initiatives. Q: How to realize the emancipatory potential of heterotopias (beyond absolute space)?
Representations of space (conceived)	Metaphorical space built via integration of multiple SSE practices – jumping scale	Economic integration of multiple SSE projects (e.g., local SSE producer–distributor–consumer networks discussed in the text) to produce larger "economic space" allowing economic subjects to conceive of an alternative economic life. Q: How to develop linkages among SSE and build a vast social space for envisioning change?
Spaces of representation (lived)	Lived space sustained by spatiotemporal dynamics of economic subjects practicing alternative economies	Participants in SSE collectively produce a sustained "lived space" allowing economic subjects to go through self-transformation and simultaneously effect transformation of the world around us. Q: Building the "conditions of possibility" for instigating political transcendence?

Finally, moving from conceived space to lived space, this is the sphere where personal transformation and transformation of the world would occur. Solidarity economy, in effect, is to *make economic democracy a lived practice*, and it is only through sustained effort in getting involved in economic practices – to engage in the ethical dynamic of decision-making and collective visioning – that personal political transformation and transcendence may occur. In all, as emphasized by Harvey, the three dimensions of space (material, conceived, and lived) are linked with one another, and all are critical in our effort to build a utopian vision for solidarity economy and to realize its vision on earth. As numerous writings and analyses have shown (Clark and Teachout 2012; Eisenstein 2011; Bollier and Helfrich 2012), capitalism is so successful in conquering the world space precisely because of its ability to transcend the space dimensions and manage to transform people while transforming the global economic system. To create the conditions of possibility for effecting a counter-movement, it requires us to pay attention to the different spatiotemporalities of the diverse space dimensions, and to set in motion the right kinds of spatiotemporal dynamics that can change the lived experience of economic subjects, and make the solidarity economy movement a practicable and realizable utopian project.

Charting economic alterity in Hong Kong: lessons learned thus far

Ever since Hong Kong's economy took off during the final three decades of the twentieth century, the former British colony has been trumpeted as the world's best showcase of *laissez-faire*, free-wheeling capitalism, and this image has not changed following its reunification with China on July 1, 1997. If anything, China's own market reforms and economic liberalization have greatly strengthened the power of the capitalist class in the small city-state, and it is no secret that the Beijing government has long forged an unholy alliance with local business tycoons so that total political control may be assumed through the formation of a tightly knit state–capital nexus. Following the handover, income disparity and economic marginalization continue to worsen to the point that Hong Kong now records the highest Gini-coefficient among all developed economies.[5]

The image of *laissez-faire* capitalism, repeatedly advertised and reinforced through rhetoric such as "positive non-interventionism" or "Small Government, Big Market," is, of course, highly misleading. For instance, the hegemonic capitalist class, commonly referred to as "property hegemony" in recent years, given the heinous power of the property developers in town, has dominated market sectors and the entire urban space, and the expression "free market" has become a mere footnote to remind us of the weak state administration which allows the property developers and other big businesses to roam free in the market, transforming the urban space and forming a network of monopolies that sucks out the life-blood of city dwellers.

At the same time, the image also obscures the multitude of social relations always embedded in the informal economy, which also play a vital role in the processes of economic transformation. Essentially a migrant society, self-help and mutual help via indigenous groupings (e.g., clansman associations) and local economic organizing at the neighborhood level (e.g., local lending clubs that were popular before the 1980s) characterize solidarity-based economic activities that are ignored by the dominant imaginary of economic development driven by risk-taking and entrepreneurialism of the capitalist class and, over time, people have come to accept and even embrace the fable of the "trickle-down economy" supposedly contributing to economic prosperity and benefitting all members of society. The social and solidarity economy, then, is an entirely foreign concept to most people, and building a movement around economic alternatives is close to being a total fantasy if not owing to the waves of economic hardship resulting from the Asian Financial Crisis which hit Hong Kong shortly after the political handover, leading to the disillusionment among economic subjects suffering from escalating economic oppression.

Background of the Social Economy Action Research Project

Eager to find ways to assist the economically marginalized, community organizers and local activists began their experimentations with grassroots economic initiatives, often relying on philanthropy or even on government seed funding. Under the broad banner "community economic development projects," many small-scale initiatives sprang up in the aftermath of the 1997 to 1998 Asian financial crisis. The government, as expected, would still adhere to the dominant economic discourse and emphasized neoliberalist rhetoric, such as welfare-to-work and self-reliance, to justify budget cuts while providing short-term relief funding to transient social economy projects. Many projects would eventually cease operations after the initial funding dried up, and some were absorbed into mainstream welfare programs. Yet many social economy projects do survive and show a high degree of resiliency, continuing to display characteristics distinct from dominant economic praxis.

The 2007 to 2010 global financial tsunami offered yet another wake-up call for the local population to rethink the mainstream economic praxis dominating Hong Kong for several decades. The predatory nature of endless capital accumulation and the unjust political regime that helps sustain the economic system in its current form were laid bare before everyone's eyes. More enlightened segments of the citizenry including the economically oppressed, the younger generations, and a good proportion of the middle class have grown increasingly critical of the dominant economic praxis, and many of them became more open to envisioning economic alternatives in their longing for a change of scenery. It certainly feels as if the seed of economic democracy has been sown emerging from the internal contradictions of the capitalist system. However, devoid of access to any viable avenues for practicing economic democracy, few could envision real change to happen to the system and to oneself. There is a pressing need, therefore, to open up the urban space for allowing economic alternatives to develop and prosper, so that the more aware sections of the citizenry are granted the opportunity to support and become engaged participants in the solidarity economy movement. Only then can we collectively build and experience a "lived space" that would lay the "conditions of possibility" for political translation and transcendence.

The development of solidarity economy initiatives in Hong Kong has thus reached a critical stage that requires a comprehensive study to evaluate their achievements, as well as to understand the challenges and dilemmas they face. Against this background, the Social Economy Action Research Project, steered by the Hong Kong Polytechnic University Research Team, initiated its study of the social and solidarity economy in Hong Kong in mid-2010.[6] The research aims to identify and track the trajectories of a range of alternative economic praxis, and it is also working to build a joint action platform with organizers to ponder the prospect of developing a scalable and sustainable social/solidarity economy alterity in Hong Kong and China that works toward countering mainstream capitalist economy.

The mapping exercise and the accompanying research work thus far undertaken by the Project serve a few purposes. First, it is a stock-take exercise informing the nature, size, and variety of alternative economic practices. Second, through building an exchange and learning platform between movement practitioners, self-reflection can occur and knowledge sharing will be encouraged. Third, in studying the similarities as well as the differences between the distinct practices, the idea of a collective movement can be interrogated and critiqued on an ongoing basis and the movement's relationship with the mainstream economy debated. Finally, and perhaps most relevant to the present discussion, case stories of alternative economic practices detailing the nature of the struggles and strategies deployed to overcome hurdles are collected.

In the following section, four very short case histories are provided addressing two aspects of our present interest, namely: (1) the production of heterotopian spaces for alternative economic practices, and (2) the creation and consolidation of economic spaces (hence, movement spaces) for inducing political translation and transcendence. The case materials will connect us back to the various space conceptions examined earlier in Tables 14.1 and 14.2.

Local social economy praxis in Hong Kong

Since we are still in the early stages of our inquiry, we are yet to develop a thorough understanding of the multiple ways through which the production and use of urban space could possibly shape the progression and realization of the ideals of the solidarity economy movement. Yet, some preliminary case findings are assembled which indicate the significance of space- and place-making to the movement. In the following, four short case narratives are provided in relation to the production and use of heterotopian spaces and the formation of two producer–distributor–consumer (PDC) networks in Hong Kong.[7]

Running co-op tuck-shops inside college campuses

Established in 1989, the Hong Kong Women Workers Association is an NGO situated in the dynamics of women's and labor movements advocating the rights of women workers in Hong Kong. By the late 1990s, the post-industrialization era coincided with the Asian economic turmoil, and the working class was threatened by job loss and aggravating work conditions, resulting in low wages, job insecurity, and the lack of social and legal protection. In an effort to experiment with alterity emphasizing the economic autonomy of workers, the Association organized its first producers' cooperative comprising 10 women members to run a tuck-shop on the Chinese University of Hong Kong campus.

The initiative aims to provide a new option for those at the grassroots level to work together, based on the principle of equality, democratic decision-making, and mutual respect. It also aims to create decent job opportunities, and helps make visible the contributions of women's labor. In realizing an alternative economic praxis, it also manifests itself as a source of gendered local resistance, echoing the international labor and cooperative movements, working to reclaim the political and socio-economic space colonized by the capitalist system. In promoting the culture of ethical consumption, the women's co-op regularly collaborates with various student bodies to organize activities on campus to raise awareness on the living conditions of grassroots workers, promote fair trade, and launch critiques of corporate monopoly. Recently, in 2010, the Association founded another cooperative tuck-shop on the new Hong Kong College of Technology campus using the same model.

NGO-run social businesses in public hospitals

Adopting the social enterprise model, MentalCare Connect was established in 2002 to provide job opportunities for the socially disadvantaged. Its annual revenue reached US$5 million in 2009/2010, as it employed over 220 workers, half of them former mentally-ill patients. It is a subsidiary of the Mental Health Association of Hong Kong, a well-known welfare NGO attending to the needs of the mentally ill through running a variety of service programs, including sheltered workshops, supported employment, and other mainstream rehabilitation services.

The NGO has long attempted to launch retail businesses as a means to offer job opportunities to its clients. By way of open bidding tenders administered by public hospitals, the social enterprise got the opportunity to open convenience stores and retail outlets selling rehabilitation products inside the premises of public hospitals. With the brand name Cheers Gallery, it suggested a happy workplace for the disadvantaged. With the success of its initial hospital shops, the enterprise has now expanded its operations to other shop spaces across various geographical locations and developed an online platform to sell its rehabilitation products. Through the gradual development of its retail businesses, the ideals of work integration for community rehabilitation are successfully practiced.

Forging a producer–distributor–consumer network using community currency

Community Oriented Mutual Economy (COME) is a LETS local community currency project launched by the St. James' Settlement NGO with initial funding support from the local Oxfam after Hong Kong was hit hard by the Asian financial crisis, which seriously affected the livelihood of many grassroots people. The COME project prints its own currency, which it issues to members in exchange for services and other labor work offered by them. The residents are actively engaged in the management committee and various working groups to achieve self-management of the grassroots project.

The local currency (called "hours-credit coupon" or time-dollar) gradually gained recognition and wide community support and, over time, has evolved into a unique producer–distributor–consumer network allowing other solidarity economy producers to circulate their products within the system. For instance, organic farmers in the rural areas established ties to the LETS network and a community-supported agriculture system was formed. Using time-dollar as a medium of exchange, the local residents in Wanchai will also provide labor work for the farmers both in the fields (during peak harvest season) and in a small food-processing facility in Wanchai, and, as a result, farmers can increase their income with the sale of processed farm products. In return, with the time-dollars earned, the local residents are also able to consume the premium organic produce for a combination of time-dollars and real-dollars, produce which otherwise would be too expensive. In this way, in the spirit of solidarity and reciprocity, the producers and consumers are engaged in alternative economic practices which are totally distinct from the dominant economic praxis.

Producer–distributor–consumer network in community-supported agriculture

Life in Harmony is a not-for-profit social enterprise established in 2007 by a group of ecologically conscious "housewives" who for some years have developed a consumer cooperative in promoting green and healthy living while pursuing a life of simplicity. An important aspect of the enterprise's work is the development of a cross-border community-supported agriculture (CSA) network, connecting small rural farmers in southern China with ethical purchasing groups in Hong Kong, including residents, labor groups, schools, and NGOs across the territory.

Through collaborating with a rural development agency, Life in Harmony established direct connections with local farmers and arranged the supply of healthy and good-quality agricultural produce to be shipped to customers in Hong Kong. Other than relying on faceless accreditation systems, the enterprise emphasizes building social relations and person-to-person contacts in its effort to ensure that acceptable agricultural practices are adhered to by the farmers. Visitation trips are organized from time to time for members of the Hong Kong cooperative to visit the farmers and build personal relationships. A production–circulation–consumption chain is thus established, upon which the ideals of CSA and the ethical consumption movement are promoted. For the three years before the enterprise decided to cease operations early this year, it procured high-quality farm produce from China and Taiwan, such as soya beans, rice, and vinegar, together with other locally made products. It also worked with a local bean curd workshop to make and supply the only organic handmade tofu in Hong Kong. The project is currently undergoing a process of deep evaluation to draw lessons from its three years of experience, while its businesses have been transferred to other collective purchase and CSA groups, including the PDC network in Wanchai, maintained by the COME project.

Making sense of the early case findings

In selecting the above cases, we intend to return to the earlier discussions about different concepts of space as offered above. The women's co-ops and the NGO-run social enterprise running solidarity-based businesses in college campuses and public hospitals allow us to readily outline parallels with the absolute/relative/relational and material/conceived/lived space concepts.

In Hong Kong, workers' co-ops and social enterprises represent economic alterity (there are very few of them) and they are rarely encountered in the urban space. The privatization of previously publicly managed properties and unending gentrification projects have together eliminated the urban space that these enterprises might occupy. In the two presented cases, practitioners seized the opportunity to set up their operations as a result of special tendering policies adopted by the colleges and the public hospitals, both of which are semi-public organizations. Such an exceptional policy window thus created the policy space (a relative space) that materialized into the absolute space of alternative economies when shops and retail outlets were offered support to open businesses. The absolute space of alternative economies, in turn, became the breeding ground for the creation of social and metaphorical spaces, which allowed other economic subjects (for instance, members of women's co-ops and college students) to engage in an alternative economic praxis. The material space of the heterotopias thus manages to shape and have a sustained impact on the conceived and lived spaces, which are owned individually and collectively by the economic subjects.

The producer–distributor–consumer networks offer yet another illustration of the production of "economic spaces" at multiple scales, manifesting the social, symbolic, and experiential dimensions of space. While the configurations vary in their detail, the two PDC networks serve the important function of realizing the integration of solidarity-based economies and build "actual" economies. In contrast to the tuck-shops and retail outlets that operate at the firm level, the scale of operations of the PDC networks move onto another level and run across multiple geographical spaces. As discussed earlier, the political significance of conceived and lived space (the economic spaces built and sustained by the PDC networks) lies in the fact that it allows the economic subjects to become fully immersed in alternative economic praxis, thus becoming able to build new identities and gradually negotiate their everyday economic decisions according to new values and new practices.

This rather positive analysis notwithstanding, the above case findings do not support the view that social and solidarity economy is flourishing in Hong Kong. The cases reveal how a multitude of social relations are rediscovered and re-established in economic life, as practitioners and economic participants seek to revive the spirit of solidarity and place it at the center of economic exchange. But in the context of achieving political translation and transcendence, the numbers of organizers and the scale of their operations are still immaterial vis-à-vis the dominant economic praxis. There are difficult constraints on numerous fronts, including local struggles in the use of urban space, the lack of avenues allowing transformed economic citizens to practice economic democracy on a "deep" and continuing basis, not to mention the long-fought battle over ideologies on economic imperatives. Yet, if our analysis has any traction, the case findings would definitely suggest that local organizers have adopted appropriate strategies (transcending the various space dimensions in organizing their struggles) and are heading in the right direction in their mission to instigate spatio-temporal dynamics that would contribute to and provide for the "conditions of possibility" for the creation of a transformational politics.

Not a conclusion: some lingering questions

In closing, it is worthwhile to refer again to Miller's closing comments, his message being equally relevant to our investigation:

> As a political and economic project, solidarity economy is both humble and ambitious. It is humble in the sense that solidarity economy movements do not claim to have all of the answers, recognizing instead that our strength lies in coming together with creativity and courage to experiment and learn. Its ambition lies in aspiring to build strong linkages across multiple sectors of society and economy, to build coordinated social movements in which opposition to injustice is intimately bound up with the creation of practical and inspiring alternatives, and to ultimately transform the current socio-economic order.
>
> (Miller 2010, 41)

Following on from our explorations in earlier sections of this chapter, two questions related to the Social Economy Action Research Project are examined here, serving as a tentative conclusion to this initial inquiry. First, given the analysis provided in this (incomplete) review, how are social economy organizers to react to the current situation and prepare for the next stage of the movement in Hong Kong? Second, what is the fitting scale, or the strategic level of intervention organizers should adopt and push for their movement's agendas? Should more emphasis be put on the local sites, or would a regional perspective (like the Hong

Kong–Pearl River Delta imaginary as proposed by the research) serve important strategic purposes for the advancement of the collective movement?

In Hong Kong, the development of social and solidarity economy has been realized without detailed planning or any blueprint provided by a central authority. This, of course, is considered a strength rather than a weakness, an imperative for building an open movement as we have argued above. Emerging initially as place-based politics at particular sites, the local struggles contemplate place-making as their initial intervention tactics in realizing economic alterity. In the process, they built alternative place and space – the heterotopias of economic alterity – that allowed participants to practice economic democracy employing multiple means.

As the organizers achieved some successes at the initial stage and level of operations, they moved on to form alliances and networks with other like-minded practitioners and further expanded the "economic spaces" where economic subjects could deepen their practices and become involved in the collective vision for a better future. In this way, the hurdles hindering progress of the movement are transcended, as the initially place-based politics are infused with emerging development trajectories and turned into spatiotemporal dynamics with the intermingling of time and space.

Our findings reveal such a development trend, and on this basis we argue that the local solidarity economy movement is heading in the right direction. The movement has and will continue to have setbacks (like the recent closure of Life in Harmony, a key actor in the local struggles), but as long as the movement is adhering to a path of transcendence and continues to fuel and sustain the positive spatiotemporal dynamics, the tendency for the local struggles to degenerate into reactionary and exclusionary politics is minimized. In other words, in preparing to carry the movement to the next level, local organizers should all be ready to launch struggles at multiple levels and scales, with an imperative to focusing on building and sustaining a transcendence politics that is advancing the spatiotemporal scale.

This brings us to the second point regarding the appropriate level of intervention and the fitting scale for envisioning further progression of the solidarity economy movement. As we have argued, it is inevitable that practitioners and organizers have to prepare for struggles at multiple levels, and the fiercest of the struggles is most likely to be at the local level. Yet, there are many reasons for the need to think beyond the local and allow our imagination to jump scales and consider building a movement (and the utopianism) at multiple spatiotemporal scales as we have argued and as illustrated in some of the recent literature referred to above.

The solidarity economy is inherently a global movement, an invitation tendered to all. It is a place-based politics that takes its time to transcend scales, and, as we argue in this chapter, it embodies a utopian vision that is explicitly spatiotemporal, infusing it with a mixture of social, spatial, and processual ingredients that provide for the conditions of possibility for political translation and transcendence. There are certain important "internal dynamics" within the movement that represent the necessary conditions for allowing the movement the vision to realize, and it is very likely that, as we arrive at specific moments (of the movement), these internal dynamics will only function well at matching spatiotemporal scales. For instance, history has reminded us that many past struggles were organized at the city scale, and for good reason. If we now consider the case for solidarity economy, the act of *collecting visioning* (a central internal dynamic) initially may work well at the local level and then advance all the way up to the city level as the movement progresses. But if the movement remains at a standstill at one scale, dreams may run dry (because of unavoidable local constraints), and the once robust internal dynamic of actors' collective visioning could stall, shattering the path of political transcendence and allowing pathways back to reactionary and exclusionary politics to set in.

Attempting to offer any conclusion to the question of scale, the strategic level for envisioning and effecting change may not coincide with the level that appears to be the most "logical" or "handy" from practical or geographical points of view. Given the character of social and solidarity economy and of its unique dynamics, adopting a regional perspective may, in fact, offer most strategic sense at this particular moment in time, not in terms of achieving a proper division of labor or economies of scale (as mainstream economics would teach us), but because the internal dynamics of the movement coupled with the development trajectory of the historical struggles may require us to navigate onto a larger geographical scale. We cannot ascertain whether our speculation is adequate, and all we can do is to continue to experiment and engage in our collective visioning exercise, as mandated by the solidarity economy movement.

Notes

1 In this chapter we choose not to get into the debate over definitions, and will not make a distinction between "social economy," "solidarity economy," and "social and solidarity economy," as we use these terms interchangeably throughout the text. In its accepted usage, social economy is normally regarded as a broader formulation that also covers the whole of the solidarity economy movement (see, e.g., Fonteneau *et al.* 2010). This chapter was originally published as an article in 2012, in *New Community Quarterly* 10(4), 30–40.

2 See Miller (2010) for a diagrammatical expression of a "map" of the solidarity economy cycle showing linkages of the five activity spheres.

3 See Harvey (2009, ch. 7) for a discussion of these three conceptions of space.

4 See Harvey (2009, ch. 7) for a discussion of the three space concepts put forward by Henri Lefebvre.

5 Quoting data from the U.N. Development Program, the October 2009 issue of *Business Week* reported that Hong Kong has the highest income disparity in the world (the UNDP used 2006 figures as the base in calculating the Gini-coefficients).

6 The project received funding support from the Research Grants Council, and is part of a larger SPPR research project entitled "Forging New Trans-border Links: Social/Community Economies in Hong Kong and the Pearl River Delta," which aims to examine the development of social and community economies in both Hong Kong and the Pearl River Delta.

7 The websites of the organizations/projects are as follows. Relevant information was also gathered from study groups and research workshops organized by the Social Economy Action Research Project with the participation of local practitioners.

HKWWA: www.hkwwa.org.hk/.
MentalCare Connect: www.mentalcare.com.hk/.
Project COME: http://come.sjs.org.hk/cht/section010/.
Life in Harmony: www.lifeinharmony.hk/.

References

Amin, A. 2009. "Extraordinarily Ordinary: Working in the Social Economy." *Social Enterprise Journal* 5(1), 30–49. doi: 10.1108/17508610910956390.

Bollier, D., and S. Helfrich, eds. 2012. *The Wealth of the Commons: A World beyond Market and State*. Amherst, MA: Levellers Press.

Boulet, J. 2009. "Community Economic Development outside the Capitalist Square." *New Community Quarterly* 8(1): 24–32. Available online at: www.newcq.org/database/sites/default/files/ncq%20outside%2081.pdf.

Castells, M. 2012. *Networks of Outrage and Hope: Social Movements in the Internet Age*. Cambridge: Polity Press.

Chan, P.F.Y. 2006. "Hong Kong Women's Cooperative as Alternative Economic Practice." Paper presented at the thirty-third World Congress of Schools of Social Work on "Growth and Inequality," Santiago, Chile, August 28–31.

Clark, S., and W. Teachout. 2012. *Slow Democracy: Rediscovering Community, Bringing Decision Making Back Home*. White River Junction, VT: Chelsea Green Publishing.

De Young, R., and T. Princen, eds. 2012. *The Localization Reader: Adapting to the Coming Downshift*. Cambridge, MA: MIT Press.

Eisenstein, C. 2011. *Sacred Economics: Money, Gift and Society in the Age of Transition*. Berkeley, CA: Evolver Editions.

Elster, J. 1989. "From Here to There; or, If Cooperative Ownership is so Desirable, Why are There so Few Cooperatives?" *Social Philosophy and Policy* 6: 93–111.

Featherstone, D. 2012. *Solidarity: Hidden Histories and the Geographies of Internationalism*. London: Zed Books.

Fonteneau, B., N. Neamtan, F. Wanyama, L.P. Morais, and M. de Poorter. 2010. *The Reader 2010: "Social and Solidarity Economy: Building a Common Understanding."* Turin, Italy: International Training Centre of the International Labour Organization.

Gibson-Graham, J.K. 2002. "Beyond Global vs. Local: Economic Politics outside the Binary Frame." In *Geographies of Power: Placing Scale*, edited by A. Herod and M.W. Wright (pp. 25–60). Malden, MA: Wiley-Blackwell.

Gibson-Graham, J.K. 2006. *A Postcapitalist Politics*. Minneapolis: University of Minnesota Press.

Gibson-Graham, J.K., and G. Roelvink. 2009. "Social Innovation for Community Economies." In *Social Innovation and Territorial Development*, edited by D. MacCallum, F. Moulaert, J. Hillier, and S.V. Haddock (pp. 25–38). Farnham: Ashgate.

Harvey, D. 2000. *Spaces of Hope*. Berkeley and Los Angeles: University of California Press.

Harvey, D. 2008. "The Right to the City." *New Left Review* 53, 23–40. Available online at: http://newleftreview.org/II/53/david-harvey-the-right-to-the-city.

Harvey, D. 2009. *Cosmopolitanism and the Geographies of Freedom*. New York: Columbia University Press.

Harvey, D. 2010. *The Enigma of Capital and the Crisis of Capitalism*. Oxford: Oxford University Press.

Heise, U.K. 2008. *Sense of Place and Sense of Planet: The Environmental Imagination of the Global*. Oxford: Oxford University Press.

Hui, Po Keung. 2004. "In Search of a Communal Economic Subject: Reflections on a Local Community Currency Project." In *Remaking Citizenship in Hong Kong: Community, Nation and the Global City*, edited by A.S. Ku and N. Pun (pp. 191–208). Abingdon: Routledge.

Kemmis, D. 1990. *Community and the Politics of Place*. Norman: University of Oklahoma Press.

Kohn, M. 2003. *Radical Space: Building the House of the People*. Ithaca, NY: Cornell University Press.

Lebowitz, M.A. 2010. *The Socialist Alternative: Real Human Development*. New York: Monthly Review Press.

Levitas, R. 2003. "On Dialectical Utopianism." *History of the Human Sciences* 16(1), 137–150. doi: 10.1177/0952695103016001011.

Leyshon, A., R. Lee, and C.C. Williams, eds. 2003. *Alternative Economic Spaces*. London: Sage.

Miller, E. 2004. "Solidarity Economics: Strategies for Building New Economics from the Bottom-up and the Inside-out." Available online at: http://base.socioeco.org/docs/doc-7377_en.pdf.

Miller, E. 2010. "Solidarity Economy: Key Concepts and Issues." In *Solidarity Economy I: Building Alternatives for People and Planet: Papers and Reports from the 2009 U.S. Forum on the Solidarity Economy*, edited by E. Kawano, T.N. Masterson, and J. Teller-Elsberg (pp. 25–42). Amherst, MA: Center for Popular Economics.

Myers, J. 2009. *In Search of… Exploration of the Boundaries, Scope and Definitions of the Social Economy: A Discussion Paper*. Paper 2009–4 of Social Economy and Sustainability Research Network Working Paper Series. Halifax: Social Economy and Sustainability Research Network.

Neamtan, N. 2010. "The Solidarity Economy, State Organization and Political Power." In *Solidarity Economy I: Building Alternatives for People and Planet: Papers and Reports from the 2009 U.S. Forum on the Solidarity Economy*, edited by E. Kawano, T.N. Masterson, and J. Teller-Elsberg (pp. 341–350). Amherst, MA: Center for Popular Economics.

Pierson, P. 2004. *Politics in Time: History, Institutions, and Social Analysis*. Princeton, NJ: Princeton University Press.

Ramos, J.M. 2012. "Deep Democracy, Peer-to-peer Production and our Common Futures." *Futura* 31.

Tremblay, C. 2009. *Advancing the Social Economy for Socio-economic Development: International Perspectives*. No. 1 of Canadian Social Economy Research Partnerships Centre Public Policy Paper Series. Victoria, BC: Canadian Social Economy Hub at the University of Victoria.

Wright, E.O. 2006. "Compass Points: Towards a Socialist Alternative." *New Left Review* 41, 93–124. Available online at: www.ssc.wisc.edu/~wright/Published%20writing/New%20Left%20Review%20paper.pdf.

Wright, E.O. 2010. *Envisioning Real Utopias*. London: Verso.

Yuen, T.Y.K. 2012. "An Overview of Social Enterprise Development in China and Hong Kong." Paper presented at the International Symposium on East Asia in Transition organized by Ritsumeikan University, Kyoto, Japan, March 24–25.

Index

Page numbers in *italics* denote tables, those in **bold** denote figures.

For Product Safety Concerns and Information please contact our EU
representative GPSR@taylorandfrancis.com
Taylor & Francis Verlag GmbH, Kaufingerstraße 24, 80331 München, Germany

www.ingramcontent.com/pod-product-compliance
Ingram Content Group UK Ltd.
Pitfield, Milton Keynes, MK11 3LW, UK
UKHW020017200926
475702UK00014B/1926
9780367598471